BANKRUPTCY: THE CASE FOR RELIEF IN AN ECONOMY OF DEBT

A decade after the Global Financial Crisis and Great Recession, developed economies continue to struggle under excessive household debt. While exacerbating inequality and political unrest, this debt—when combined with wage stagnation and a shrinking welfare state—has played a key role in maintaining economic growth and allowing households faced with rising costs of living to make ends meet. In *Bankruptcy: The Case for Relief in an Economy of Debt*, Joseph Spooner examines this economic model and finds it increasingly unsustainable. In a call to action to reduce debt burdens, he turns to bankruptcy law, which is uniquely situated as a mechanism of social insurance against the risks of a debt-dependent economy. This book should be read by anyone interested in understanding the problem of consumer debt and how best to address it.

JOSEPH SPOONER is an Assistant Professor at the London School of Economics Law Department. He researches issues of law, policy and politics relating to household debt and over-indebtedness. He has worked on the World Bank's Report on the Treatment of the Insolvency of Natural Persons (2013) and the Law Reform Commission of Ireland's project on personal debt management (2010-2012). He has published articles on the law and politics of bankruptcy and household debt in leading journals including the Journal of Law and Society and The Modern Law Review.

CAMBRIDGE UNIVERSITY PRESS

Series Editors

Professor Eilis Ferran, University of Cambridge
Professor Niamh Moloney, London School of Economics and Political Science
Professor Howell Jackson, *Harvard Law School*

International Corporate Law and Financial Market Regulation

Corporate law and financial market regulation have major implications for how the modern economy is organised and regulated and for how risk is managed and distributed – domestically, regionally and internationally. This Series seeks to inform and lead the vibrant scholarly and policy debate in this highly dynamic area by publishing cutting-edge, timely and critical examinations of the most pressing and important questions in the field.

BANKRUPTCY: THE CASE FOR RELIEF IN AN ECONOMY OF DEBT

JOSEPH SPOONER

London School of Economics and Political Science

CAMBRIDGE
UNIVERSITY PRESS

CAMBRIDGE
UNIVERSITY PRESS

University Printing House, Cambridge CB2 8BS, United Kingdom

One Liberty Plaza, 20th Floor, New York, NY 10006, USA

477 Williamstown Road, Port Melbourne, VIC 3207, Australia

314–321, 3rd Floor, Plot 3, Splendor Forum, Jasola District Centre, New Delhi – 110025, India

79 Anson Road, #06–04/06, Singapore 079906

Cambridge University Press is part of the University of Cambridge.

It furthers the University's mission by disseminating knowledge in the pursuit of education, learning, and research at the highest international levels of excellence.

www.cambridge.org
Information on this title: www.cambridge.org/9781107166943
DOI: 10.1017/9781316711484

First published 2019

Printed and bound in Great Britain by Clays Ltd, Elcograf S.p.A.

A catalogue record for this publication is available from the British Library.

Library of Congress Cataloging-in-Publication Data
Names: Spooner, Joseph Tobias, 1985– author.
Title: The law of consumer bankruptcy : a critical approach / Joseph Spooner, London School of Economics and Political Science.
Description: Cambridge, United Kingdom ; New York, NY, USA : Cambridge University Press, 2019. | Series: International corporate law and financial market regulation | Based on author's thesis (doctoral – University College, London, 2014) issued under title: Personal insolvency law in the modern consumer credit society : English and comparative perspectives. | Includes bibliographical references and index.
Identifiers: LCCN 2018049855 | ISBN 9781107166943 (hardback)
Subjects: LCSH: Bankruptcy – England. | Debt relief – England. | Consumer credit – Law and legislation – England. | Bankruptcy – Economic aspects. | Finance, Personal – Government policy | BISAC: LAW / Corporate.
Classification: LCC KD2139 .S69 2019 | DDC 346.4207/8–dc23
LC record available at https://lccn.loc.gov/2018049855

ISBN 978-1-107-16694-3 Hardback

To Henrietta, Jenni and Seamus.

CONTENTS

FIGURES

PREFACE AND ACKNOWLEDGMENTS

Ten years ago, I began a role as a legal researcher at the Law Reform Commission of Ireland, where my brief was a project on the enforcement of judgment debts. This seemed like quite an interesting aspect of civil procedure and a topic that would allow some exploration of how issues of private law and the administration of justice impact on social and economic life. After two weeks on the job, the Lehman Brothers bank collapsed. Within the first month, the Irish banking system followed suit, leading the Irish Government to issue a blanket guarantee of Irish banks' liabilities. Suddenly questions of how the law regulates household debt and default became more obviously pressing and captivating matters, and this research project was quickly expanded to a wider enquiry, including proposals to overhaul Irish bankruptcy law. If this was perhaps a dramatic beginning to a research career and a vivid introduction to the political, economic, social, and legal significance of household debt, it was merely indicative of the realisations regarding the role of debt in our economy with which we all (and particularly those of my generation) were confronted following the Global Financial Crisis of 2008 and Great Recession. This book is a product of this experience, both personal and societal.

Many debts have been incurred in the writing of this book. Particular thanks are due to Professor Ian Fletcher, who sadly passed away during the completion of this project. Professor Fletcher supervised my Ph.D project in which many ideas explored in this book were first developed. His work has been an inspiration and his generous mentorship offered a wonderful introduction to the academic world. It is a great regret that he will not read this book. I also thank Alison Diduck, Robert Stevens, Nigel Balmer, Lucinda Miller and the University College London Faculty of Laws for their help and encouragement during my Ph.D studies. I am very grateful to my colleagues at the LSE Law Department, many of whom have read and commented on drafts of various chapters. Neil Duxbury, Niki Lacey, Paul MacMahon, Susan Marks, Niamh Moloney,

Linda Mulcahy, Sarah Paterson, Nick Sage, and Edmund Schuster have been particularly generous and constructive.

Special thanks are due to Iain Ramsay, who contributed greatly to the development of the book through insightful comments and many detailed discussions. I also thank for their input andencouragement Stephanie Ben-Ishai, Susan Block-Lieb, Jason Kilborn, David Milman, Saul Schwartz and Ted Janger. The Household Finance Collaborative Research Network, convening at the Law and Society Association annual meeting, has been an excellent forum for discussing ideas developed in the book. I remember in particular the contribution to this group of Jean Braucher, who is sadly no longer with us. I also thank Melbourne Law School (particularly Paul Ali, Lucinda O'Brien, Ian Ramsay and John Tobin) and Queensland University of Technology School of Law (particularly Ros Mason, Nicola Howell and Michael Murray), where I spent periods during the writing of this book. I thank Dr José Garrido for inviting me to participate on the World Bank Insolvency and Creditor/Debtor Regimes Task Force project on the Treatment of the Insolvency of Natural Persons, from which I obtained valuable insight. Ideas explored in this book have been discussed to varying degrees in articles in the *Journal of Law and Society* and the *Modern Law Review*, and I thank the editors and reviewers of these publications. I am also grateful for the support and understanding of Cambridge University Press staff including Matt Galloway, Jackie Grant, Kim Hughes and Gemma Smith, as well as series editors Eilis Ferran, Niamh Moloney and Howell Jackson.

My family have been a huge help and support throughout my studies and career, and I am very grateful to my parents Caitríona and Jody, and siblings Álmath, Muirne, Eithne and Cormac.

Henrietta Zeffert has been a fount of inspiration, patience, insight, and encouragement throughout this project. I am immensely grateful for her belief and support.

All errors and omissions remain my responsibility.

1

Introduction

1.1 The Debt Economy: Household Debt and Crises of Financialised Capitalism

This book arrives a decade after the global financial crisis of 2007–8 and the beginning of the Great Recession, at a time when much of the world still labours under problems vividly brought to light by these events. In recent years, book after book appears to have been published identifying fundamental crises in the contemporary economic and political order, from a range of political and ideological perspectives.[1] Mainstream opinion presents a global economy struggling from economic stagnation, significant and widening inequality, and related political discord.[2] Economic growth remains sluggish in advanced economies, with particular problems of low productivity growth and weak demand.[3] Inequality came into sharp focus following the crisis,[4] with US President Barack Obama even proclaiming it 'the defining

[1] See e.g. R. G. Rajan, *Fault Lines: How Hidden Fractures Still Threaten the World Economy* (Princeton University Press, 2011); D. Harvey, Seventeen Contradictions and the End of Capitalism (Oxford University Press, 2014); R. B. Reich, *Saving Capitalism: For the Many, Not the Few* (Knopf Publishing Group, 2015); W. Streeck, *How Will Capitalism End?: Essays on a Failing System* (Verso Books, 2016); C. Crouch, *Can Neoliberalism Be Saved From Itself?* (Social Europe Edition, 2017); E. Posner and E. Weyl, *Radical Markets: Uprooting Capitalism and Democracy for a Just Society* (Princeton University Press, 2018).

[2] See e.g. 'Subdued Demand: Symptoms and Remedies', *World Economic Outlook* (International Monetary Fund, 2016) xvi.

[3] S. Lo and K. S Rogoff, 'Secular Stagnation, Debt Overhang and Other Rationales for Sluggish Growth, Six Years On' (Bank for International Settlements, 2015) 482 www.bis.org/publ/work482.pdf.

[4] T. Piketty, *Capital in the Twenty-First Century* (Harvard University Press, 2014) 1; A. B. Atkinson, *Inequality* (Harvard University Press, 2015) 1.

challenge of our time'.[5] Macroeconomic policymakers have taken new interest in issues of inequality and distribution following the crisis,[6] while there has been an outpouring of high profile academic literature on the topic.[7] Undoubtedly related to economic sluggishness and inequality, political instability further threatens prosperity, as most clearly exemplified by the Brexit referendum and the election of President Donald Trump.[8]

The starting point of this book is that there is now significant evidence to link these pressing policy problems of economic stagnation, inequality and political discord to high levels of household debt. Perhaps the contribution of debt to these issues is unsurprising, given that commentators such as Nancy Fraser argue that the 'defining feature' of our contemporary regime of financialised capitalism is the 'new centrality of debt'.[9] The increasing recognition of high household debt levels as a key aspect of contemporary advanced economies gives new significance to bankruptcy or personal insolvency law, as a unique point of contact between the legal system and the problem of excessive household debt.[10]

[5] B. Obama, 'Remarks by the President on Economic Mobility' (The Arc, Washington DC, 4 December 2013) https://obamawhitehouse.archives.gov/node/248126 accessed 14 June 2018.

[6] See e.g. G. Vlieghe, 'Debt, Demographics and the Distribution of Income: New Challenges for Monetary Policy – Speech by Gertjan Vlieghe, Bank of England' (Department of Economics and Centre for Macroeconomics public lecture, London School of Economics, 18 January 2016) 7–8 www.bankofengland.co.uk/publications/pages/speeches/2016/872.aspx accessed 19 January 2016; J. Yellen, 'Macroeconomic Research After the Crisis' ('The Elusive "Great" Recovery: Causes and Implications for Future Business Cycle Dynamics' 60th Annual Economic Conference, Federal Reserve Bank of Boston, Boston, Massachusetts, 14 October 2016) www.federalreserve.gov/newsevents/speech/yellen20161014a.htm?emailid=55ccb821090bff0300e78b62&segmentid=1e887e34-00a5-c328-481c-7a09b5553d9c accessed 25 October 2016; S. Keen, *Can We Avoid Another Financial Crisis?* (Polity Press, 2017) 25–38.

[7] Piketty (n. 4); Atkinson (n. 4); J. Stiglitz, *The Price of Inequality: The Avoidable Causes and Invisible Costs of Inequality* (Allen Lane, 2012).

[8] 'Gaining Momentum?' *World Economic Outlook* April 2017 (International Monetary Fund, 2017) xvi.

[9] N. Fraser, 'Contradictions of Capital and Care', *New Left Review* 99 (2016) 112.

[10] This book largely uses the terms 'bankruptcy' and 'insolvency' interchangeably. An exception is when specific references are made to insolvency procedures under English law. Here the bankruptcy procedure is one of four procedures together forming 'personal insolvency law' (alongside the Individual Voluntary Arrangement, Debt Relief Order and County Court Administration Order procedures): I. F. Fletcher, *The Law of Insolvency* 4th revised edn (Sweet & Maxwell, 2009) pt. 1. For reasons set out later in this Chapter related to the need to distinguish issues discussed here from the unrelated field of corporate insolvency, the book considers the term bankruptcy – and particularly consumer bankruptcy – most appropriate. The meaning of 'consumer bankruptcy' in this

The subject of this book is the place of bankruptcy law – and particularly what this chapter later describes as consumer bankruptcy law – in the contemporary financialised economy, and its ability to offer a response to the economic, social and political problems inherent to this regime.[11]

The statement that our current economic order is 'financialised' may be understood in various ways.[12] Financialisation can describe the shift between two major economic regimes – from the post-war Keynesian demand management economy to the contemporary post-Keynesian or neoliberal regime that emerged from the late 1970s.[13] The neoliberal and financialised eras have become synonymous, particularly after the global financial crisis.[14] Financialisation can also refer to the expanded role that financial services play at the household level, and the extent to which households must use financial products (chiefly credit) in order to access essential services, maintain a reasonable living standard, build wealth and participate in society. One aspect of this trend has seen financial risks individualised through the withdrawal of collective and public risk management mechanisms.[15] In this sense, the process has implications for the way in which households use credit and encounter debt difficulty, and so too for the models of credit use and debtor behaviour informing policy-making. Another related aspect of financialisation is the extent to which the logic of finance has permeated our daily lives.[16] This manifests, for example, in the neoliberal paradigm of the individual as an enterprise, an

book is discussed below. Therefore, references to bankruptcy are more frequent than references to insolvency, and include not just the specific bankruptcy procedure, but general legal approaches to regulating the factual insolvency of an individual debtor; or what the World Bank calls 'the constellation of potential approaches to treating that condition': World Bank, *Report on the Treatment of the Insolvency of Natural Persons* (2013) para. 17. Chapter 4 discusses further the range of personal insolvency procedures.

11 While the focus is on English law as located in the UK economy, the economic and political trends discussed are common to many advanced economies, and the book hopes that much of its discussion and argument are more widely applicable.

12 M. Prasad, *Land of Too Much* (Harvard University Press, 2012) 197; M. Sawyer, 'What Is Financialization?', *International Journal of Political Economy* 42 (2013) 5.

13 Sawyer (n. 12); C. Berry, 'Citizenship in a Financialised Society: Financial Inclusion and the State before and after the Crash', *Policy & Politics* 43 (2015) 509, 512; P. Pathak, 'Ethopolitics and the Financial Citizen', *The Sociological Review* 62 (2014) 90, 92.

14 W. Davies, 'Neoliberalism: A Bibliographic Review', *Theory, Culture & Society* 31 (2014) 309, 316.

15 Berry (n. 13) 512; J. S. Hacker, *The Great Risk Shift: The New Economic Insecurity and the Decline of the American Dream* Revised edn (Oxford University Press, 2008).

16 R. Martin, *Financialization of Daily Life* (Temple University Press, 2002); G. F. Davis, *Managed by the Markets: How Finance Re-Shaped America* reprint (Oxford University Press, 2011).

'entrepreneur of the self' or an investor of her human capital.[17] It may lead policymakers and judges to adopt particular characterisations of debtors as 'financial subjects',[18] judging debtor conduct in accordance with norms of individualisation and responsibilisation,[19] including 'responsibility to the self and the population at large to reduce the collective burden on the welfare state'.[20] Moving from official decision making to the individual, we may also internalise this logic and allow financialisation to shape our individual behaviour.[21] Another perspective views financialisation as the manner in which the financial sector has come to occupy a disproportionate position in the economy, accounting for an increasing share of national income and demonstrating a notable rise in profits relative to other activities (e.g. trade and commodity production).[22] With such economic heft, the financial sector also acquires increasing power and political influence.[23] It holds the ability to shape, for example, the legal and regulatory norms governing household debt and bankruptcy.[24] These various understandings of financialisation are mutually reinforcing.

The financialisation process has involved a dramatic debt expansion, to the point where UK household debt has grown from less than 30 per cent of GDP in the late 1970s to a peak of over 95 per cent per cent during the global financial crisis (Figure 1.1).[25] Household debt-to-disposable incomes had reached 100 per cent by the mid-1990s, before peaking at 175 cent around

[17] M. Lazzarato and J. D. Jordan, *The Making of the Indebted Man: Essay on the Neoliberal Condition* reprint edn (Massachusetts Institute of Technology Press, 2012) 33; W. Brown, *Undoing the Demos: Neoliberalism's Stealth Revolution* (Massachusetts Institute of Technology Press, 2015) 32–45; I. Ramsay, *Personal Insolvency in the 21st Century: A Comparative Analysis of the US and Europe* (Hart Publishing, 2017) 28.

[18] Pathak (n. 13) 96.

[19] S. Soederberg, *Debtfare States and the Poverty Industry: Money, Discipline and the Surplus Population* (Routledge, 2014) 51.

[20] Pathak (n. 13) 97.

[21] Berry (n. 13) 510.

[22] A. Turner, *Between Debt and the Devil: Money, Credit, and Fixing Global Finance* (Princeton University Press, 2015) 19–21; Prasad (n. 12) 197.

[23] C. Deutschmann, 'Limits to Financialization', *European Journal of Sociology/Archives Européennes de Sociologie* 52 (2011) 347; J. Hopkin and K. A. Shaw, 'Organized Combat or Structural Advantage? The Politics of Inequality and the Winner-Take-All Economy in the United Kingdom', *Politics & Society* 44 (2016) 345.

[24] J. Spooner, 'The Quiet-Loud-Quiet Politics of Post-Crisis Consumer Bankruptcy Law: The Case of Ireland and the Troika', *Modern Law Review* 81 (2018) 790–824.

[25] 'BIS Statistics Explorer: Table F3.1: Total Credit to Households (Core Debt) as a Percentage of GDP' (Bank for International Settlements) https://stats.bis.org/statx/srs/table/F3.1?c=&p=20174&m= accessed 8 July 2018.

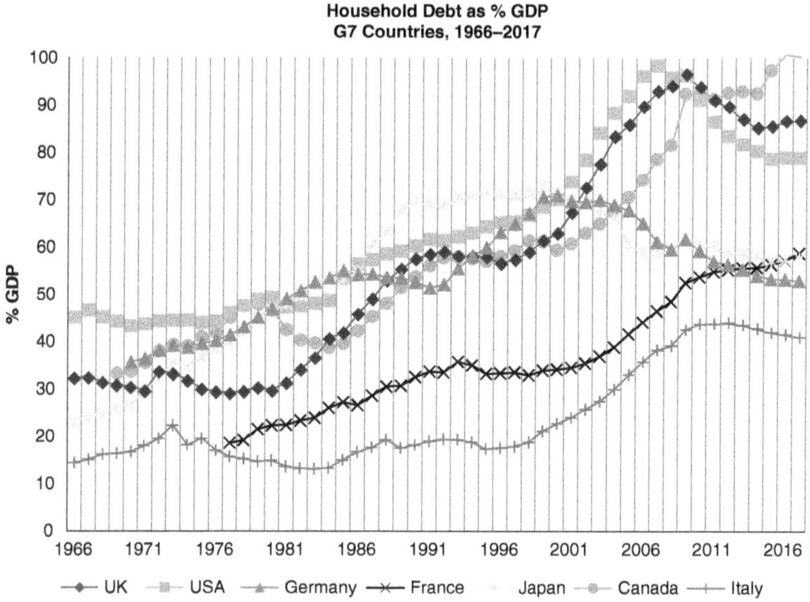

Figure 1.1: Household debt as percentage of GDP. Source: Bank for International Settlements

a decade later (Figure 1.2).[26] Mainstream institutions such as the Council of Europe can now state that 'member states have entered an era where the use of credit has become an essential part of their economies'.[27] Maurizio Lazzarato characterises contemporary conditions as forming a 'debt economy', with neoliberalism 'making the creditor–debtor relationship a centrepiece of politics' and developing debt into the 'archetype of social relations'.[28] Despite the neoliberal era being widely seen as characterised by a renewed embrace of free marketised exchange,[29] Lazzarato (similarly to David Graeber[30]) argues that it is debt – rather than exchange – which forms the 'constitution of society' and represents the most general and global power relation, and the site of contemporary class struggle.[31] On this view, the

[26] 'Household Accounts – Household Debt – OECD Data' (Organisation for Economic Cooperation and Development) http://data.oecd.org/hha/household-debt.htm accessed 10 July 2018.

[27] Council of Europe, 'Recommendation CM/Rec(2007)8 of the Committee of Ministers to Member States on Legal Solutions to Debt Problems'.

[28] Lazzarato and Jordan (n. 17) 20, 23, 33.

[29] See e.g. Davies (n. 14).

[30] D. Graeber, *Debt: The First 5,000 Years* (Melville House, 2012).

[31] Lazzarato and Jordan (n. 17) 39, 89.

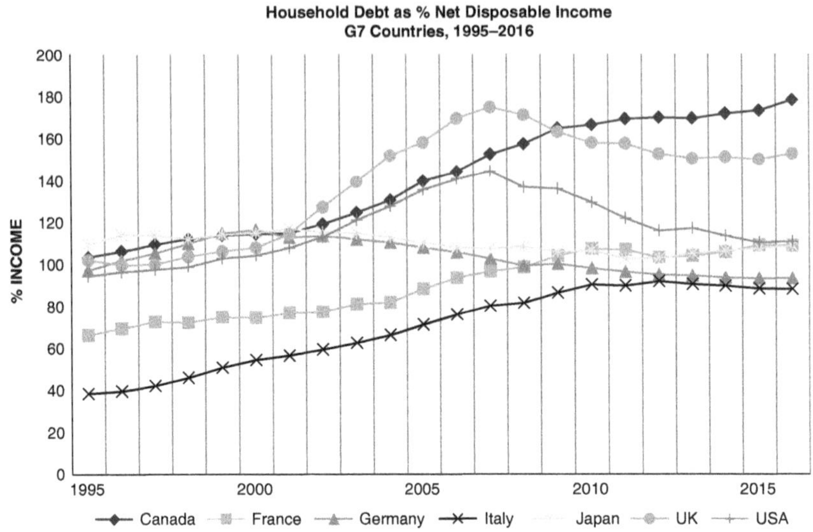

Figure 1.2: Household debt as percentage of disposable income. Source: OECD

dominance of debt explains the condition of contemporary society more effectively than other distinctions such a shift from production to consumption.[32] Many of our contemporary relationships and interactions have been reduced to debtor–creditor dynamics, including those between capital and labour, welfare state services and citizens, and businesses and consumers.[33] Wolfgang Streeck characterises contemporary advanced societies as taking the form of 'debt states', under which neoliberal reforms have reduced taxation and increased public borrowing, but also reduced state public service provision and triggered a rise in household debt to pay for newly marketised social rights.[34] Susanne Soederbergh similarly describes a 'debtfare' economic regime, under which official policies support the expansion of credit markets to augment or replace wages for the poor in the face of income stagnation and inequality.[35]

[32] George Ritzer, '"Hyperconsumption" and "Hyperdebt": A "Hypercritical" Analysis' in *A Debtor World: Interdisciplinary Perspectives on Debt* (Oxford University Press, 2012) 61–2; L. Cohen, *A Consumers' Republic: The Politics of Mass Consumption in Postwar America* (Vintage Books, 2004).

[33] Lazzarato and Jordan (n. 17) 30.

[34] W. Streeck, *Buying Time: The Delayed Crisis of Democratic Capitalism* (Verso Books, 2014) 73.

[35] Soederberg (n. 19).

A range of perspectives therefore identify a 'debtor world', characterised by 'the global phenomenon of increased indebtedness and societal dependence thereon'.[36] Many questions are raised by the central role of high levels of household debt, even regarding the sustainability of this financialised economic order.[37] The global financial crisis did not involve the rethinking of principles of economic organisation that many would have expected, and our financialised economy has not been overhauled. Nonetheless, the prolonged economic slump of the Great Recession has convinced mainstream technical opinion, if not yet politicians and policymakers, to depart from the pre-crisis consensus that widespread access to credit and extensive household debt are always welfare enhancing. International institutions now recognise that many of the pressing problems of financialised capitalism can be linked to excessive household debt, including economic stagnation, inequality and political instability inherent in a debt-dependent economy. The focus of this book lies on these problems, and on the policy role that bankruptcy law and policy might play in response.

1.1.1 *Debt and Economic Stagnation*

Excessive household debt is now recognised as a leading explanation for the prolonged global economic slump following the financial crisis of the late 2000s.[38] Recent reports issued by the Bank for International Settlements note that a 'growing body of evidence points to the existence of a "boom and bust" pattern in the relationship between household debt and GDP growth [under which an] increase in credit predicts higher growth in the near term but lower growth in the medium term'.[39] The global financial crisis brought into sharp relief the risks to financial stability caused by mass household indebtedness,[40] and the build-up of household (both mortgage and unsecured) debt remains 'a key source of

36 R. Brubaker, R. M. Lawless and C. J. Tabb (eds.), *A Debtor World: Interdisciplinary Perspectives on Debt* (Oxford University Press USA, 2012) ix.

37 M. Blyth and M. Matthijs, 'Black Swans, Lame Ducks, and the Mystery of IPE's Missing Macroeconomy', *Review of International Political Economy* 24 (2017) 203.

38 Lo and Rogoff (n. 3) 8.

39 A. Zabai, 'Household Debt: Recent Developments and Challenges' *Bank for International Settlements Quarterly Review* 39 (2017) 47; 'The Global Economy: Maturing Recoveries, Turning Financial Cycles?' (Bank for International Settlements, 2017).

40 Financial Stability Board, *Consumer Finance Protection with Particular Focus on Credit* (2011); R. J. Shiller, *The Subprime Solution* (Princeton University Press, 2012); A. Mian and A. Sufi, *House of Debt* (University of Chicago Press, 2014).

risk to financial and economic stability'.[41] In recent years scholars and policy institutions have increasingly recognised a 'debt overhang' problem, and the contribution of excessive household debt to sluggish economic growth and slow 'recovery' throughout the Great Recession and its aftermath.[42] Mian and Sufi argue that common understandings of the Great Recession as being caused by a banking crisis are misplaced, and instead it represented a crisis of consumer spending as heavily indebted households reduced expenditure in response to economic shocks.[43] Debt contracts carry many inherent risks,[44] including shifting the costs of economic downturns away from creditors (whose claims remain unaffected) onto society's debtors (who lose equity in homes and whose obligations remain intact while income and assets diminish). When society's debtors are those with the highest marginal propensity to consume and the least ability to self-insure, the shifting of losses from creditors to debtors reduces society's overall consumption levels.[45] This effect has continued after the immediate shock of the crisis to produce longer term effects, as highly leveraged households focus resources on debt service rather than consumer spending.[46]

1.1.2 Debt and Inequality

A fascinating development in recent policy literature has been the recognition of the negative aggregate effects of inequality for the overall economy

[41] 'Financial Stability Report: June 2017' (Bank of England 2017) 41 1, 1–19 'Fiscal Monitor – Debt: Use It Wisely' (International Monetary Fund, 2016) www.imf.org/external/pubs/ft/fm/2016/02/fmindex.htm accessed 4 January 2017; 'Household Debt and Financial Stability', Global Financial Stability Report October 2017 (International Monetary Fund, 2017); Zabai (n. 39) 48–51.

[42] See e.g. ' Dealing with Household Debt', World Economic Outlook 2012 (International Monetary Fund, 2012) www.imf.org/external/pubs/ft/weo/2012/01/pdf/c3.pdf; World Bank (n. 10); Mian and Sufi (n. 40); Turner (n. 22); P. Bunn and M. Rostom, 'Household Debt and Spending in the UK' (Bank of England, 2015) 554; Lo and Rogoff (n. 3) 10; International Monetary Fund, 'Fiscal Monitor – Debt: Use It Wisely' (n. 38); 'The Global Economy: Maturing Recoveries, Turning Financial Cycles?' (Bank for International Settlements, 2017) 48–9; International Monetary Fund, 'Household Debt and Financial Stability' (n. 38). The 'debt overhang' externality of household debt is discussed in more detail in Chapter 3 (text to notes 165–78).

[43] Mian and Sufi (n. 40) 46–59.

[44] Turner (n. 22) 54–7.

[45] International Monetary Fund, 'Dealing with Household Debt' (n. 42) 9–13; Zabai (n. 39) 43–6.

[46] Bunn and Rostom (n. 42); International Monetary Fund, 'Household Debt and Financial Stability' (n. 41); Zabai (n. 39).

and society, and the breakdown of the long-held consensus that there is a necessary trade-off between efficiency and equity.[47] An understanding of the effects of excessive household debt furthers this recognition, given how the inequality of debt may exacerbate negative aggregate economic effects. A primary mechanism through which excessive debt jeopardises economic prosperity is through its unequal distribution of economic risks onto the least well-resourced members of society. Technical accounts explain that in terms of aggregate demand, the distribution of debt among households is crucial, since most negative effects arise where high debt levels are concentrated among households with the most limited resources and 'less scope for self-insurance'.[48] This means that links between excessive debt and economic stagnation turn on the fact that the economy's debtors are those with a higher marginal propensity to consume and limited recourse to wealth reserves to protect themselves against economic downturns. The imposition of financial losses on this group will cause them to reduce expenditure significantly, reducing aggregate demand upon which economic growth depends.

Both the structure of debt contracts and the wider structure of household credit markets can contribute to inequality. Caplovitz taught us half a century ago that contemporary credit markets are both born of inequality and exacerbate the unequal distribution of resources.[49] At the supply side, rising inequality allows increasingly wealthy, high income groups to invest income in financial assets backed by loans extended to low income groups, creating a need for more profitable household debt to provide further fields for reinvestment.[50] Meanwhile growing income inequality intensifies the demand for credit among lower income households who receive an increasingly small proportion of aggregate income.[51] Rising household borrowing partly involves attempts by low and middle income

[47] Atkinson (n. 4) 243–62. For recognition of the macroeconomic risks of inequality, see e.g. International Monetary Fund, 'Gaining Momentum? '*World Economic Outlook* April 2017 (n. 8); Era Dabla-Norris and others, 'Causes and Consequences of Income Inequality: A Global Perspective' (IMF 2015) IMF Staff Discussion Note.

[48] Zabai (n. 39) 45.

[49] D. Caplovitz, *Poor Pay More: Consumer Practices of Low Income Families* (Free Press, 1968); N. I. Silber, 'Discovering That the Poor Pay More: Race Riots, Poverty, and the Rise of Consumer Law Symposium: How the Poor Still Pay More – A Reexamination of Urban Poverty in the Twenty-First Century', *Fordham Urban Law Journal* 44 (2017) 1319.

[50] Dabla-Norris and others (n. 47) 8; M. Kumhof, R. Rancière and P. Winant, 'Inequality, Leverage, and Crises', *American Economic Review* 105 (2015) 1217.

[51] P. Lucchino and S. Morelli, *Inequality, Debt and Growth* (Resolution Foundation, 2012) 2; Turner (n. 22) 119–24.

households to maintain both their absolute standards of living and relative standards of consumption[52] and bridge the gap between stagnant wages and rising costs of living.[53] Joseph Stiglitz identifies a key role for contemporary credit markets in exacerbating inequality through the rent-seeking activities of consumer lenders in 'preying upon [poor and uninformed] groups with predatory lending and abusive credit card practices'.[54] Stiglitz also points to creditor-friendly US bankruptcy law as amplifying these effects.[55] David Harvey notes that consumer marketplaces are new sites for class conflict and exploitation, arguing that collective gains workers may win from capital in the workplace can quickly be erased through excess value extracted from consumers by businesses in the marketplace.[56] Soederberg advances this idea, arguing that while workplaces involve primary exploitation of labour by capital, consumer credit markets (particularly those used among low-income groups) produce 'secondary forms of exploitation whereby workers' real income can be modified ... in the sphere of exchange through the extraction of interest and fees from a loan'.[57] In this way debt creates inequality, while also arising *from* existing inequality.[58]

At a more basic level, some commentators argue that fundamental features of our legal system establish so-called 'ground rules' of capitalism that tend towards inequality.[59] Various basic laws of capitalism give excessive market power to certain parties, while protecting and

52 A. Barba and M. Pivetti, 'Rising Household Debt: Its Causes and Macroeconomic Implications – a Long-Period Analysis', *Cambridge Journal of Economics* 33 (2009) 113, 122; T. A Sullivan, 'Debt and the Simulation of Social Class' in R. Brubaker, R. M. Lawless and C. J. Tabb (eds.), *A Debtor World: Interdisciplinary Perspectives on Debt* (Oxford University Press, 2012) 54.

53 See Barba and Pivetti (n. 52) 124–5; Lucchino and Morelli (n. 51) 2.

54 Stiglitz (n. 7) 37. See Chapter 3's discussion of failures in consumer credit markets (text to notes 97–138).

55 ibid. The changes to bankruptcy law were enacted by the Bankruptcy Abuse Prevention and Consumer Protection Act of 2005. See e.g. R. M. Lawless and others, 'Did Bankruptcy Reform Fail – An Empirical Study of Consumer Debtors', *American Bankruptcy Law Journal* 82 (2008) 349.

56 D. Harvey, *The Enigma of Capital: And the Crises of Capitalism* (Profile Books, 2011) 66–8.

57 Soederberg (n. 19) 37.

58 S. Soederberg, 'The US Debtfare State and the Credit Card Industry: Forging Spaces of Dispossession', *Antipode* 45 (2013) 493, 494.

59 For example, Campbell points to monopoly rights granted through intellectual property law, and the privileges afforded to managers of public companies by principles of limited liability and the separation of ownership and control: D. Campbell, 'The Fetishism of Divergence: A Critique of Piketty', *Journal of Corporate Law Studies* 15 (2015) 183, 212–13. Reich (n. 1) xiii; D. S. Grewal, 'Book Review – The Laws of Capitalism', *Harvard Law Review* 128 (2014) 626.

perpetuating that power through the enforcement of rights acquired in the market. The 'private law' norms of contract law can be considered among such ground rules, which structure market outcomes and distribute resources.[60] Contracts are mechanisms used to shift risks and costs through legal rights and obligations. Mian and Sufi have pointed to the manner in which legal rules regarding the enforcement of debt contracts shift the costs of economic downturn from society's well-resourced creditors to debtors of more limited means.[61] In contrast to other arrangements such as equity financing, debt contracts involve no sharing of loss. If circumstances change during the performance of a debt contract, the debtor remains liable for full repayment and forfeiture of security, while the creditor retains a claim to the full sum owed plus interest, as well as to any security interest. This subjects debtors to the risks of economic volatility. Rigorous enforcement of debt contracts by the legal system invariably involves the distribution of resources upwards from the debtor class to holders of capital.

1.1.3 Debt and Political Instability

A wide range of observers note the political instability linked to contemporary inequality.[62] Various authors caution that the effects of economic crisis and inequality may be to undermine the social fabric or the 'trust modern societies need for growth and stability'.[63] One manifestation of political unrest was the emergence of the 'Occupy' movement following the financial crisis, which in disparate forms campaigned against inequality.[64] A focal point was protest against the debt burden carried by households, leading to offshoots such as 'Strike Debt', which sought to mobilise a debtor movement against a creditor class.[65] Indeed, Mark Blyth and Matthias Matthijs attribute the 2016 populist shock to debtor–creditor politics, with votes in the UK, USA, Austria, Italy and elsewhere arising in the context of 'anti-creditor pro-

60 I. Ramsay, 'Consumer Credit Law, Distributive Justice and the Welfare State', *Oxford Journal of Legal Studies* 15 (1995) 177, 178–89.
61 Mian and Sufi (n. 40) 18–19; A. Mian and A. Sufi, 'The Macroeconomic Advantages of Softening Debt Contracts', *Harvard Law & Policy Review* 11 (2017) 11.
62 Dabla-Norris and others (n. 47) 8–9; International Monetary Fund, 'Gaining Momentum?' *World Economic Outlook April 2017* (n. 8) xv–xvii; Reich (n. 1) vii–viii.
63 Shiller (n. 40) 2; Reich (n. 1) xii.
64 Todd Gitlin, 'Occupy's Predicament: The Moment and the Prospects for the Movement', *The British Journal of Sociology* 64 (2013) 3; N. Chomsky, Occupy (Penguin, 2012).
65 Y. McKee, 'DEBT: Occupy, Postcontemporary Art, and the Aesthetics of Debt Resistance', *South Atlantic Quarterly* 112 (2013) 784.

debtor political coalitions that have been systematically eating away at mainstream centre-left and centre-right party vote shares since the [financial] crisis'.[66] Populist uprisings can be seen as 'a political reaction to the reversal of power between creditors and debtors' represented in decades of policy consensus producing 'a creditors' paradise' of high household debt, ultra-low inflation and a reduced share of growth for labour.[67] The sense of political disillusionment was not helped by policymakers post-crisis failures to rescue financially troubled households while 'bailing out' the financial sector.[68] When the Obama administration ultimately abandoned post-crisis plans to amend bankruptcy law to allow mortgage debt reduction ('cram-down'), certain US authors described this move as representing 'a stark choice of supporting Wall Street [over] Main Street interests',[69] and even a 'great betrayal' of voters.[70] From another perspective, commentators suggest that political opposition to proposed assistance for perceived irresponsible debtor households fuelled the rise of a populist right.[71]

Such flaring of political opinion and polarisation can lead to policy paralysis.[72] The role of financial sector influence over both political processes and the technocratic decision making that operates when politicians leave a 'policy void'[73] may work to maintain a favourable status quo.[74] A lack of political responsiveness may explain the growth of civil society groups and organisation outside of mainstream political parties,[75] including movements advancing ideas of debt resistance as a challenge to financialisation and its

66 Blyth and Matthijs (n. 37) 218.

67 ibid, 219.

68 Ramsay, '*21st Century*' (n. 17) 10; 'Financial Stability Review' (European Central Bank, 2015) 148; I. Martin and C. Niedt, Foreclosed America (Stanford University Press, 2015) ch. 4.

69 J. Taub, *Other People's Houses: How Decades of Bailouts, Captive Regulators, and Toxic Bankers Made Home Mortgages a Thrilling Business* (Yale University Press, 2014) 263–6; Mian and Sufi (n. 40) 135–7; A. J. Levitin, 'The Politics of Financial Regulation and the Regulation of Financial Politics: A Review Essay', *Harvard Law Review* 127 (2013) 1991, 2022–3.

70 J. Taub, *Other People's Houses* (Yale University Press, 2014) 247–66.

71 ibid, 263–6; Mian and Sufi (n. 40) 135–7; Levitin (n. 69) 1991, 2022–3.

72 A. Mian, A. Sufi and F. Trebbi, 'Resolving Debt Overhang: Political Constraints in the Aftermath of Financial Crises', *American Economic Journal: Macroeconomics* 6 (2014) 1.

73 J. Montgomerie and others, 'The Politics of Indebtedness in the UK' (Goldsmiths University of London, 2014) 4.

74 Spooner, 'The Quiet-Loud-Quiet Politics of Post-Crisis Consumer Bankruptcy Law: The Case of Ireland and the Troika' (n. 24).

75 F. de Witte, 'EU Law, Politics, and the Social Question', *German Law Journal* 14 (2013) 581, 591; C. Crouch, 'From Markets versus States to Corporations versus Civil Society?' in

effects.[76] The alternative appears to be for indebted households to join 'anti-creditor, pro-debtor coalitions-in-waiting that are ripe for the picking by insurgents and opportunists of both the left and the right'.[77] In either case, this can result in political conflict and instability. In short, excessive levels of household debt generate sensitive political problems, and it has long been the case that 'debt is social dynamite'.[78]

1.1.4 *The Case for Debt Relief*

Recognition by international and domestic policymakers of the dangers of high levels of household debt marks a striking departure from the prior consensus in favour of credit market expansion[79] and the 'democratisation of credit',[80] towards a nascent understanding that 'less finance can be better'.[81] Acceptance of the problems of excessive debt creates a compelling policy case for household debt relief initiatives and suggests a central economic role for personal insolvency or bankruptcy law. The discharge of debt in bankruptcy constitutes 'an extraordinary exception to the usual obligation orientation of the law'.[82] The rest of the legal system is directed towards enforcing contractual obligations central to the preservation of a debt-dependent society and power relations of debt.[83] By contrast bankruptcy law has the potential to, and in fact does, counter the principle of debt itself – it is a unique societal institution that offers debt relief routinely and as of right. Once this aspect of its nature is recognised, bankruptcy can reduce household indebtedness and

W. Streeck and A. Schäfer (eds.), *Politics in the Age of Austerity* (Polity Press, 2013); Montgomerie and others (n. 73) 4.

76 See e.g. A. Ross, *Creditocracy: And the Case for Debt Refusal* 1st edn (OR Books, 2014); E. Hoekstra, 'Andrew Ross on the Anti-Debt Movement' in D. Hartmann and C. Uggen (eds.), *Owned* (W W Norton & Company, 2015); Montgomerie and others (n. 73) 31–6.

77 Blyth and Matthijs (n. 66) 219; G. Standing, The Precariat: The New Dangerous Class, New edn (Bloomsbury Academic, 2016) 1.

78 T. Sullivan, E. Warren and J. L. Westbrook, As We Forgive Our Debtors: Bankruptcy and Consumer Credit in America (Beard Books, 1989) 334.

79 Turner (n. 22) 99.

80 Soederberg (n. 19) 61–5.

81 Turner (n. 22) 17. See also Mian and Sufi (n. 40) 127.

82 M. Howard, 'A Theory of Discharge in Consumer Bankruptcy', *Ohio State Law Journal* 48 (1987)1047, 1047–8.

83 See e.g. the emphasis in Law and Finance literature on investor and creditor enforcement rights as influencing 'development': e.g. R. La Porta, F. Lopez-de-Silanes and A. Shleifer, 'The Economic Consequences of Legal Origins', *Journal of Economic Literature* 46 (2008) 285.

so address related problems. This depends, however, on policymakers concerned with the dangers of excessive household debt recognising bankruptcy law as a tool for addressing these risks, alongside (and perhaps even in preference to) other policy measures of a monetary or fiscal nature.[84] Economic policymakers increasingly advocate the merits of household debt relief policies, though often seeing 'no economy-wide tools available for large-scale debt restructuring'.[85] Bankruptcy is such a tool, however, at least when appropriately deployed (and perhaps expanded). Consumer bankruptcy literature has long argued the case for household debt discharge, and some institutions such as the World Bank have accepted this perspective.[86] Now these arguments could potentially be given deeper support and a wider audience by contemporary broad recognition of the macroeconomic policy benefits of debt relief. An ambition of the book is to argue this case, while examining how broader ideas regarding the policy benefits of debt relief can be given concrete shape through the detail of bankruptcy law.

The ability of the law to respond to contemporary policy challenges also depends, however, on lawmakers (legislative, administrative and judicial) within the bankruptcy system recognising the public policy case for extensive household debt relief. The latter chapters of this book present a story of English bankruptcy law's failure to accept its contemporary role as a social insurance mechanism against the risks associated with a debt-dependent economy. The book reveals a law continuing to prioritise the aim of debt collection and maximising returns to creditors despite the pressing contemporary case for focusing on objectives of debt relief and providing a 'fresh start' to financially troubled debtors. The historical origins of the law in corporate and commercial insolvency obscure how the law is now called upon to address distinct problems related to non-business household debt. While conditions of financialisation create a need for household debt relief, the accompanying neoliberal ideas of individual responsibility and minimalist state intervention in (financial) markets have militated against the law's delivery of such relief. Before the book progresses to these criticisms, the remainder of this

[84] See text to notes 195–9 below and Chapter 3, text to notes 263–83.

[85] G. Vlieghe, 'Debt, Demographics and the Distribution of Income: New Challenges for Monetary Policy' (Public lecture, London School of Economics, 18 January 2016) 3 www.bankofengland.co.uk/publications/Pages/speeches/2016/872.aspx accessed 11 November 2018.

[86] World Bank (n. 10). For discussion of what the books refers to as 'consumer bankruptcy' literature, see footnote 144 below and accompanying text.

chapter takes the first steps in building the argument in favour of bankruptcy's prioritisation of an objective of debt relief, by presenting an account of the extent and distribution of household debt and over-indebtedness. It then illustrates how these conditions argue for a new law of consumer bankruptcy.

1.2 An Indebted Society: High Household Debt Levels and Over-Indebtedness

1.2.1 Household Debt Levels

Even a brief analysis of the empirical picture in the UK illustrates the central role of household debt in contemporary advanced economies. UK household indebtedness stands at historically high levels, with household debt to income ratios standing at 140 per cent in 2017 compared to less than 80 per cent in 1987.[87] The Office for Budget Responsibility predicts this figure to rise to 153 per cent by early 2022, as debt levels increase and wages grow slowly (if at all).[88] By the measure of debt servicing – i.e. interest payments as a share of household income after living costs – household debt burdens may be more severe than even before the global financial crisis.[89]

Mortgages constitute approximately 70 per cent of this debt load and, reducing slightly from the pre-crisis peak, the stock of mortgage debt remains almost double that of the late 1980s.[90] Following an immediate post-crisis slowdown, unsecured consumer credit has returned to its fastest annual growth rate since boom times of 2005, outpacing wage growth considerably.[91] Half of new lending is by banks, primarily credit cards (34 per cent of the total consumer credit stock), personal loans and overdrafts, with rapid growth also in dealership car finance (now representing 30 per cent of the consumer credit stock).[92] Credit availability standards in these categories have loosened continuously from 2012 to 2017, for example through increasingly attractive balance transfer offers.

87 Bank of England (n. 41) 3.
88 Office for Budget Responsibility, 'Office for Budget Responsibility Economic and Fiscal Outlook March 2017' (2017) Cm 9024 65 https://obr.uk/efo/economic-fiscal-outlook-march-2017/ accessed 11 November 2018.
89 D. Gibbons, 'Britain in the Red: Why We Need Action to Help over-Indebted Households' (Centre for Responsible Credit (commissioned by TUC and Unison) 2016) 4.
90 Bank of England (n. 41) 4–5.
91 ibid, 14.
92 ibid, 14, 18–19.

Credit quality has not improved, even though interest rates have been falling (querying common understandings of 'risk-based pricing').[93] These circumstances have left the Financial Conduct Authority (FCA) concerned at consumers' long-term indebtedness. For example, it found that two million credit card borrowers are in 'persistent debt', and an even larger number carry balances that will take ten years to clear.[94]

The past decade of recession and sluggish growth has brought changes in the types of debts leading households into financial difficulty. The FCA has extended its scrutiny beyond credit cards to problems in bank overdraft and high cost credit markets (including rent-to-own services, home-collected (doorstep) credit and catalogue credit).[95] The early post-crisis period saw a surge in high-cost short-term ('payday') lending, (from a value of £900 million in 2008–9 to £2–2.2 billion by 2011/12[96]), and accompanying problems in this debt category.[97] Regulatory responses in this sector appear to have been successful.[98] Financial difficulties continue to manifest in other ways, however, and UK households have increasingly encountered problems in relation to essential obligations such as rent arrears and debts owed to central and local government.[99] These obligations, associated with low-income groups, are sometimes termed 'hidden' debt problems[100] and tend to receive less academic and policy attention than other issues such as credit card and mortgage debt.[101] Chapters 2 and 6 show in more detail how this

[93] See e.g. P. A. McCoy, 'Rethinking Disclosure in a World of Risk-Based Pricing', *Harvard Journal on Legislation* 44 (2007) 123.

[94] 'Credit Card Market Study: Interim Report' (Financial Conduct Authority, 2015) MS14/6.2; 'Credit Card Market Study: Final Findings Report' (Financial Conduct Authority, 2016) MS14/6.3; 'Credit Card Market Study: Consultation on Persistent Debt and Earlier Intervention Remedies' (Financial Conduct Authority, 2017) CP17/10.

[95] 'High-Cost Credit: Including Review of the High-Cost Short-Term Credit Price Cap' (Financial Conduct Authority, 2017) FS17/2.

[96] *Payday Lending: Compliance Review Final Report* (Office of Fair Trading, 2013) 9.

[97] ibid, 5.

[98] Financial Conduct Authority, 'High-Cost Credit: Including Review of the High-Cost Short-Term Credit Price Cap' (n. 95) 8. See Chapter 2, text to notes 72–4.

[99] See e.g. London Assembly, Economy Committee, 'Final Demand: Personal Problem Debt in London' (Greater London Authority 2015); 'Council Tax Debts: How to Deal with the Growing Arrears Crisis Tipping Families into Problem Debt' (StepChange Debt Charity 2015); 'Changing Household Budgets' (Money Advice Trust 2014).

[100] LSE Housing and Communities, 'Facing Debt: Economic Resilience in Newham' (LSE Centre for Analysis of Social Exclusion 2014) CASE Report 83 19 http://sticerd.lse.ac.uk/dps/case/cr/casereport83.pdf accessed 11 November 2018.

[101] For exceptions, see S. Ben-Ishai and S. Schwartz, 'Bankruptcy for the Poor?', *Osgoode Hall Law Journal* 45 (2007) 471, 473–4; S. Ben-Ishai, S. Schwartz and J. Barretto,

trend has been influenced by the politics of austerity, the privatisation of public services,[102] the marketisation of public agencies,[103] and the consequent financialisation of welfare.[104] Meanwhile Chapter 6 focuses on the impact of government creditors' increasing tendency to act as aggressive self-interested debt collectors in pursuit of austerity policies. For now, these developments highlight some of the changing challenges to which bankruptcy law must respond. The rise of debt problems outside the financial sector, for example, shows difficulties in addressing problematic debt solely through financial regulatory measures. This highlights a key role for personal insolvency's collective, holistic approach to individual debt.

1.2.2 Distribution of Household Debt

Macro-level measures of household debt (e.g. debt-to-GDP and debt-to-wealth ratios) 'underestimate the true burden of indebted households'.[105] The highest debt-to-income, debt-to-assets and debt-service ratios have been found among low- and middle-income households, both before and after the financial crisis see Figure 1.3.[106] Indebtedness is also unevenly spread among generations, with highest rates in the 25–34 and 35–44 groups (49 per cent owing non-mortgage debt) and lowest among the over-65s (13 per cent).[107] Office for National Statistics surveys find that under 6 per cent of individuals in the highest net income decile (3 per cent in the highest wealth decile) report a heavy debt burden, contrasting with almost 34 per cent of

'The Role of Government as a Creditor of the Disadvantaged' in W. Backert, S. Block-Lieb and J. Niemi (eds.), *Contemporary Issues in Consumer Bankruptcy* (Peter Lang, 2013) 201; I. Ramsay and T. Williams, 'Inequality, Market Discrimination and Credit Markets' in I. Ramsay (ed.), *Consumer Law in the Global Economy* (Aspen, 1997).

102 See e.g. I. Ramsay, 'A Tale of Two Debtors: Responding to the Shock of Over-Indebtedness in France and England – a Story from the Trente Piteuses', *The Modern Law Review* 75 (2012) 212, 247; D. Levi-Faur, 'The Welfare State: A Regulatory Perspective', *Public Administration* 92 (2014) 599; H. Haber, 'Regulation as Social Policy: Home Evictions and Repossessions in the UK and Sweden', *Public Administration* 93 (2015) 806.

103 See e.g. C. Crouch, *Post-Democracy* 1st edn (Polity Press, 2004) 40–1.

104 See e.g. J. Montgomerie and M. Büdenbender, 'Round the Houses: Homeownership and Failures of Asset-Based Welfare in the United Kingdom', *New Political Economy* Vol. 20, No. 3, 2015, p. 386–405.

105 International Monetary Fund, 'Household Debt and Financial Stability' (n. 41) 62.

106 Barba and Pivetti (n. 52) 113–4; 'Household Debt Inequalities' (Office for National Statistics, 2016) www.ons.gov.uk/peoplepopulationandcommunity/personalandhouseholdfinances/debt/articles/householddebtinequalities/2016-04-04 accessed 16 June 2017.

107 Office for National Statistics (n. 106) 16.

individuals in the lowest income decile (almost 40 per cent in the lowest wealth decile).[108] The poorest decile of the population spent almost half of its income on debt repayments during the Great Recession while the wealthiest decile spent just under one tenth.[109] Recent years have seen debt servicing costs relative to income (DSI) grow four times more quickly for lowest income households than those of highest incomes.[110] High household debt levels are clearly distributed regressively, with the heaviest burden of debt falling on the poorest.

The quality of this debt is also unequally distributed throughout society. Drawing on Caplovitz' lesson that the Poor Pay More,[111] market segmentation, price differentiation and cross-subsidisation contribute to the regressive nature of consumer credit markets.[112] This adds inequality of value to original inequality of income.[113] Low-income debtors are often segmented into high-interest product categories. Pricing structures on products such as credit cards often involve the extraction of extra fees and charges from those debtors already struggling financially, culminating in the 'sweat box' of credit card lending identified by Ronald Mann.[114] Credit card and banking pricing systems mean that financially comfortable consumers, the 'convenience users' rather than borrowers, obtain services at little to no cost, subsidised by those in financial difficulty.[115] While all individuals are subject to biases in decision-

108 Office for National Statistics, 'The Burden of Financial and Property Debt, Great Britain, 2010 to 2012' (2015) www.ons.gov.uk/ons/rel/was/wealth-in-great-britain-wave-3/the-burden-of-property-debt-in-great-britain–was/rpt-the-burden-of-financial-and-property-debt–great-britain–2010-to-2012.html accessed 16 September 2015.

109 Matthew Whittaker, 'On Borrowed Time? Dealing with Household Debt in an Era of Stagnant Incomes' (Resolution Foundation 2012) 3 www.resolutionfoundation.org/publications/borrowed-time-dealing-household-debt-era-stagnant-incomes/ accessed 15 September 2014.

110 Gibbons (n. 89) 35–6.

111 Caplovitz (n. 49); Silber (n. 49).

112 As discussed in Chapter 7 (text to notes 266–306), such regressive effects may be exacerbated by credit scoring processes in the era of Big Data: D. K. Citron and F. Pasquale, 'The Scored Society: Due Process for Automated Predictions Essay', *Washington Law Review* 89 (2014) 1; M. Fourcade and K. Healy, 'Seeing like a Market', *Socio-Economic Review* 15 (2017) 9.

113 I. Ramsay, *Consumer Law and Policy: Text and Materials on Regulating Consumer Markets* (3rd revised edn (Hart Publishing, 2012) 70–7.

114 R. J. Mann, 'Bankruptcy Reform and the Sweat Box of Credit Card Debt', *University of Illinois Law Review* 2007 (2007) 375, 385–7.

115 ibid, 384. The FCA recently found that 10 per cent of customers generate between one third and half of bank account profits: 'Strategic Review of Retail Banking Business Models: Progress Report' (Financial Conduct Authority,2018).

making, survey data[116] supports the theoretical assumption that educated consumers and those with access to advisors are less likely to make suboptimal credit product choices than those with more limited resources.[117] In this regard, in the US subprime mortgage market of the 2000s inferior quality mortgage loans were more common among low income borrowers, ethnic minorities and women.[118] Marginal costs are also higher for low-income consumers due to their greater need of access to funds outside of low wages to pay for necessities.[119]

If high aggregate household debt levels raise policy concerns, evidence of the distribution of debt exacerbates such worries. Aside from social justice concerns raised by the heaviest debt load falling on lowest income groups, this regressive distribution threatens aggregate demand and so economic prosperity. Arguments presented by Mian and Sufi and international institutions regarding the 'debt overhang' problem are inherently distributional, based on the position that aggregate welfare is harmed by the manner in which debt contracts impose losses on society's debtors.[120] They point to negative overall consequences of reduced spending among households with the highest marginal propensity to consume – i.e. those who will spend almost all available resources and reduce expenditure sharply when resources are reduced. The lower wealth debtors on whom Mian and Sufi concentrate are mortgage debtors, while similar analysis in the UK finds significant 'debt overhang' effects on consumption and growth only in respect of mortgage debt (albeit while acknowledging some data limitations in relation to unsecured debt).[121] Neither Mian and Sufi nor Bank of England researchers explore macroeconomic implications of debt overhang for households of those less wealthy than heavily leveraged homeowners. Other accounts seem more open to the idea that similar effects should arise from reduced expenditure among the lowest income households, who carry the heaviest debt

[116] See e.g. N. O'Donnell and M. Keeney, 'Financial Capability: New Evidence for Ireland' (Central Bank and Financial Services Authority of Ireland, 2009) 98–9.

[117] O. Bar-Gill and E. Warren, 'Making Credit Safer', *University of Pennsylvania Law Review* 157 (2008) 1, 64.

[118] O. Bar-Gill, 'The Law, Economics and Psychology of Subprime Mortgage Contracts', *Cornell Law Review* 94 (2008) 1073, 1138–9.

[119] Bar-Gill and Warren (n. 117) 64.

[120] Mian and Sufi (n. 40) 46–59; International Monetary Fund, 'Dealing with Household Debt' (n. 42) 9.

[121] Bunn and Rostom (n. 33) 11, 18; Bank of England (n. 41) 3–4, 16. See Chapter 3, text to notes 167–78.

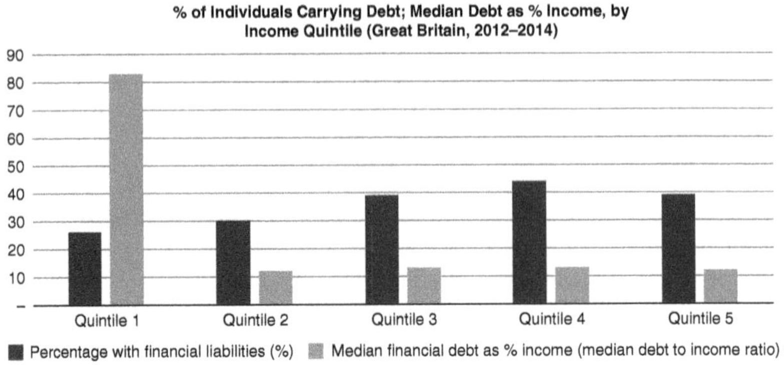

Figure 1.3: 'Household Debt Inequalities', 4 April 2016. Source: Office for National Statistics

loads, hold the highest marginal propensity to consume and have limited ability to self-insure.[122] While further study in relation to this group would be valuable, it is clear that the distribution of debt throughout an economy is significant.

1.2.3 Debt and Over-Indebtedness

Prior to the global financial crisis, high levels of household debt *per se* rarely caused policy concern.[123] Instead, where policymakers addressed household debt they focused on the risks of default and *over-indebtedness*.[124] Over-indebtedness is not a legal term of art but is commonly used in policy discourse in the UK and Europe when discussing the economic and social problems of financially overburdened households. Despite the well-established nature of the concept, no single

[122] Zabai (n. 39) 45.

[123] In the macroeconomic context, a Bank of England staff member can note that a decade ago it was controversial to suggest that 'debt matters': Vlieghe (n. 6).

[124] See e.g. Elaine Kempson, *Over-Indebtedness in Britain: A Report to the Department of Trade and Industry* (Personal Finance Research Centre, 2002) www.pfrc.bris.ac.uk/Reports/Overindebtedness_Britain.pdf accessed 11 November 2018; 'Tackling Overindebtedness: An Action Plan 2004' (Department of Trade and Industry; Department for Work and Pensions 2004); Department of Trade and Industry, *Over-Indebtedness in Britain: A DTI Report on the MORI Financial Services Survey 2004* (2005); European Commission and others, *Towards A Common Operational European Definition of Over-Indebtedness* (European Commission, Directorate-General for Employment, Social Affairs and Equal Opportunities 2008); European Commission and others, *Over-Indebtedness: New Evidence from the EU-SILC Special Module* (2010).

accepted definition exists.[125] Common core elements of definitions point to circumstances in which a household is unable to meet recurring expenses under all contracted financial commitments on a structural (i.e. persistent and ongoing) basis without reducing its minimum standard of living, and where the household is unable to remedy the situation through recourse to assets or other financial resources such as further borrowing.[126]

No consensus exists as to the appropriate method of measuring over-indebtedness,[127] with studies adopting a range of objective and/or subjective indicators of financial difficulty. Objective measures used include indicators such as high aggregate levels of debt-to-income or debt-to-asset ratios,[128] high debt service ratios, arrears in repaying debts and/or bills,[129] write-downs of debt by creditors,[130] and participation in legal personal insolvency or debt collection procedures.[131] Subjective measures use survey responses in which debtors or households identify themselves as experiencing difficulty in repaying obligations,[132] suffering

125 See European Commission and others, *Over-Indebtedness: New Evidence from the EU-SILC Special Module* (n. 124) 3; European Commission and others, *Towards A Common Operational European Definition of Over-Indebtedness* (n. 124) 33; R. Disney, S. Bridges and J. Gathergood, *Drivers of Over-Indebtedness, Report to the Department for Business, Enterprise and Regulatory Reform* (University of Nottingham, 2008) 11; Department of Trade and Industry (n. 124) 3.

126 European Commission and others, *Towards A Common Operational European Definition of Over-Indebtedness* (n. 124) 37.

127 Department for Business, Innovation and Skills, *Credit, Debt & Financial Difficulty in Britain, 2009/10: A Report Using Data from the YouGov DebtTrack Survey* (2011) 40; European Commission and others, *Towards A Common Operational European Definition of Over-Indebtedness* (n. 124) 38.

128 Kempson (n. 124) 24, 27–30; European Commission and others, *Over-Indebtedness: New Evidence from the EU-SILC Special Module* (n. 124) 30; Financial Inclusion Centre, *Report 1: Debt and Household Income* (2011) 19–30; Department of Trade and Industry (n. 124) 3–4.

129 Department of Trade and Industry (n. 124) 3–4; Department for Business, Innovation and Skills (n. 127) 40–2; Disney, Bridges and Gathergood (n. 125) 41; B. Duygan-Bump and C. Grant, 'Household Debt Repayment Behaviour: What Role Do Institutions Play?', *Economic Policy* 24 (2009) 107, 113.

130 A. E. Dawsey and L. M. Ausubel, 'Informal Bankruptcy' (2002) SSRN eLibrary http://papers.ssrn.com/sol3/papers.cfm?abstract_id=332161 accessed 11 November 2018; L. M. Ausubel, 'Credit Card Defaults, Credit Card Profits, and Bankruptcy', *American Bankruptcy Law Journal* 71 (1997) 249.

131 Department for Business, Innovation and Skills (n. 127) 42–3.

132 G. Betti and others, 'Consumer Over-Indebtedness in the EU: Measurement and Characteristics', *Journal of Economic Studies* 34 (2007) 136, 144–6; Disney, Bridges and Gathergood (n. 125) 41; Department for Business, Innovation and Skills (n. 127) 45–9.

from 'financial stress',[133] or finding bills and credit commitments a heavy burden.[134] Despite these differences, studies throughout the 2000s and 2010s have reached broadly constant estimates,[135] that between 10 per cent and 20 per cent of UK households can be considered over-indebted.[136]

Such high levels of over-indebtedness raise extensive social costs, given the negative effects on the financial security, housing, health and productivity of debtors and those around them.[137] This position challenges bankruptcy or personal insolvency law to offer policy solutions, as the legal institution charged with regulating situations of 'insolvency'. The concept of 'insolvency' does not overlap perfectly with over-indebtedness; it constitutes a factual condition that has become a legally defined term of art and gateway to legal procedures.[138] It is rarely used in social and economic contexts to describe or measure situations of financial difficulty.[139] A distinction between what the law recognises as insolvency and the social and economic reality of over-indebtedness helps assuage typical concerns that expansive bankruptcy laws cause excessive losses to creditors – defaults and losses are not created by bankruptcy law but are empirical facts.[140] A focus on over-indebtedness rather than insolvency also might highlight the socioeconomic context in which the law operates – by addressing the financial difficulties of low- and middle-income households, bankruptcy law has evolved from its origins in corporate and commercial law to become

[133] Disney, Bridges and Gathergood (n. 125) 41.

[134] Department for Business, Innovation and Skills (n. 127) 45–9.

[135] Kempson (n. 124); Department of Trade and Industry (n. 124); Disney, Bridges and Gathergood (n. 125).

[136] Kempson (n. 124); Department of Trade and Industry (n. 124); Disney, Bridges and Gathergood (n. 125); Department for Business, Innovation and Skills (n. 127); 'Indebted Lives: The Complexities of Life in Debt' (Money Advice Service 2013) www.moneyadviceservice.org.uk/en/static/indebted-lives-the-complexities-of-life-in-debt-press-office accessed 11 November 2018.

[137] For just one example of an account of these costs, see K. Porter, 'The Damage of Debt', *Washington and Lee Law Review* 69 (2012) 979. See further Chapter 3, text to notes 139–86.

[138] As a factual condition, insolvency can be distinguished from a purely legal concept such as 'bankruptcy': Fletcher (n. 10) paras. 1-012–13. It is difficult to isolate the concept from its legal context, however, and drafters of a recent World Bank report used 'insolvency' to encapsulate both 'the distressed condition of the debtor' *and* the range of measures to addressing that condition: World Bank (n. 10) para. 17.

[139] For one recent exception, see S. Albanesi and J. Nosal, 'Insolvency after the 2005 Bankruptcy Reform' (Federal Reserve Bank of New York Staff Report No. 725, 2015).

[140] See Chapter 3, text to notes 230–48.

a social insurance mechanism.[141] The distinction between over-indebtedness and insolvency also shifts intractable debates as to whether insolvency filing rates are 'too high'[142] to the more constructive question of how the law performs against an objective standard of the over-indebtedness levels prevailing in the economy. This allows one to see, for example, a striking discrepancy between continuously high levels of over-indebtedness and the recent sharp decline in bankruptcies in England and Wales.[143] This book argues that in a financialised economy in which debt is central to household welfare, bankruptcy can offer a vital safety net against inevitable widespread household over-indebtedness. Later this book will show the distance the law must still travel in order to fulfil this role.

1.3 A Law of Consumer Bankruptcy

The framing of this book around the topic of consumer bankruptcy situates it within a relatively recent tradition of comparative consumer bankruptcy literature.[144] This scholarship adopts interdisciplinary and empirical perspectives on the operation of the law as a policy response to household finance problems, viewed in the context of global social and economic trends. US law holds exceptional status in this field as the most developed and studied consumer bankruptcy system,[145] under which the 'fresh start' policy and the principle of household debt relief is most fully established.[146] This has influenced the literature's adoption of the US terminology of 'bankruptcy'. The focus on consumer bankruptcy

[141] See Chapter 3.

[142] J. Braucher, 'Theories of Overindebtedness: Interaction of Structure and Culture', *Theoretical Inquiries in Law* 7 (2006) 323, 328; D. A. Moss and G. A. Johnson, 'The Rise of Consumer Bankruptcy: Evolution, Revolution, or Both', *American Bankruptcy Law Journal* 73 (1999) 311, 349.

[143] Chapters 4 and 5 examine and explain these trends.

[144] W. Backert, S. Block-Lieb and J. Niemi, *Contemporary Issues in Consumer Bankruptcy* 1st edn (Peter Lang GmbH, 2013); J. Niemi, I. Ramsay and W. C. Whitford, *Consumer Credit, Debt and Bankruptcy: Comparative and International Perspectives* (Hart Publishing, 2009); K. Anderson, 'The Explosive Global Growth of Personal Insolvency and the Concomitant Birth of the Study of Comparative Consumer Bankruptcy', *Osgoode Hall Law Journal* 42 (2004) 661; J. S. Ziegel, *Comparative Consumer Insolvency Regimes: A Canadian Perspective* illustrated edn (Hart Publishing, 2003); I. Ramsay, W. C. Whitford and J. Niemi-Kiesilainen, *Consumer Bankruptcy in Global Perspective* (Hart Publishing, 2003).

[145] Ramsay, '*21st Century*' (n. 17) 27.

[146] However, policy developments in the past two decades have tested this position: J. Westbrook, 'The Retreat of American Bankruptcy Law', *Queensland University of*

also highlights key themes of this book. Since at least the 1980s, English law has claimed that it 'emphasises the importance of the rehabilitation of the individual insolvent'.[147] Since the early 2000s, the majority of cases under all personal insolvency procedures (bankruptcies, Individual Voluntary Arrangements and Debt Relief Orders) have involved debtors legally regarded as consumers,[148] in the sense of individuals who entered credit contracts for purposes outside of their trade or profession.[149] This book's emphasis on consumer bankruptcy shows how these two developments have not been in harmony, however, as in many ways the law has never truly recognised the importance of the rehabilitation of non-business debtors.

A focus on consumer bankruptcy also highlights consumer debt as an area of policy significance. It highlights how crisis and recession have called into question the neoliberal focus on supply-side economics and drawn attention to the importance to economic prosperity of protecting consumers as well as producers (or financiers[150]). Indeed, it is in the very capacity of consumers who have reduced expenditure that households' personal financial difficulties transmit into a wider 'debt overhang' problem. After previous economic crises policymakers primarily concerned themselves with corporate debt and corporate insolvency law reform.[151] This approach is clearly insufficient in a country like the UK that has long since switched from a producer to a consumer economy.[152] Similarly, the contribution of excessive household debt to the Great Recession ruptures the apparent consensus that protecting banks from losses and

Technology Law Review 17 (2017) 40; W. C. Whitford, 'Changing Definitions of Fresh Start in US Bankruptcy Law', *Journal of Consumer Policy* 20 (1997) 179.

147 *Smith (A Bankrupt)* v. *Braintree District Council* [1989] 3 WLR 1317, [1990] 2 AC 215, 237–8.

148 In the early 2000s, the majority of bankruptcies involved consumer debtors rather than traders. By the mid-2000s the vast majority of Individual Voluntary Arrangements similarly involved consumers, while almost all Debt Relief Orders fall into this category also. Chapter 3 discusses further the nature and key features of these three procedures.

149 This is a widely-used legal definition of 'consumer': see e.g. Consumer Rights Act 2015 (2015 c.15), s.2(3); Directive 2008/48/EC of the European Parliament and of the Council of 23 April 2008 on Credit Agreements for Consumers and Repealing Council Directive 87/102/EEC Art.3(a) (2008).

150 See e.g. R. Foroohar, *Makers and Takers: The Rise of Finance and the Fall of American Business* (Crown Business, 2016).

151 See e.g. Halliday and Carruthers' study of policy responses to the Asian financial crisis of the late 1990s: T. C. Halliday and B. G. Carruthers, *Bankrupt: Global Lawmaking and Systematic Financial Crisis* (Stanford University Press, 2009).

152 Ritzer (n. 32); J. Q. Whitman, 'Consumerism versus Producerism: A Study in Comparative Law', *Yale Law Journal* 117 (2007) 340.

safeguarding their intermediary function holds the key to economic recovery.[153] Mainstream observers seem now to accept what Marxian perspectives have long argued: the unsustainability of protecting business and financial sectors over households while simultaneously shifting responsibility for driving growth onto household expenditure funded by debt.[154] This book shows how there is now wide recognition that negative outcomes arise where the costs of an economy built on high debt levels are pushed onto groups with the highest marginal propensity to consume and least capacity to 'self-insure' against these losses and the volatility of their financial positions. Negative outcomes result where losses are allowed to fall on those on the wrong side of information asymmetries, on those subject to behavioural biases leading to sub-optimal decisions, and on those lacking the resources to correct these contracting failures.[155] These factors effectively highlight the public policy case for offering debt relief to consumers, but more so to anyone falling with in a category of 'average' debtors outside high net worth status – Teresa Sullivan, Elizabeth Warren and Jay Westbrook's 'Fragile Middle Class' or the Occupy movement's 'ninety-nine percent'.[156] A stronger case exists for debt relief for this group than the characters who populate both media coverage and Law Reports on personal insolvency law:[157] high-flying

153 Mian and Sufi (n. 40) 133.

154 Harvey, *The Enigma of Capital* (n. 56).

155 See Chapter 3 (text to notes 97–138) for discussion of how these factors lead to failures in consumer credit markets.

156 T.A. Sullivan, E. Warren and J. L. Westbrook, *The Fragile Middle Class: Americans in Debt* (Yale University Press, 2000); C. Calhoun, 'Occupy Wall Street in Perspective', *The British Journal of Sociology* 64 (2013) 26. A useful concept to give legal form to the category of debtors covered by the book might be the 'high net worth' debtor as contained in FCA regulatory rules and related legislation, which allows rules to be disapplied for borrowers who, *inter alia*, have earned over £150,000 in the previous year. Such an income would place a borrower in the top 98–99 per cent of UK pre-tax incomes: HM Revenue & Customs, 'Percentile Points from 1 to 99 for Total Income before and after Tax' (*GOV.UK*, 2018) www.gov.uk/government/statistics/percentile-points-from-1-to-99-for-total-income-before-and-after-tax accessed 16 July 2018; Financial Services and Markets Act 2000 (Regulated Activities) Order 2001 (SI 2001/544), art. 60H; FCA Handbook CONC (Consumer Credit Sourcebook), App. 1.4.

157 The presence of these individuals in the Law Reports is most likely because these are the debtors – or the bankruptcy estates – with the means to fund litigation capable of giving rise to reported case law. Cases of 'bankruptcy tourism' in particular are likely to be highly resource-intensive: see e.g. A. Walters and A. Smith, 'Bankruptcy Tourism' under the EC Regulation on Insolvency Proceedings: A View From England and Wales', *International Insolvency Review* 19 (2010) 181, 186, 193. For a rare example of a cross-border bankruptcy case involving a debtor of more modest means, see *Official Receiver v. Keelan* [2012] BPIR 613.

corporate investors,[158] multi-million property speculators,[159] well-resourced 'bankruptcy tourists',[160] or riches-to-rags fallen tycoons.[161] The material conditions of debtors are more relevant to theoretical and policy discussions than legal distinctions between consumers and traders that existed in England historically and persist in certain European jurisdictions.[162] Therefore this book's idea of consumer bankruptcy includes self-employed debtors or traders outside the high net worth category, whose financial circumstances often show little material difference compared to consumer counterparts.[163]

In any case, neoliberalism has blurred lines between consumers and producers through its ideological framing of the individual as the 'entrepreneur of the self', whose choices and actions are presented as the management of her human capital, including the negotiation of risk.[164] Contemporary financialised capitalism also breaks down other distinctions such as that between the worker and the consumer, given how debt repayment requires the growth of human capital and 'work on the self'.[165] The consumer debtor

[158] See J. Kilpi, *The Ethics of Bankruptcy* (Routledge, 1998) 141–162.

[159] See e.g. *Kemsley* v. *Barclays Bank Plc and Others* [2013] EWHC 1274 (Ch); *McConnon* v. *Zurich Bank* [2012] IEHC 587.

[160] See e.g. *O'Donnell & O'Donnell* v. *The Governor and Company of the Bank of Ireland*, [2012] EWHC 3749 (Ch) (2012); *ACC Bank Plc.* v. *McCann* [2013] NIMASTER 1.

[161] See e.g. *Irish Bank Resolution Corporation Limited* v. *Quinn* [2012] NICh 1; *Quinn & Others* v. *Irish Bank Resolution Corporation Limited & Others* [2012] IEHC 261; C. Paulus, *Shaping the Contours of a Hybrid Concept – Mr Quinn's COMI: Irish Bank Resolution Corporation* v. *Quinn* [2012] NICh 1, 25 INSOLV. INT. 75 (2012).

[162] Recent European Commission initiatives towards the harmonisation of substantive insolvency law draw a distinction between business and consumer insolvency. The European Commission initially suggested that legislation should extend to consumer insolvency, but its latest Proposal limits its application to corporate and 'entrepreneur' debtors, while 'inviting' Member States to extend the application of debt discharge provisions to consumers: 'Initiative on Insolvency: Inception Impact Assessment' (European Commission, 2016) 2016/JUST/025 – Insolvency II 5; 'Proposal for a Directive of the European Parliament and of the Council on Preventive Restructuring Frameworks, Second Chance and Measures to Increase the Efficiency of Restructuring, Insolvency and Discharge Procedures and Amending Directive 2012/30/EU' (European Commission, 2016) 2016/0359 (COD) COM (2016) 723 final 14. See also N. J. Herman Huls, Overindebtedness of Consumers in the E.C. Member States : Facts and Search for Solutions (Centre de Droit de la Consommation, 1994) 100; J. J. Kilborn, '*La Responsabilisation de l'Economie*: What the United States Can Learn from the New French Law on Consumer Overindebtedness', *Michigan Journal of International Law* 26 (2004) 619, 628.

[163] See e.g. R. M Lawless, 'Striking Out on Their Own: The Self-Employed in Bankruptcy' in *Broke: How Debt Bankrupts the Middle Class* (Stanford University Press 2012).

[164] Ramsay, '*21st Century*' (n. 17) 28.

[165] Lazzarato and Jordan (n. 17) 33.

of this book is thus a consumer, a producer/entrepreneur of the self, a worker, and a citizen, as the dynamic of debt increasingly governs relations between capital and labour, the state and its citizens, and businesses and their customers.[166]

This term consumer bankruptcy holds another advantage of distancing the subject matter of this book from corporate insolvency. Private law generally views itself as market facilitating, establishing ground rules for free exchange and enforcing market bargains. A non-interventionist ideology of contractual freedom dominates.[167] In contrast, the starting point of consumer law is that markets are imperfect and that the law must intervene to correct failures, internalise social costs and produce more efficient (or more equal[168]) allocations. A similar contrast can be drawn between corporate insolvency law's regulation of the presumptively efficient realm of business-to-business contracting, and a consumer insolvency law that assumes it will be required to correct imperfect market allocations. In highlighting the discrete policy issues applicable to personal insolvency, the book departs from the orthodoxy in England and Wales and elsewhere that there is a single body of *insolvency* law. The book criticises judicial and administrative decisions that apply similar principles or analogous reasoning to corporate and personal insolvency procedures. It argues that dangers arise when adopting identical approaches in cases of an average household's financial problems and, say, the insolvency of a group of mining companies owing debts of £4.4 billion.[169] English policymakers, lawyers and judges persist in

166 ibid, 30. While Chapters 4, 5 and 7 show how neoliberalism has transformed traditional aspects of the justice system into services and contractual arrangements, the transformation of state-citizen interaction into creditor-debtor relationships is clearest in Chapter 6.

167 The Australian High Court has, for example, noted that developments in consumer protection require the common law to evolve from its traditional free market ideology, stating that 'this pattern of remedial legislation suggests the need for caution in dealing with the unwritten law as if *laissez faire* notions of an untrammelled "freedom of contract" provide a universal legal value'. *Andrews* v. *Australia and New Zealand Banking Group Ltd* [2012] HCA 30 [5]. On this theme generally, see J. N. Adams and R. Brownsword, 'The Ideologies of Contract' *Legal Studies* 7 (1987) 205; Ramsay, 'Consumer Credit Law, Distributive Justice and the Welfare State' (n. 60); C. Willett, 'General Clauses and the Competing Ethics of European Consumer Law in the UK', *The Cambridge Law Journal* 71 (2012) 412.

168 T. Prosser, 'Regulation and Social Solidarity', *Journal of Law and Society* 33 (2006) 364.

169 See *Tucker* v. *Gold Fields Mining LCC* [2009] Court of Appeal, England and Wales [2009] EWCA Civ 173, [2010] BCC 544. The English courts have held that the same principles of interpretation and application should apply to Company Voluntary Arrangement and Individual Voluntary Arrangement procedures: In *Re NT Gallagher & Sons Ltd* [2002] EWCA Civ 404, [2002] 1 WLR 2380.

applying commercial law assumptions in this area, however, failing to embrace bankruptcy's new role of providing relief to over-indebted individuals as a form of social insurance against the risks of an economy dependent on high levels of household debt.

The book uses the term 'consumer' cautiously and sparingly, however. Iain Ramsay, drawing on Lendol Calder, notes that descriptions of 'consumer' credit and debt replaced 'consumptive' debt in US discourse during the 1930s, as part of efforts by opinion makers to legitimise and normalise household borrowing.[170] The success of such normalisation has provoked responses from conservative commentators critical of the alleged reduction of stigma associated with debt,[171] who seek to link the language of consumer credit to irresponsible spending and 'over-consumption'.[172] A term like *household debt* might better reflect how problem debt extends beyond such clichéd accounts of spending splurges and credit card binges.[173] Rather, subsequent chapters (particularly Chapter 6) illustrate the difficulties increasingly arising in relation to all manner of household costs – including housing costs (mortgage debt and rent arrears), credit cards and personal loans, bank overdrafts, car finance, tax, and social welfare overpayments. Use of the term consumer shows how the law directs its focus to a natural or legal person, necessarily individualising problems even where they may be collective in nature.[174] This may, for example, conceal the pooling of financial resources across a household[175] and obscure wider issues of gender and

170 Ramsay, *Personal Insolvency in the 21st Century* (n. 17) 27, citing Lendol Calder, *Financing the American Dream: A Cultural History of Consumer Credit* new edn (Princeton University Press, 2001).

171 See e.g. Judge E. H. Jones and T. J. Zywicki, 'It's Time for Means-Testing', *Brigham Young University Law Review* 1999 (1999) 177.

172 See E. Warren, 'The Over-Consumption Myth and Other Tales of Economics, Law, and Morality', *Washington University Law Quarterly* 82 (2004) 1485.

173 See e.g. I. Ramsay, '"Wannabe WAGS" and "Credit Binges": The Construction of Overindebtedness in the UK' in J. Niemi, I. Ramsay and W. C. Whitford (eds.), Consumer Credit, Debt and Bankruptcy: Comparative and International Perspectives (Hart Publishing, 2009).

174 Soederberg (n. 19) 86–90; I. Ramsay, 'Towards an International Paradigm of Personal Insolvency Law? A Critical View', *Queensland University of Technology Law Review* 17 (2017) 15, 38.

175 The law in places acknowledges the factual circumstances of *household* over-indebtedness, for example allowing joint insolvency petitions: see e.g. 11 USC §302. For discussion of the prevalence of joint bankruptcy filings under US law, see e.g. E. Warren, 'What Is a Women's Issue? Bankruptcy, Commercial Law, and Other Gender-Neutral Topics', *Harvard Women's Law Journal* 25 (2002) 19, 27–8; Sullivan, Warren and Westbrook (n. 156) 36–7. Laws also generally provide for asset exemptions

family raised by debt and its centrality in contemporary capitalism.[176] Certain critical scholars identify the concept of the consumer as a depoliticising rhetorical tool, used to conceal differences and inequalities of class and identity, and particularly to hide conflict between capital and labour.[177] Soederberg argues that the long-recognised primary exploitation of labour by capital is less visible when it takes the form of secondary exploitation in consumer finance markets, where debtors are conceptualised as consumers exercising their market sovereignty by choosing freely to enter into formally and apparently neutral debt contracts.[178] This is why Lazzarato argues in favour of 'viewing debt as the archetype of social relations' since this 'means conceiving economy and society on the basis of an asymmetry of power and not on that of a commercial exchange that implies and presupposes equality'.[179] Harvey notes similarly that gains made in the workplace through collective bargaining can be quickly lost in a less politically visible manner in the marketplace through rent seeking and exploitative business practices.[180]

Arguably the term 'consumer' need not operate in this manner. There is a case for politicising consumer markets, highlighting the contribution of market failures not just to inefficient economic outcomes but also to inequality and political disenfranchisement. Post-crisis developments show some support for the potential of debtor mobilisation and political activism.[181] The label 'consumer' may be an even more effective banner than the 'debtor' around which actors may be more comfortable gathering,[182] allowing a wider

which protect a reasonable standard of living for the debtor's dependents: e.g. Insolvency Act 1986, s.283(2); Fletcher (n. 10) paras. 8–076 to 8–080. In England and Wales, insolvent couples can also enter interlocking Individual Voluntary Arrangements (IVAs).

[176] See e.g. M. Cooper, *Family Values: Between Neoliberalism and the New Social Conservatism* (Zone Books – The MIT Press, 2017); Fraser (n. 9); A. Roberts, 'Financing Social Reproduction: The Gendered Relations of Debt and Mortgage Finance in Twenty-First-Century America', *New Political Economy* 18 (2013) 21; Warren (n. 175).

[177] Ramsay, '*21st Century*' (n. 17) 27.

[178] Soederberg (n. 19).

[179] Lazzarato and Jordan (n. 17) 33.

[180] Cross-refer to footnote 56.

[181] Montgomerie and others (n. 73); Hoekstra (n. 76); L. Stanley, J. Deville and J. Montgomerie, 'Digital Debt Management: The Everyday Life of Austerity', *New Formations* 87 (2016) 64.

[182] For difficulties of debtor organisation, see e.g. T. C. Halliday, S. Block-Lieb and B. G. Carruthers, 'Missing Debtors: National Lawmaking and Global Norm-Making of Corporate Bankruptcy Regimes' in *A Debtor World: Interdisciplinary Perspectives on Debt* (Oxford University Press, 2012); J. Spooner, 'Long Overdue: What the Belated

collective political identity to be developed. The debtor, and particularly the insolvent debtor, is an identity that continues to hold significant negative connotations, making it a difficult concept for people to associate around.[183] A desire to distinguish ourselves from debtors may result from a need to reassure ourselves that we could never fall into such hardship.[184] Even among new online debtor communities, the goal of achieving a 'debt free day' – and so a transition out of the class of debtor – lies at the heart of the advice and support members provide to one another.[185] In contrast, civil society action amongst consumers might compensate for lack of political representation.[186]

This book presents what it hopes is a convincing theoretical case for debt relief, based on current policy and academic ideas. It makes no claim that its arguments will be politically successful. Nonetheless it presents a utilitarian argument for debt relief measures based on the negative effects of excessive household leverage on aggregate consumption and growth. This focus on *consumer* bankruptcy may offer a useful political frame for promoting the public interest in debt reduction beyond benefits to individual debtors. The idea of 'spending for one's country' is well established.[187] As discussed throughout this book, processes of financialisation, fiscal austerity and the commercialisation and privatisation of public services have drawn a wider group of households and activities into financial markets in recent decades. These trends have blurred lines between concepts such as consumer, entrepreneur, citizen and resident. What once were public law rights of citizens may now be consumer rights of individuals subjected to 'market justice'.[188] Mobilisation as consumers may offer a means of unified collective action across various fields of activity in a 'regulatory welfare state'.[189] Bankruptcy can act as generalised

Reform of Irish Personal Insolvency Law Tells Us about Comparative Consumer Bankruptcy', *American Bankruptcy Law Journal* 86 (2012) 243; Spooner, 'The Quiet-Loud-Quiet Politics of Post-Crisis Consumer Bankruptcy Law: The Case of Ireland and the Troika' (n. 24).

183 Halliday, Block-Lieb and Carruthers (n. 182).

184 K. Gross, 'Demonizing Debtors: A Response to the Honsberger-Ziegel Debate', *Osgoode Hall Law Journal* 37 (1999) 263, 272.

185 Stanley, Deville and Montgomerie (n. 181).

186 Crouch, 'From Markets versus States to Corporations versus Civil Society?' (n. 75).

187 Most famously in President Bush's call on Americans to fulfil their patriotic duty by shopping in the aftermath of the September 11 terrorist attacks: K. C. Engel and P. A. McCoy, The Subprime Virus: Reckless Credit, Regulatory Failure, and Next Steps (Oxford University Press USA, 2011) 19.

188 Streeck (n. 34) 61.

189 Levi-Faur (n. 102); Haber (n. 102).

consumer or social protection of last resort across many sectors,[190] as all our relationships increasingly become reduced to debtor–creditor dynamics.[191]

1.4 Debt Overhang and the Limits of Bankruptcy

Another reason for this book's focus on consumer bankruptcy is to question the limitation of English law's provision of debt relief to insolvency procedures. As noted above, a decade ago high levels of household debt were rarely seen as problematic.[192] Policymakers tended to draw distinctions between *debt* (often discussed in terms of welfare-enhancing *credit*) and *problem debt*. Concerns were reserved for the latter situation in which default moved households from indebtedness to over-indebtedness. Most policy in fact focused on ensuring and encouraging 'access' to the former.[193] Lessons from the Great Recession have demonstrated the dangers of high levels of household debt *per se*, as well as the difficulties in responding to the consequent problem of debt overhang. The effect of excessive household leverage in stymying economic growth means that a vicious cycle prevents natural household de-leveraging from taking place without policy intervention.[194] Various policy documents point towards regulatory measures that can prevent debt from reaching problematic levels in future, but do less to tackle the historic debt mountain.[195] There are limits as to what can be achieved via monetary policy; and politicians in many countries, particularly in the UK, have shown little appetite for the public expenditure involved in tackling debt overhang via progressive fiscal measures.[196] Macroeconomists

[190] W. C. Whitford, 'The Ideal of Individualized Justice: Consumer Bankruptcy as Consumer Protection, and Consumer Protection in Consumer Bankruptcy', *American Bankruptcy Law Journal* 68 (1994) 397.

[191] Lazzarato and Jordan (n. 17) 30.

[192] See e.g. n. 100 above.

[193] See generally G. Trumbull, 'Credit Access and Social Welfare The Rise of Consumer Lending in the United States and France', *Politics & Society* 40 (2012) 9, 125–50; I. Ramsay and T. Williams, 'The Crash That Launched a Thousand Fixes: Regulation of Consumer Credit After the Lending Revolution and the Credit Crunch' in N. Moloney and K. Alexander (eds.), *Law Reform and Financial Markets* (Elgar, 2011) 223; I. Ramsay, 'To Heap Distress upon Distress? Comparative Reflections on Interest-Rate Ceilings', *University of Toronto Law Journal* 60 (2010) 707.

[194] Lo and Rogoff (n. 3) 10.

[195] Bunn and Rostom (n. 42); International Monetary Fund, 'Household Debt and Financial Stability' (n. 41).

[196] International Monetary Fund, 'Dealing with Household Debt' (n. 42) 13.

increasingly advocate the merits of household debt relief policies yet do so while seeing 'no economy-wide tools available for large-scale debt restructuring'.[197] Even documents that advocate debt relief measures often explicitly limit themselves to proposing consensual debt restructuring schemes,[198] which Chapters 4 and 5 argue have a poor track record in delivering the kind of extensive debt relief necessary to address debt overhang problems. In a context in which 'all policy levers appear to be blocked',[199] bankruptcy offers one remaining option for an 'economy-wide tool' to address the debt overhang problem.

Is bankruptcy up to this challenge?[200] Mian, Sufi and Trebbi argue that it is an inadequate response to the large debtor–creditor imbalances that emerge during financial crises and recessions.[201] As the debt discharge offered in bankruptcy is conditional on the liquidation of the debtor's assets for the benefit of creditors, these authors argue that a 'fire sale' of assets in mass bankruptcies could exacerbate economic problems and a spiral of falling house prices, household wealth and consumption.[202] Most relevantly, they argue that bankruptcy comes into effect too late to address debt overhang problems of reduced expenditure among leveraged households responding to economic shocks.[203] Debtors enter bankruptcy only after they have fallen into default and over-indebtedness and taken the step of seeking assistance. This moment might arise long after they have cut back significantly on expenditure in an effort to struggle through debt problems.[204] These authors express the problem in US terms. There, bankruptcy has traditionally lacked an 'insolvency' requirement and instead has relied on the debtor's own decision to petition for bankruptcy as evidence that her financial circumstances are

197 Vlieghe (n. 6) 3.

198 International Monetary Fund, 'Dealing with Household Debt' (n. 42); J. R. Andritzky, 'Resolving Residential Mortgage Distress: Time to Modify?' (International Monetary Fund, 2014) IMF Working Paper WP/14/226 www.imf.org/external/pubs/cat/longres.aspx?sk=42532.0 accessed 11 November 2018; International Monetary Fund, 'Fiscal Monitor – Debt: Use It Wisely' (n. 41).

199 Turner (n. 22) 12.

200 See discussion of these points in somewhat different context: J Spooner, 'Recalling the Public Interest in Personal Insolvency Law: A Note on Professor Fletcher's Foresight', *Nottingham Insolvency Business Law eJournal* 3 (2015) 537, 542–4.

201 Mian, Sufi and Trebbi (n. 72) 21.

202 ibid, 20.

203 ibid. See further Chapter 3, text to notes 167–78.

204 For discussion of the sacrifices and reductions in expenditure undertaken by US debtors before filing for bankruptcy, see P. Foohey and others, 'Life in the Sweatbox', *Notre Dame Law Review* (94 Notre Dame Law Review 219 (2018)).

such as to give rise to social costs warranting debt relief.[205] This problem is more pronounced in England and Wales, where a financially troubled debtor must wait until formally insolvent before she may enter a procedure. If bankruptcy is to address the debt overhang problem, it would need to lose its identity as an insolvency law and undergo a fundamental change in extending relief to households regarded as cash-flow solvent.[206]

Expanding beyond the realms of insolvency may be too radical a change for contemporary bankruptcy law to contemplate. At the very least these considerations argue that bankruptcy must offer as extensive relief as possible to insolvent debtors in the situations where it currently applies. Responses to the crisis and recession in the UK have included monetary policy centred on low interest rates, forbearance policies and mortgage debt support schemes to prevent mass home repossessions,[207] and regulatory reforms designed to prevent future crises.[208] These measures have pursued and partly achieved worthy aims of keeping people in their homes and reducing moderately the future accumulation of debt. Nonetheless these measures could be accused of representing a historical pattern under which states have

> insisted on legislating around the edges, softening the impact, eliminating obvious abuses like debt slavery, using the spoils of empire to throw all sorts of extra benefits at their poorer citizens . . . so as to keep them more

[205] C. G. Hallinan, 'The Fresh Start Policy in Consumer Bankruptcy: A Historical Inventory and an Interpretive Theory', *University of Richmond Law Review* 21 (1986) 49, 109, 130–1.

[206] On the current cash-flow insolvency test, see Insolvency Act 1986, s.263H; Fletcher (n. 10) paras. 6–088; *Re Coney* (1998) [1998] BPIR 333.

[207] M. Whittaker and K. Blacklock, 'Hangover Cure: Dealing with the Household Debt Overhang as Interest Rates Rise' (Resolution Foundation, 2014) 22–30 www.resolutionfoundation.org/publications/hangover-cure-dealing-with-the-household-debt-overhang-as-interest-rates-rise/ accessed 15 September 2014; I. Ramsay, 'Two Cheers for Europe: Austerity, Mortgage Foreclosures and Personal Insolvency Policy in the EU' in H. W. Micklitz and I. Domurath (eds.), Consumer Debt and Social Exclusion (2015) 210–12. Policy efforts to prevent evictions of homeowners have not extended to tenants, with evictions and homelessness rising among the renting population : J. Spooner, 'Seeking Shelter in Personal Insolvency Law: Recession, Eviction and Bankruptcy's Social Safety Net', Journal of Law and Society 44 (2017) http://onlinelibrary.wiley.com/journal/10.1111/(ISSN)1467-6478/ accessed 26 January 2017.

[208] In the area of conduct of business regulation, see e.g. *Mortgage Market Review* (Financial Services Authority, 2009). From a prudential perspective, Bank of England staff members conclude that the potential for high debt levels to impact aggregate demand requires prudential regulatory responses to prevent future build-up of debt: Bunn and Rostom (n. 22) 28–9.

> or less afloat – but all in such a way as never to allow a challenge to the principle of debt itself.[209]

These policies have done little either to reduce the persistently high household debt burden or more extensively to reshape financialised capitalism and reduce our contemporary economic and political over-reliance on high levels of household debt. By discharging debt, bankruptcy in contrast cuts to the heart of these problems. Indeed, an optimistic view might see bankruptcy's challenge to the principle that 'surely one has to pay one's debts'[210] as potentially pointing the way towards a re-orientation of our legal, social and economic structures away from the current dependence on household debt.

1.5 Conclusion

To confront problematic contemporary structures in this manner, or even to act merely as a necessary release valve against the pressures built into the existing economic order, bankruptcy law must overcome aspects of contemporary legal ideology and political economy that militate against the full acceptance of its debt relief function. As Chapter 2 discusses, processes associated with the neoliberal turn and financialisation – such as privatisation, fiscal consolidation, and the marketisation of public services – have increased household debt difficulties and the need for debt relief. The associated ideology, however, has pushed bankruptcy policy and institutions in an opposite direction, reducing the availability and extent of debt relief.

Path dependency and the historical origins of the law as a commercial debt collection mechanism have prevented the law from evolving into the new role it now plays as a safety net for households seeking protection from the risks of financialisation and a 'fresh start'. For much of its long past bankruptcy law has been understood as forming part of private law and commercial law, a view that this book shows to persist among certain stakeholders. This means that ideas and assumptions underpinning the law have tended to be drawn from private law orthodoxy founded upon the sanctity of contract and the enforcement of obligations.[211] Bankruptcy is often

[209] Graeber (n. 30) 390–1.
[210] ibid, 2.
[211] 'Discharge of legal obligations is an extraordinary exception to the usual obligation orientation of the law . . . ': Howard (n. 82) 1047.

categorised alongside corporate restructuring as forming an overall law of insolvency, despite fundamental differences between these two areas. While corporate insolvency can be understood as a 'win-win' for creditors, other stakeholders and the wider community, bankruptcy's debt discharge represents redistribution from creditor to debtor.[212] Chapter 3 presents the resultant confusion lying at the heart of English law, showing how its aims are divided between creditor wealth maximisation and debtor relief; and its identity is split between a commercial tool for enforcing market bargains and its current operation as part of the social safety net.

Chapters 4 to 7 illustrate how these factors of confusion regarding the law's core aims and identity, path dependency, and the neoliberal ideology of financialised capitalism have prevented bankruptcy law from embracing fully the importance of its debt reduction function. These factors have influenced key features of the law including access conditions and the question of whether debt relief should be provided publicly as of right or available only via private bargaining and 'market-based debt resolution' (Chapters 4 and 5). These factors also shape the treatment of 'priority debts' by the law, including those owed to government, and the extent of protection and debt relief offered through the law's stay of creditor enforcement and debt discharge (Chapter 6). Finally, the regulation of debtor (mis)conduct and the law's safeguards against 'moral hazard' have been influenced heavily by neoliberal ideas of personal responsibility and new public management techniques, as well as the law's underlying historical attitudes (Chapter 7).

Bankruptcy law has not recognised that contemporary public policy challenges require it to reorientate itself towards the goal of offering extensive debt relief to financially troubled households. This book criticises bankruptcy law for failing to fulfil its progressive potential, given its ability to contribute to the redistribution of the risks inherent in a debt-dependent economy in a more efficient and equitable manner. Authors and international institutions increasingly diagnose crises of contemporary financialised capitalism, whether manifesting in economic stagnation, extreme inequality or political unrest. These problems all relate to some degree to excessive

[212] Ramsay, '*21st Century*' (n. 17) 16; S. Block-Lieb, 'Austerity, Debt Overhang, and the Design of International Standards on Sovereign, Corporate and Consumer Debt Restructuring Symposium', *Indiana Journal of Global Legal Studies* 22 (2015) 487, 536.

household debt. Bankruptcy law cannot turn its back on this wider context when faced directly with questions of whether it should uphold the dominant ideology of debt, or alternatively offer the debt relief demanded by contemporary policy challenges, and the thousands of households who turn to the law in need.

2

Financialised Capitalism and the Centrality of Household Debt

2.1 Eras of Capitalism: Political Economy of the Household Debt Expansion

The expansion of household debt central to contemporary financialised capitalism[1] can be linked to 'the rather obvious shift from national Keynesian demand management systems to the neoliberal order of global supply side economics that has been analysed to death . . . '[2] It appears at times that judges, lawyers, and bankruptcy policymakers are among those who have not yet analysed these developments to death, however. A lack of contextual scrutiny of the place of household debt in the political and economic order, and a failure to recognise the implications for bankruptcy of fundamental economic shifts, limits the law's ability to respond to contemporary socio-economic conditions. By exploring the wider political economy that has led to a systemic dependence on high household debt levels, this chapter aims to offer a sense of the structural environment influencing household over-indebtedness and insolvency. This illustrates the risks inherent in a model of financialised capitalism requiring ever-expanding household debt to maintain economic growth and household living standards, and the consequent need for insurance mechanisms against these inevitable dangers. The presentation of this structural account is a first step towards arguing for bankruptcy's role as such an insurance mechanism of last resort.

The legal system and related government policy on over-indebtedness can be criticised for overemphasising individual debtor behaviour while

[1] N. Fraser, 'Contradictions of Capital and Care', *New Left Review* 99 (2016) 100.

[2] M. Blyth and M. Matthijs, 'Black Swans, Lame Ducks, and the Mystery of IPE's Missing Macroeconomy', *Review of International Political Economy* 24 (2017) 203, 209.

giving insufficient recognition to 'ever-worsening structural constraints' such as stagnant incomes, reduced social welfare provision, precarious employment and rising living costs.[3] By its nature, the law also tends to focus on the microeconomic picture of interactions between individual debtors and creditors, with only cursory consideration of wider issues such as the impact of legal rules on credit availability and aggregate welfare. There seems to be value in developing a broader macroeconomic picture in order to place the law in context.[4] English private law also tends to adopt an apolitical view of 'a "natural" level of credit availability or market structure' and a strong sense of duty to protect this environment and ensure 'access to credit'.[5] Instead, this book's account seeks to illustrate how outcomes are shaped by the 'ground rules of consumer credit law', the 'contractual culture' and the surrounding politics from which credit markets can never exist independently.

The shift in regimes of political economy is often understood as a response to the instabilities, contradictions or crises of capitalist economies of the late 1970s.[6] It represented an attempt to produce economic growth and stability by reconciling the profit expectations of capital owners with the employment expectations of wage-earners, who capitalism also requires to act as confident mass consumers.[7] Following financial crisis and recession, researchers and policy institutions have increasingly recognised that this shift to an economy centred on household debt merely 'bought time' and stored up problems for the future, which have become our current policy challenges.[8] This understanding reveals the role that bankruptcy can play in compensating for, and

[3] P. Pathak, 'Ethopolitics and the Financial Citizen', *The Sociological Review* 62 (2014) 90, 91.

[4] In this way the chapter follows the developing law-and-macroeconomics literature: Z. Liscow, 'Counter-Cyclical Bankruptcy Law: An Efficiency Argument for Employment-Preserving Bankruptcy Rules', *Columbia Law Review* 116 (2016) 1461; J. S. Masur and E. A. Posner, 'Should Regulation Be Countercyclical?', *Yale Journal on Regulation* 34 (2017) 857; Y. Listokin, 'Law and Macroeconomics: The Law and Economics of Recessions', *Yale Journal on Regulation* 34 (2017) 791.

[5] I. Ramsay, 'Consumer Credit Law, Distributive Justice and the Welfare State', *Oxford Journal of Legal Studies* 15 (1995) 177, 178.

[6] C. Crouch, 'Privatised Keynesianism: An Unacknowledged Policy Regime', *The British Journal of Politics & International Relations* 11 (2009) 382; D. Harvey, Seventeen Contradictions and the End of Capitalism (Profile Books, 2014); Fraser (n. 1).

[7] Crouch (n. 6) 382; W. Streeck, Buying Time: The Delayed Crisis of Democratic Capitalism (Verso Books, 2014) 23.

[8] Streeck (n. 7); D. Harvey, *The Enigma of Capital: And the Crises of Capitalism* (Profile Books, 2011) 106–16; Blyth and Matthijs (n. 2); Fraser (n. 1).

ameliorating, problems inherent in the modern regime of financialised capitalism. Of course, law also emanates from, and implements, prevailing ideas and rationalities.[9] Many key features of contemporary bankruptcy law are based on the same ideas underpinning the neoliberal framework now exposed as deeply problematic, undermining the ability of the law to deliver effective policy solutions to contemporary challenges. In order to critique the law's operation and to suggest directions for reform, it is necessary to understand the justifications underpinning the political and economic regime in which it has developed.

2.1.1 Post-War Consensus in Keynesian Demand Management

Various accounts describe the post-war period of managed capitalism in the USA and much of western Europe as a time when economic growth was steady and politics stable, as 'Keynesian fiscal expansionism was an orthodoxy shared by left and right'.[10] An equilibrium was reached based on a policy priority of full employment.[11] This involved government intervention in the business cycle and political planning to ensure growth, redistribution, and household protection from market instability, along with low interest rates and profit margins (as labour took a large share of GDP).[12] Advances in industrial technology and work organisation enabled productivity increases among workers. Under a 'virtuous spiral'[13] this facilitated domestic consumption both through rising wages and cheaper production.[14]

Originally both the investor class and the voting public accepted this situation of high economic growth produced jointly by labour and capital, alongside secure employment, growing wages and expansive social protection through the development of the welfare state.[15] In an economy more tightly controlled by the state, capital's movement was limited – enabling it to be taxed and redistributed.[16] Central banks were dependent and subject to political influence, and so to this political pact.

[9] W. Brown, *Undoing the Demos: Neoliberalism's Stealth Revolution* (Zone Books – The MIT Press 2015) 151–2.

[10] M. Cooper, *Family Values: Between Neoliberalism and the New Social Conservatism* (Zone Books – The MIT Press, 2017) 44.

[11] Blyth and Matthijs (n. 2) 208.

[12] Streeck (n. 7) 24–5; Blyth and Matthijs (n. 2) 208–15.

[13] Crouch (n. 6) 384.

[14] ibid; Fraser (n. 1) 104; Blyth and Matthijs (n. 2) 208.

[15] Streeck (n. 7) 32.

[16] Blyth and Matthijs (n. 2) 209.

As wages and welfare payments grew to keep pace with rising prices, offering households the security necessary to consume freely, households had less need to borrow than currently. In the USA, conditions of stable employment, growing incomes and rising prices made household 'borrowing for prosperity' attractive, however, and credit enabled middle class households to borrow to fund consumption of newly marketed domestic goods to enhance their lifestyles.[17] Meanwhile in the UK, households remained relatively unburdened by debt in the post-war period, until borrowing began to soar in the 1980s.[18]

Many commentators explain the departure from this regime as arising from the widespread acceptance amongst influential observers and policymakers of the perception that it held inherent tendencies towards high inflation and low profitability, undermining the system's technical capacity to produce economic growth.[19] The tipping point was a crisis of high inflation combined with weak growth ('stagflation'), which policymakers attributed to a 'ratchet effect' caused by increasing wages and government spending.[20] Critical perspectives argue, however, that the post-war economic regime was undermined less by an inherent technical incapacity to produce growth, and more by the unravelling of the political consensus regarding its distributive equilibrium.[21] Contrary to the orthodox narrative that inflation represented a threat to all classes,[22] inflation had in fact amplified redistributive policies and assisted working households by reducing the cost of debt repayments, contributing to a post-war economic regime described as a 'debtors' paradise'.[23] Inflation produced negative effects for the creditor and investor classes, however, who launched a 'revolt' against what they saw as a 'covert tax' designed to transfer wealth from investors to workers.[24] This political opposition drove the shift towards neoliberalism and 'a fundamental restructuring' of the capitalist political economy.[25]

[17] L. Hyman, *Debtor Nation: The History of America in Red Ink* (Princeton University Press, 2011) ch. 5.
[18] C. R. Geisst, *Beggar Thy Neighbor: A History of Usury and Debt* (University of Pennsylvania Press, 2013) 301.
[19] Crouch (n. 6); Blyth and Matthijs (n. 2) 211–213; W. Davies, 'Neoliberalism: A Bibliographic Review', *Theory, Culture & Society* 31 (2014) 309, 314.
[20] Crouch (n. 6) 386.
[21] Cooper (n .10) 26.
[22] ibid.
[23] Blyth and Matthijs (n. 2) 215; Cooper (n. 10) 125.
[24] Cooper (n. 10) 127.
[25] Streeck (n. 7) 27.

2.1.2 The Neoliberal Turn and Inflation Targeting

What followed was the era of neoliberalism, a regime 'most commonly understood as enacting an ensemble of economic policies in accord with its root principle of affirming free markets'.[26] Brown explains that neoliberalism can be conceptualised as 'a historically specific economic and political reaction against Keynesianism and democratic socialism'. Marxian perspectives explain this 'reaction' as a class project involving the mobilisation of the state in pursuit of the aim of restoring the rate of profit.[27] Beyond a focus on specific periods and policies, however, neoliberalism also can be understood as 'a more generalised practice of "economising" spheres and activities heretofore governed by other tables of value'.[28] This reflects the Foucauldian analysis that neoliberalism represents 'an attempt to remake social and personal life in its entirety, around an ideal of enterprise and performance'.[29]

Whichever understanding one adopts, following the inflation 'crisis' neoliberal ideas were widely disseminated by mainstream economists and accepted by policymakers of various leanings. It became clear a new consensus had been formed to organise the economy on opposite principles to the prior regime.[30] A new policy priority of inflation targeting was instituted,[31] which required reducing government spending, stifling wage growth and significantly increasing unemployment, while allowing asset values to soar.[32] A key feature of this policy shift was the rise of independent central banks and the new dominance of monetary policy under a trend of 'monetarism'.[33] The US Federal Reserve led through measures to restrict money supply and drive up interest rates, addressing the inflationary 'ratchet effect' problem perceived to have been produced by the influence of politics over monetary policy.[34] Independent central banks could stand up to governments and exert discipline over fiscal policy, lowering interest rates in response to

[26] Brown, *Undoing the Demos* (n. 9) 28.
[27] Davies (n. 19) 314.
[28] Brown, *Undoing the Demos* (n. 9) 21.
[29] Davies (n. 19) 314–5.
[30] Cooper (n. 10) 19; D. Harvey, *A Brief History of Neoliberalism* new edn (Oxford University Press, 2007) 19–31; Blyth and Matthijs (n. 2) 215.
[31] Blyth and Matthijs (n. 2) 215; Cooper (n. 10) 133; Crouch (n. 6) 388–9.
[32] Colin Hay, 'Good Inflation, Bad Inflation: The Housing Boom, Economic Growth and the Disaggregation of Inflationary Preferences in the UK and Ireland', *The British Journal of Politics & International Relations* 11 (2009) 461.
[33] Blyth and Matthijs (n. 2) 217; Cooper (n. 10) 132–9.
[34] Cooper (n. 10) 132–9.

austerity and responding to increased government spending by raising rates to compensate bondholders with a premium to ensure capital returns outmatched any resulting inflation.[35] This bondholder class grew at this time as tax reductions outpaced government spending cuts, which increased government recourse to borrowing. This both expanded financial markets and effectively transformed society's wealthier groups from taxpayers to creditors.[36] A cycle of policies was thus instituted that favoured the interests of capitalists, creating a 'creditors' paradise', in which the real value of debt is maintained by low inflation and the majority of economic growth accrues to capital rather than labour.[37]

2.1.3 Neoliberal Regulation and the Legal Foundations of a Debt-Dependent Economy

A further element of the creditors' paradise policy regime was a deregulatory agenda which created new investment opportunities and facilitated the financialisation of the economy.[38] Deregulation created a reverse 'ratchet effect' by increasing capital mobility, driving down labour's bargaining power and causing governments to adopt ever more investor-friendly policies in fear of capital flight.[39] Financial deregulation is widely recognised as a key factor in the expansion of household credit.[40] The US Supreme Court decision of *Marquette* v. *First Omaha*,[41] which overturned state interest rate limits, is often cited as the catalyst for unprecedented consumer lending and soaring bankruptcy filing rates in the USA.[42] In recent decades UK regulatory regimes at both prudential

35 ibid, 142.
36 S. B. Hager, *Public Debt, Inequality, and Power* (University of California Press, 2016) 6–8.
37 Blyth and Matthijs (n. 2) 215.
38 J. Hopkin and K. A. Shaw, 'Organized Combat or Structural Advantage? The Politics of Inequality and the Winner-Take-All Economy in the United Kingdom', *Politics & Society* 44 (2016) 345.
39 Blyth and Matthijs (n. 2) 216–217; Crouch (n. 6) 389–390.
40 See e.g. G. Trumbull, 'Credit Access and Social Welfare The Rise of Consumer Lending in the United States and France', *Politics & Society* 40 (2012) 9, 13–14; K. T. Leicht, 'Borrowing to the Brink: Consumer Debt in America', *Broke: How Debt Bankrupts the Middle Class* (Stanford University Press, 2012).
41 *Marquette Nat Bank of Minneapolis* v. *First Omaha Service Corp* (1978) 439 US 299 (Supreme Court of the United States).
42 D. Ellis, 'The Effect of Consumer Interest Rate Deregulation on Credit Card Volumes, Charge-Offs, and the Personal Bankruptcy Rate' *Bank Trends* No. 98-05; A. A. Dick and A. Lehnert, 'Personal Bankruptcy and Credit Market Competition', *The Journal of Finance* 65 (2010) 655.

and consumer protection levels have facilitated household borrowing. In respect of UK mortgage lending, prudential deregulation included the removal of direct Government controls over building society lending and of restrictions on the powers of these institutions.[43] It also involved the introduction of open competition in mortgage credit markets through the abolition of exchange controls, credit supply limits,[44] building society tax advantages, and a legalised cartel-type arrangement of common interest rates in the building society sector.[45] Reforms in the early 2000s placed all mortgage lending under the supervision of a single regulator, the Financial Services Authority (FSA – since replaced by the Financial Conduct Authority (FCA)[46]).[47] The FSA's initial regulatory policy had been to facilitate an expansion of mortgage lending;[48] and was founded upon a non-interventionist philosophy that markets are in general self-correcting.[49] It imposed prudential capital requirements which it subsequently confessed were exposed as insufficient by the global financial crisis.[50] The regulator's approach to consumer protection was also 'light-touch' in nature, relying on non-interventionist information disclosure – mere requirements that consumers be provided with information concerning a mortgage product before purchasing it.[51] The regulator rejected more intensive product design regulation, such as limiting the sale of high loan-to-value (LTV) or loan-to-income (LTI)

[43] M. Stephens, 'Mortgage Market Deregulation and Its Consequences', *Housing Studies* 22 (2007) 201, 207–8.

[44] ibid, 201.

[45] ibid, 206.

[46] *A New Approach to Financial Regulation: Consultation on Reforming the Consumer Credit Regime* (Department for Business, Innovation and Skills, 2010); *A New Approach to Financial Regulation: Transferring Consumer Credit Regulation to the Financial Conduct Authority* (HM Treasury and Department for Business, Innovation and Skills, 2013).

[47] Financial Services and Markets Act 2000 (2000 c.8)

[48] See generally, Lord Turner, *The Turner Review: A Regulatory Response to the Global Banking Crisis* (Financial Services Authority 2009); *Mortgage Market Review* (Financial Services Authority, 2009).

[49] Turner (n. 48) 87.

[50] Financial Services Authority (n. 48) 25–6.

[51] A detailed account of regulatory provisions under the Financial Services and Markets Act 2000 lies outside the scope of this book. The regulatory structure consists of a three-tier approach of overarching principles, explanatory codes and detailed rules relating to licensing, supervision and enforcement. Conduct of business rules relating to mortgage loans are contained in the Mortgage and Home Finance: Conduct of Business Sourcebook (MCOB) section of the FCA Handbook: www.handbook.fca.org.uk/handbook/MCOB .pdf accessed 10 November 2018. See S. Nield, 'Responsible Lending and Borrowing: Whereto Low-Cost Home Ownership', *Legal Studies* 30 (2010) 610, 613–14.

mortgage loans, allowing such products to proliferate and facilitate the rapid expansion of mortgage debt in the 2000s.[52] Similarly, the FSA did not prescribe rigorous requirements regarding the affordability assessments which lenders should undertake when lending.[53] This led to lax creditworthiness measurements by lenders and an over-reliance on security rather than on mortgage borrowers' ability to pay, particularly in subprime mortgage markets.

Similar trends prevailed in respect of unsecured credit regulation in the UK, under a regime inspired by the Crowther Committee's neoclassical economic paradigm favouring free markets.[54] This Committee expressly prioritised the open supply of credit over consumer protection, considering that the law should not 'restrict [the majority's] freedom of access to credit in order to protect the relatively small minority who get into difficulties'.[55] The Consumer Credit Act 1974 was based around market-facilitating, non-interventionist measures such as information disclosure regulation.[56] It relied on informed and 'confident' consumers, rather than substantive regulatory rules, to drive competitive markets through free exchange.[57] More intensive regulatory approaches,[58] such as price controls limiting interest rates on consumer loans, had traditionally been rejected since the middle of the nineteenth century, under the classical economic argument that such

52 Financial Services Authority (n. 48) 37–49.

53 ibid, 50–5.

54 For a comparative overview of consumer credit regulatory philosophies in the UK and France, see I. Ramsay, 'To Heap Distress upon Distress? Comparative Reflections on Interest-Rate Ceilings', *University of Toronto Law Journal* 60 (2010) 707. See Crowther Committee on Consumer Credit, *Consumer Credit: Committee Report* (Stationery Office Books, 1971).

55 Crowther Committee on Consumer Credit (n. 54) para. 1.3.5.

56 Regulations establish prescriptive rules regarding the form and content of pre-contractual information disclosure by lenders: I. Ramsay, *Consumer Law and Policy: Text and Materials on Regulating Consumer Markets* 3rd revised edn (Hart Publishing 2012) 411–4. See e.g. Consumer Credit (Disclosure of Information) Regulations 2004, SI 2004/1481; Consumer Credit (Agreements) (Amendment) Regulations 2004, SI 2004/1482; Consumer Credit Act 1974, Part IV.

57 I. Ramsay, 'From Truth in Lending to Responsible Lending' in A. Janssen and G. Howells (eds.), *Information Rights and Obligations: The Impact on Party Autonomy and Contractual Fairness* (Avebury Technical, 2005) 48.

58 Historically, control orders had set rules on terms of such loans as hire-purchase arrangements, stipulating the down payments or deposits required, the finance charges and maximum term of repayment. See S. Brown, 'Using the Law as a Usury Law: Definitions of Usury and Recent Developments in the Regulation of Unfair Charges in Consumer Credit Transactions', *Journal of Business Law* (2011) 91, 95.

measures could limit access to credit unduly.[59] Controls of interest rates have been limited to private law mechanisms for overturning contracts based upon 'extortionate' interest rates[60] or 'unfair credit relationships'.[61] The approach of the English courts to such provisions has been non-interventionist, as they have tended to rely on market rates in upholding high-interest credit contracts.[62] Limited regulation of interest rates facilitated a rapid expansion of high-cost consumer credit markets in the UK in recent years following the financial crisis.[63] Political pressure mounted in response to this trend, effectively forcing the UK Conservative and Liberal Democrat coalition government to direct the Financial Conduct Authority to introduce an interest rate cap in this market.[64]

Just as in the mortgage credit market, product design regulation has been limited, primarily confined to the general control of unfair terms in consumer contracts under EU law.[65] While this legislation can control some allegedly unfair pricing practices such as credit card default charges and other risky product features,[66] its regulatory power is limited by its inapplicability

[59] Ramsay, 'To Heap Distress upon Distress?' (n. 54) 715–7; Brown, 'Using the Law as a Usury Law: Definitions of Usury and Recent Developments in the Regulation of Unfair Charges in Consumer Credit Transactions' (n. 58) 112; D. Cayne and M. J. Trebilcock, 'Market Considerations in the Formulation of Consumer Protection Policy', *University of Toronto Law Journal* 23 (1973) 396, 411–8. See also the Usury Laws Repeal Act 1854 (17 & 18 Vict., c 90).

[60] See Consumer Credit Act 1974, ss. 137–140 (repealed); Ramsay, 'To Heap Distress upon Distress?' (n. 53) 716.

[61] See Consumer Credit Act 1974, ss.140A–140D; S. Brown, 'The Unfair Relationship Test, Consumer Credit Transactions and the Long Arm of the Law', *Lloyds Maritime and Commercial Law Quarterly* 60 (2009) 90.

[62] E. Lomnicka, 'Unfair Credit Relationships: Five Years On', *Journal of Business Law* 8 (2012) 713, 728.

[63] National Audit Office, *Regulating Consumer Credit* (The Stationery Office, 2012) 8.

[64] See e.g. 'CP14/10: Proposals for a Price Cap on High-Cost Short-Term Credit – Financial Conduct Authority' (2014) www.fca.org.uk/news/cp14-10-proposals-for-a-price-cap-on-high-cost-short-term-credit accessed 11 November 2018; P. Ali, C. Hay McRae and I. Ramsay, 'Payday Lending Regulation and Borrower Vulnerability in the United Kingdom and Australia', *Journal of Business Law* 2015 (2015) 223; A. K. Aldohni, 'The UK New Regulatory Framework of High-Cost Short-Term Credit: Is There a Shift Towards a More "Law and Society" Based Approach?', *Journal of Consumer Policy* 40 (2017) 321.

[65] EU Council Directive 93/13/EEC on unfair terms in consumer contracts 1993, implemented into domestic law in the Consumer Rights Act 2015, Part 2.

[66] For example, the Court of Justice of the European Union has indicated that a national court could assess the fairness in a mortgage loan contract of an acceleration clause, a default interest rate clause, and a clause providing for unilateral quantification of unpaid debt: see *Mohamed Aziz* v. *Catalunyacaixa* [2013] Case C-41511 (Court of Justice of the

to 'core' terms of consumer credit contracts.[67] Furthermore, it was not until 2006, with the enactment of the Consumer Credit Act 2006, that lenders came under a duty to assess a consumer's ability to afford a loan before selling the loan to the consumer; although the banking industry had agreed that such an assessment should form part of the sales process under the voluntary Banking Code.[68] Responsible lending rules are now enforced by the Financial Conduct Authority under their Conduct of Business Sourcebook[69] The Authority has found that the majority of lenders use appropriate affordability assessments, but that there 'is evidence of under-compliance with . . . rules'. Closer scrutiny and tighter rules have led to FCA enforcement activity against high-cost lenders,[70] with some firms struggling to maintain their business models while complying with new affordability rules.[71] The Financial Conduct Authority's introduction of interest rate caps in the high-cost short-term credit sector has brought benefits for consumers,[72] and is a significant departure from traditional regulatory philosophy.[73] The Authority acknowledges that problems remain of expansion in other high-

European Union). Default charges can be controlled under the Consumer Rights Act 2015, Sched. 2, Part 1, para. 6. In the mid-2000s, The Office of Fair Trading set out its regulatory policy for monitoring such credit card charges for fairness: *Calculating Fair Default Charges in Credit Card Contracts* (Office of Fair Trading, 2006).

67 See e.g. *The Office of Fair Trading* v. *Abbey National plc & Others* [2010] 1 AC (UK Supreme Court 2009), discussed at text to notes 81–3 below.

68 Banking Code superseded by 'Lending Code', paras. 50–6; 'Lending Code' paras. 50–6 www.lendingstandardsboard.org.uk/res-cat/lc-archive/ accessed 12 November 2018; G. McMeel, 'Conduct of Banking Business Brought into the FSA Fold', *Lloyds Maritime and Commercial Law Quarterly* (2010) 431, 434–6. The Banking Code was first issued in 1992 but replaced by the Lending Code in 2009).

69 'Assessing Creditworthiness in Consumer Credit: Summary of Research Findings' (Financial Conduct Authority, 2017) Summary of Research Findings; 'Assessing Creditworthiness in Consumer Credit: Proposed Changes to Our Rules and Guidance' (Financial Conduct Authority, 2017) Consultation Paper CP17/27.

70 'Wonga to Make Major Changes to Affordability Criteria Following Discussions with the FCA' (Financial Conduct Authority, 2014) Press Release www.fca.org.uk/news/press-releases/wonga-make-major-changes-affordability-criteria-following-discussions-fca accessed 15 February 2018; 'Rent-to-Own Provider BrightHouse to Provide over £14.8 Million in Redress to around 249,000 Customers' (Financial Conduct Authority, 2017) Press Release www.fca.org.uk/news/press-releases/rent-to-own-provider-brighthouse-14-8-million-redress-249000-customers accessed 15 February 2018.

71 Z. Wood, 'BrightHouse Admits Affordability Checks Are Hurting Business Model', *The Guardian* (4 October 2016) www.theguardian.com/money/2016/oct/04/brighthouse-admits-affordability-checks-are-hurting-business-model accessed 15 February 2018.

72 'High-Cost Credit: Including Review of the High-Cost Short-Term Credit Price Cap' (Financial Conduct Authority, 2017) Feedback Statement FS17/2.

73 Ramsay, 'To Heap Distress upon Distress?' (n. 54).

cost credit markets not subject to this cap.[74] Recent reforms follow decades of regulation prioritising innovation and market access, however, which undoubtedly facilitated the expansion of household debt.[75] Debt levels remain high, and problems of high-cost and persistent debt remain. Chapter 1 shows how debt problems can move from the regulated financial sector into other areas such as debts relating to utilities and government services. Neoliberal regulatory approaches have always been aware that the legitimacy of the deregulatory regime depends on a paradoxical need for interventions in response to crisis and scandal, and recent reforms might fit this pattern.[76] Even if one takes the alternative position that the extensive activity of the FCA represents a shift from pre-crisis regulatory approaches, its effects are limited in light of the acceleration in recent years of structural trends under which debt compensates for low wages and insufficient welfare state provision (as discussed below).[77]

At the level of private law, English courts have shown favourable attitudes towards new product features and business practices which facilitated the expansion of household debt. Early in the neoliberal era, Atiyah noted that 'Freedom of Contract seems to have been re-established as the ideology of the common law', and that 'the message of the New Right [was] being heard in the law courts as well as in the City of London'.[78] In setting the common law 'ground rules' of consumer credit markets,[79] English courts have followed classical

[74] Financial Conduct Authority, 'High-Cost Credit: Including Review of the High-Cost Short-Term Credit Price Cap' (n. 72); 'High-Cost Credit Review – Update' (Financial Conduct Authority, 2018) Feedback Statement FS17/2.

[75] I. Ramsay and T. Williams, 'The Crash That Launched a Thousand Fixes: Regulation of Consumer Credit After the Lending Revolution and the Credit Crunch' in N. Moloney and K. Alexander (eds.), *Law Reform and Financial Markets* (Elgar, 2011).

[76] ibid, 225. Often responses to crises and 'atrocity stories' can take the form of non-interventionist neoliberal regulatory techniques such as disclosure: O. Ben-Shahar and C. E. Schneider, *More Than You Wanted to Know: The Failure of Mandated Disclosure* (Princeton University Press, 2014) ch. 9.

[77] I. Ramsay, 'Household Finances: Income, Saving and Debt Inquiry – Written Evidence Submitted by Professor Iain Ramsay' (Treasury Committee 2018) (HHF0043) www.parliament.uk/business/committees/committees-a-z/commons-select/treasury-committee/inquiries1/parliament-2017/household-finances-17–19/publications/ accessed 15 June 2018.

[78] P. S. Atiyah, 'Freedom of Contract and the New Right', Essays on Contract (Oxford University Press, 1986) 366, 363.

[79] Ramsay, 'Consumer Credit Law, Distributive Justice and the Welfare State' (n. 5) 177–8; G. Howells and S. Weatherill, *Consumer Protection Law* 2nd revised edn (Avebury Technical, 2005) 3; R. Brownsword, *Contract Law: Themes for the Twenty-First Century* 2nd edn (Oxford University Press, 2006) 48–9.

contract law and basic neo-classical economics ideas in seeing their role as being to facilitate free exchange and uphold marketplace bargains 'neutrally'. This has helped to create a 'contractual culture' giving maximum freedom to lenders to expand household lending.[80] Courts have approved untested product features such as acceleration clauses and new business models based increasingly on default charges as being compatible with traditional contract law doctrines.[81] In finding that unauthorised overdraft fees on current accounts were charges for services rather than (invalid) penalties for default, and so exempt from unfair terms regulation, Lord Phillips, in a Supreme Court decision, partly based his view on the importance of the charges as sources of bank revenue. This was a striking vote of approval by the common law for bank freedom to develop new opportunities for consumer lending profits.[82] This decision involved the UK Supreme Court rejecting the claim of specialist consumer credit regulator the Office of Fair Trading, and holding that the private law authorised business practices that continue to cause consumer harm a decade later.[83] On occasion courts have malleably dis-applied or moulded long-standing common law doctrines and principles by reference more to policy concerns than legal precedent,[84] while motivated by the view that it is 'important that lenders should feel able to advance money'.[85] Even in interpreting consumer protection legislation

[80] Ramsay, 'Consumer Credit Law, Distributive Justice and the Welfare State' (n. 5) 178.

[81] *Wadham Stringer Finance* v. *Meaney* High Court of Justice, England and Wales, Queen's Bench [1980] 3 All ER 789, [1981] 1 WLR 39, 46, discussed in Ramsay, 'Consumer Credit Law, Distributive Justice and the Welfare State' (n. 5) 183; *The Office of Fair Trading* v. *Abbey National plc & Others* (n. 67).

[82] Lord Phillips stated that 'whatever may have been the position in the past, the Banks now rely on the Relevant Charges as an important part of the revenue they generate from the current account services ... ', *Office of Fair Trading* v. *Abbey National plc and Others* [2010] 1 AC 696, [88]. The decision of the UK Supreme Court contrasts both in its ultimate finding and its reasoning with the Australian High Court decision of *Andrews* v. *ANZ Banking*. Here the court noted that while the decision was to be decided in accordance with private law rules, the enactment of relevant consumer protection measures meant that 'this pattern of remedial legislation suggests the need for caution in dealing with the unwritten law as if *laissez faire* notions of an untrammelled "freedom of contract" provide a universal legal value': [2012] HCA 30, [5].

[83] Financial Conduct Authority, 'High-Cost Credit Review – Update' (n. 74).

[84] H. Collins, 'Regulating Contract Law' in C. Parker and others (eds.), Regulating Law (2004).

[85] *Royal Bank of Scotland Plc* v. *Etridge (No 2)* [2001] UKHL 44, [2002] 2 AC 773, [2], per Lord Nicholls. Lord Hobhouse commented that '[t]he law has, in order to accommodate the commercial lenders, adopted a fiction which nullifies the equitable principle [of undue influence] and deprives vulnerable members of the public of the protection which equity gives them.' See *Etridge*, [115].

specifically designed to augment the common law, English courts have adhered to ideas of arm's length bargaining based on trader self-interest and consumer self-reliance,[86] in regarding market forces as the best indicators of the fairness of terms such as interest rates.[87] Furthermore, English courts have held firm to the *caveat emptor* principle in finding that lenders owe no common law duty to consider whether a loan is in a borrower's best interests.[88] This has allowed lenders to feel able to increase the supply of credit to consumers without fear of legal recrimination should this result in over-indebtedness.

2.1.4 Neoliberal Regulation, Market Innovation and the Consumer Lending Revolution

These regulatory and judicial trends follow a principle that 'excessive regulation can stifle innovation'.[89] The financial innovation facilitated by neoliberal regulatory approaches have contributed to expanding household debt levels, shifting default risk away from lenders, and ending the relational nature of household borrowing. A supply-side consumer lending 'revolution' developed significant new practices of 'securitisation, the application of sophisticated computer technology to develop predictive credit scores and risk-based pricing, and the increasing spread of all-purpose credit cards'.[90] In terms of the latter, the transactional structure of credit cards departed significantly from traditional understandings of *caveat emptor* and rational weighing of risk and reward by consumers.[91] By making revolving credit available to households in a manner previously impossible, credit cards broke the historical link between repayment and the period of use of purchased goods, while also removing the discipline of a fixed repayment plan.[92] A leading account identifies credit cards as 'unique contributors to the over-indebtedness problem', with

[86] See e.g. C. Willett, 'General Clauses and the Competing Ethics of European Consumer Law in the UK', *The Cambridge Law Journal* 71 (2012) 412.

[87] Lomnicka (n. 62) 728.

[88] See e.g. J. Wadsley, 'Bank Lending and the Family Home: Prudence and Protection', *Lloyds Maritime and Commercial Law Quarterly* 3 (2003) 341, 352.

[89] Ramsay and Williams (n. 75) 226–7.

[90] ibid, 221.

[91] R. J. Mann, *Charging Ahead: The Growth and Regulation of Payment Card Markets around the World* 1st edn (Cambridge University Press, 2007) 182.

[92] I. Ramsay, 'Consumer Credit Society and Consumer Bankruptcy: Reflections on Credit Cards and Bankruptcy in the Informational Economy' in J. Niemi, I. Ramsay and W. C. Whitford (eds.), *Consumer Bankruptcy in Global Perspective* (Hart Publishing, 2003) 22.

evidence refuting any suggestion that credit cards substitute benignly for less efficient borrowing alternatives.[93]

The development of sophisticated credit reporting and scoring technologies has expanded credit supply,[94] claiming to address the lack of information available to lenders regarding borrower creditworthiness, which Stiglitz and Weiss identified as leading to credit rationing.[95] The arrival of the era of Big Data has enhanced lending potential by allowing lenders to segment customer groups and identify profit opportunities among 'undersold' customers.[96] Computerised credit scoring techniques mark a shift from relational banking to automated, and ultimately algorithmic, lending of a more transactional nature. This change was furthered by the development of securitisation and 'originate-to-distribute' lending,[97] as financial technologies have allowed debt originators to transfer default risk.[98] Securitisation promised the potential reduction of overall credit risk through diversification,[99] and opened new fields for investors to seek profit.[100] For present purposes, securitisation contributed to the expansion of household debt by allowing banks to grow their loan books by accessing liquidity while shifting risk to investors and more readily complying with capital requirements regulation. Securitisation aside, other secondary markets in household debt developed through debt collection and debt purchasing industries.[101] Lenders pass approximately £20bn of debt to debt

93 Mann (n. 91) 182.

94 J. Lauer, *Creditworthy: A History of Consumer Surveillance and Financial Identity in America* (Columbia University Press, 2017).

95 J. E. Stiglitz and A. Weiss, 'Credit Rationing in Markets with Imperfect Information', *The American Economic Review* 71 (1981) 393.

96 J. Lauer, *Creditworthy: A History of Consumer Surveillance and Financial Identity in America* (Columbia University Press, 2017) 209.

97 A. Berndt and A. Gupta, 'Moral Hazard and Adverse Selection in the Originate-to-Distribute Model of Bank Credit', *Journal of Monetary Economics* 56 (2009) 725.

98 A. Sufi, 'Lender Incentives, Credit Risk, and Securitization: Evidence from the Subprime Mortgage Crisis' in R. Brubaker, R. M. Lawless and C. J. Tabb (eds.), *A Debtor World: Interdisciplinary Perspectives on Debt* (Oxford University Press, 2012) 87.

99 M. Cerrato and others, 'Why Do UK Banks Securitize?' (Social Science Research Network, 2012) SSRN Scholarly Paper ID 2051379 2 https://papers.ssrn.com/abstract=2051379 accessed 25 July 2017.

100 E. Dabla-Norris and others, 'Causes and Consequences of Income Inequality: A Global Perspective' (International Monetary Fund, 2015) IMF Staff Discussion Note 8; M. Kumhof, R. Rancière and P. Winant, 'Inequality, Leverage, and Crises', *American Economic Review* 105 (2015) 1217.

101 For discussion of the development of US debt buying and collection industries, and their influence on the use of bankruptcy, see D. Jimenez, 'Dirty Debts Sold Dirt Cheap', *Harvard Journal on Legislation* 52 (2015) 41; P. Foohey and others, 'Life in the Sweatbox', *Notre Dame Law Review* (94 Notre Dame Law Review 219 (2018)).

collectors in the UK annually.[102] Large amounts of household debt are also sold outright to debt purchasers, with large growth in such firms in recent years, often backed by private equity.[103] Approximately £900m of purchased debt was *recovered* by debt buyers in 2014, meaning that the bad debts originally sold by lenders were of a substantially higher original value. Large debt buying firms now occupy key roles as the largest unsecured creditors in the English bankruptcy system.[104] Technological advances and innovations in business practices have thus transformed household credit markets from the position prevailing just decades ago. Today's markets are nothing like those of nineteenth century classical law contract law theory, and even resemble little the credit markets existing when law-and-economics ideas gained popularity in the 1970s.

2.1.5 Justifying a Debt-Dependent Economy

As generally with the rise of neoliberal ideas,[105] political support and voter consent for expanded household debt were accompanied by support of policymakers and academic economists.[106] General prevailing faith in the efficient market hypothesis led to a view that *access to credit* was welfare-enhancing for borrowing households and beneficial to the wider economy. Under this view, increased household borrowing was always economically rational, but was only possible due to the favourable regulatory structures and financial innovation facilitated by the neoliberal turn. The 'dominant conceptual framework' supporting this position was the 'consumption smoothing', 'life cycle' or 'permanent income hypothesis' neo-classical economic model.[107] This framework views increased household debt

102 'Sector Views 2017' (Financial Conduct Authority, 2017) 20.

103 D. Gibbons, 'Britain in the Red: Why We Need Action to Help over-Indebted Households' (Centre for Responsible Credit (commissioned by TUC and Unison) 2016) 16.

104 I. Ramsay, *Personal Insolvency in the 21st Century: A Comparative Analysis of the US and Europe* (Hart Publishing, 2017) 74.

105 Cooper (n. 10) 18–19.

106 Turner (n. 21) 1. See also L. Zingales, 'Presidential Address: Does Finance Benefit Society?', *The Journal of Finance* 70 (2015) 1327.

107 G. Betti and others, 'Consumer Over-Indebtedness in the EU: Measurement and Characteristics', *Journal of Economic Studies* 34 (2007) 136, 138; G. Bertola, R. Disney and C. Grant, 'The Economics of Consumer Demand and Supply', *Economics of Consumer Credit* (Massachusetts Institute of Technology Press, 2006) 4.

as a rational response to uncertain fluctuations of income over time by forward-looking actors seeking to maximise their long-term preferences.[108] As households accumulate and lose wealth at different rates throughout the course of the life cycle,[109] those engaging in utility-maximising behaviour should organise their income flows over their lifespan to *smooth* their consumption. This involves borrowing when income is low and saving at times of high income so that consumption levels remain constant.[110] Borrowing under this model can 'be just as sensible as saving' and raise household welfare.[111] A second strand of the consumption smoothing theory views consumer credit as a form of insurance, a means of maintaining desired levels of consumption in the face of *temporary* 'income shocks' or deviations from the long-run income trend.[112] During a time in which a household's income has fallen due to temporary unemployment, for example, it may be economically rational for the household to borrow so as to allow consumption to remain constant in this intermediate low-income period.[113] Some versions of the consumption smoothing thesis in turn explain household *over*-indebtedness as arising from borrower behaviour deviating from perfect rationality.[114] Neoliberal regulators respond benignly to these divergences by 'upskilling' consumers to fit their role as sovereign and empowered drivers of markets, using information disclosure legislation and pursuing the 'international crusade' of financial literacy policies.[115]

[108] A. Barba and M. Pivetti, 'Rising Household Debt: Its Causes and Macroeconomic Implications—a Long-Period Analysis', *Cambridge Journal of Economics* 33 (2009) 113, 114; Bertola, Disney and Grant (n. 107) 1, 4–5; D. G. Baird, 'Technology, Information, and Bankruptcy', *University of Illinois Law Review* 2007 (2007) 305, 310–1; F. H. Buckley, 'Book Review: The Debtor as Victim', *Cornell Law Review* 87 (2001) 1078, 1081.

[109] R. Disney, S. Bridges and J. Gathergood, Drivers of Over-Indebtedness, Report to the Department for Business, Enterprise and Regulatory Reform (University of Nottingham 2008) 14.

[110] Barba and Pivetti (n. 108) 119; Baird (n. 108) 310.

[111] Bertola, Disney and Grant (n. 107) 2, 12.

[112] Barba and Pivetti (n. 108) 120.

[113] Disney, Bridges and Gathergood (n. 109) 15. Chapter 3 questions the assumptions of perfect rationality and information on the part of the borrower on which this theory depends: see Chapter 3, text to notes 118–38.

[114] Barba and Pivetti (n. 108) 121.

[115] Ramsay and Williams (n. 75) 224, 234–7.

2.2 Contradictions of the Debt-Dependent Economy

2.2.1 *Privatised Keynesianism and Loans for Wages*

Critical perspectives describe the shift of economic regime in quite different terms. Rather than the rise in household debt delivering prosperity, it merely papered over present economic problems while storing up risks for the future.[116] At a macro level, the aftermath of the financial crisis and Great Recession produces increasing evidence that the post-Keynesian neoliberal economic regime contains internal contradictions and tensions that question its sustainability. Meanwhile from a household perspective, the expansion of household debt has not necessarily led to enhanced living standards.

For many commentators, the expansion of household debt was merely a fix that temporarily sustained the capitalist order through its transition from the stagflation crisis to a new equilibrium of low wage inflation and high asset value appreciation.[117] Suppressed wages and government withdrawal of public service spending threatened both to stifle the mass consumption necessary for economic growth, however, and to reduce household living standards below the politically acceptable minimum required for the legitimacy of the economic regime.[118] Household borrowing offered a solution to this contradiction through a model of 'privatised Keynesianism'. Debt allowed aggregate consumption and household living standards to be maintained in the face of stagnating wages for the middle and working classes and increased income inequality.[119] Thus extensive household borrowing, both through unsecured consumer debt and equity release loans secured on rising home values,[120] enabled 'the best outcome from the point of view of the capitalist system': low wages coexisting with sustained high levels of aggregate demand, all without state intervention and mass redistribution.[121]

During this period of suppressed wage growth, living costs continued to rise. Household credit became necessary not just at a macroeconomic level to support aggregate demand, but also at the household level to meet

[116] M. Prasad, *Land of Too Much* (Harvard University Press, 2012) 196.
[117] Harvey, *The Enigma of Capital* (n. 8) 106–118.
[118] Blyth and Matthijs (n 2) 217; Streeck (n. 7) 38; Crouch (n. 6) 390–1.
[119] Crouch (n. 6); P. Lucchino and S. Morelli, *Inequality, Debt and Growth* (Resolution Foundation 2012); J. D. Wisman, 'Wage Stagnation, Rising Inequality and the Financial Crisis of 2008', *Cambridge Journal of Economics* 37 (2013) 921; Kumhof, Rancière and Winant (n. 100).
[120] Hay (n. 32).
[121] Barba and Pivetti (n. 108) 126–7.

essential costs and sustain household living standards. This trend is vividly illustrated by Warren's empirical findings that in the mid-2000s US families were spending more 'on the basics of being middle class' than had been the case in the 1970s.[122] Asset price inflation means that while in the late 1970s the ratio of UK house prices to household gross disposable incomes stood at under 3:1, at present it is closer to 5:1.[123] Rental housing costs are historically high, with approximately one third of renters reporting that payments amount to at least 30 per cent of their pre-tax incomes.[124] The wave of privatisation that formed a key feature of the neoliberal turn may also have added to rising costs.[125] Rising household borrowing on this account results from attempts by low- and middle-income households to maintain both their absolute standards of living and relative standards of consumption. Debt has temporarily bridged gaps created by conditions of rising costs of living, wage stagnation and increased volatility of income and employment.[126]

2.2.2 Credit/Welfare Trade-Off

Commentators also link the expansion of household debt in recent decades to a 'credit/welfare state trade-off'.[127] In a 'debtfare' economy in which debt substitutes for welfare provision,[128] households become increasingly reliant on a 'debt safety net' in the face of a shrinking social

[122] E. Warren, 'The Over-Consumption Myth and Other Tales of Economics, Law, and Morality', *Washington University Law Quarterly* 82 (2004) 1485, 1502.

[123] 'Financial Stability Report: June 2017' (Bank of England, 2017) Financial Stability Report 41 (2).

[124] ibid. For a discussion of contemporary problems of rental debt and bankruptcy's response, see Chapter 6 and J. Spooner, 'Seeking Shelter in Personal Insolvency Law: Recession, Eviction and Bankruptcy's Social Safety Net', Journal of Law and Society 44 (3) (2017) 374–405.

[125] See e.g. estimates that UK water costs are 40 per cent higher for households in real terms since privatisation: P. Kenway and A. Tinson, 'A Socially Responsible Water Industry?' (New Policy Institute, 2015).

[126] Barba and Pivetti (n. 108) 122; T. A. Sullivan, 'Debt and the Simulation of Social Class' in R. Brubaker, R. M. Lawless and C. J. Tabb (eds.), *A Debtor World: Interdisciplinary Perspectives on Debt* (Oxford University Press, 2012) 54; M. Crain and M. Sherraden, *Working and Living in the Shadow of Economic Fragility* (Oxford University Press, 2014); G. Standing, *The Precariat: The New Dangerous Class* New edn (Bloomsbury Academic 2016); J. Morduch and R. Schneider, *The Financial Diaries: How American Families Cope in a World of Uncertainty* (Princeton University Press, 2017).

[127] Prasad (n. 116) 227–45.

[128] S. Soederberg, *Debtfare States and the Poverty Industry: Money, Discipline and the Surplus Population* (Routledge, 2014) 89.

safety net.[129] A key element of what can be termed the neoliberal economic regime was a reduction in state spending and a rolling back of the welfare state, in a shift of risk from the state to the individual.[130] The reduction in funding of public services increased financial pressure on households already beginning to suffer from suppressed wage growth.[131] Debt becomes a means of accessing – via markets – services previously provided publicly to citizens in the form of social rights,[132] as, for example, public housing and pension provision are replaced by 'asset-based welfare' policies.[133] Household credit then resembles the 'ultimate market-based social welfare programme'.[134] State welfare provision fulfils a 'consumption smoothing' function,[135] and fits the life cycle model of household consumption described above which constitutes the most common justification for consumer borrowing. These trends followed the general neoliberal aim of rolling back state involvement in the economy, while also fitting with political notions of individual responsibility and policymakers' desire to move a wider range of households from public services into the asset-holding investor class.[136] The relationship between household debt and (a lack of) welfare state provision is vivid in the US context of limited public healthcare provision, as medical debt features prominently among debtors entering bankruptcy.[137] Chapter 5 shows how austerity policies of the past decade have accelerated these trends and made more visible the links between cuts to government welfare provision and household debt.

[129] Lucchino and Morelli (n. 119). Cooper suggests that 'The government promotion of consumer credit has long played a unique role in America's public-private welfare state, standing alongside social insurance as one of the key redistributive mechanisms developed under the New Deal.' See Cooper (n. 10) 143.

[130] J. S. Hacker, *The Great Risk Shift: The New Economic Insecurity and the Decline of the American Dream* revised edn (Oxford University Press, 2008).

[131] Cooper (n. 10) 137.

[132] Soederberg (n. 128) 89; Streeck (n. 7) 39, 73.

[133] J. Montgomerie and M. Büdenbender, 'Round the Houses: Homeownership and Failures of Asset-Based Welfare in the United Kingdom', *New Political Economy* 20 (2015) 386.

[134] Sullivan (n. 126) 138.

[135] John Hills, *Good Times, Bad Times: The Welfare Myth of Them and Us* (Policy Press, 2014) 49–61.

[136] J. D. G. Wood, 'The Integrating Role of Private Homeownership and Mortgage Credit in British Neoliberalism', *Housing Studies* 33 (7) (2018) 993–1013.

[137] Sullivan (n. 126) 141–171; R.J. Landry III and A. K. Yarbrough, 'A Struggling Social Safety Net: Global Lessons from Bankruptcy and Healthcare Reforms in the United States, France and England', *The Future of Consumer Credit Regulation: Creative Approaches to Emerging Problems* (Ashgate Publishing Limited, 2008).

2.2.3 'Let Them Eat Credit': A Time-Limited Credit Consensus

One would have thought that the global financial crisis would have strengthened these critiques and exposed the unsustainability of substituting debt for income growth and social protections, but as Graeber notes, 'the Great Conversation that many were expecting never took place'.[138] The financial crisis did not cause a rethink of financialisation, and its aftermath may even have intensified prior trends.[139] Household debt levels have increased in both emerging and advanced economies since the crisis.[140] Austerity policies represent a continuation of neoliberal ideology and an intensification of the substitution of private debt for public debt begun in the pre-crisis decades.[141] Through the suppression of wages and reduction of social welfare payments,[142] pro-cyclical austerity policies have produced the worst decade for real wage growth in two centuries,[143] and trends are in line for the worst rise in inequality since the 1980s.[144] The 'privatised Keynesian' growth model of debt-based consumption persists,[145] as seen in the 2010 Coalition Government and 2015 and 2017 Conservative Governments' reliance on familiar policies such as the Help to Buy mortgage subsidy scheme.[146] Cuts to social welfare provision under austerity measures have been linked to increased debt as households use credit to fill new gaps, with several reports pointing to evidence of specific cuts pushing households into debt.[147]

[138] Graeber (n. 10) 381. See also Davies (n. 9) 316 and the sources cited.

[139] C. Berry, 'Citizenship in a Financialised Society: Financial Inclusion and the State before and after the Crash', *Policy & Politics* 43 (2015) 509, 511.

[140] 'Household Debt and Financial Stability', *Global Financial Stability Report October 2017* (International Monetary Fund, 2017) 54.

[141] Streeck (n. 7) 38–40; Barba and Pivetti (n. 108); M. Blyth, *Austerity: The History of a Dangerous Idea* (Oxford University Press USA 2013) 152–77.

[142] Blyth and Matthijs (n. 2) 218.

[143] 'Public and Family Finances Squeezes Extended Well into the 2020s by Grim Budget Forecasts' (Resolution Foundation) www.resolutionfoundation.org/media/press-releases/public-and-family-finances-squeezes-extended-well-into-the-2020s-by-grim-budget-forecasts/ accessed 3 October 2017.

[144] A. Corlett and S. Clarke, 'Living Standards 2017: The Past, Present and Possible Future of UK Incomes' (Resolution Foundation, 2017) www.resolutionfoundation.org/publications/living-standards-2017-the-past-present-and-possible-future-of-uk-incomes/ accessed 3 October 2017.

[145] Bank of England (n. 123) 14–5.

[146] Berry (n. 139) 518–9.

[147] See Chapter 6, text to notes 29–40.

As post-crisis rebuilding appears to produce neither significant growth nor satisfactory living standards, questions arise as to how long further this regime can be sustained. The temporary success of the 'privatised Keynesianism' model depended on support from mainstream economic opinion regarding its welfare enhancing effects. It also required political consensus under the promise that increased access to credit could maintain or even raise living standards,[148] without more substantive and redistributive reforms that would be difficult to achieve and politically contentious.[149] Deregulation, privatisation and the expansion of household debt moved the task of delivering positive outcomes from state institutions to markets, and the mantra of 'let them eat credit'[150] permitted politicians to evade responsibility for negative economic events and difficult distributional questions.[151] Political attention turned away from the capital-labour struggle and from questions of government redistribution,[152] towards campaigns for the extension of credit access to previously excluded groups (whether based on gender, race or class).[153] These campaigns pushed on an open door, being welcomed both by governments and by a financial services industry keen to find fresh fields for return on capital (since increased inequality risked 'over-accumulation' problems for the asset-holding class).[154] As the scope of activity of democratic institutions (and so of democratic rights[155]) receded, voters were appeased through the 'democratisation of credit' or *financial inclusion*.[156] Soederberg argues that this *debtfarism* regime

[148] Berry (n. 139) 514–5.

[149] R. G. Rajan, *Fault Lines: How Hidden Fractures Still Threaten the World Economy* (Princeton University Press, 2011) 8, 9, 31; Lucchino and Morelli (n. 119) 3; Cooper (n. 10) 139.

[150] Rajan (n. 149) 21.

[151] G. R. Krippner, *Capitalizing on Crisis* Gld edn (Harvard University Press, 2012) 147; Prasad (n. 116) 196–7.

[152] Streeck (n. 7) 76–8; Soederberg (n. 128) 55, 60–1.

[153] M. Cooper, *Family Values: Between Neoliberalism and the New Social Conservatism* (Zone Books - The MIT Press 2017) 144–54; M. Prasad, *Land of Too Much* (Harvard University Press, 2012) 221–6. These developments seem consistent with Fraser's account of 'a "progressive" neoliberalism, which celebrates "diversity", meritocracy and "emancipation" while dismantling social protections and re-externalizing social reproduction ... [and redefining] emancipation in market terms'. N. Fraser, 'Contradictions of Capital and Care', *New Left Review* 100 (2016) 99, 113.

[154] Soederberg (n. 128) 27.

[155] C. Crouch, Post-Democracy 1st edn (Polity Press, 2004) 80–5.

[156] ibid, 61. On financial inclusion in the UK, see e.g. C. Berry, 'Citizenship in a Financialised Society: Financial Inclusion and the State before and after the Crash', *Policy & Politics* 43 (2015) 509.

depoliticises debt relations among the poor by moving conflict to the ostensibly apolitical market, and 'safeguards the illusions of market freedoms and equality to ensure that all *consumers* may benefit from standards of fairness, competition, transparency and accountability'.[157] Developments in credit markets mean that reality departs frequently from this 'illusion' however, and as this becomes increasingly visible political consensus can break down.

Rather than guaranteeing prosperity to all bar a small group of deviant or irrational debtors, structural conditions of high debt levels have made mass over-indebtedness inevitable. Repeated studies have generally found that the primary cause of over-indebtedness is a fall in a leveraged household's income – an 'income shock'.[158] These shocks are most commonly attributable to such 'life accidents' as a loss of employment, a relationship breakdown, or ill health; which render previously manageable commitments unaffordable. The need for households to carry heavy debt loads, in the face of wage stagnation and reduced social provision, means that the occurrence of such a life accident can push them over the edge into financial difficulty. A second significant cause of over-indebtedness is a household's low income.[159] Again, studies based on debtor self-reporting,[160] qualitative case studies and interviews,[161] and quantitative analysis of aggregate household financial data,[162] show a link between over-indebtedness and the condition of living on a low income for a prolonged period. While research generally identifies a third category of causes of over-indebtedness broadly encompassing household financial mismanagement,[163] even this apparently behavioural factor cannot be understood outside structural conditions. Certain studies, for example, characterise as financial mismanagement a debtor's failure to reduce expenditure in the face of falling income or rising living costs (one stark example categorises as

157 Soederberg (n. 128) 61.

158 See e.g. European Commission and others, *Towards A Common Operational European Definition of Over-Indebtedness* (European Commission, Directorate-General for Employment, Social Affairs and Equal Opportunities 2008) 23–4.

159 ibid, 24–5.

160 E. Kempson, Over-Indebtedness in Britain: A Report to the Department of Trade and Industry (Personal Finance Research Centre, 2002) 30–1 www.pfrc.bris.ac.uk/Reports/Overindebtedness_Britain.pdf accessed 11 November 2018.

161 C. Dearden and others, *Credit and Debt in Low-Income Families* (Joseph Rowntree Foundation, 2010) www.jrf.org.uk/publications/credit-debt-low-incomes-families accessed 11 November 2018.

162 European Commission and others, *Over-Indebtedness: New Evidence from the EU-SILC Special Module* (European Commission, 2010) 33–4.

163 European Commission and others (n. 158) 25–7.

'financial imprudence' a failure of household to adjust its fuel consumption as oil prices rise[164]).[165] This assumes that households are living at a heightened standard of living which they can lower as costs rise, a situation divorced from the reality of households struggling to make ends meet, and at odds with the macro trends discussed here.[166] Over-indebtedness is a structural problem in an economy dependent on high household debt levels, rather than a minority issue among 'a deviant group of chronic failures'.[167]

The possibility of wealth democratisation through credit has been called into question following the global financial crisis. A net decline in American median wealth was generated by the subprime crisis of 2007,[168] while the UK sees historically low homeownership rates in conditions of continued asset price inflation and falling real wages.[169] The privatised Keynesianism regime relied on a change of attitude so that 'debt was no longer feared', but many features of expanded credit markets mean that fearlessness may be misplaced as debt retains its historic status as a 'potentially damaging tool that alters the borrowers' lifestyles and future prospects'.[170] While access to credit may have been democratised, the terms on which this credit is available remain discriminatory.[171] Expensive and high-risk products have been targeted at lower-income borrowers under the age-old position that 'the poor pay more'.[172] Rather than providing mutually beneficial outcomes for borrower

[164] Disney, Bridges and Gathergood (n. 109) 30.

[165] European Commission and others (n. 158) 27.

[166] J. S. Hacker, 'The Middle Class at Risk' in K. Porter (ed.), *Broke: How Debt Bankrupts the Middle Class* (Stanford University Press, 2012) 230–4.

[167] Leicht (n. 40) 215. See the discussion of improvident borrower behaviour in Chapter 7.

[168] Cooper (n. 10) 157.

[169] A. Corlett and L. Judge, 'Home Affront: Housing across the Generations' (Resolution Foundation 2017) www.resolutionfoundation.org/publications/home-affront-housing-across-the-generations/ accessed 3 October 2017.

[170] Geisst (n. 18) 299.

[171] For discussion of how UK regulation has prioritised *access* over *consumer protection* in credit markets, see G. Trumbull, 'Consumer Protection in French and British Credit Markets' (2008) UCC08-17 www.jchs.harvard.edu/publications/finance/understanding_consumer_credit/papers/ucc08-17_trumbull.pdf accessed 11 November 2018.

[172] I. Ramsay, *Consumer Law and Policy: Text and Materials on Regulating Consumer Markets* 2nd revised edn (Hart Publishing, 2007) 88–92; O. Bar-Gill and E. Warren, 'Making Credit Safer', *University of Pennsylvania Law Review* 157 (2008) 1, 64; O. Bar-Gill, 'The Law, Economics and Psychology of Subprime Mortgage Contracts', *Cornell Law Review* 94 (2008) 1073, 1138–9; D. Caplovitz, *Poor Pay More: Consumer Practices of Low Income Families* (Free Press, 1968); N. I. Silber, 'Discovering That the Poor Pay More: Race Riots, Poverty, and the Rise of Consumer Law Symposium: How the Poor Still Pay More: A Reexamination of Urban Poverty in the Twenty-First Century', *Fordham Urban Law Journal* 44 (2017) 1319.

and lender, developments in contemporary credit markets have caused creditor and debtor interests to diverge more than ever. The ability to shift risk through secondary markets,[173] and the development of lending practices such as the 'sweat box' model of credit card lending,[174] mean that lenders can profit significantly from defaulting customers and those carrying persistent levels of debt.[175] In these circumstances consumer behaviour is not welfare enhancing, but rather constitutes a form of 'subsistence' borrowing driven by necessity.[176] Advances in behavioural research allow lenders to design products,[177] and advertising methods,[178] that exploit consumer behaviour falling short of economic rationality, as 'lenders today understand far better than they did even 10 years ago about the possibility of consumer error and how profitable it could be'.[179] New technology facilitates these processes, as lenders and credit reporting agencies can record vast amounts of data regarding individual borrowers, customising products and marketing for maximum profit.[180] In the worst cases this can lead to negative outcomes of persistent debt and over-indebtedness, in the best cases the benefits we receive from credit are exchanged for a disciplinary system in which all of our financial behaviour is logged and judged (see Chapter 7). The lived experience of a debt-dependent economy can therefore contrast with the promise of the democratisation of credit.[181] The lack of fulfilment of this promise risks reinforcing social and political division,[182] as the temporary political 'peace' bought by the privatised Keynesian model may be coming to

[173] Berndt and Gupta (n. 97); Sufi (n. 98).

[174] R. J. Mann, 'Bankruptcy Reform and the Sweat Box of Credit Card Debt', *University of Illinois Law Review* 2007 (2007) 375.

[175] 'Credit Card Market Study: Consultation on Persistent Debt and Earlier Intervention Remedies' (Financial Conduct Authority,2017) CP17/10 48.

[176] A. Freeman, 'Payback: A Structural Analysis of the Credit Card Problem Financial Reform During the Great Recession: Dodd-Frank, Executive Compensation, and the Card Act', *Arizona Law Review* 55 (2013) 151.

[177] O. Bar-Gill, 'Seduction by Plastic', *Northwestern University Law Review* 98 (2003) 1373; Bar-Gill (n. 172); R. Harris and E. Albin, 'Bankruptcy Policy in Light of Manipulation in Credit Advertising', *Theoretical Inquiries in Law* 7 (2006) 431.

[178] 'From Advert to Action: Behavioural Insights into the Advertising of Financial Products' (Financial Conduct Authority, 2017) Occasional Papers 26.

[179] E. Warren, 'Balance of Knowledge' in R. Brubaker, R. M. Lawless and C. J. Tabb (eds.), *A Debtor World: Interdisciplinary Perspectives on Debt* (Oxford University Press, 2012) 295.

[180] ibid, 295–8.

[181] W. Davies, J. Montgomerie and S. Wallin, 'Financial Melancholia – Mental Health and Indebtedness' www.perc.org.uk/project_posts/financial-melancholia-mental-health-and-indebtedness/ accessed 20 July 2017.

[182] Cooper (n. 10) 157.

a close. Surprise election and referenda results in countries such as the UK, US and Germany may result from the manner in which the 'creditor's paradise' of this economic regime produces a disillusioned debtor class whose grievances can be mobilised by political extremists.[183] Streeck may be correct in arguing that 'it is becoming ever less possible to stimulate social justice by feeding fictive resources into the distributional conflict while allowing market justice to prevail'.[184]

If the privatised Keynesianism model may be no longer politically sustainable, it also seems to have lost mainstream economic policy support. This book began by illustrating the problems of economic stagnation, inequality and political instability that are increasingly recognised as inherent to an economic structure reliant on high levels of household debt. The financial crisis and subsequent Great Recession have exposed the 'institutional pathologies that are endogenous to [this] regime'.[185] Evidence mounts that debt booms of the kind necessitated by neoliberal privatised Keynesianism inevitably lead to severe financial crises.[186] The 'loans for wages' growth model eventually eats itself, as heavily leveraged households reach limits of their capacity to borrow and service debt, creating a debt overhang problem that stifles further growth. Evidence appears to be mounting that this economic regime is unsustainable, merely offering a temporary 'fix' to tensions inherent to capitalism, storing up problems for the future and producing inevitable crises.[187]

2.3 Conclusions

The 'privatised Keynesianism' model of financialised capitalism appeared initially to deliver growth and 'political peace' following the crises of the Keynesianism demand management model that preceded it.[188] Recent years have exposed the limits of this model, however. If the aims of the shift to privatised Keynesianism were to quell the disquiet of the capital holding class, then it may have been successful in the wealth it has

[183] Blyth and Matthijs (n. 2) 219.
[184] Streeck (n. 7) 61.
[185] Blyth and Matthijs (n. 2) 211, 222–3.
[186] A. Mian and A. Sufi, *House of Debt* (University of Chicago Press, 2014); Ò. Jordà, M. Schularick and A. M. Taylor, 'The Great Mortgaging: Housing Finance, Crises, and Business Cycles' (National Bureau of Economic Research 2014) Working Paper 20501 www.nber.org/papers/w20501 accessed 11 July 2018; International Monetary Fund (n. 140) 66–8.
[187] Barba and Pivetti (n. 108); Hay (n. 32); Streeck (n. 7) 46, 61; Blyth and Matthijs (n. 2) 222.
[188] Prasad (n. 116) 197.

generated for the top end of the distribution curve. This has come at the cost of heightened household and macroeconomic instability, economic stagnation and levels of inequality that are deeply problematic in their own right and politically dangerous. The short-term benefits of wider access to household debt appear to have been reversed in the long run,[189] and evidence increasingly argues that the expansion of debt has been excessive.[190]

Social costs of over-indebtedness and debt overhang problems are unavoidable when structures of political economy depend on high levels of household borrowing to maintain economic growth and household living standards in the face of wage repression and a shrinking welfare state. These developments call for mechanisms for internalising the considerable externalities of expanded household credit markets. This creates a significant role for bankruptcy law, as an important response to the inevitable need for 'insurance-style guarantees against downside risks' of financialisation.[191] The emergence of a phenomenon of mass household over-indebtedness coincided with increased recourse to personal insolvency law by financially troubled consumers seeking relief and a 'fresh start', as households increasingly turned to bankruptcy as a 'social insurer of last resort'.[192] It is time that policymakers and the legal system similarly turned towards conceptualising bankruptcy in this way as a stabiliser against the macroeconomic risks of a debt-dependent economy, and as a safety net for the households it pushes into financial difficulty. As Chapter 3 argues, this involves the law accepting the primacy of the 'fresh start' policy and its debt relief objective, which it has traditionally sought to balance with the conflicting aim of maximising returns to creditors.

While the bankruptcy system might potentially act as a counterweight to risks of our financialised economic order, it nonetheless forms part of this regime and cannot be considered outside the prevailing political economy.[193] When financialisation is shaping an entire economic and political order towards maximising returns to creditors, it is understandable that bankruptcy might tilt itself towards prioritising this objective. Ideas underpinning neoliberal financialisation – privatisation, individualisation of risk, the rolling back of the welfare state, and the commercialisation of public services – shape the design and operation of the

[189] International Monetary Fund (n. 140) 53.
[190] Zingales (n. 106) 1341.
[191] Berry (n. 139) 521.
[192] Spooner (n. 124).
[193] Brown, *Undoing the Demos* (n. 9) ch. 5.

contemporary bankruptcy system. The neoliberal turn has also revived freedom of contract as the 'paramount value' in private law,[194] and has involved the moulding of law and regulation by supportive neo-classical economic or pseudo-economic principles.[195] Bankruptcy law's historical origins in commercial law made its interpretation and application particularly receptive to the revival of these ideas, even as both practice and theory suggest it now should be understood as a consumer or social welfare law, both of which start far from assuming the efficiency of private ordering and market allocations.

Where, then, does bankruptcy fit in this political economy of financialisation? Critical accounts cast bankruptcy as an element of the 'rhetorical and regulative features of the ... debtfare state', which 'play a strategic role in constructing, mediating the tensions within, and socially reproducing' consumer credit industries.[196] The logic of the 'democratisation of credit' and financial inclusion can spread to judges and bankruptcy policymakers, who accordingly seek to deploy bankruptcy as a tool for expanding, rather than correcting, credit markets. Bankruptcy laws can even be co-opted by creditors and market forces 'to discipline the surplus population to the exigencies of the market'.[197] Certainly, elements of these criticisms are evident in English law. Policymakers and judges have overseen the marketisation of the bankruptcy or personal insolvency system, with the consequence that public provision of debt relief (through the bankruptcy and Debt Relief Order procedures) has been marginalised. Debtors are increasingly diverted into 'market-based debt resolution' involving long-term repayment plans negotiated along a contractual basis and productive of high returns to creditors (Chapters 4 and 5). Austerity policies have exacerbated financial difficulties and caused particular problems with for 'priority' debts relating to essential household services, which bankruptcy law has struggled to accommodate within its existing structures. Meanwhile government agency creditors have sought to redeploy bankruptcy law as a tool for collecting such liabilities in pursuit of fiscal consolidation targets (Chapter 6). Finally, neoliberal ideas of individual responsibility and the marketisation of

[194] Atiyah (n. 78). Note, however, the scholarly consensus that neoliberal thought is distinct from the Victorian liberalism from which it takes inspiration, and where Atiyah locates the zenith of freedom of contract: Davies (n. 19) 310.

[195] See e.g. J. Kwak and S. Johnson, *Economism: Bad Economics and the Rise of Inequality* (Pantheon Books, 2017); Brown, *Undoing the Demos* (n. 9) 151 *et seq.*

[196] Soederberg (n. 128) 101.

[197] ibid.

public services have reshaped bankruptcy's regulation of debtor (mis) conduct. This leaves debtors subject to an opaque and stigmatising array of public sanctions by government agencies and omniscient supervision by credit reporting firms (Chapter 7).

As problems of economic stagnation, inequality and political unrest expose the limitations of the 'privatised Keynesianism' model of financialised capitalism, so they illustrate the difficulties of a bankruptcy system overly influenced by this model. These problems at the very least call on bankruptcy to reconceptualise itself as a safety valve to release pressures inherent in the contemporary economic order and to accept that its public policy benefits lie in its ability to act as a bulwark against the negative effects of a 'creditor's paradise' economy, rather than in perpetuating the pursuit of such paradise. Perhaps recognition of these problems also progresses further to argue the case that bankruptcy, by offering debt relief and so contesting the principle of debt itself, can point a path towards a new economic equilibrium less dependent on excessive levels of household borrowing. Either approach must begin by building the case for the public policy merits of household debt relief, and the argument for bankruptcy to deliver such relief. The following chapter aims to argue this case.

3

Consumer Bankruptcy Theory and the Case for Debt Relief

3.1 Introduction: Ambivalent Aims and an Identity Crisis of Personal Insolvency Law and Policy

In a political economy in which increased household debt compensates for stagnating wages and a shrinking welfare state, consumer bankruptcy can act as an 'insurer of last resort' against the risk and instability such an economic structure necessarily involves. Through its provision of debt relief, bankruptcy forms part of the (otherwise shrinking) social safety net for financially distressed households. Indeed, in practice the law operates in this manner, as debtors of little income and few assets resort to insolvency procedures in seeking relief from financial difficulties and creditor pressure. Moving from the household to the wider economy, recent years have seen increasingly widespread arguments that household debt relief policies – and so bankruptcy – can play an important role as 'economic stabilisers' at the macroeconomic level.[1]

English policymakers, judges and commentators have not wholly accepted the extent to which personal insolvency law currently fulfils this role, however, and certainly have not fully recognised the potential of the law to deliver further public policy benefits by offering more expansive household debt relief. Instead, English law is ambivalent in its aims, and these stakeholders tend to treat the law as serving two contrasting purposes: on the one hand *debt collection* and the maximisation of returns to creditors, and on the other the provision of *debt relief* to over-indebted individuals under the 'fresh start' policy. The tension is clear between these 'different and perhaps competing philosophical bases for

[1] 'Dealing with Household Debt', World Economic Outlook 2012 (International Monetary Fund, 2012) 12–14 www.imf.org/external/pubs/ft/weo/2012/01/pdf/c3.pdf accessed 1 November 2018.

the one legal process'.[2] This leads to uncertainty as to which of these aims should most inform the law's design and application,[3] and legislation has not developed a clear hierarchy of policy priorities.[4] This chapter argues that in the contemporary environment of an economy and society straining under the effects of high levels of household debt, a strong case exists for prioritising the debt relief aim of bankruptcy, and so orientating the law firmly towards the fresh start policy and its role as insurance against risks inherent in contemporary financialised capitalism.

3.1.1 Bankruptcy: Debt Collection or Debt Relief?

Express policy statements show English law's adherence to a 'firmly established tenet of time-worn bankruptcy lore ... that the bankruptcy system serves two functions: the protection and payment of creditors; and the provision of shelter and a "fresh start" to overburdened debtors'.[5] After initial primacy of the debt collection objective,[6] the law's historical development has consisted of efforts to seek 'an appropriate balance of bankruptcy's collection and debtor rehabilitation goals'.[7] This balance has tilted at particular points in history.[8] Early bankruptcy legislation focused on the core feature of the surrender of all debtor assets for the benefit of

[2] P. Shuchman, 'An Attempt at a "Philosophy of Bankruptcy"', *UCLA Law Review* 21 (1973) 403, at 414.

[3] C. G. Hallinan, 'The Fresh Start Policy in Consumer Bankruptcy: A Historical Inventory and an Interpretive Theory', *University of Richmond Law Review* 21 (1986) 49, 144.

[4] D. Milman, 'The Challenge of Modern Bankruptcy Policy: The Judicial Response' in S. Worthington (ed.) Commercial Law & Commercial Practice (Hart Publishing, 2003) 396.

[5] Hallinan (n. 3) at 50. See also E. Warren, 'A Principled Approach to Consumer Bankruptcy', American *Bankruptcy Law Journal* 71 (1997) 483, at 483; I. Fletcher, 'Bankruptcy Law Reform: The Interim Report of the Cork Committee, and the Department of Trade Green Paper', *The Modern Law Review* 44 (1981) 77, at 81.

[6] M. Howard, 'A Theory of Discharge in Consumer Bankruptcy', *Ohio State Law Journal* 48 (1987) 1047, 1049; C. J. Tabb, 'The Historical Evolution of the Bankruptcy Discharge', *American Bankruptcy Law Journal* 65 (1991) 325; A. J. Duncan, 'From Dismemberment to Discharge: The Origins of Modern American Bankruptcy Law', *Commercial Law Journal* 100 (1995) 191.

[7] Howard (n. 6) at 1082. See also D. Skeel, Debt's Dominion: A History of Bankruptcy Law in America (Princeton University Press, 2001) 210.

[8] D. McKenzie Skene, 'Plus Ça Change, Plus C'est La Même Chose? The Reform of Bankruptcy Law in Scotland', *Nottingham Insolvency Business Law eJournal* 3 (2015) 285, at 297.

creditors,[9] while adding harsh penalties to coerce repayment.[10] Three key conditions essential to modern consumer bankruptcy were absent from the law prior to the eighteenth century. No debt discharge was provided to the debtor, with creditors retaining their collection rights after the proceedings had concluded.[11] Only involuntary proceedings brought by creditor petition were possible, while procedures were applicable only to traders or business debtors, rather than consumers.[12] Debt discharge was established in 1705,[13] before subsequently voluntary bankruptcy was introduced in 1844.[14] Bankruptcy was finally extended to non-traders in 1861.[15]

The introduction in 1976 of *automatic* debt discharge for debtors on completion of the bankruptcy process,[16] irrespective of creditor consent or the level of returns produced for creditors,[17] was a landmark in establishing debt relief as 'a legitimate independent objective'.[18] The Insolvency Act 1986 added to the range of personal insolvency procedures by introducing Individual Voluntary Arrangements alongside bankruptcy. It also advanced the debt relief objective further, by reducing the debtor's waiting period for bankruptcy discharge to just three years.[19] This reform built on the recognition by the seminal Cork Report of the fresh start principle as a basic aim of the law.[20] More recent policy developments have tilted the balance ever further towards this objective, while continuing nonetheless to emphasise the importance of debt collection. The Enterprise Act 2002 lowered the discharge waiting

[9] Duncan (n. 6) 194.
[10] ibid, 194–5; Tabb (n. 6) 330–2.
[11] Tabb (n. 6) 332.
[12] Duncan (n. 6) 195.
[13] An Act to Prevent Frauds Frequently Committed by Bankrupts 1705, 4 & 5 Anne, c. 17.
[14] An Act to amend the Law of Insolvency, Bankruptcy, and Execution, 7 & 8 Vict., c. 96, §41 (1844), Tabb (n. 6) 353–4.
[15] See An Act to amend the law relating to bankruptcy and insolvency in England, 24 & 25 Vict. c. 134; V. Countryman, 'A History of American Bankruptcy Law', *Commercial Law Journal* 81 (1976) 226, 229; Sir Kenneth Cork, *Insolvency Law and Practice: Report of the Review Committee* (HMSO, 1982) para. 42.
[16] Insolvency Act 1976 ss. 7–8; I. F. Fletcher, *Law of Bankruptcy* (Macdonald & Evans Ltd, 1978) 308–9.
[17] Duncan (n. 6) 199; Tabb (n. 6) 337.
[18] Hallinan (n. 3) 60; English law eliminated the creditor consent condition in 1842 (5 & 6 Vict., c. 122, s. 39 (1842)), but reintroduced it in 1869 (32 & 33 Vict., c. 71, s. 48 (1869)). It was revoked in 1883 but replaced by a system of limited, conditional and suspended debt discharges: Tabb (n. 6) 354.
[19] Insolvency Act 1986 s. 279.
[20] Cork (n. 15) 192.

period in bankruptcy to just one year.[21] It also replaced the automatic restrictions and disqualifications previously applicable to all bankrupts with a narrower system of sanctions for culpable debtors.[22] When justifying these reforms, policymakers expressly referred to the 'fresh start' or 'second chance' philosophy, arguing that a more generous debt discharge would promote entrepreneurship by encouraging business risk taking.[23] Nonetheless, policymakers reiterated the principle that debtors who 'can pay, should pay' as a 'key element of our bankruptcy system'.[24] While giving a more lenient discharge with one hand, reforms simultaneously enhanced requirements for bankrupt debtors to contribute income to creditors for up to three years.[25] Attempts by Government agency the Insolvency Service to modernise the Individual Voluntary Arrangement (IVA) insolvency procedure evidence similar concern that concessions to debtors are balanced by the advancement of creditor interests . Proposals advanced in the mid-2000s acknowledged the need both 'to support the concept of a fresh start' and 'to ensure the debtor pays the maximum affordable contribution'.[26] The establishment of the Debt Relief Order procedure (DRO) in 2009 seemed to represent a more complete evolution.[27] As confirmed by courts, 'the purpose of the DRO scheme is unadulterated debt relief',[28] and it involves no contributions to creditors from the debtor's assets or income. Instead, under this means-tested procedure, low-income debtors with very few assets owing limited amounts of debt simply obtain initial provisional protection from enforcement for one year, followed by full discharge of all non-excluded

[21] Enterprise Act 2002 s. 256, substituting Insolvency Act 1986 s. 279.

[22] Enterprise Act 2002 s. 257, Schd. 20, inserting Insolvency Act 1986, s. 281A, Schd. 4A. See Chapter 7 for a detailed discussion of the Bankruptcy Restrictions Order/Undertaking system.

[23] Productivity and Enterprise: Insolvency – A Second Chance Cm 5234 (The Insolvency Service; Department for Trade and Industry, 2001).

[24] ibid, 1.9.

[25] Enterprise Act 2002 s. 260, inserting Insolvency Act 1986 s. 310A.

[26] *Improving Individual Voluntary Arrangements* (Insolvency Service, 2005) paras. 13, 21. For insight into the IVA procedure, see A. Walters, 'Individual Voluntary Arrangements: A "Fresh Start" for Salaried Consumer Debtors in England and Wales', *International Insolvency Review* 18 (2009) 5.

[27] See Tribunals Courts and Enforcement Act 2007 (2007 c. 15), Ch 5 Part 3, Schds. 18–9; Insolvency Act 1986, Part VIIA, Schds. 4ZA-4ZB; *Relief For The Indebted – An Alternative To Bankruptcy* (The Insolvency Service, 2005); *A Choice Of Paths: Better Options to Manage Over-Indebtedness and Multiple Debt* (Department of Constitutional Affairs, 2004)

[28] *R (Cooper and Payne)* v. *Secretary of State for Work and Pensions* Court of Appeal, England and Wales [2010] EWCA Civ 1431, [2011] BPIR 223 [85].

debts.[29] Even in proposing this mechanism for debtors lacking payment capacity, policymakers reiterated 'that people who can pay . . . should do', and indicated that the bankruptcy procedure would ensure debtors of greater means make repayments to creditors.[30] A Call for Evidence issued by the Insolvency Service in 2014 further exemplifies this disunity of purpose. It considered simultaneously a relaxation of the restrictive means-based DRO access conditions (thus expanding debt relief), and tweaks to the bankruptcy petition procedure that left unquestioned bankruptcy's status as the 'strongest of debt recovery tools'.[31]

3.1.2 Bankruptcy: Commercial Law or Social Safety Net?

Uncertainty in ranking the primary aims of bankruptcy law reflects uncertainty as to the law's very identity. Underpinning the debt collection objective is a conception of the law as a market facilitation tool and the view that insolvency should produce outcomes involving 'as few dislocations as possible' from pre-bankruptcy market allocations.[32] A vision prioritising this aim sees bankruptcy as part of the commercial law, fitting alongside corporate insolvency into a single law of insolvency.[33] The fresh start policy, in contrast, understands that 'in its proper context ... the law of personal insolvency functions as a mechanism of redistribution'.[34] To prioritise this vision is to recognise that the vast majority of debtors using personal insolvency procedures have not fallen into debt difficulty due to business activities. Rather they have encountered everyday financial problems arising in an economy in which borrowing has become necessary to compensate for suppressed wages and reduced social support. These debtors are consumers, tenants,

[29] A debtor can be sanctioned and subjected to the suspension of her discharge in the event of misconduct.

[30] The Insolvency Service (n. 27) para. 22.

[31] 'Insolvency Proceedings: Debt Relief Orders and the Bankruptcy Petition Limit: Call for Evidence' (Insolvency Service, 2014) Call for Evidence Foreword www.gov.uk/government/consultations/insolvency-proceedings-review-of-debt-relief-orders-and-the-bankruptcy-petition-limit accessed 1 November 2018.

[32] T. H. Jackson, *The Logic and Limits of Bankruptcy Law* (Harvard University Press, 1986) 253.

[33] Private law textbooks tend to treat personal and corporate insolvency together, dedicating much discussion to rules regarding the distribution of debtor assets to creditors in both areas. See e.g. M. Bridge, 'Insolvency' in A. Burrows (ed.), *English Private Law* 3rd edn (Oxford University Press, 2013) ch. 19.

[34] I. F. Fletcher, *The Law of Insolvency* 4th revised edn (Sweet & Maxwell, 2009) paras. 3–002.a

taxpayers, citizens/welfare users, meaning that bankruptcy is far from a commercial law – instead it can be considered as a consumer law, a social welfare law, or a 'law of hardship'.[35] Processes of privatisation and marketisation of public services associated with neoliberalism mean that in the 'regulatory welfare state' the lines between these categories of consumer law and social welfare law have in any case been blurred.[36] Regulatory norms and consumer protection measures can provide a 'safety net of last resort', for those who fall through the increasingly wide cracks in welfare state provision.

Many other jurisdictions clearly accept the position of bankruptcy in the social safety net. In contrast to English law,[37] bankruptcy procedures were not open to non-traders in many European jurisdictions when mass household over-indebtedness first emerged in the late 1980s. Governments responded by enacting bespoke consumer debt-adjustment laws,[38] which offered previously unavailable debt relief to troubled households and 'were seen as part of the welfare state protection'.[39] For example, French authors characterise the country's law as 'un droit social',[40] and reforms in that country formed part of much wider legislation targeting social exclusion.[41] A seminal empirical study of the US system found that bankruptcy 'must be understood within a broad range of social support systems',[42] and that it is 'clear that many lawyers see it just that way'.[43] Contemporary US authors can

[35] J. Braucher, 'Response to Eric Posner', *Fordham Journal of Corporate & Financial Law* 7 (2001) 463, 463.

[36] H. Haber, 'Regulation as Social Policy: Home Evictions and Repossessions in the UK and Sweden', *Public Administration* 93 (2015) 806.

[37] English law extended bankruptcy to non-traders in 1861: see An Act to amend the law relating to bankruptcy and insolvency in England, 24 & 25 Vict. c. 134; Cork (n. 15) para. 42.

[38] See e.g. J. Kilborn, 'Two Decades, Three Key Questions, and Evolving Answers in European Consumer Insolvency Law: Responsibility, Discretion, and Sacrifice', in J. Niemi and others (eds.), *Consumer Credit, Debt and Bankruptcy* (Hart Publishing, 2009) 307.

[39] J. Niemi-Kiesilainen, 'Consumer Bankruptcy in Comparison: Do We Cure a Market Failure or a Social Problem', *Osgoode Hall Law Journal* 37 (1999) 473, 481.

[40] I. Ramsay, 'A Tale of Two Debtors: Responding to the Shock of Over-Indebtedness in France and England – a Story from the Trente Piteuses', *The Modern Law Review* 75 (2012) 212, 234.

[41] *Projet de loi d'orientation relative à la lutte contre les exclusions, (Projet de loi n° 1055); Loi n° 2003-710 du 1er août 2003 d'orientation et de programmation pour la ville et la renovation urbaine.*

[42] T. Sullivan, E. Warren and J. L. Westbrook, *As We Forgive Our Debtors: Bankruptcy and Consumer Credit in America* (Beard Books, 1989) 333.

[43] T. A. Sullivan, E. Warren and J. L. Westbrook, *The Fragile Middle Class: Americans in Debt* (Yale University Press, 2000) 169.

go so far as to describe 'consumer bankruptcy [as] one of the largest social insurance programs', offering more assistance to households than all state unemployment insurance programs combined.[44] Even in neighbouring Scotland, policymakers are comfortable conceptualising the law in welfare state terms, with recent personal insolvency reforms presented as forming part of a national 'financial health service', with obvious analogy to the National Health Service.[45]

English courts and policymakers have yet to embrace wholly this conception of bankruptcy law, however. Confusion regarding the very nature of the law can be seen by examining two judicial decisions that indirectly asked courts to consider this question. In the *Lightfoot* case, a debtor challenged, as running contrary to the right of access to the courts, the requirement that debtors seeking to petition for bankruptcy must pay a deposit towards costs of the Official Receivers administering debtors' cases.[46] The Court of Appeal rejected the debtor's claim, holding that this fee was not payable for access to the courts, but rather reflected the costs charged for services provided to the debtor petitioning for bankruptcy. The courts here characterised bankruptcy as a form of public service assisting debtors in difficulty, rather than a judicial process. In the first instance judgment, Laws J stated that the relevant insolvency law provisions

> belong to a self-standing statutory scheme designed both for the fair treatment of creditors and for the relief of debtors. If the scheme (or its predecessors) had never been enacted, the rule of law would not itself in the least be affronted. It is not concerned with the adjudication of general disputes. Its premise is that the debts are already owed. It constitutes a benign administrative system to make fair and practical sense of the case where the debtor, by his own fault or not, cannot pay his undisputed creditors.[47]

For this judge, there was nothing inherently judicial about bankruptcy, and it was 'perfectly possible in theory to envisage a system, designed for the same ends, which would be run by administrators under

[44] W. Dobbie and J. Song, 'Debt Relief and Debtor Outcomes: Measuring the Effects of Consumer Bankruptcy Protection', *American Economic Review* 105 (2015) 1272, 1272.

[45] Skene (n. 8) 292.

[46] *R* v. *Lord Chancellor, ex parte Lightfoot* [2000] QB 597 (Court of Appeal (England and Wales)); J. Tribe, 'The Lightfoot Paradox: Financing the Cost of Personal Insolvency Relief through Bankruptcy Revenue Stamps and Sliding Scales – Part A', *Insolvency Intelligence* 29 (2016) 97. See the discussion of bankruptcy fees in Chapter 4.

[47] *R* v. *Lord Chancellor, ex parte Lightfoot* (n. 46) 609.

a government department'.[48] One might read in these words a judicial acceptance that bankruptcy's primary function had evolved into the provision of relief to debtors, and an understanding of the law as a public assistance scheme similar to other welfare state services.

Such an understanding was not evident in the more recent case of *R (Howard)* v. *Official Receiver* concerning the nature of the DRO procedure.[49] One might expect this procedure to be even more readily categorised as a social service due to its provision of debt relief without conditions of repayment to creditors, and its non-judicial nature.[50] When a debtor argued that the Official Receiver administering DROs was subject to the same 'equality duty' as other public authorities when considering debtor cases,[51] however, the High Court held that an Official Receiver's decision to make or revoke a DRO constituted a 'judicial function', involving an adjudication of the competing rights of the debtor and her creditors. This finding arose in the context of a claim brought by a debtor when an Official Receiver revoked a DRO that had been made in her favour, as the official judged that her late receipt of previously underpaid working tax credits took her outside the means-testing criteria of the DRO procedure. The debtor's argument was that her health issues meant that equality legislation applied to the Official Receiver's decision to revoke the DRO. In finding for the Official Receiver, the court rejected the claimant's arguments that the official's decision making was analogous to the decisions made by an administrative officer distributing various public services and payments under welfare state schemes.[52] The High Court distinguished the position of such an officer from the Official Receiver by stating that the latter's decision was not in response to a claim by a debtor for a benefit, and that it 'determines the rights of a creditor or creditors as well as the rights and liabilities of the debtor'.

[48] ibid.

[49] *Howard, R (on the application of)* v. *The Official Receiver* [2013] EWHC 1839 (Admin), [2014] QB 930.

[50] The DRO procedure is administered by the Insolvency Service with applications submitted through debt advice charities designated as 'approved intermediaries'. See Chapter 4, pages 118–119, 122–125.

[51] The Official Receiver argued that the decision was an exercise of a judicial function and so was not subject to the equality duty of public authorities to eliminate discrimination, advance equality of opportunity and foster good relations between those with protected characteristics and others who do not share such characteristics. See Equality Act 2010, s. 149.

[52] *Howard, R (on the application of)* v. *The Official Receiver* [2013] EWHC 1839 (Admin) (n. 49) 115–6.

The judge emphasised that it is 'in the very nature of a DRO and an order revoking a DRO that they affect and at least temporarily determine competing rights and liabilities of the debtor and creditor(s)'.[53] For judge Sir Nicholas Stadlen, 'the process by which a person's rights and/ or liabilities are determined with binding legal effect is ... materially different' from public officials' 'difficult questions of allocating scarce resources'.[54]

The court's central point that the making and revoking of a DRO involves a determination of debtor and creditor rights seemingly conflicts directly with the statement of the court in *Lightfoot* that bankruptcy does not involve the adjudication of disputes. These two decisions share little common ground and are difficult to reconcile. Their inconsistency illustrates the identity crisis at the heart of English bankruptcy law. The law sometimes views itself as an administrative scheme providing public assistance to troubled households, and other times as a judicial process for the determination of competing rights, and particularly for the protection of the rights of creditors as commercial investors. It may be notable that the only common ground in the judicial decisions was the manner in which they rejected debtor claims and circumscribed access to debt relief, an outcome common in judicial decisions discussed throughout this book.

3.2 Developing a Hierarchy of Policy Priorities

The confusion regarding bankruptcy law's core identity and objectives is deeply problematic since most policy decisions and litigated questions involve a direct choice of one of the law's aims above the other. Uncertainty regarding the purposes the law should pursue creates tension and risks failure to achieve one or both objectives, and the concern of this book lies in how bankruptcy's debt relief objective can be obscured and outweighed by concerns of maximising returns to creditors. To reconcile these aims and to evaluate how the law should prioritise one primary objective, it is necessary to interrogate their respective theoretical underpinnings. This requires a common framework, which this book develops by relying largely on a law-and-economics perspective, incorporating socio-legal insight and elements of political theory. Commentators and policy-makers have drawn on a wide range of rationales in theorising bankruptcy

[53] ibid, 193.
[54] ibid, 163.

and in particular valuable accounts in support of the fresh start policy have been advanced across a range of theoretical perspectives.[55] This book adopts an approach that aims to acknowledge this theoretical pluralism and bridge a division in academic literature between law-and-economics and socio-legal scholars, and between macrodata and microdata.[56] In so doing, it aims to avoid unresolvable disputes between parties adopting different normative perspectives and failing to engage one another in constructive debate.[57] By focusing on economic analyses of household debt and bankruptcy, the book's approach allows the case for debt relief to meet economic justifications for primacy of the debt collection objective on their own terms. Commentators adopting a critical perspective may condemn how promoters of a neoliberal political agenda have used neo-classical economic ideas – often of an overly simplistic and fundamentalist nature[58] – instrumentally, selectively[59] and partially,[60] in support of their interests.[61] These voices oppose outright the framing of issues in economic terms, as this risks subordinating 'democratic state commitments to equality, liberty, inclusion and constitutionalism' to 'the project of economic growth, competitive positioning, and capital

[55] Howard (n. 6) 1048; J. M. Czarnetzky, 'The Individual and Failure: A Theory of the Bankruptcy Discharge', *Arizona State Law Journal* 32 (2000) 393, 394; J. J. Kilborn, 'Mercy, Rehabilitation, and Quid Pro Quo: A Radical Reassessment of Individual Bankruptcy', *Ohio State Law Journal* 64 (2003) 855, 861; R. E. Flint, 'Bankruptcy Policy: Toward a Moral Justification for Financial Rehabilitation of the Consumer Debtor', *Washington and Lee Law Review* 48 (1991) 515, 519. For justifications for debt relief in bankruptcy based on ethic and virtue-based perspectives, see e.g. H. M. Hurd, 'The Virtue of Consumer Bankruptcy' in R. Brubaker, R. M. Lawless and C. J. Tabb (eds.), *A Debtor World: Interdisciplinary Perspectives on Debt* (Oxford University Press USA, 2012); K. Gross, *Failure and Forgiveness: Rebalancing the Bankruptcy System* (Yale University Press 1997); J. Kilpi, *The Ethics of Bankruptcy* (Routledge, 1998). Important treatments of the consumer credit and bankruptcy system have also emerged from critical theory: see e.g. S. Soederberg, *Debtfare States and the Poverty Industry: Money, Discipline and the Surplus Population* (Routledge, 2014).

[56] Skeel (n. 7) 199; S. Block-Lieb and E. J. Janger, 'The Myth of the Rational Borrower: Rationality, Behavioralism, and the Misguided Reform of Bankruptcy Law', *Texas Law Review* 84 (2005) 1481.

[57] A. Mechele Dickerson, 'Can Shame, Guilt, or Stigma Be Taught: Why Credit-Focused Debtor Education May Not Work', *Loyola of Los Angeles Law Review* 32 (1998) 945, 1871.

[58] J. Kwak and S. Johnson, *Economism: Bad Economics and the Rise of Inequality* (Pantheon Books, 2017).

[59] C. Crouch, *Can Neoliberalism Be Saved From Itself?* (Social Europe Edition, 2017).

[60] D. Campbell, 'Welfare Economics for Capitalists: The Economic Consequences of Judge Posner', *Cardozo Law Review* 33 (2012) 2233.

[61] W. Brown, *Undoing the Demos: Neoliberalism's Stealth Revolution* (Massachusetts Institute of Technology Press, 2015) 22–8; J. R. Hackney, 'Law and Neoclassical Economics: Science, Politics, and the Reconfiguration of American Tort Law Theory', *Law and History Review* 15 (1997) 275.

enhancement'.[62] Since neo-classical economic ideas have been co-opted in neoliberal processes of the financialisation of everything,[63] critical perspectives might fear that their deployment might inevitably advance interests of the financial sector.

While acknowledging this perspective, this book considers that there are advantages to engaging with economic analysis in support of progressive positions. As Davies suggests, under normative neoliberalism 'neoclassical economics becomes a soft constitution for government'.[64] This opens the possibility for progressive voices to use tools of economic analysis to hold such a government to its own standards and to critique it on its own terms.[65] Deployment of the framework of *market failure*, which has come to dominate policy making,[66] lends more weight to critique than arguments originating from alternative theoretical starting points. It is difficult even for neoliberal policymakers to ignore, with any legitimacy, evidence that increased hardship for households in our 'creditor's paradise' economy also comes with significant economic cost. Events of the past decade have cast into doubt the traditional acceptance of an efficiency-equity trade-off,[67] and have increasingly illustrated how unequal distributions of risk and loss throughout the economy can produce negative effects not just for disadvantaged individuals, but for aggregate welfare. This recognition has been facilitated both by a macroeconomic turn in law-and-economics,[68] and the increased recognition in macroeconomic policy of the significance of distributional issues.[69] At this point, socio-legal and political economy approaches can enhance market failure analysis.

[62] Brown (n. 61) 26.

[63] W. Davies, 'Neoliberalism: A Bibliographic Review', *Theory, Culture & Society* 31 (2014) 309, 316; Brown (n. 61) 28.

[64] W. Davies, 'The New Neoliberalism', *New Left Review* (2016) 121, 128.

[65] Crouch argues that most 'weaknesses of the neoliberal approach' are 'fully recognised in the neoclassical economic theory on which neoliberalism draws': Crouch (n. 59) 12.

[66] T. Prosser, 'Regulation and Social Solidarity', *Journal of Law and Society* 33 (2006) 364, 366–71; I. Ramsay, *Consumer Law and Policy: Text and Materials on Regulating Consumer Markets* 3rd revised edn (Hart Publishing, 2012) 49.

[67] A. B. Atkinson, *Inequality* (Harvard University Press, 2015) 243–63.

[68] A. Mian and A. Sufi, *House of Debt* (University of Chicago Press, 2014); A. Mian and A. Sufi, 'The Macroeconomic Advantages of Softening Debt Contracts', *Harvard Law and Policy Review* 11 (2017) 11; P. A. McCoy, 'Countercyclical Regulation and Its Challenges', *Arizona State Law Journal* 47 (2015) 1181; Y. Listokin, 'Law and Macroeconomics: The Law and Economics of Recessions', *Yale Journal on Regulation* 34 (2017) 791.

[69] G. Vlieghe, 'Debt, Demographics and the Distribution of Income: New Challenges for Monetary Policy – Speech by Gertjan Vlieghe, Bank of England' (Department of Economics and Centre for Macroeconomics Public Lecture, London School of

They can offer more insight into, for example, individual behaviour and environmental and relational constraints than economic models relying solely on assumptions of individual rationality and of conduct as reflective of individual preferences.

Longstanding economic analyses supporting the prioritisation of bankruptcy's debt relief function have now been have been augmented by lessons from the global financial crisis and Great Recession. Radical post-crisis activism has over time been joined by mainstream commentary in highlighting the negative effects of unduly high debt levels.[70] International institutions line up to illustrate how 'debt overhang' is stifling economic growth, and to urge national policymakers to enact extensive household debt relief policies.[71] These ideas undermine key assumptions of the debt collection objective, which are further weakened by evidence of the contemporary practice of household debt and bankruptcy developed in both economic and socio-legal studies. Together these sources suggest a strong public policy case for tilting the balance of

Economics, 18 January 2016) www.bankofengland.co.uk/publications/Pages/speeches/2016/872.aspx accessed 6 November 2018; J. Yellen, 'Macroeconomic Research After the Crisis' ('The Elusive "Great" Recovery: Causes and Implications for Future Business Cycle Dynamics' 60th Annual Economic Conference, Federal Reserve Bank of Boston, Boston, Massachusetts, 14 October 2016) www.federalreserve.gov/newsevents/speech/yellen20161014a.htm?emailid=55ccb821090bff0300e78b62&segmentId=1e887e34-00a5-c328-481c-7a09b5553d9c accessed 5 November 2018; S. Keen, Can We Avoid Another Financial Crisis? (Polity Press, 2017) 25–38.

70 For example, 'debt refusal' campaigns featured amongst the activities of the post-crisis Occupy movement, while other debtor activist and civil society groups have also developed in recent years: see e.g. T. Gitlin, 'Occupy's Predicament: The Moment and the Prospects for the Movement', *The British Journal of Sociology* 64 (2013) 3; E. Hoekstra, 'Andrew Ross on the Anti-Debt Movement' in D. Hartmann and C. Uggen (eds.), *Owned* (W W Norton & Company, 2015); J. Montgomerie and others, 'The Politics of Indebtedness in the UK' 31–6. For more mainstream conversion to this view, see e.g. P. Bunn and M. Rostom, 'Household Debt and Spending in the UK' (Bank of England, 2015) 554; S. Lo and K. S. Rogoff, 'Secular Stagnation, Debt Overhang and Other Rationales for Sluggish Growth, Six Years On' (Bank for International Settlements, 2015) 482 10 www.bis.org/publ/work482.pdf; ' The Global Economy: Maturing Recoveries, Turning Financial Cycles?' (Bank for International Settlements, 2017) 48–50; 'Financial Stability Report: June 2017' (Bank of England, 2017) Financial Stability Report 41 1–49. The scholarship of Mian and Sufi has been particularly influential in disseminating this realisation: see e.g. A. Mian and A. Sufi, *House of Debt: How They (and You) Caused the Great Recession, and How We Can Prevent It from Happening Again* (University of Chicago Press, 2014).

71 See e.g. International Monetary Fund, 'Dealing with Household Debt' (n. 1); 'Fiscal Monitor – Debt: Use It Wisely' (International Monetary Fund, 2016) www.imf.org/external/pubs/ft/fm/2016/02/fmindex.htm accessed 5 November 2018.

the law towards debt relief, and for accepting its important role as an insurance mechanism against risks of contemporary financialised capitalism.

3.2.1 Creditor Wealth Maximisation and Bankruptcy as Debt Collection

Certain commentators nonetheless continue to state the 'standard justification for bankruptcy'[72] as being to maximise returns to creditors by enforcing pre-bankruptcy debt contracts to the greatest extent possible. This may result from the position that in a surprisingly under-theorised area of law, scholarship is dominated by Professor Jackson's contractarian 'creditors' bargain' theory,[73] which advocates for creditor wealth maximisation as the law's sole goal.[74] This theory is contractarian on two levels. Firstly, the model is founded in neo-classical economic reasoning and the efficient market hypothesis, considering that bankruptcy's basic function is to produce a collective outcome for creditors that reflects as closely as possible their prior market positions.[75] In acting as a tool for enforcing market allocations, it shares classical contract law's view that voluntary contractual exchange will produce more efficient outcomes than centralised decision making, based on the Hayekian insight that government policymakers inevitably lack information regarding party preferences.[76] Under this view, seller responses to purchaser preferences will lead to mutually beneficial (*Pareto superior*) transactions between sellers and buyers (with at least one party's position improving and no one's deteriorating) until the optimum point of efficiency (*Pareto optimality*)[77] is reached, beyond which no further transactions will benefit one party without causing a loss to

[72] A. Walters, 'Personal Insolvency Law after the Enterprise Act: An Appraisal', *Journal of Corporate Law Studies* 5 (2005) 65, 69.

[73] Jackson (n. 32).

[74] See e.g. A. J. Levitin, 'Bankrupt Politics and the Politics of Bankruptcy', *Cornell Law Review* 97 (2011) 1399, 1404–5; R. J. Mokal, 'The Authentic Consent Model: Contractarianism, Creditor's Bargain, and Corporate Liquidation', *Legal Studies* 21 (2001) 400, 401–2.

[75] Jackson (n. 32) 253; D. Milman, *Personal Insolvency Law, Regulation and Policy* (Ashgate Publishing Limited, 2005) 4.

[76] M. Trebilcock, *The Limits of Freedom of Contract* new edn (Harvard University Press, 1997) 8–16; S. Storm, 'Financialization and Economic Development: A Debate on the Social Efficiency of Modern Finance', *Development and Change* 49 (2018) 1, 5–7.

[77] M. L. Stearns and T. J. Zywicki, *Stearns and Zywicki's Public Choice Concepts and Applications in Law* (West Publishing Company, 2009) 16.

another.[78] This reasoning forms 'the core of the legitimacy of the market as an allocative mechanism, for it shows allocations reached at general competitive equilibrium to be perfectly efficient' and so to produce positive welfare outcomes.[79] To this end, the law must support the market mechanism by clearly defining property rights,[80] establishing ground rules[81] which allow these rights to be transferred freely,[82] and enforcing contractual bargains (with any contractual excuses for non-payment construed narrowly) in order to protect the market expectations of parties.[83] Hence the maximisation of returns to creditors in bankruptcy should best approximate the efficiency of market allocation.

The second contractarian aspect of the 'creditors' bargain' heuristic is its foundation in the idea that insolvency law is a mechanism beneficial to creditors as a group, and thus a mechanism to which all creditors (acting under an ethic of commercial self-interest that is the hallmark of classical contractual theory[84]) would hypothetically accept as offering them the best outcome in the event of the debtor's default. Here the efficiency of bankruptcy lies in its *collective* nature, and the solution it offers to the 'prisoner's dilemma' and 'tragedy of the commons' problems raised by competition among creditors for a defaulting debtor's limited resources.[85] Both of these games drawn from economic theory consider situations where a joint welfare-maximising solution would be reached for all parties through their cooperation, but where each self-interested party has an incentive to operate in a non-cooperative manner.[86] Under the creditors' bargain model, creditor cooperation is desirable to produce the joint welfare maximising outcome (of the greatest possible returns to creditors). The incentives created for each creditor to pursue individual enforcement against a debtor in the hope of full recovery may result in

78 ibid, 16–17; Trebilcock (n. 76) 7. These sources also explain the more relaxed Kaldor-Hicks efficiency standard.

79 D. Campbell, 'The Relational Constitution of the Discrete Contract' in *Contract and Economic Organisation: Socio-legal Initiatives* (Dartmouth Publishing Co Ltd, 1996) 52.

80 Trebilcock (n. 76) 9–15; Stearns and Zywicki (n. 77) 18.

81 J. N. Adams and R. Brownsword, 'The Ideologies of Contract', *Legal Studies* 7 (1987) 205, 206–7.

82 Trebilcock (n. 76) 9, 15–7.

83 G. Howells and S. Weatherill, *Consumer Protection Law* 2nd revised edn (Avebury Technical, 2005) 8; Czarnetzky (n. 55) 415.

84 Chris Willett, 'General Clauses and the Competing Ethics of European Consumer Law in the UK', *The Cambridge Law Journal* 71 (2012) 412; Adams and Brownsword (n. 81).

85 Jackson (n. 32) 10–4; Trebilcock (n. 76) 10–5.

86 Trebilcock (n. 76) 11.

the joint welfare-minimising outcome, however. Individual enforcement efforts may reduce the total value of the debtor's assets (the size of the common pool), and lead to additional costs as creditors compete to be the first to collect from the debtor, including the costs of monitoring both the debtor and competing creditors.[87] Bankruptcy solves the prisoner's dilemma and tragedy of the commons problems by offering a collective and compulsory procedure which compels creditor cooperation.[88] All creditors benefit from the law's stay on individual enforcement efforts, centralised acquisition and sharing of information regarding a debtor's assets, and distribution of these assets among creditors on a pro rata basis.[89] Pro rata distribution is most appropriate, 'because it mimics the value of [creditors'] expected positions immediately before bankruptcy'.[90] The law in this way avoids wasteful costs of creditor competition and monitoring, while also facilitating business planning and more accurate pricing of credit by guaranteeing a minimum (and predictable) amount of recovery to creditors instead of uncertain outcomes of races to court.[91]

Under this perspective, personal insolvency law thus enhances the welfare of all creditors, which is expected to lead to wider credit availability at lower cost.[92] The case for maximising returns to creditors rests on the view that this will produce optimal outcomes. It relies heavily on assumptions of the efficiency of financial markets, and the welfare-enhancing effects of 'financial deepening' and high levels of household debt or 'open access to credit'.[93] It also involves a view of the centrality to the economy of the financial intermediation role performed by banks, a perspective that held 'tremendous support among some in the economics profession' in their analyses of the global financial crisis and Great Recession, influencing policymakers to view 'hurting banks [as] the worst thing for the economy'.[94] Under this view, in the face of widespread household debt default, insolvency law should avoid the crystallisation of losses through debt write-downs. Instead it should aim to minimise creditor losses and stabilise the system, while 'letting banks recognise

87 Jackson (n. 32) 16; Trebilcock (n. 76) 12.
88 Jackson (n. 32) 13.
89 See e.g. V. Finch, *Corporate Insolvency Law: Perspectives and Principles* 2nd edn (Cambridge University Press, 2009) 32–7.
90 Jackson (n. 32) 30–1; Kilpi (n. 55) 14–5.
91 Jackson (n. 32) 14–6.
92 ibid, 14.
93 See pages 51–53 above.
94 Mian and Sufi, *House of Debt* (n. 68) 133.

losses over time against earnings'.[95] Other policymakers and institutions concerned with bank losses and Non-Performing Loans (NPLs) go somewhat further in considering bankruptcy alongside debt enforcement mechanisms and arguing for its deployment towards the facilitation of creditor asset recovery.[96]

3.2.2 *Consumer Credit Market Failures and the Creditors' Bargain Model*

The previous chapters have shown how contemporary conditions of household debt challenge the optimality of 'financial deepening' and the efficiency of financial markets. In so doing, evidence of subsistence borrowing, debt overhang, and mass over-indebtedness undermine assumptions underpinning the creditors' bargain model and the justification for prioritising bankruptcy's debt collection objective.[97] Ideas of market efficiency occupy a paradigmatic world of contractual agreements freely agreed, understood, and negotiated to mutual benefit, between equally well-informed parties of equal bargaining power.[98] Corporate insolvency's world of efficient business-to-business contracting may approximate this ideal. The contemporary world of household debt contrasts strongly with this ideal. It is trite to state that consumer credit markets are prone to failures, and active regulators seem to uncover one sector after another in which consumer detriment and suboptimal outcomes arise.[99] Diagnoses of market failures circulated widely in

95 A. J. Levitin, 'Politics of Financial Regulation and the Regulation of Financial Politics: A Review Essay', *Harvard Law Review* 127 (2013) 1991, 2006.

96 S. Aiyar and others 'A Strategy for Resolving Europe's Problem Loans' (International Monetary Fund, 2015) Staff Discussion Note SDN/15/19 18–20, 28–9.

97 The model can also be criticised for its tendency to lead towards Posnerian ideas of wealth maximisation which have been faulted for failures to take account developments in welfare economics, as well as being politically partial in nature and protective of businesses, rather than of markets: Campbell (n. 60).

98 M. J. Radin, *Boilerplate: The Fine Print, Vanishing Rights, and the Rule of Law* (Princeton University Press, 2012) 3–18.

99 As one illustration, in recent years the Financial Conduct Authority has found problems warranting intervention in payday lending, credit card, rent-to-own finance, doorstep lending, home catalogue credit, store credit cards, and bank overdraft markets: 'CP14/10: Proposals for a Price Cap on High-Cost Short-Term Credit – Financial Conduct Authority' (Financial Conduct Authority, 2014) www.fca.org.uk/news/cp14-10-proposals-for-a-price-cap-on-high-cost-short-term-credit accessed 5 November 2018; 'Credit Card Market Study: Consultation on Persistent Debt and Earlier Intervention Remedies' (Financial Conduct Authority, 2017) CP17/10; 'High-Cost Credit Review – Consultation on Rent-to-Own, Home-Collected Credit, Catalogue Credit and Store Cards, and

consumer credit and bankruptcy literature for decades, but have been made more broadly and starkly visible by the financial crisis and subsequent recession. International organisations such as the International Monetary Fund (IMF) now critique the permanent income theory's assertion of the efficiency of household credit, pointing out that 'newer theories and empirical evidence show that the relationship between household debt and macro-financial stability can also be negative'. The tendency for credit markets to produce suboptimal outcomes is revealed when one 'relax[es] some of the assumptions of the permanent income model and consider[s] the consequences of borrowing constraints, negative externalities and behavioural biases'.[100] These factors illustrate the risks inherent in an economy dependent on high levels of household debt, and the important role of bankruptcy as an insurance mechanism for reallocating these risks by acting as a macroeconomic stabiliser and safety net for distressed households.

Conditions in contemporary household credit markets mean that credit contracts depart from the ideal of mutually beneficial exchange between borrower and lender.[101] Creditors can profit from contracts that lead to debtor default, with products designed accordingly.[102] Relational banking is a thing of the past, and debtor–creditor relationships are mediated by third parties such as debt collectors and purchasers, credit reporting agencies, securitisation vehicles and loan servicers.[103] Creditor interests can be advanced by contracts that produce significant negative outcomes for debtors. Discussions of the debt economy and

Alternatives to High-Cost Credit' (Financial Conduct Authority, 2018) Consultation Paper CP18/12; 'High-Cost Credit Review – Overdrafts' (Financial Conduct Authority, 2018) Consultation Paper CP18/13.

100 International Monetary Fund, 'Household Debt and Financial Stability' (n. 103) 56–7. On testing the creditors' bargain model in this way by relaxing its assumptions, see S. Block-Lieb, 'Fishing in Muddy Waters: Clarifying the Common Pool Analogy as Applied to the Standard for Commencement of a Bankruptcy Case', *American University Law Review* 42 (1992) 337, 430.

101 See pages 49–51 above.

102 R. J. Mann, 'Bankruptcy Reform and the Sweat Box of Credit Card Debt', *University of Illinois Law Review* 2007 (2007) 375; Financial Conduct Authority, 'Credit Card Market Study: Consultation on Persistent Debt and Earlier Intervention Remedies' (n. 99) 48.

103 See e.g. A. Berndt and A. Gupta, 'Moral Hazard and Adverse Selection in the Originate-to-Distribute Model of Bank Credit', *Journal of Monetary Economics* 56 (2009) 725; A. Sufi, 'Lender Incentives, Credit Risk, and Securitization: Evidence from the Subprime Mortgage Crisis' in R. Brubaker, R. M. Lawless and C. J. Tabb (eds.), *A Debtor World: Interdisciplinary Perspectives on Debt* (Oxford University Press, 2012); P. Foohey and others, 'Life in the Sweatbox', *Notre Dame Law Review* (94 (2018) forthcoming).

contemporary household credit markets also cast doubt on the assumption of free market entry and exit. The 'loans for wages' and 'credit/welfare trade-off' ideas illustrate how household living standards depend on borrowing,[104] with the privatisation and marketisation of public services contributing further to these trends. This suggests a form of 'subsistence borrowing' under which households have little option but to enter credit markets, and little freedom to leave.[105]

Information failures and information asymmetry abound in consumer credit markets, as lenders possess significantly more information than borrowers in respect of credit products. Information may be particularly expensive to access and process for consumers in credit markets,[106] in which products are complex and a wide range of products are marketed.[107] In addition, consumers' knowledge of product features may be inaccurate due to lenders' ability to change credit products at low cost and their ability to vary even the terms of existing products through contract amendments.[108] Lenders also offer different terms to different consumers, further reducing transparency regarding available products.[109] The 'learning effect' said to be a feature of market action is reduced in consumer credit markets, due to the fact that large loan transactions such as mortgages are entered into infrequently by consumers.[110] Also, learning possibilities are limited as people tend to feel uncomfortable discussing financial

[104] A. Barba and M. Pivetti, 'Rising Household Debt: Its Causes and Macroeconomic Implications – a Long-Period Analysis', *Cambridge Journal of Economics* 33 (2009) 113; Monica Prasad, *Land of Too Much* (Harvard University Press, 2012); J. Montgomerie, 'America's Debt Safety-Net', *Public Administration* 91 (2013) 871; Soederberg (n. 55).

[105] A. Freeman, 'Payback: A Structural Analysis of the Credit Card Problem Financial Reform During the Great Recession: Dodd-Frank, Executive Compensation, and the Card Act', *Arizona Law Review* 55 (2013) 151.

[106] See generally J. E. Stiglitz, 'The Contributions of the Economics of Information to Twentieth Century Economics', *The Quarterly Journal of Economics* 115 (2000) 1441, 34; I. Ramsay, *Consumer Law and Policy: Text and Materials on Regulating Consumer Markets* 2nd revised edn (Hart Publishing, 2007) 65.

[107] O. Bar-Gill and E. Warren, 'Making Credit Safer', *University of Pennsylvania Law Review* 157 (2008) 1, 10, 16.

[108] The unilateral variation of consumer contract terms is regulated by unfair contract terms legislation, however. See Consumer Rights Act 2015, pt. 2 and Schd. 2, implementing EU Council Directive 93/13/EEC on Unfair Terms in Consumer Contracts (1993).

[109] Bar-Gill and Warren (n. 107) 16.

[110] C. Scott and J. Black, *Cranston's Consumers and the Law* 3rd edn (Butterworths 2000) 33; P. Lunn, 'Can Policy Improve Our Financial Decision-Making?' (Economic and Social Research Institute 2012).

affairs generally,[111] with those in financial difficulty often experiencing particular shame.[112] Even where consumers are provided with information in advance of borrowing, empirical surveys show that consumers do not fully understand the information provided, and tend not to use it.[113] Searching and process costs discourage consumers from 'shopping around' for credit products, and even when engaging in price comparisons consumers usually search based on headline interest rates. This does not prevent what is known as a 'market for lemons'[114] developing, since consumers are less likely to have regard to the quality of products and in particular the presence of certain potentially 'risky' product features. Such features could include future interest rate rises as well as charges and penalty interest rates for missed and/or late repayments, all of which can contribute to a consumer falling into over-indebtedness.[115] Lenders do not compete on these less visible charges, since borrowers pay little attention to them at the *ex ante* purchasing stage, and switching costs render borrowers captive at the *ex post* stage when such charges have been incurred.[116] A voluminous literature illustrates how consumer credit regulatory rules which require the disclosure of information to consumers do not succeed in curing information failures and producing optimal outcomes.[117]

111 M. De Muynck, 'Credit Cards, Overdraft Facilities and European Consumer Protection – A Blank Cheque for Unfairness?', *European Review of Private Law* 18 (2010) 1181, 1194–5.

112 See e.g. B. T. White, 'Underwater and Not Walking Away: Shame, Fear, and the Social Management of the Housing Crisis', *Wake Forest Law Review* 45 (2010) 971; P. Ali, L. O'Brien and I. Ramsay, '"Short a Few Quid": Bankruptcy Stigma in Contemporary Australia', *University of New South Wales Law Journal* 38 (2015) 1575. Note, however, how online fora offer opportunities for debtors to share experiences and offer mutual support: L. Stanley, J. Deville and J. Montgomerie, 'Digital Debt Management: The Everyday Life of Austerity', *New Formations* 87 (2016) 64.

113 A. Atkinson and others, *Levels of Financial Capability in the UK: Results of a Baseline Survey* (Financial Services Authority, 2006); N. O'Donnell and M. Keeney, *Financial Capability: New Evidence for Ireland* (Central Bank and Financial Services Authority of Ireland, 2009); Illuminas (for the FSA), *Disclosure in the Prime Mortgage Market* (Financial Services Authority, 2008).

114 See G. A. Akerlof, 'The Market for "Lemons": Quality Uncertainty and the Market Mechanism', *The Quarterly Journal of Economics* 84 (1970) 488.

115 O. Bar-Gill, 'The Law, Economics and Psychology of Subprime Mortgage Contracts', *Cornell Law Review* 94 (2008) 1073, 1096–102, 1107, 1119–23; Mortgage Market Review (Financial Services Authority, 2009) 4, Annex 2.

116 Payday Lending: Compliance Review Final Report (Office of Fair Trading, 2013) 13.

117 See generally *inter alia* S. Block-Lieb and R. L. Wiener, 'Disclosure as an Imperfect Means for Addressing Over-Indebtedness: An Empirical Assessment of Comparative

Evidence from credit markets also challenges the assumption of rational choice lying at the heart of the efficient market hypothesis: that each individual is motivated by 'rational' self-interest, meaning that she will always make decisions which advance her preferences.[118] In contrast, the developing behavioural economics literature argues that outcomes of decisions are influenced strongly by context, such that people's preferences are not clear, stable and organised, and 'contextual influences [may even] render the very meaning of the term "preferences" unclear'.[119] Under the process of hyperbolic discounting, individuals exhibit time-inconsistent preferences, so that their cost-benefit evaluations tend to overvalue immediate benefits while discounting future costs.[120] Another particularly robustly confirmed finding in cognitive and social psychology[121] is the optimism bias which causes us to adopt an over-optimistic approach to decision-making and to discount unduly the possibility of adverse events occurring.[122] These factors may lead consumers to overvalue the benefit of present access to funds and undervalue future costs and risks (even if informed of them). Such risks and costs may include the difficulty of making future repayments, the likelihood of an 'income shock' or 'life accident' occurring,[123] and the potentially severe economic, social and health consequences of over-indebtedness.[124] Institutional lenders exploit these factors through the design of product features such as low introductory 'teaser' interest rates on mortgage or credit card loans, which attract borrowers holding unrealistically optimistic estimates of future income, rises in home values, interest rates and credit scores.[125] In extreme cases, unexpected charges may create a debt spiral

Approaches' in *Consumer Credit, Debt and Bankruptcy* (Hart Publishing, 2009); O. Bar-Gill, 'Seduction by Plastic', *Northwestern University Law Review* 98 (2003) 1373; Bar-Gill (n. 115); O. Ben-Shahar and C. E. Schneider, *More Than You Wanted to Know: The Failure of Mandated Disclosure* (Princeton University Press, 2014). See pages 42–47 above.

118 Trebilcock (n. 76) 3–4.

119 C. R. Sunstein and R. H. Thaler, 'Libertarian Paternalism Is Not an Oxymoron', *University of Chicago Law Review* 70 (2003) 1159, 1161.

120 Ramsay, *Consumer Law and Policy* (n. 106) 72.

121 R. Harris and E. Albin, 'Bankruptcy Policy in Light of Manipulation in Credit Advertising', *Theoretical Inquiries in Law* 7 (2006) 431, 434–6.

122 Ramsay, *Consumer Law and Policy* (n. 106) 73; I. Ramsay, 'From Truth in Lending to Responsible Lending' in A. Janssen and G. Howells (eds.), *Information Rights and Obligations: The Impact on Party Autonomy and Contractual Fairness* (Avebury Technical, 2005) 53; Harris and Albin (n. 121) 434.

123 Bar-Gill (n. 117) 1400.

124 Ramsay, 'From Truth in Lending to Responsible Lending' (n. 122) 52.

125 Lunn (n. 110) 24–5; Bar-Gill (n. 115) 1119–21; Bar-Gill and Warren (n. 107) 34–5; Bar-Gill (.n 117) 1396–400; 'From Advert to Action: Behavioural Insights into the

sufficient to trap borrowers in the 'sweat box' of negatively amortising revolving credit.[126] Some use of high cost or risky products may be rational in the context of an individual's precarious circumstances,[127] as contemporary research into decision making under conditions of scarcity shows that conditions sometimes require the prioritisation of immediate needs over consideration of long-term outcomes.[128] Behavioural biases also lead to negative outcomes after the initial borrowing decision has been made. Traits of loss aversion and status quo bias mean that borrowers will often try to maintain a lifestyle long after an economically rational actor would make changes.[129] A recent study also shows significant departures from economic rationality in the ways in which debtors prioritise the repayment of various debts, suggesting limited ability to work their way out of debt.[130]

Together all of these factors render impossible the rational planning of a household's financial needs throughout a lifetime,[131] exposing the weakness of the 'permanent income hypothesis' or 'life cycle' model used to justify expanded household debt as welfare enhancing.[132] They mean that many consumer borrowers err systematically in making credit decisions, guaranteeing a certain number of inefficient consumer borrowing decisions, and a portion of consumer borrowers inevitably falling into over-indebtedness.[133] When combined with informational asymmetries, these behavioural trends

Advertising of Financial Products' (Financial Conduct Authority, 2017) Occasional Papers 26.

126 Mann (n. 102).

127 R. Mann, 'Assessing the Optimism of Payday Loan Borrowers', *Supreme Court Economic Review* 21 (2014) 105.

128 S. Mullainathan and E. Shafir, Scarcity: Why Having Too Little Means so Much (Penguin Books, 2013).

129 I. Ramsay, 'Consumer Credit Society and Consumer Bankruptcy: Reflections on Credit Cards and Bankruptcy in the Informational Economy' in J. Niemi, I. Ramsay and W. C. Whitford (eds.), *Consumer Bankruptcy in Global Perspective* (Hart Publishing, 2003) 24.

130 J. Gathergood and others, 'How Do Individuals Repay Their Debt? The Balance-Matching Heuristic' (National Bureau of Economic Research, 2017) Working Paper 24161 www.nber.org/papers/w24161 accessed 5 November 2018.

131 Harris and Albin (n. 121) 441.

132 See pages 51–53 above.

133 While I have focused primarily on failures in the markets for consumer loans, it is clear that the same behavioural traits may lead to problems in respect of other forms of credit, such as arrears of utility bills and rental housing. See e.g. J. Spooner, 'Seeking Shelter in Personal Insolvency Law: Recession, Eviction and Bankruptcy's Social Safety Net', *Journal of Law and Society* 44 (2017) 401–3 https://onlinelibrary.wiley.com/doi/full/10.1111/jols.12035 accessed 5 November 2018.

weaken the ability of consumers to discipline providers of suboptimal products and so to police market efficiency. They also cast light on studies that find a significant cause of over-indebtedness to be 'over-commitment',[134] 'failures of money management',[135] 'financial imprudence',[136] or the Insolvency Service's category of 'living beyond means'.[137] Where these sources elaborate on the meaning of these concepts, they tend to describe them as being composed of factors (lack of financial literacy and an understanding of product terms among borrowers) which can from a different perspective be seen as *market failures*. These factors are more indicative of market features productive of widespread suboptimal outcomes, rather than aberrant financial mismanagement among an incompetent or deviant minority.[138]

3.2.3 *Externalities*

This inevitable over-indebtedness creates externalities, since not all costs and benefits are contained internally within credit market transactions, and products are not priced to reflect the true cost to society of their production.[139] In terms of third party costs, family members of over-indebted individuals suffer severe consequences,[140] while significant costs may be incurred by public social welfare systems in providing for

[134] E. Kempson, Over-indebtedness in Britain: A Report to the Department of Trade and Industry (Personal Finance Research Centre, Bristol, 2002) 32.

[135] E. Kempson and S. Collard, *Managing Multiple Debts: Experiences of County Court Administration Orders among Debtors, Creditors and Advisors* (Department for Constitutional Affairs, 2004) 11–2 www.bristol.ac.uk/geography/research/pfrc/themes/advice/administration-orders.html accessed 5 November 2018.

[136] R. Disney, S. Bridges and J. Gathergood, Drivers of Over-Indebtedness (University of Nottingham, 2008) 27–30.

[137] 'Individual Insolvencies by Age, Gender, and Cause of Insolvency, England and Wales 2015' (Insolvency Service, 2016) www.gov.uk/government/statistics/individual-insolvencies-by-location-age-and-gender-england-and-wales-2015 accessed 5 November 2018.

[138] K. T. Leicht, 'Borrowing to the Brink: Consumer Debt in America', *Broke: How Debt Bankrupts the Middle Class* (Stanford University Press, 2012) 215. See the discussion of improvident borrower behaviour in Chapter 7.

[139] R.t Baldwin, M. Cave and M. Lodge, *Understanding Regulation: Theory, Strategy, and Practice* 2nd edn (Oxford University Press, 2011) 18; Ramsay, Consumer Law and Policy (n. 106) 56.

[140] Bar-Gill and Warren (n. 111) 59–61; Harris and Albin (n. 126) 452–4. Over-indebtedness is more common among households with children: European Commission and others, *Over-Indebtedness: New Evidence from the EU-SILC Special Module* (2010) 35–7.

the basic needs of financially troubled households.[141] Additional burdens may be placed on healthcare systems,[142] as connections between debt difficulties and ill health have been widely recognised in relevant literature.[143] Wider macroeconomic externalities or negative systemic consequences of consumer credit markets provide the 'most powerful driving concerns',[144] however, and form the basis of the primary economic justifications for debt relief through bankruptcy.

The US Supreme Court's classic statement of the fresh start policy advocated the public benefit of giving 'the honest but unfortunate debtor ... a new opportunity in life and a clear field for future effort'.[145] Contemporary policy discussion builds on this traditional justification by increasingly linking excessive household debt to productivity losses, advocating debt relief policies 'to restore the debtor to economic productivity and viable participation in the open credit economy'.[146] First, individuals in severe debt difficulty may be less productive in their employment. When the product of a debtor's labour accrues to creditors, rather than to the debtor's own benefit, her incentives to work may be reduced.[147] The burden of creditor collection efforts may drive the debtor to forgo work entirely to rely on social welfare assistance or on non-taxed cash economy work.[148] Externalities then result through a drain on public social welfare resources and/or reduced contributions to tax revenues.[149] While commentators have questioned

[141] U. Reifner and others, *Consumer Overindebtedness and Consumer Law in the European Union* (Institute for Financial Services, Erasmus University of Rotterdam, University of Helsinki 2003) 62.

[142] S. Emami, 'Consumer Over-Indebtedness and Health Care Costs: How to Approach the Question from a Global Perspective', World Health Report Background Paper 3 (World Health Organisation, 2010).

[143] See e.g. B. Duygan-Bump and C. Grant, 'Household Debt Repayment Behaviour: What Role Do Institutions Play?', *Economic Policy* 24 (2009) 107; 'Women, Debt & Health' (Women's Health Council and MABS, 2007); N. Balmer and others, 'Worried Sick: The Experience of Debt Problems and Their Relationship with Health, Illness and Disability', *Social Policy and Society* 5 (2006) 39; P. Pleasence and N. J. Balmer, 'Mental Health and the Experience of Social Problems Involving Rights: Findings from the United Kingdom and New Zealand', *Psychiatry, Psychology and Law* 16 (2009) 123.

[144] Report on the Treatment of the Insolvency of Natural Persons (World Bank, 2013) para. 77.

[145] *Local Loan Co.* v. *Hunt*, 292 U.S. 234, 244 (1934), *per* Sutherland J.

[146] Howard (n. 16) 1069.

[147] Jackson (n. 32) 244; Hallinan (n. 3) 119.

[148] R. M. Hynes, 'Non-Procrustean Bankruptcy', *University of Illinois Law* Review 2004 (2004) 301, 342.

[149] World Bank (n. 144) paras. 102–5.

the reality of the assumption that creditor collection of debtor income reduces debtors' incentive to work,[150] some empirical evidence shows strong links between households being in arrears and leaving paid employment.[151] A relationship between long-term unemployment and over-indebtedness has also been recognised.[152] Even allowing for such uncertainty, greater concerns may be based on the reduced *ability* of debtors to work due to the stress and health difficulties associated with over-indebtedness.[153] Policymakers appear concerned by this social cost, with a 2003 report by the UK Government noting that the decline in productivity resulting from over-indebtedness could be conservatively estimated at 30 per cent of an individual's salary, approximating to 1 per cent of GDP when extrapolated to the over-indebted portion of the population.[154] An active debt relief policy can address these concerns by restoring debtor employment incentives[155] and alleviating the stress and health problems which may compromise a debtor's workplace productivity.[156]

Policymakers from countries such as England and Australia, as well as institutions such as the World Bank and European Commission, have been drawn to similar arguments that bankruptcy's debt relief can serve economic productivity by facilitating entrepreneurship.[157] From an *ex ante* perspective,

[150] Hynes (n. 148) 323.

[151] E. Kempson, S. McKay and M. Willitts, Characteristics of Households in Debt and the Nature of Indebtedness (Department for Work and Pensions; Bristol University Personal Finance Research Centre, 2004) 5 www.bristol.ac.uk/geography/research/pfrc/themes/credit-debt/characteristics.html accessed 5 November 2018.

[152] Duygan-Bump and Grant (n. 143) 121–2.

[153] Balmer and others (n. 143); C. Fitch, S. Hamilton and R. Davey, *Debt and Mental Health: What Do We Know? What Should We Do?* (Royal College of Psychiatrists; Money Advice Trust; Rethink; Finance and Leasing Association, 2009); Emami (n. 142).

[154] Department of Trade and Industry, Fair, Clear and Competitive: The Consumer Credit Market in the 21st Century (White Paper) (HMSO, 2003) 138.

[155] Hallinan (n. 3) 70; World Bank (n. 144) 37–40.

[156] K. Porter, 'The Pretend Solution: An Empirical Study of Bankruptcy Outcomes', *Texas Law Review* 90 (2011) 103, 142–4.

[157] Czarnetzky (n. 55); The Insolvency Service; Department for Trade and Industry (n. 23); World Bank (n. 144) paras. 106–10; 'Commission Recommendation of 12.3.2014 on a New Approach to Business Failure and Insolvency' (European Commission, 2014) C(2014) 1500 final Commission, 'Initiative on Insolvency: Inception Impact Assessment' (European Commission, 2016) 2016/JUST/025 – Insolvency II; 'Proposal for a Directive of the European Parliament and of the Council on Preventive Restructuring Frameworks, Second Chance and Measures to Increase the Efficiency of Restructuring, Insolvency and Discharge Procedures and Amending Directive 2012/30/EU' (European Commission, 2016) 2016/0359 (COD) COM(2016) 723 final; P. Ali, L. O'Brien and I. Ramsay, 'Misfortune or Misdeed: An Empirical Study of Public

the availability of debt discharge can encourage individuals to take the risks necessary to engage in profitable business activity, thus reducing disincentives to economic activity created by potential over-indebtedness in a business context in which some failure is inevitable, irrespective of fault.[158] From an *ex post* perspective, over-indebtedness may lead to lost economic activity among entrepreneurs who are actually over-burdened with debt due to failed business ventures, and unable to pursue business opportunities for this reason. Over-indebtedness may leave such individuals practically unable to raise credit and obtain business investment, while also reducing incentives for such individuals to pursue economic activity, since any benefits may accrue to their creditors. The justification for debt discharge based on restoring business people to economic productivity has long proved influential,[159] and notably inspired the liberalisation of the English bankruptcy procedure under the Enterprise Act 2002. Policy makers aimed to use debt discharge to 'encourage those who have failed, through no fault of their own, to try again', so that people can risk their capital, energy and time in creating a 'dynamic and successful economy'.[160]

Policy makers have grasped less readily the realisation that following the shift from producer to consumer economies,[161] these considerations now apply equally, if not to an even greater degree, to household (non-business) debt. Given contemporary volatile economic conditions,[162] and the necessity of household borrowing in the face of 'loans for wages' and 'credit/welfare trade-off' trends, 'simply engaging in modern economic life is a sort of entrepreneurial risk',[163] in a neoliberal framework in which individuals

Attitudes Towards Personal Bankruptcy', *University of New South Wales Law Journal* 40 (2017) 1098, 1107–10.

[158] Czarnetzky (n. 55) 412.

[159] See e.g. how Blackstone justified debt discharge as necessary protection against business risk and a means of restoring a failed trader to a 'useful member of the Commonwealth'. See Jay Cohen (1982), 161, citing William Blackstone, *Commentaries on the Laws of England* vol. 2 (1765–1769), 484.

[160] The Insolvency Service; Department for Trade and Industry (n. 23) 1.

[161] J. Q. Whitman, 'Consumerism versus Producerism: A Study in Comparative Law', *Yale Law Journal* 117 (2007) 340; G. Ritzer, '"Hyperconsumption" and "Hyperdebt": A "Hypercritical" Analysis', *A Debtor World: Interdisciplinary Perspectives on Debt* (Oxford University Press, 2012).

[162] I. Ramsay, 'Comparative Consumer Bankruptcy' *University of Illinois Law Review* 2007 (2007) 241, 244–5; M. Crain and M. Sherraden, *Working and Living in the Shadow of Economic Fragility* (Oxford University Press, 2014); J. Morduch and R. Schneider, *The Financial Diaries: How American Families Cope in a World of Uncertainty* (Princeton University Press, 2017).

[163] World Bank (n. 144) para. 109.

are pressured to be 'entrepreneurs of the self'.[164] Meanwhile, under the 'privatised Keynesianism' economic model, growth is dependent on high levels of consumer spending. At an *ex ante* level, this requires 'confident consumers', and bankruptcy's debt relief can form part of a suite of protection measures necessary to encourage consumption.[165] *Ex post*, the Great Recession has laid clear how debt overhang can stifle economic growth when households become so heavily burdened by debt as to reduce consumption.[166] Mian and Sufi offer the most developed account on this point, illustrating empirically how the Great Recession in the USA appears less related to a financial sector crisis and a retraction in bank lending, and more accurately attributable to falling consumption among highly indebted households.[167] In response to the key question of what causes severe economic downturn, the authors advance a 'levered losses' framework,[168] under which significant rises in household debt followed by extensive losses in asset values cause households to cut back on spending.[169] This model explains reduced consumption through a 'wealth effects' mechanism, with wealth destruction (in the form of a housing market collapse) leading to reduced consumption as households both seek to save in order to rebuild wealth, and are unable to continue spending at high levels due to tighter constraints on further borrowing.[170] Similar effects of excessive leverage have been found in other countries and relying on alternative transmission channels. Some accounts link households' reduced expenditure with concerns regarding their ability to meet existing debt repayments.[171] Others consider that household expenditure falls simply due to inability of households to service high debt levels, meaning that affordability of debt ('cash flow' insolvency) may be is more significant to economic growth than household wealth (or 'balance sheet' insolvency).[172] All recognise that debt-burdened households are precisely those with a higher marginal propensity

[164] Brown (n. 61) 32–5.

[165] See e.g. Empowering and Protecting Consumers (Department for Business, Innovation and Skills, 2011).

[166] International Monetary Fund, 'Dealing with Household Debt' (n. 1) 3, 7–8; Mian and Sufi, *House of Debt* (n. 68); Lo and Rogoff (n. 70) 8–10; International Monetary Fund, 'Fiscal Monitor – Debt: Use It Wisely' (n. 71); Bank for International Settlements (n. 70) 48–50; International Monetary Fund, 'Household Debt and Financial Stability' (n. 100).

[167] Mian and Sufi, *House of Debt* (n. 68).

[168] ibid, 46–59.

[169] ibid, 51.

[170] ibid.

[171] Bunn and, Rostom (n. 70).

[172] International Monetary Fund, 'Household Debt and Financial Stability' (n. 100) 65; Bank for International Settlements (n. 70) 49.

to consume than society's creditors, so that over-indebtedness, or even heavy leverage among solvent borrowers, may deprive an economy of its main spenders.[173] Debt contracts shift the costs of economic downturn from creditors to debtors, as creditors retain claims to full repayment and any security, while debtors lose any equity held in secured assets and continue to owe entire sums borrowed with interest.[174] In order to restore aggregate demand, appropriate policy responses in economic crises might require the redistribution of losses more evenly – this would require extensive household debt relief, rather than focusing policy efforts (and fiscal resources) on propping up banks. *Ex ante* regulation and contract design could prevent debt overhang problems from building up in future.[175] In the absence of such foresight and in the teeth of crisis, however, difficulties must be addressed primarily through aggressive debt relief,[176] which can 'substantially mitigate the negative effects of household deleveraging on economic activity'.[177] As society's chief institution for the provision of debt relief, bankruptcy might deliver positive economic outcomes not through a creditors' bargain, but through a 'debtors' bargain'. It can address the collective action problem that arises when borrowing households do not internalise the potential impact of their actions on aggregate demand and other households.[178]

The creditors' bargain model is further weakened by its failure to recognise these potential negative macroeconomic effects of debt markets. Such problems are concealed by the methodological individualism of the early law-and-economics framework from which this theory emanates, and its tendency to ignore distributional and macroeconomic issues.[179] Where they even addressed distributional questions, conventional accounts from this perspective omitted them from legal analysis under the view that redistribution through taxation-and-transfer was

[173] International Monetary Fund, 'Dealing with Household Debt' (n. 1) 9–10; Mian and Sufi, *House of Debt* (n. 68) 50–1, 131–3, 140–8.

[174] Mian and Sufi, *House of Debt* (n. 68) 18–20, 50–2.

[175] Mian and Sufi, 'The Macroeconomic Advantages of Softening Debt Contracts' (n. 68); International Monetary Fund, 'Household Debt and Financial Stability' (n. 100) 70.

[176] Mian and Sufi, *House of Debt* (n. 68) 135–51.

[177] International Monetary Fund, 'Dealing with Household Debt' (n. 1) 3.

[178] International Monetary Fund, 'Household Debt and Financial Stability' (n. 100) 58.

[179] J. R. Hackney, 'Law and Neoclassical Economics Theory: A Critical History of the Distribution/Efficiency Debate', *The Journal of Socio-Economics* 32 (2003) 361; M. T. McCluskey, F. A. Pasquale and J. Taub, 'Law and Economics: Contemporary Approaches' (Social Science Research Network, 2016) SSRN Scholarly Paper ID 2728030 https://papers.ssrn.com/abstract=2728030 accessed 5 November 2018.

more effective than via private law rules.[180] In contrast, Mian and Sufi's argument regarding the macroeconomic benefits of debt relief is overtly distributional, while bodies such as the IMF agree that higher levels of income inequality exacerbate the negative effects of rising household debt on growth.[181] More recently, scholars have increasingly highlighted inefficient and inequitable distributive effects of private law 'ground rules', and argued that their reform could produce more equitable and economically optimal distributions.[182] The financial crisis caused early law-and-economics scholars such as Posner to admit that their approaches 'missed' the danger that the deregulatory policies they advocated on microeconomic grounds might increase the risk of recession.[183] Now a number of scholars join Mian and Sufi in adopting macroeconomic perspectives on legal analysis and policy design.[184] This turn to law-and-macroeconomics has coincided with an increased recognition among macroeconomists of the significance of distributional issues.[185] Evidence increasingly emerges to suggest that debt markets distribute losses in a manner that is not only inequitable, but also productive of harmful macroeconomic outcomes. The economic principle of enhancing aggregate welfare by shifting costs and risks away from those with the highest marginal propensity to consume thus mirrors the ethical

[180] I. Ramsay, 'Consumer Credit Law, Distributive Justice and the Welfare State', *Oxford Journal of Legal Studies* 15 (1995) 177, 178; Hynes (n. 148) 328. This position is also central to neoliberal approaches to regulation, and to arguments for supporting freedom of contract advanced by Thatcher's 'New Right': I. Ramsay and T. Williams, 'The Crash That Launched a Thousand Fixes: Regulation of Consumer Credit After the Lending Revolution and the Credit Crunch' in N. Moloney and K. Alexander (eds.), *Law Reform and Financial Markets* (Edward Elgar, 2011) 227 http://papers.ssrn.com/sol3/papers.cfm ?abstract_id=1474036 accessed 5 November 2018; P. S. Atiyah, 'Freedom of Contract and the New Right', Essays on Contract (Clarendon Press, 1986) 360 www .amazon.co.uk/Essays-Contract-Clarendon-Paperbacks-Atiyah/dp/019825444X/ ref=ntt_at_ep_dpt_7 accessed 5 November 2018.

[181] International Monetary Fund, 'Household Debt and Financial Stability' (n. 100) 69–70.

[182] See e.g. R. B. Reich, *Saving Capitalism: For the Many, Not the Few* (Knopf Publishing Group, 2015).

[183] R. A. Posner, 'On the Receipt of the Ronald H. Coase Medal: Uncertainty, the Economic Crisis, and the Future of Law and Economics', *American Law and Economics Review* 12 (2010) 265, 268.

[184] Z. Liscow, 'Counter-Cyclical Bankruptcy Law: An Efficiency Argument for Employment-Preserving Bankruptcy Rules', *Columbia Law Review* 116 (2016) 1461; Listokin (n. 68); J. S. Masur and E. A. Posner, 'Should Regulation Be Countercyclical?', *Yale Journal on Regulation* 34 (2017) 857; R. Van Loo, 'Consumer Law As Tax Alternative' (Social Science Research Network, 2017) SSRN Scholarly Paper ID 3090800 https://papers.ssrn.com/abstract=3090800 accessed 5 November 2018.

[185] Yellen (n. 69); Vlieghe (n. 69); Keen (n. 69).

principle of maximising the distributive entitlements of society's least well-off members.[186] The ability of bankruptcy's debt relief to redistribute losses from debtors to creditors therefore has a dual appeal of promising both efficient and progressive policy outcomes.

3.3 Bankruptcy as Social Insurance

Failures in credit markets and the accompanying externalities necessitate macroeconomic stabilising mechanisms,[187] while households require 'insurance-style guarantees against downside risks' of financialisation.[188] This necessitates a role for bankruptcy law as a form of such insurance against the risks of an economy dependent on high levels of household debt.[189] At a theoretical level, bankruptcy operates according to an insurance model in transferring risk from debtors (the insured) to creditors (insurers) through the discharge of debt, on the payment by debtors of a risk-adjusted premium taking the form of an interest rate.[190] At a more practical level, one could understand bankruptcy as *functionally* operating as social insurance, filling gaps left by the welfare state.[191] In terms of macroeconomic effects, the IMF presents both 'automatic stabilisers' of social transfer payments and 'bold household debt restructuring programmes' as alternative methods to reduce defaults, debt service burdens and problems of lower aggregate demand.[192] As the 'loans for wages' and 'credit/welfare trade-off' ideas illustrate, debt has come to play an essential role in maintaining household living standards, and in the face of a shrinking social safety net may represent the 'ultimate market-based social welfare programme'.[193] Given the propensity for high leverage levels to lead to default, however, perhaps credit is merely a penultimate safety net, with bankruptcy acting as the protection of last resort for financially troubled households. Processes of privatisation and the marketisation of public services

186 Kilpi (n. 55) 73–4.
187 International Monetary Fund, 'Dealing with Household Debt' (n. 1).
188 C. Berry, 'Citizenship in a Financialised Society: Financial Inclusion and the State before and after the Crash', *Policy & Politics* 43 (2015) 509, 521.
189 Hallinan (n. 3) 98–109; Jackson (n. 32) 229–32; T. Eisenberg, 'Bankruptcy Law in Perspective', *UCLA Law Review* 28 (1980) 953, 981–3; Hynes (n. 148) 327–31.
190 A. Feibelman, 'Defining the Social Insurance Function of Consumer Bankruptcy', *American Bankruptcy Institute Law Review* 13 (2005) 129, 130.
191 See e.g. Braucher (n. 35) 466.
192 International Monetary Fund, 'Dealing with Household Debt' (n. 1) 13, 26.
193 Sullivan, Warren and Westbrook (n. 43) 138.

increasingly move the State from service provider to regulator,[194] and create a 'regulatory welfare state'.[195] Bankruptcy forms part of this system of legal norms that offer protection against calamities no longer covered by the social insurance system of the Welfare State, or new risks of financialisation against which such systems were never designed to protect.[196] This is the role demanded of bankruptcy by the thousands of households who turn to it for assistance unavailable elsewhere.

The insurance theory of bankruptcy illustrates how the law's debt discharge function can allocate efficiently the *losses/costs* of default in the *ex post* situation of a debtor's over-indebtedness, while also incentivising the efficient allocation of the *risk* of the debtor's future inability to pay in the *ex ante* creditor–debtor contracting process.[197] While debt contracts allocate all risks of changing circumstances and default onto debtors, a discharge of debt insures the debtor by transferring such risks from debtor to creditors, as the superior bearers of risk.[198] Insurance enhances efficiency not merely through the transfer of risk from the insured to the insurer, but also via the insurer's pooling or spreading of risks,[199] substituting several small losses for a single disastrously large loss.[200] Insurance also reduces uncertainty costs by allowing statistical predictions of loss levels among a portfolio of similar risks, converting incalculable uncertainty into actuarial risk.[201] Uncertain losses of a debt economy can be transformed by the insurance function of bankruptcy into certain costs both for debtors (in the 'premium' payments they make in the form of interest rates/prices) and for creditors (in the form of predicted losses in personal insolvencies).[202] The premium paid by the insured should reflect the risk she represents, and so through 'risk-based pricing' lenders segment borrowers into categories based on their creditworthiness, charging interest rates broadly reflecting risk of non-payment.[203]

194 Ramsay (n. 40) 247.
195 Haber (n. 36).
196 J. J. Kilborn, 'Comparative Cause and Effect: Consumer Insolvency and the Eroding Social Safety Net', *Columbia Journal of European Law* 14 (2007) 563.
197 Hallinan (n. 3) 98; T. Baker, 'On the Genealogy of Moral Hazard', *Texas Law Review* 75 (1996) 237, 272–5.
198 Hallinan (n. 3) 100.
199 ibid, 101.
200 ibid; World Bank (n. 144) para 95.
201 L. H. White, 'Bankruptcy as an Economic Intervention', *Journal of Libertarian Studies* 1 (1977) 281, 285.
202 Hallinan (n. 3) 102.
203 ibid, 106; In practice, risk-based pricing may differ from this theoretical explanation however, as interest rates ostensibly based on repayment risk may in fact be influenced

Insurance theory begins with a starting point that if contractual relationships are to allocate resources efficiently, the party best able to prevent a loss from occurring should be required by law to bear the risk of that loss.[204] Traditional views of the creditor–debtor relationship considered the debtor to be better placed to prevent default, given her perceived greater knowledge and control of her financial circumstances than her creditor.[205] As discussed above, in modern consumer credit markets information asymmetries and behavioural biases mean that institutional lenders are significantly better judges than debtors of the nature and effects of complex credit products. Debt contracts have long departed from paradigms of freely negotiated mutually beneficial agreements, and constitute products designed by creditors for maximum profitability.[206] As discussed in Chapter 7, gaps in information held by creditors, causing them to make adverse selections[207] in the past, have been overcome by technological advances and advanced credit scoring systems.[208] Institutional creditors are now better equipped than debtors

by other factors such as mortgage broker remuneration, discrimination among borrowers, and rent-seeking: P. A. McCoy, 'Rethinking Disclosure in a World of Risk-Based Pricing', *Harvard Journal on Legislation* 44 (2007) 123, 127; The high interest rates charged on loans to low-income borrowers may not be based on an elevated risk of default, but rather on profitability concerns arising from high marginal administrative costs of providing loans of small amounts: G. Trumbull, 'Credit Access and Social Welfare The Rise of Consumer Lending in the United States and France', *Politics & Society* 40 (2012) 9, 25–6.

204 Eisenberg (n. 189) 981; R. A. Posner and A. M. Rosenfield, 'Impossibility and Related Doctrines in Contract Law: An Economic Analysis', *Journal of Legal Studies* 6 (1977) 83, 83. In theory, legal intervention might not be necessary if parties themselves could design their contracts to allocate risks more efficiently between debtors and creditors: Mian and Sufi, 'The Macroeconomic Advantages of Softening Debt Contracts' (n. 68). Difficulties arise, however, from the fact that individual creditors and even debtors see the current structure of debt contracts as benefitting their interests: A. Turner, *Between Debt and the Devil: Money, Credit, and Fixing Global Finance* (Princeton University Press, 2015) 192–4. Contracting failures described in this chapter also illustrate the difficulties in relying on private contracting to allocate risk efficiently, since generally lenders will leverage imperfect borrower decision making to shift risk onto borrowers.

205 Eisenberg (n. 189) 982.

206 E. Warren, 'Balance of Knowledge' in R. Brubaker, R. M. Lawless and C. J. Tabb (eds.), *A Debtor World: Interdisciplinary Perspectives on Debt* (Oxford University Press, 2012).

207 J. E. Stiglitz and A. Weiss, 'Credit Rationing in Markets with Imperfect Information', *The American Economic Review* 71 (1981) 393.

208 See e.g. D. K. Citron and F. Pasquale, 'The Scored Society: Due Process for Automated Predictions Essay', *Washington Law Review* 89 (2014) 1; M. Fourcade and K. Healy, 'Seeing like a Market', *Socio-Economic Review* 15 (2017) 9; J. Lauer, *Creditworthy: A History of Consumer Surveillance and Financial Identity in America* (Columbia University Press, 2017).

to access the actuarial and statistical knowledge necessary to predict the likelihood of a particular borrower falling into over-indebtedness,[209] particularly given that the primary causes of over-indebtedness are 'life accidents' external to the debtor.[210] By transforming de facto default into de jure losses, bankruptcy's debt discharge may crystallise costs for creditors in a manner that incentivises responsible lending.[211] Since lenders are the best judges of the risk involved in a credit transaction, they can adjust their creditworthiness standards in order to extend credit only where risks of over-indebtedness are sufficiently small.[212] Ideally lenders (if they held perfect information) would price each credit transaction in a manner which accounts for the risk of default involved, in which case there would be no need for the legal system to regulate default.[213] The advent of Big Data means that this possibility is approaching,[214] though in many cases lenders remain limited to information enabling only pricing based on statistical average risk or default rates.[215]

An insurance theory of bankruptcy also advocates the re-orientation of the law towards debt relief due to the disparate abilities of creditors and debtors to bear the costs of default and insure against it. Creditors design credit products to shift losses onto debtors, while also developing sophisticated mechanisms for spreading and diversifying risk, as well as passing it to third parties. The mandatory insurance of bankruptcy is justified since information asymmetries and behavioural biases limit the ability of debtors to acquire insurance against the causes of over-indebtedness and the catastrophic losses it may involve.[216] Debtors would tend to substitute 'self-insurance' for market insurance,[217] most likely involving under-resourced debtors passing on costs to others in society (family members, social welfare and healthcare systems), thus generating

[209] Howard (n. 6) 1063; J. A. E. Pottow, 'Private Liability for Reckless Consumer Lending', *University of Illinois Law Review* 2007 (2007) 405, 432–4.

[210] See pages 58–61 above.

[211] By aligning legal and de facto losses, debt discharge can serve to ensure accurate account valuation, impacting significantly on the value of lender's assets. See World Bank (n. 144) paras. 79–84.

[212] Howard (n. 6) 1064.

[213] A. A. Leff, 'Injury, Ignorance and Spite–The Dynamics of Coercive Collection', *Yale Law Journal* 80 (1970) 1, 26–8.

[214] Fourcade and Healy (n. 208) 11.

[215] Howard (n. 6) 1064.

[216] World Bank (n. 144) para. 95.

[217] Hallinan (n. 3) 113–16; Jackson (n. 32) 237–41; Hynes (n. 148) 343–4.

externalities.[218] A significant mis-selling scandal in the UK payment protection insurance market suggests that the potential for such failures are not just theoretical, but very real.[219] Negative macroeconomic effects of excessive household leverage and debt overhang are most severe when debt is distributed most heavily among those with limited ability to self-insure.[220] The rigidity of debt contracts, under which a debtor's liability is total and not contingent on future events, mean that credit markets transfer risk to society's debtors in a manner productive of inefficient outcomes.[221] If markets cannot offer effective insurance against these risks, then a strong case exists for bankruptcy to provide the insurance that markets cannot provide, re-allocating more efficiently the risks inherent in our debt-dependent economy.

3.4 Objections to Debt Relief

Despite increasing acceptance of the economic costs of household over-indebtedness, two key objections tend to oppose full acceptance of debt relief policies and the embrace of bankruptcy's social insurance function. The first worries that debtors will abuse any system of debt relief, while the second cautions that such a system will raise the costs of, and reduce access to, credit.[222] These are common arguments against consumer protection and social insurance measures generally,[223] mirroring classic concerns that reforms will produce opposite effects to policymakers' intended outcomes.[224] An insurance framework offers a unified theory of bankruptcy, however, that not only presents the policy merits of debt

[218] Hallinan (n. 3) 118–25; Hynes (n. 148) 340–2. For an example of what might happen in a 'world without bankruptcy', survey evidence from the time before Ireland enacted its first functioning bankruptcy law in 2012 showed that households lacked provision for future income reductions or expenses and pointed to the social welfare system as their only means of dealing with financial shortfalls: O'Donnell and Keeney (n. 113) 45–9.

[219] The mis-selling practices and regulatory response are discussed in the English cases of *R (British Bankers Association) v. The Financial Services Authority and Ors* [2011] EWHC 999 (Admin), and *Plevin v. Paragon Personal Finance Ltd* [2014] UKSC 61.

[220] A. Zabai, 'Household Debt: Recent Developments and Challenges', *Bank for International Settlements Quarterly Review* 2017 (2017) 39, 45.

[221] International Monetary Fund, 'Household Debt and Financial Stability' (n. 100) 56; Mian and Sufi, 'The Macroeconomic Advantages of Softening Debt Contracts' (n. 68).

[222] See e.g. E. A. Posner, 'Comment on Means Testing Consumer Bankruptcy by Jean Braucher', *Fordham Journal of Corporate & Financial Law* 7 (2001) 457, 458–9.

[223] Kilborn, 'Comparative Cause and Effect' (n. 196) 595.

[224] A. Hirschman, *The Rhetoric of Reaction: Perversity, Futility, Jeopardy* (Harvard University Press, 1991) 11. Baker notes that moral hazard is used similarly to caution against 'the perverse consequences of well-intentioned efforts to share the burdens of

relief, but also includes internal responses to these objections and incorporates means of addressing the concerns they raise.

3.4.1 Moral Hazard

Even economic policy documents advocating bold household debt relief policies caution that any measures must guard against the risk of *moral hazard*.[225] The concept of moral hazard in fact originates in insurance theory,[226] where it explains that protection against a relevant risk can both reduce the insured's incentives to take precautions to prevent such an event, and increase the insured's incentives to exaggerate the extent of a loss which has occurred.[227] In the bankruptcy context, moral hazard concerns arise as to the extent to which the discharge, by relieving the debtor of the burden of over-indebtedness, creates incentives at the *ex post* stage for the debtor to enter an insolvency procedure at the first sign of financial difficulty (potentially in the absence of true need). The availability of discharge similarly raises *ex ante* moral hazard concerns that the debtor may over-borrow in the first place.[228] A full understanding of moral hazard theory illustrates, however, how insurance contracts can be structured so as to reduce and guard against the perverse incentives potentially created by protection against loss. In a similar manner, bankruptcy law incorporates a number of features which are designed to raise the costs of debt relief in order to encourage appropriate use, and to sanction 'abuse', of the benefits of debt relief. Chapter 7 considers in detail the question of moral hazard. It argues that while concerns in this area are legitimate, an application of moral hazard theory to the conditions of contemporary bankruptcy and credit markets suggests that they receive undue emphasis in policy discussions. Disciplinary

life': T. Baker, 'On the Genealogy of Moral Hazard', *Texas Law Review* 75 (1996) 237, 239.

225 International Monetary Fund, 'Dealing with Household Debt' (n. 1) 14; Y. Liu and C. B. Rosenberg, 'Dealing with Private Debt Distress in the Wake of the European Financial Crisis: A Review of the Economics and Legal Toolbox' (International Monetary Fund, 2013) IMF Working Paper WP/13/44 20, 17–18; J. R. Andritzky, 'Resolving Residential Mortgage Distress: Time to Modify?' (International Monetary Fund, 2014) IMF Working Paper WP/14/226 6 www.imf.org/external/pubs/cat/longres.aspx?sk=42532.0 accessed 5 November 2018; International Monetary Fund, 'Fiscal Monitor – Debt: Use It Wisely' (n. 71) 20.

226 See generally Baker (n. 197); J. E. Stiglitz, 'Risk, Incentives and Insurance: The Pure Theory of Moral Hazard', *The Geneva Papers on Risk and Insurance – Issues and Practice* 8 (1983) 4.

227 Hallinan (n. 3) 84, 92, 103; Hynes (n. 148) 329; Feibelman (n. 190) 136–7.

228 Hallinan (n. 3) 92.

debt markets exert extensive control over debtor behaviour in manners unprecedented and extending beyond the abilities of any legal measures. Meanwhile bankruptcy law contains robust safeguards against abuse. Indeed bankruptcy has always concerned itself with policing debtor misconduct, and some accounts identify alongside debt collection and debt relief a third traditional objective of upholding 'commercial morality' and protecting the public from dishonest debtors.[229] The advantage of the social insurance understanding of bankruptcy is that it offers a common framework to address this concern within a single overriding debt relief objective, rather than forcing the law to serve multiple independent aims.

3.4.2 'Lenders Should Feel Able to Advance Money'

The risk-sharing involved in an insurance framework also provides a response to another limb of opposition to debt relief policies and the re-orientation of bankruptcy towards this aim – the claim that such reforms will increase the cost of, and reduce access to, household credit.[230] As shown above, new awareness of the externalities of debt markets, as highlighted by the financial crisis and subsequent recession, have cast doubt on the once ubiquitous assumption that wide access to credit is welfare enhancing. Those doubting the merits of wide availability of debt at a price concealing its true social costs[231] build on the pre-crisis development of the principle of responsible lending.[232] The appropriate role of bankruptcy may be not to enforce market bargains without question in the hope of facilitating credit markets, but precisely to slow debt flows and cause markets to internalise their costs through truer pricing. In this way, those outcomes feared by those who argue that the 'sky will fall'[233] if creditors' rights are unduly restricted should actually benefit the wider

[229] Cork (n. 15) para. 1734 *et seq.*; Fletcher, *The Law of Insolvency* (n. 34) paras. 11–031.

[230] J. Goodman and A. Levitin, 'Bankruptcy Law and the Cost of Credit: The Impact of Cramdown on Mortgage Interest Rates', *Journal of Law and Economics* 57 (2014) 139, 139–42; J. Taub, *Other People's Houses* (Yale University Press, 2014) 117–8; J. Spooner, 'Seeking Shelter in Personal Insolvency Law: Recession, Eviction, and Bankruptcy's Social Safety Net', *Journal of Law and Society* 44 (2017) 374, 387–90.

[231] Mian and Sufi, *House of Debt* (n. 68) 182; Turner (n. 204) 61–73.

[232] See e.g. Ramsay, 'From Truth in Lending to Responsible Lending' (n. 122); K. Fairweather, 'The Development of Responsible Lending in the UK Consumer Credit Regime' in James Devenney and Mel Kenny (eds.), *Consumer Credit, Debt and Investment in Europe* (Cambridge University Press, 2012).

[233] L. Lupica, 'The Consumer Debt Crisis and the Reinforcement of Class Position', *Loyola University Chicago Law Journal* 40 (2008) 557, at 604.

economy, while also providing valuable over-indebtedness insurance for individual debtors.[234] The tensions and contradictions of debt dependence may require the sky of pre-crisis policy consensus to fall. In turn, it may be necessary for English law to abandon its article of faith that it is 'important that lenders should feel able to advance money'[235] and to realise the fragility of the justification for its 'enduring pro-creditor bias'.[236] If our society cannot afford credit at a price reflecting its true social costs, then serious questions arise as to whether we would be better off moving towards an economic regime less reliant on cheap household debt.

It seems increasingly difficult to support the view that a reduction in supply of cheap household credit would cause greater economic harm than the fall in demand caused by overly leveraged households' declining consumption.[237] Even if one retains this view, however, it must be noted that despite the centrality to policy discussions of the influence of bankruptcy rules on credit supply, empirical evidence is 'surprisingly limited'.[238] Some studies produce unclear results,[239] while others find minor increases in mortgage prices attributable to variations in

234 Goodman and Levitin (n. 230) 156–7.

235 *Royal Bank of Scotland Plc* v. *Etridge (No 2)* [2001] UKHL 44, [2002] 2 AC 773, [2], *per* Lord Nicholls. In this decision, Lord Hobhouse criticised this trend, arguing at [115] that '[t]he law has, in order to accommodate the commercial lenders, adopted a fiction which nullifies the equitable principle [of undue influence] and deprives vulnerable members of the public of the protection which equity gives them'.

236 L. Fox O'Mahoney, J. Devenney and M. Kenny, 'England and Wales' in S. Weatherill and A. C. Ciacchi (eds.), *Regulating Unfair Banking Practices in Europe: the Case of Personal Suretyships* (Oxford University Press, 2010) 170. See e.g. Collin's discussion of case law relating to the doctrine of undue influence, in which courts have reached decisions not based on precedent, but on overt policy discussions and a view that the ability of small businesses to access credit should outweigh the protection of individuals from exploitation by their partners: H. Collins, 'Regulating Contract Law' in C. Parker and others (eds.), Regulating Law (Oxford University Press, 2004).

237 This is the very argument rejected by authors such as Mian and Sufi in arguing that the severity of the Great Recession can be explained by policymakers' sole focus on protecting banking sectors, involving the shifting of losses onto leveraged households: Mian and Sufi, *House of Debt* (n. 68) 133, 46–59.

238 Goodman and Levitin (n. 230) 141. This is particularly surprising since incentives to conduct research supporting the correlation between debtor protections and increases in borrowing costs have been high. In similar circumstances Zingales invokes the 'dog that didn't bark' principle to suggest that the lack of published evidence can be safely interpreted as a lack of correlation: L. Zingales, 'Presidential Address: Does Finance Benefit Society?', *The Journal of Finance* 70 (2015) 1327, 1342.

239 T. A. Durkin and others, *Consumer Credit and the American Economy* (Oxford University Press USA 2014) 613–4.

bankruptcy laws.[240] Yet more determine that, given contemporary lender practices of securitisation and diversification of investment, 'the scope of the bankruptcy discharge has very little impact on the price or availability of credit except at the margins'.[241] Creditors can spread and minimise risk in a manner unavailable to individual debtors,[242] for whom an adverse financial event can prove disastrous and will most likely be uninsured.[243] Regulatory rules oblige financial creditors to hold capital reserves designed to protect against such losses.[244] As shown in Chapter 1, there are an estimated 8.8 million over-indebted people in the UK,[245] while lenders charge off approximately £2.75 billion in non-mortgage debt annually as bad debts.[246] In this context, losses attributable to England and Wales' 100,000 annual personal insolvencies reflect only a small portion of lenders' costs, but offer great benefit to those debtors supported. These considerations suggest that losses to creditors caused by greater debt relief in bankruptcy should reduce lender economic activity (i.e. credit supply) to a lesser extent than imposing costs on debtors (through the usual structure of debt contracts) will affect over-indebted individuals' behaviour (i.e. consumer spending), especially considering debtors' higher marginal propensity to consume. Debt relief through bankruptcy can then operate as an efficient insurance mechanism by transferring losses onto creditors as the party best placed to bear loss.[247] A further lesson of the Great Recession is that moving losses onto *debtors* may even slow credit flows by stifling *demand*, since a two-sided view of credit markets sees that boom-time borrowers will reduce recourse to credit when economic conditions worsen.[248]

240 Goodman and Levitin (n. 230).
241 Adam J Levitin, 'Resolving the Foreclosure Crisis: Modification of Mortgages in Bankruptcy', *Wisconsin Law Review* 2009 (2009) 565, 648, 601–2.
242 L. E. Willis, 'Will the Mortgage Market Correct – How Households and Communities Would Fare If Risk Were Priced Well', *Connecticut Law Review* 41 (2008) 1177, 1182; Levitin, 'Resolving the Foreclosure Crisis' (n. 241) 648.
243 Mian and Sufi, *House of Debt* (n. 68) 46–59.
244 See e.g. 'Financial Stability Report: June 2018' (Bank of England, 2018) 43 33–4.
245 'Indebted Lives: The Complexities of Life in Debt' (Money Advice Service, 2013) www.moneyadviceservice.org.uk/en/static/indebted-lives-the-complexities-of-life-in-debt-press-office accessed 5 November 2018.
246 'Bankstats (Monetary & Financial Statistics) – Latest Tables, Bank of England' (Bank of England) www.bankofengland.co.uk/statistics/Pages/bankstats/current/default.aspx accessed 5 November 2018.
247 World Bank (n. 144) paras. 94–8; Eisenberg (n. 189) 981; Posner and Rosenfield (n. 204).
248 See e.g. Bunn and Rostom (n. 70).

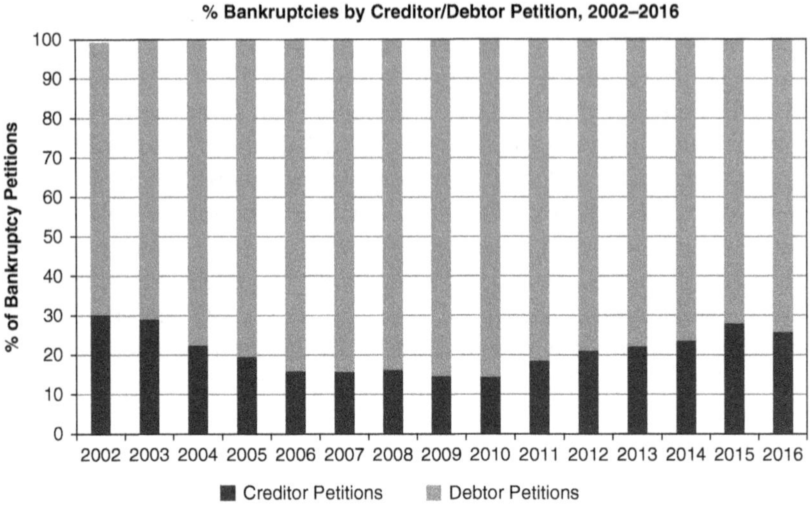

Figure 3.1: Despite relatively high numbers of creditor petitions, bankruptcy is primarily invoked by debtors. Source: Insolvency Service

3.4.3 *A True Tragedy: The Practice of Bankruptcy When There Is Nothing Left to Collect*

Contemporary personal insolvency practice offers a further compelling factor in favour of understanding bankruptcy as a form of social insurance and of emphasising its debt relief objective. All Debt Relief Order (DRO) and Individual Voluntary Arrangement (IVA) cases, and the vast majority of bankruptcies,[249] involve consumer debtors seeking protection by voluntarily invoking these procedures, rather than creditors coercively petitioning for bankruptcy to recover debts (Figures 3.1 and 3.2).[250] Conditions of the 'insolvency marketplace' described in Chapters 4 and 5 mean not only that any debtors with repayment capacity tend to be diverted out of bankruptcy and DROs into IVAs and/or Debt Management Plans (DMPs), but also that intermediary business models have evolved to the point where even low-income debtors are 'sold' IVAs and DMPs as 'solutions' to their financial problems. All DRO debtors and most bankruptcy

[249] Approximately 10–20 per cent of bankruptcy debtors have sufficient income to be required to contribute to creditors: Insolvency Service, *Insolvency Statistics: April to June 2016* (28 July 2016).

[250] See Chapter 5's discussion of (government) creditors' persistent use of bankruptcy as a debt collection device.

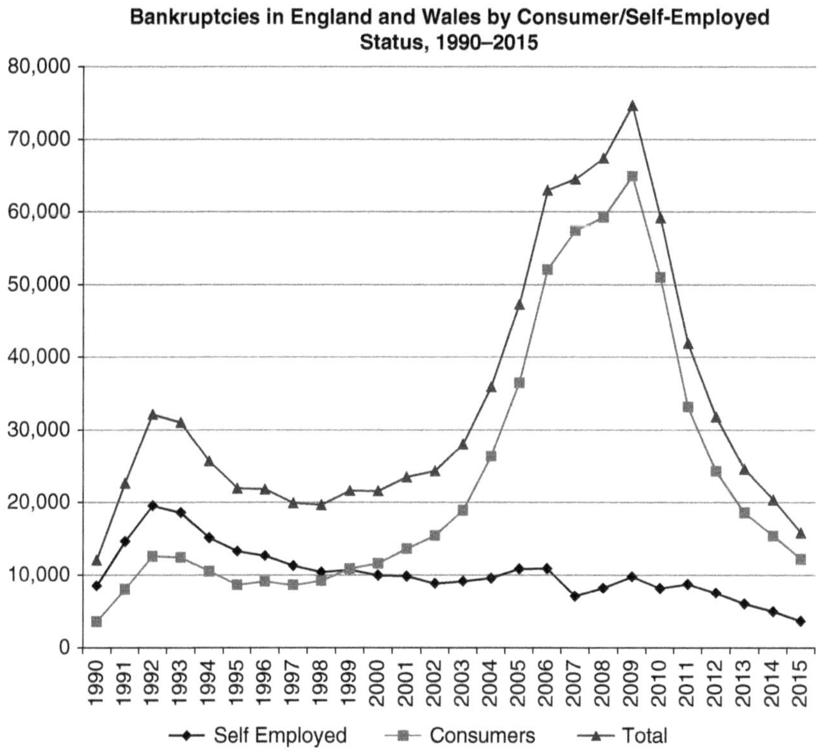

Figure 3.2: Consumer debtors are the majority users of bankruptcy. Source: Insolvency Service

debtors have few, if any, non-essential assets available for distribution to creditors (Figure 3.3). From the perspective of debtors invoking insolvency procedures, the 'predominant purpose – if not the sole purpose – of individual bankruptcy today is to effect the discharge of debts – to give the debtor a "fresh start"'.[251] With the exception of a small unrepresentative minority of high value cases, by the time debtors enter the bankruptcy procedure there is simply nothing left to collect.

The position is somewhat more complicated in respect of IVAs, which were designed to be invoked by debtors and continue to be sold and bought as a debt relief product. As the following chapters illustrate, this may involve some bait-and-switch marketing, as the IVA has been moulded into a mechanism increasingly protective of creditor interests.

[251] Kilborn, 'Mercy, Rehabilitation, and Quid Pro Quo' (n. 55) 866.

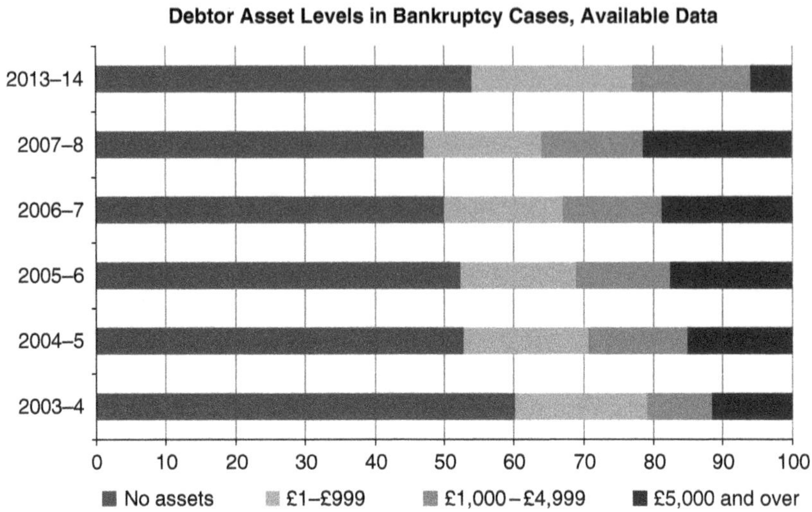

Figure 3.3: Most debtors entering bankruptcy have few, if any, assets available for liquidation. Source: Insolvency Service

Chapters 4 and 5 show that where IVAs produce substantial returns to creditors, the externalities generated by such arrangements call into question whether the public interest would be better served by these debtors availing of the bankruptcy and DRO procedures.

Historically, personal insolvency law may have operated alongside corporate insolvency law as a commercial or corporate law aiming to recover returns to investors from failed business debtors. Any English commercial law or legal theory textbook that continues to discuss the law as a method of liquidating assets for creditors' benefit, however, focuses on only a small minority of cases and ignores the everyday practice of the law.[252] It now operates as a safety net for financially troubled households. Debt charities view insolvency procedures as a 'lifeline'[253] for impoverished clients and part of a 'debt solutions landscape',[254] rather than legal or judicial processes. Similarly, in its recent review of this landscape, the

[252] See e.g. Bridge (n. 33) ch. 19; J. Finnis, Natural Law And Natural Rights 2nd edn (Oxford University Press USA, 2011) 188–93.

[253] 'A Guide to the CAP's Official Response to the Insolvency Service's Call for Evidence' (Christians Against Poverty, 2014) 3.

[254] 'Money Advice Trust Consultation Response: Insolvency Service - DROs and the Bankruptcy Petition Limit' (Money Advice Trust, 2014) 4.

Financial Conduct Authority treated 'insolvency/statutory solutions' as just one of many options for addressing problem debt.[255] As a specialist credit regulator, the FCA situated bankruptcy at one end of a spectrum of options, many of which are indisputably welfarist in nature, such as 'help with budgeting'. In this context, one can see 'consumer insolvency law [as] a new member of the family of programs [*sic*] designed to deal with the financial dangers of a changing world'.[256]

3.5 Conclusions: The Case for Debt Relief

A recent IMF review opens with a statement that 'although finance is generally believed to contribute to long-term economic growth, recent studies have shown that the growth benefits start declining when aggregate leverage is high'.[257] At this point 'increases in private sector credit, including household debt, may raise the likelihood of a financial crisis and could lead to lower growth'. An understanding of bankruptcy law as a debt collection mechanism is based on a view of credit as the 'lifeblood of the economy' and the protection of creditor rights as the key to financial and economic development.[258] The evidence of the past decade reveals, however, that an economic structure involving excessive household debt 'truncates the flow of money, the lifeblood of capitalism', since 'future income used to pay old debts means less money circulating in the economy'.[259] Of course our economy and society require households to pay their debts, but only until a point arises when it would be counterproductive for them to do so. While some authors argue that this point arrives at an even earlier stage,[260] we can be certain that it has been

[255] 'Quality of Debt Management Advice' (Financial Conduct Authority, 2015) Thematic Review TR15/8 para. 2.13.

[256] Kilborn, 'Comparative Cause and Effect' (n. 196) 595.

[257] International Monetary Fund, 'Household Debt and Financial Stability' (n. 100) 53.

[258] 'Obama: Credit Flow Is Economy's "Lifeblood"' http://politicalticker.blogs.cnn.com/2009/02/24/obama-credit-flow-is-economys-lifeblood/ accessed 5 November 2018; 'Principles for Effective Insolvency and Creditor Rights Systems' (World Bank, International Finance Corporation 2005) 2; H. MaCartney, 'From Merlin to Oz: The Strange Case of Failed Lending Targets in the UK', *Review of International Political Economy* 21 (2014) 820, 837.

[259] L. Coco, 'Debtor's Prison in the Neoliberal State: Debtfare and the Cultural Logics of the Bankruptcy Abuse Prevention and Consumer Protection Act of 2005', *California Western Law Review* 49 (2012) 1, 48.

[260] A. Mian, A. Sufi and F. Trebbi, 'Resolving Debt Overhang: Political Constraints in the Aftermath of Financial Crises', *American Economic Journal: Macroeconomics* 6 (2014) 1, 20–1.

reached by the time a debtor falls into over-indebtedness or insolvency. At the moment an individual enters insolvency, the law should focus on addressing the externalities of over-indebtedness. Understanding bankruptcy as social insurance transforms the objective of the law into making extensive debt relief widely available to over-indebted individuals. While this objective must be subject to limitations in order to address concerns regarding moral hazard, it is unconstrained by competing aims and the goal of maximising returns to creditors disappears from consumer bankruptcy law.[261] Where debtors are required to make contributions to creditors from assets and income, this is not in pursuit of an independent debt collection objective, but is merely one of several safeguards to raise the costs of debt relief to ensure appropriate use.[262]

Even among those who accept the policy need to address the social costs of excessive household debt, doubts arise as to whether bankruptcy is the most appropriate tool for doing so. Some policy actors advocate regulatory (both prudential and conduct of business) measures that can prevent debt from reaching problematic levels in future,[263] and it is undoubtedly true that *ex ante* regulation is a more precise tool than bankruptcy for controlling credit supply and ensuring responsible lending. Barring occasional compensatory debt relief remedies,[264] however, regulation can do little to reduce existing high levels of historic debt. Contract design features offering flexibility or debt relief would have the advantage of coming into effect earlier than insolvency procedures, thus potentially acting in a timely manner before households have cut back spending drastically.[265] Given the contracting failures in consumer credit markets, however, the likelihood of such contractual arrangements being reached must be limited. Meanwhile, both regulatory and contractual solutions suffer from the disadvantage of addressing specific sectors

[261] For an argument supporting a similar position, see J. Westbrook, 'The Retreat of American Bankruptcy Law', *QUT Law Review* 17 (2017) 40. As clarified in Chapter 5, the approach argued here applies only to the 'consumer' debtor cases with which this book is concerned. Convincing arguments may exist for the persistence of a debt collection objective in respect of high net worth debtors.

[262] Hallinan (n. 3) 144.

[263] Bunn and Rostom (n. 70); International Monetary Fund, 'Household Debt and Financial Stability' (n. 100).

[264] 'Wonga to Pay Redress for Unfair Debt Collection Practices' (Financial Conduct Authority, 2014) Press Release www.fca.org.uk/news/press-releases/wonga-pay-redress-unfair-debt-collection-practices accessed 5 November 2018.

[265] Mian and Sufi, 'The Macroeconomic Advantages of Softening Debt Contracts' (n. 68).

or even individual debtor–creditor contracts and may depend for enforcement on a debtor undertaking a series of litigation in respect of each account. In contrast, bankruptcy can apply to the full range of an individual's obligations in a single procedure.[266] Traditional law-and-economics perspectives see private law as an inefficient means of addressing the macroeconomic and distributive issued raised,[267] which would instead be better managed through monetary and fiscal policy responses. Literature now increasingly recognises, however, that law can contribute importantly to macroeconomic outcomes when monetary policy runs against the 'zero lower bound' and the power of central banks to reduce interest rates is limited.[268] Furthermore, monetary policy is limited by the fact that interest rate changes are 'likely to have asymmetrical effects in a high debt economy', meaning that interest rate reductions may not spur heavily leveraged households into spending to the same degree that rate increases will reduce consumption.[269] In terms of other monetary measures, the Bank of England has admitted that quantitative easing was skewed towards the upper ends of the income distribution,[270] and so its ability to stimulate growth was limited by the fact that it benefitted those with the lowest marginal propensity to consume.[271]

Fiscal policy can address debt overhang problems effectively, for example through the provision of 'automatic stabilisers' through social welfare transfers.[272] Bankruptcy is at best an incomplete substitute for a robust social welfare system.[273] In a political environment in which

[266] W. C. Whitford, 'The Ideal of Individualized Justice: Consumer Bankruptcy as Consumer Protection, and Consumer Protection in Consumer Bankruptcy', *American Bankruptcy Law Journal* 68 (1994) 397.

[267] Ramsay, 'Consumer Credit Law, Distributive Justice and the Welfare State' (n. 180) 178; Hynes (n. 148) 328.

[268] Listokin (n. 68); J. Furman, 'How Lawyers Can Help Macroeconomists in the Wake of Three Major Challenges Keynote Address', *Yale Journal on Regulation* 34 (2017) 709.

[269] Zabai (n. 220) 45.

[270] 'The Distributional Effects of Asset Purchases' (Bank of England, 2012) www.bankofengland.co.uk/-/media/boe/files/news/2012/july/the-distributional-effects-of-asset-purchases-paper accessed 5 November 2018.

[271] This factor, combined with the contribution of quantitative easing to inequality, lead to political calls for 'quantitative easing for the people' or 'helicopter money' policies. Turner considers that 'reducing the value of debt through restructuring and writedowns ... should certainly play a role', but primarily advocates a form of "fiat money as a solution to the problem of inadequate nominal demand: Turner (n. 204).

[272] International Monetary Fund, 'Dealing with Household Debt' (n. 1) 13, 26.

[273] See e.g. P. Ali, L. O'Brien and I. Ramsay, 'Bankruptcy and Debtor Rehabilitation: An Australian Empirical Study', *Melbourne University Law Review* 40 (2017) 688.

governments are committed to austerity policies and see little available 'fiscal space',[274] however, this option is unavailable.[275] An IMF paper argues that debt relief policy measures are particularly appropriate as a substitute for fiscal policy responses in 'economies with limited scope for expansionary macroeconomic policies and in which the financial sector has already received government support'.[276] Where the necessity of debt relief policies is acknowledged, further questions arise as to the appropriate tools for delivering debt relief. Certain organisations and authors look outside bankruptcy and argue for the introduction of various forms of stand-alone consensual debt restructuring schemes to reduce debt burdens via creditor–debtor negotiation.[277] A main aim of Chapters 4 and 5 is to cast doubt on the efficacy of such schemes, given the contracting failures that arise in creditor–debtor (re)negotiation. Empirical lessons regarding the inefficacy of post-crisis mortgage restructuring policies such as the US Home Affordable Modification Program (HAMP) support this position.[278] Alternative suggestions to address the problem of excessive household debt include establishing a wholly new practice, most likely in the face of interest group opposition, and one which runs counter to the 'self-evident' logic that 'one has to pay one's debts'.[279] Consumer bankruptcy, in contrast, benefits from path dependency and in fact this practice for the release of debts has developed in an almost unintended and unobserved manner through a series of historical contingencies.[280] If consumer bankruptcy did not already exist, it would be very difficult for policymakers to introduce such a mechanism for the first time.[281] In a similar way, consumer bankruptcy

[274] Furman (n. 268) 719–20.

[275] Also, arguments can be made that fiscal measures can distort markets, while interventions (such as bankruptcy) that seek to correct market failures can enhance efficiency: Van Loo (n. 184).

[276] International Monetary Fund, 'Dealing with Household Debt' (n. 1) 27.

[277] International Monetary Fund, 'Dealing with Household Debt' (n. 1); Andritzky (n. 225); International Monetary Fund, 'Fiscal Monitor – Debt: Use It Wisely' (n. 71). See the introduction to Chapter 5 below.

[278] P. A. McCoy, 'The Home Mortgage Foreclosure Crisis: Lessons Learned' (Social Science Research Network, 2013) SSRN Scholarly Paper ID 2254672 http://papers.ssrn.com/abstract=2254672 accessed 6 August 2013; A. M. White, 'Deleveraging the American Homeowner: The Failure of 2008 Voluntary Mortgage Contract Modifications', *Connecticut Law Review* 41 (2008) 1107; Levitin, 'Resolving the Foreclosure Crisis' (n. 241).

[279] D. Graeber, *Debt : The First 5,000 Years* (Melville House, 2012) 2–4.

[280] I. Ramsay, *Personal Insolvency in the 21st Century: A Comparative Analysis of the US and Europe* (Hart Publishing, 2017) 6–7.

[281] Ramsay, 'A Tale of Two Debtors' (n. 40) 248.

has developed means of addressing several of the challenges raised to post-crisis household debt schemes, including the prevailing fear of moral hazard (see discussion in Chapter 7 below).[282] In short, using bankruptcy to address the household debt overhang problem would avoid reinventing the wheel. Evidence for this position comes from the history of bankruptcy law itself, which has seen the law being repurposed repeatedly at various points. Once the limitations of alternative measures are considered, the case for recognising bankruptcy primarily as a mechanism for delivering debt relief becomes compelling. The practical reality of the law, in which tens of thousands of families turn to insolvency procedures for relief from financial troubles, adds further to this case.

If the reader remains unconvinced regarding the ability of bankruptcy to address the market failures and externalities discussed in this chapter, one might at least acknowledge that bankruptcy law can no longer consider that it serves the public interest by unquestioningly maximising returns to creditors. Arguments that protective bankruptcy laws will raise the cost of credit are considerably weaker than they might once have been. Perspectives conceptualising bankruptcy primarily as a debt collection tool are limited not just by this increasingly unsure premise, but also by their inability to offer coherent explanation for the presence of a competing aim of debt relief and debtor rehabilitation. The 'creditors' bargain' model excludes debtors entirely from its analysis, and offers only the suggestion that the law also contains 'an independent social policy' of providing debtors with a fresh start through debt discharge.[283] While English law recognises 'the importance of the rehabilitation of the individual insolvent',[284] it is often unclear as to the justification for doing so. One is frequently left with the impression that policymakers and judges see this aim as a mere concession to the debtor's humanity and a limit placed on the efficacy of a law otherwise single-mindedly focused on maximising returns to creditors.[285]

[282] Levitin, 'Resolving the Foreclosure Crisis' (n. 241) 618–48.

[283] Jackson (n. 32) 201; Block-Lieb (n. 100) 427.

[284] *Smith (A Bankrupt)* v. *Braintree District Council* [1989] 3 WLR 1317, [1990] 2 AC 215, 237–8.

[285] For example, see comments of Simon Brown LJ in the *Lightfoot* case that 'in the more compassionate times in which we now live', access to bankruptcy might be expanded to reduce the 'hardship and worry' suffered by debtors: *Lightfoot* (n. 46) 631. This sentiment is explained further in Gross' statement that 'society may forfeit some economic efficiency now for . . . national humanity': Gross (n. 55) 138.

This chapter has aimed to address this position by offering an argument for the public policy benefits of reorientating bankruptcy towards its debt relief objective, as part of a conceptualisation of the law as a social insurance mechanism against the risks inherent in the contemporary economic regime of financialised capitalism. Chapters 1 and 2 began to present the case for debt relief policies, with the book opening by illustrating how key contemporary problems of economic stagnation, inequality and political unrest can be linked to excessive levels of household debt. These chapters illustrate the inevitability of high debt levels and over-indebtedness under the 'privatised Keynesianism' economic model, and growing realisation that this model is unsustainable. This chapter sought to narrow focus from this global perspective to the more discrete topic of bankruptcy theory, while aiming to close the jarring disconnect between bankruptcy policymaking and contemporary wider economic and social policy discussions regarding the effects of (excessive) household debt.

From this position, the remainder of the book criticises the law for its failure to fulfil its potential as a means of delivering the public policy benefits of debt relief. This chapter opened by discussing English law's ideological incoherence regarding the nature and objectives of bankruptcy, while path dependency and the law's historical origins in commercial and corporate law further obscure its contemporary nature. Finally, while policies and processes of neoliberalism and financialisation have created an unprecedented need for debt relief policies, their foundational ideas of privatisation, marketisation and fiscal consolidation (austerity) reduce the ability of the law to offer such relief. Chapters 4 and 5 apply these ideas in illustrating how the marketisation and contractualisation of the personal insolvency system has restricted access to rapid debt discharge under bankruptcy and Debt Relief Order (DRO) procedures, while pushing debtors increasingly into 'market-based debt resolution' mechanisms (Individual Voluntary Arrangements (IVAs) and Debt Management Plans (DMPs)), productive of greater returns to creditors. Chapter 6 argues that austerity policies have accelerated the 'loans for wages' and 'credit/welfare trade-off' trends discussed in Chapter 2, and that bankruptcy law has responded poorly to consequent challenges of protecting access to essential household goods and services. It also argues that austerity policies have led government agencies to adopt commercialised debt collection practices that risk shaping bankruptcy law into a debt collection tool, particularly in relation to features such as creditor bankruptcy petitions, the stay of enforcement activities, and the debt discharge. Finally, Chapter 7 considers the question of *moral hazard*, and argues that new public management practices and concerns with maximising returns to creditors have led to an ineffective regime of regulating debtor conduct in bankruptcy, while ignoring the vast private systems of debtor control created by credit reporting services. Given these criticisms, the challenges in accepting bankruptcy as a social insurance mechanism offering relief to financially troubled households are numerous. This chapters hopes to have illustrated, however, why this remains a cause worth pursuing.

4

A Consumer Bankruptcy Marketplace

4.1 Introduction: The Retreat of English Consumer Bankruptcy Law

Increasing recognition of problems associated with the high household debt levels inherent in our contemporary economic and political order present a case for household debt relief policies. As a societal institution unique in its discharge of debt routinely and as of right, bankruptcy thus gains an important role. In this context, and particularly after the role household debt played in the shock of the global financial crisis of 2008, one might have expected personal insolvency law to have featured prominently in recent policy responses. In fact, the high-water mark of debtor-friendly bankruptcy law reform came prior to the crisis with liberalisation of the bankruptcy procedure under the Enterprise Act 2002 and the introduction of the Debt Relief Order procedure under the Tribunals, Courts and Enforcement Act 2007.[1] The following two chapters argue that since this time there has been a retreat of English consumer bankruptcy law, just when the case for expansive debt relief seems strongest.[2] Subsequent chapters argue that the law fails to live up to the social insurance model of bankruptcy outlined in Chapter 3 in its regulation of debtor (mis)conduct and the limited scope of its discharge and protection

[1] Professor Fletcher describes these legislative reforms as being 'directed at providing a less harsh experience for those debtors deemed to belong to the category of "honest but unfortunate casualties of circumstance"': I. Fletcher, '"Out of Sight, out of Mind"? The Progressive Dematerialisation of Our Insolvency Procedures', *Insolvency Intelligence* 30 (2017) 81, 83.

[2] Here I borrow the term used by Professor Westbrook to describe 2005 changes that reduced the celebrated generosity of US bankruptcy law's 'fresh start' policy: J. Westbrook, 'The Retreat of American Bankruptcy Law', *QUT Law Review* 17 (2017) 40.

against creditor collection efforts. This chapter and the next argue that the law falls at the first hurdle in adopting an overall structure that limits initial debtor access to debt relief.

Policy responses to the global financial crisis and Great Recession in England and Wales did not include bankruptcy reform. Monitory policy-makers lowered interest rates, while both conduct of business and prudential regulators acted to instigate mortgage forbearance schemes and measures aimed at preventing future debt crises (including the FSA's Mortgage Market Review,[3] and the Bank of England's mortgage lending limits[4]).[5] Despite the criticisms advanced in this book, English bankruptcy law 'on the books' is more developed and progressive than laws of countries that saw drastic personal insolvency law reform as a necessary reaction to the crisis.[6] This position seems to have generated a consensus that the 'insolvency law of this country is recognised nationally and internationally ... as providing a first class system for dealing with corporate and individual financial failure'.[7] Even advocates of active responses to the debt overhang problem of the Great Recession were confident that 'the UK bankruptcy process is widely considered to offer an example of international best practice in terms of speedy discharge, flexibility and debtor recovery'.[8]

[3] *Mortgage Market Review* (Financial Services Authority, 2009); *Mortgage Market Review: Proposed Package of Reforms* (Financial Services Authority, 2011).

[4] P. Bunn and M. Rostom, 'Household Debt and Spending in the UK' (Bank of England, 2015) Staff Working Paper No. 554 28–9.

[5] M. Whittaker and K. Blacklock, 'Hangover Cure: Dealing with the Household Debt Overhang as Interest Rates Rise' (Resolution Foundation, 2014) 26–32 www.resolutionfoundation.org/publications/hangover-cure-dealing-with-the-household-debt-overhang-as-interest-rates-rise/ accessed 5 November 2018; I. Ramsay, 'Two Cheers for Europe: Austerity, Mortgage Foreclosures and Personal Insolvency Policy in the EU' in H. W. Micklitz and I. Domurath (eds.), *Consumer Debt and Social Exclusion* (Ashgate Publishing, 2015); I. Ramsay, *Personal Insolvency in the 21st Century: A Comparative Analysis of the US and Europe* (Hart Publishing, 2017) 102–3.

[6] For discussions of law reforms in Ireland, Italy and Greece, respectively, see J. Spooner, 'Long Overdue: What the Belated Reform of Irish Personal Insolvency Law Tells Us about Comparative Consumer Bankruptcy', *American Bankruptcy Law Journal* 86 (2012) 243; G. Comparato, 'The Italian Law against Over-Indebtedness: Fresh Start, Debt Advice and Financial Education' in F. Ferretti (ed.), *Comparative Perspectives of Consumer Over-Indebtedness* (Eleven International Publishing, 2016); M. J. Mouzouraki, '(Failure to Set up an Efficient) Out-of-Court System to Deal with Debtors in Financial Distress in Greece' in F. Ferretti (ed.), Comparative Perspectives of Consumer Over-Indebtedness (Eleven International Publishing, 2016).

[7] S. Baister and F. Toube, 'All Change Is Not Growth, as All Movement Is Not Forward!', *Insolvency Intelligence* 25 (2012) 49, 53.

[8] Whittaker and Blacklock (n. 5) 61.

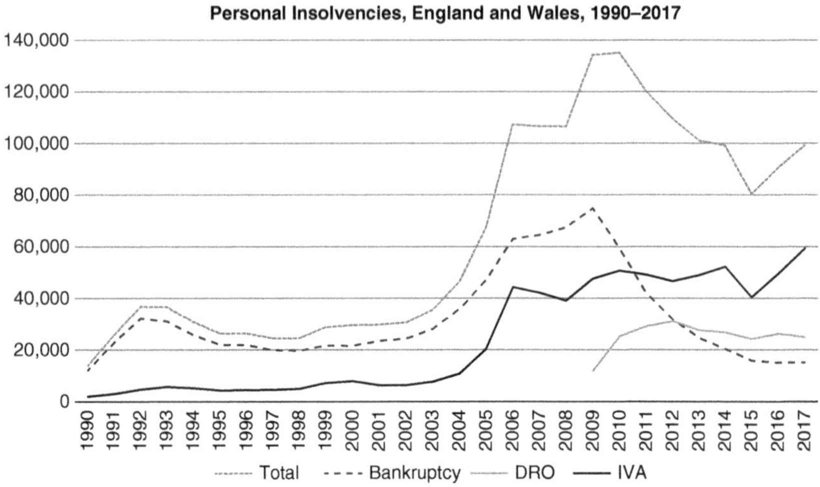

Figure 4.1: While IVAs grow in number, bankruptcy declines. Source: The Insolvency Service

The following two chapters present a picture of English bankruptcy 'law in action' to challenge this complacent image. The lived experience of personal insolvency for financially troubled debtors differs substantially from what might be suggested by the most protective features of legislative provisions. Hundreds of thousands of debtors are trapped in Debt Management Plans (DMPs) – consensual and voluntary repayment arrangements agreed with creditors and delivered by charitable or commercial intermediaries, which generally offer no debt reduction and may persist for years or even decades. Of those debtors entering statutory insolvency procedures, the majority (now almost 60 per cent and rising – see Figure 4.1) will endure only a marginally more beneficial experience under the Individual Voluntary Arrangement (IVA) statutory consensual renegotiation procedure. Approximately 30–40 per cent of IVAs will fail, ultimately denying debtors relief, often after years of them paying practitioner fees and living on a subsistence budget in order to make repayments set by creditors. Of those arrangements that 'succeed', one in three debtors may still be repaying seven years after entering the procedure, with a sizeable number continuing in repayment plans of even longer duration.[9] Just over one in four debtors accessing the formal statutory insolvency procedures (perhaps one in ten of the total entering the

[9] For discussion of how repayment can even continue after the 'completion' of an IVA, see text to notes 162–3.

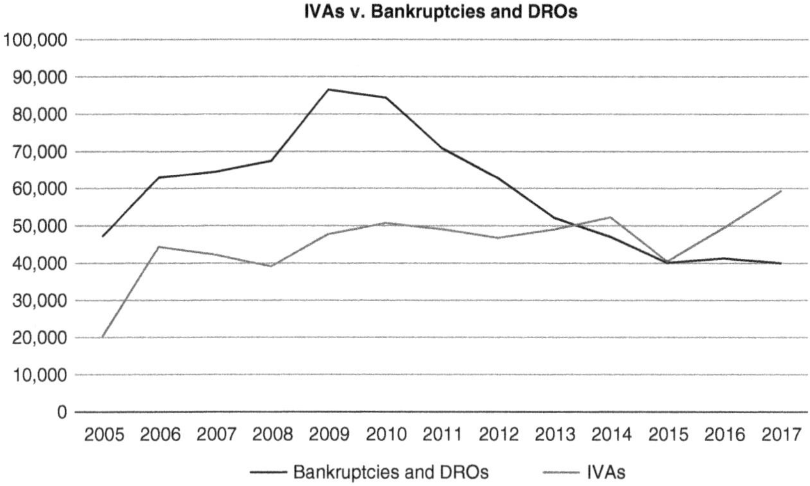

Figure 4.2: Mandatory v. consensual personal insolvency procedures, 2005–2017. Source: The Insolvency Service

'insolvency marketplace' of statutory insolvency procedures combined with DMPs) will avail of the Debt Relief Order (DRO) procedure's rapid one-year discharge without contribution to creditors. DRO numbers fall significantly short of estimates predicted by the Insolvency Service on introducing the mechanism (40 per cent lower in the fourth year of operation).[10] The generous discharge under English law fades as bankruptcy continues to 'vanish',[11] and now fewer than one in five entering formal insolvency (perhaps one in twenty entering the marketplace) will benefit from the bankruptcy procedure's debt discharge after one year (Figure 4.1). Viewed from this position, English law offers its 'speedy discharge ... and debtor recovery' to only a fraction of debtors. Meanwhile, its 'flexibility' has led to the development of a personal insolvency 'market', in which market forces and commercialised public service provision will direct debtors into 'products' offering outcomes unfavourable to debtors, but apparently satisfactory to the creditors and intermediaries who effectively set the terms of debt

[10] *Relief for the Indebted – An Alternative to Bankruptcy: Summary of Responses and Government Reply* (The Insolvency Service, 2005) 20 (on file with the author).

[11] M. Galanter, 'The Vanishing Trial: An Examination of Trials and Related Matters in Federal and State Courts', *Journal of Empirical Legal Studies* 1 (2004) 459; E. Warren, 'Vanishing Trials: The Bankruptcy Experience', *Journal of Empirical Legal Studies* 1 (2004) 913; L. Mulcahy, 'The Collective Interest in Private Dispute Resolution', *Oxford Journal of Legal Studies* 33 (2013) 59.

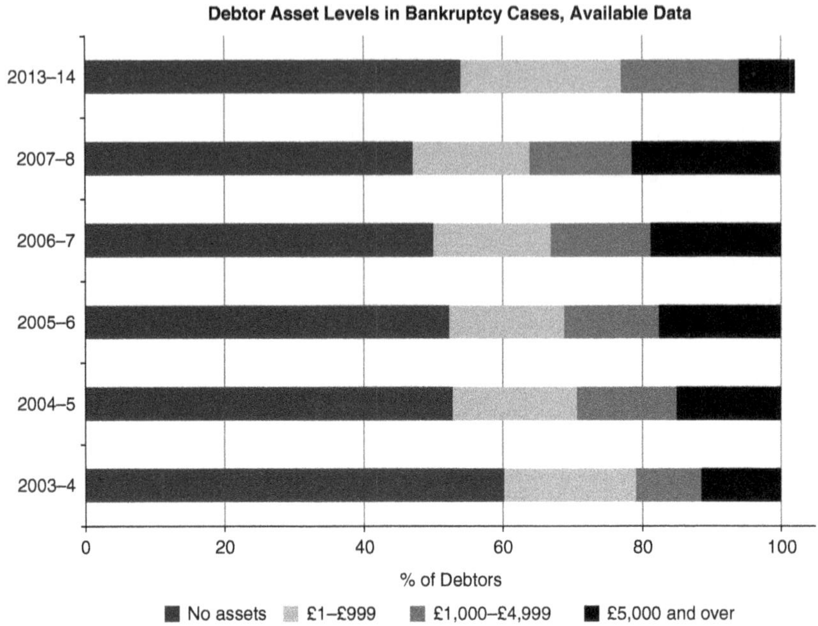

Figure 4.3: Most debtors entering bankruptcy have few, if any, assets available for liquidation. Source: The Insolvency Service

discharge. As one would expect, these actors have made discharge conditional on debtors contributing high repayments and fees over long time periods, and in so doing they have reorientated the law towards a goal of maximising returns to creditors. Debt relief is now available to most debtors only on contractarian and market terms, rather than as of right.

This book argues that a number of factors contribute to these developments. Confusion regarding the identity and core objectives of personal insolvency law has meant that policymakers, judges, and administrators never committed wholly to reforms offering more extensive debt relief. The liberalisation of the bankruptcy procedure and the introduction of the DRO mechanism were counterbalanced by efforts to maximise returns to creditors. Policymakers and courts have viewed positively the growth of 'market-based debt resolution'[12] via IVA and DMP repayment

[12] 'Dealing with Household Debt', World Economic Outlook 2012 (International Monetary Fund, 2012) 14 www.imf.org/external/pubs/ft/weo/2012/01/pdf/c3.pdf accessed 5 November 2018.

arrangements, an approach consistent with the 'creditors' bargain' model of bankruptcy as a collective process for maximising returns to creditors.[13] Path dependency has played a role,[14] as reforms facilitating debtor rehabilitation have been introduced into a law that has 'maintained the essential structures' developed in its 'formative period' of the nineteenth century.[15] Rather than overhauling personal insolvency law to respond to the new environment of financialised capitalism and mass household indebtedness, reform has been rare. The approach might be described as a 'policy of muddling through',[16] characterised by 'political and bureaucratic choices for inaction and judicial neglect'.[17] The consequence is that the contemporary operation of the law as a safety net for financially troubled households conflicts with the principles of commercial or corporate law on which it was designed.

The pendulum swing of prioritisation of the law's debt collection and debt relief aims is influenced not just by ideas arising internally from insolvency law's past, but also from prevailing ideas of political economy. A theme throughout this book is that while conditions of financialised capitalism necessitate extensive debt relief measures, the neoliberal ideas central to this economic regime – including the privatisation and commercialisation of public services, and the predominance of (financial) market logic – have contributed towards a denial of this relief. The lack of response among Policymakers and courts to the reshaping of personal insolvency law in the past decade exhibits a complementary 'desire to reduce the levels of demand upon the judicial system',[18] and confidence in markets' ability to deliver appropriate outcomes. This chapter and the next follow argue that this confidence is misplaced. In meeting these views of the efficient market hypothesis on their own terms and applying market failure theory to the conditions of contemporary household over-indebtedness, it argues that the outcomes produced by a contractarian and marketised approach to consumer bankruptcy law are far from optimal.

[13] B. E. Adler, 'Bankruptcy Primitives', *American Bankruptcy Institute Law Review* 12 (2004) 219, 235–6; T. H. Jackson, *The Logic and Limits of Bankruptcy Law* (Harvard University Press, 1986) 17.

[14] Ramsay, '*21st Century*' (n. 5) ch. 3.

[15] Fletcher, 'Out of Sight' (n. 1) 84.

[16] I. Ramsay, 'A Tale of Two Debtors: Responding to the Shock of Over-Indebtedness in France and England – a Story from the Trente Piteuses', *The Modern Law Review* 75 (2012) 212, 245.

[17] Ramsay, '*21st Century*' (n. 5) 69.

[18] Fletcher, 'Out of Sight' (n. 1) 83.

4.2 Debtor Choice and the Structure of English Law

Where a personal insolvency system is composed of a number of different procedures, a key question arises as to whether access should depend on consumer choice or decisions of public authorities regarding the appropriate procedure for a debtor applicant.[19] Unlike systems in countries such as France and Belgium,[20] and contrary to US[21] and domestic[22] proposals for a 'single portal' model, contemporary English law falls into the category of a system based on debtor choice. This choice is between the statutory procedures of bankruptcy,[23] IVAs,[24] and DROs;[25] as well as the non-statutory option of renegotiating obligations with creditors under a Debt Management Plan. Bankruptcy involves the liquidation of any non-exempt assets of the debtor, and the discharge of her debts at the end of a 12-month waiting period. The Debt Relief Order procedure (which came into effect in 2009)[26] serves no debt collection function, with no contributions to creditors from the debtor's assets/income. It is a simplified administrative insolvency procedure for 'no income, no assets' cases, under which a debtor obtains initial protection from enforcement, followed by a full discharge of all non-excluded debts after a waiting period of

[19] *Report on the Treatment of the Insolvency of Natural Persons* (World Bank, 2013) 68.

[20] J. Spooner, 'Fresh Start or Stalemate? European Consumer Insolvency Law Reform and the Politics of Household Debt', *European Review of Private Law* 21 (3) (2013) 747, 751–5.

[21] See e.g. W. C. Whitford, 'The Ideal of Individualized Justice: Consumer Bankruptcy as Consumer Protection, and Consumer Protection in Consumer Bankruptcy', *American Bankruptcy Law Journal* 68 (1994) 397; J. Braucher, 'A Fresh Start for Personal Bankruptcy Reform: The Need for Simplification and a Single Portal', *American University Law Review* 55 (2005) 1295; K. Porter, 'The Pretend Solution: An Empirical Study of Bankruptcy Outcomes', *Texas Law Review* 90 (2011) 103.

[22] Sir Kenneth Cork, *Insolvency Law and Practice: Report of the Review Committee* (HMSO, 1982) paras. 550, 272 *et seq*., more widely 545–65.

[23] I. F. Fletcher, The Law of Insolvency 4th revised edn (Sweet & Maxwell, 2009) chs. 5–13.

[24] See ibid, ch 4(I)(1); A. Walters, 'Individual Voluntary Arrangements: A "Fresh Start" for Salaried Consumer Debtors in England and Wales', *International Insolvency Review* 18 (2009) 5.

[25] This book disregards the County Court Administration Order (hereafter Administration Order) procedure, which is now very rarely used: see e.g. D. M. Skene and A. Walters, 'Consumer Bankruptcy Law Reform in Great Britain', *American Bankruptcy Law Journal* 80 (2006) 477, 487–8; I. Ramsay, 'Bankruptcy in Transition: The Case of England and Wales - The Neo-Liberal Cuckoo in the European Bankruptcy Nest?', *Consumer Bankruptcy in Global Perspective* (Hart Publishing, 2003) 212–3; Ramsay, *'21st Century'* (n. 5) ch. 3.

[26] See e.g. The Insolvency Service, *Relief for the Indebted – An Alternative to Bankruptcy* (n. 10) ; Insolvency Service, *A Choice of Paths: Better Options to Manage Over-Indebtedness and Multiple Debt* (Department of Constitutional Affairs, 2004).

one year.[27] The IVA procedure involves the debtor's submission of a proposal to her unsecured[28] creditors via a licensed Insolvency Practitioner (usually an accountant or, less frequently, a lawyer), which becomes an arrangement if approved by 75 per cent in value of creditors.[29] As discussed below, the terms of an IVA are determined by debtor–creditor negotiations, but standard terms have been developed between the consumer credit and Insolvency Practitioner (IP) industries. Commentators, policymakers and stakeholders generally repeat a consensus view that that a usual repayment plan endures for 5–6 years, in full settlement of the debtor's obligations.[30] Many IVAs endure for a much longer period, however (see Chapter 5). While the DRO is restricted to 'no income, no assets' cases, debtors otherwise largely have a free choice as to whether to enter the IVA or bankruptcy procedure.

Unlike countries such as France (in which fee-charging private debt counselling services are prohibited[31]) or Ireland (where state-funded debt counselling services have dominated[32]), an extensive industry of private and third sector debt counselling services exists in the UK.[33] Debt advice agencies and firms offer various services including money management advice and budget planning, negotiating with creditors, and more formal solutions of either statutory insolvency procedures or non-statutory DMPs.[34] A DMP consists of a (generally non-binding) agreement between a debtor and her creditors to reschedule her debts over an extended repayment period, based on the making of a monthly payment

[27] Subject to the suspension of discharge and/or the imposition of sanctions in the event of the debtor's misconduct.

[28] An IVA cannot affect the right of secured creditor to enforce its security: Insolvency Act 1986, s. 258(4).

[29] Insolvency Act 1986, s. 260; Insolvency Rules 2016/1024 reg. 15.34(6).

[30] 'Standard Conditions for Individual Voluntary Arrangements (Revised April 2012)'.

[31] *Code de la Consommation*, art. L321–1.

[32] See e.g. J. Spooner, 'Long Overdue: What the Belated Reform of Irish Personal Insolvency Law Tells Us about Comparative Consumer Bankruptcy', *American Bankruptcy Law Journal* 86 (2012) 243, 262–6.

[33] S. Collard, *An Independent Review of the Fee-Charging Debt Management Industry* (Money Advice Trust and Personal Finance Research Centre, University of Bristol, 2009); 'Debt Management Guidance Compliance Review' OFT1274 (Office of Fair Trading, 2010); P. Muller and others, *Debt Advice in the UK: Final Report for the Money Advice Service* (London Economics, 2012); B. Rowe and others, 'Financial Conduct Authority Consumer Credit Research: Payday Loans, Logbook Loans and Debt Management Services' (ESRO, Financial Conduct Authority, 2014); 'Quality of Debt Management Advice' Thematic Review TR15/8 (Financial Conduct Authority, 2015).

[34] Muller and others (n. 33) 52.

by the debtor to an agency, which is then distributed on a pro rata basis among creditors.[35] There is generally no debt write-down under a DMP, and various reports estimate long repayment periods of more than 10,[36] 20,[37] or even over 100 years.[38] Recent years have seen the IVA procedure come to dominate among statutory procedures, with almost 60 per cent of the approximately 100,000 annual personal insolvencies now using this procedure. In the wider personal insolvency 'market', however, the dominant option is the DMP. While limited data are available, the Financial Conduct Authority (FCA) estimates that at present almost half a million consumers hold debt management plans with the top 10 providers.[39] One large scale study commissioned by a representative body of DMP and IVA providers, the Debt Resolution Forum, estimated that 165,000 DMPs started in 2011.[40] While a recent regulatory clampdown by the FCA has caused some DMP providers to leave the marketplace or switch to IVA provision (since IVAs fall outside the FCA's regulatory jurisdiction),[41] it is reasonable to assume that DMPs continue to outnumber statutory insolvencies.

It is striking that there has been little discussion within the English system of questions raised by these developments. These include issues crucial to a bankruptcy system – 'rational sorting' and whether debtor choice or decision-maker adjudication should determine access to procedures;[42] whether the law should provide debt relief as of right or rely on consensual debt renegotiation; whether debt discharge should be relatively rapid and automatic or conditional on completion of a long-term repayment plan; and whether insolvency should be a public institution or a market service. The paradigm of debtor choice aligns the English system to US bankruptcy law, under which debtors choose to enter either the rapid discharge-and-liquidation procedure of Chapter 7 (of Title 11 of the US Bankruptcy Code),

35 Collard (n. 33) 2.

36 'A Consultation Document on Proposed Changes to the Individual Voluntary Arrangement (IVA) Regime' (Insolvency Service, 2007) 43.

37 'Improving Individual Voluntary Arrangements' (Insolvency Service, 2005) para. 24.

38 Financial Conduct Authority (n. 33) 25.

39 'Sector Views 2017' (Financial Conduct Authority, 2017) 20.

40 Zero-credit and Debt Resolution Forum, 'Debt Resolution in the UK' (Debt Resolution Forum, 2012) 20.

41 Financial Conduct Authority (n. 39) 23; ' Insolvency Market Trends: Review of 2017' (TDX Group, 2017).

42 See World Bank (n. 19) paras. 199–203; J. Braucher, 'A Law-in-Action Approach to Comparative Study of Repayment Forms of Consumer Bankruptcy' in J. Niemi, I. Ramsay and W. C. Whitford (eds.), *Consumer Credit, Debt and Bankruptcy: Comparative and International Perspectives* (Hart Publishing, 2009) 347–55.

or the long-term repayment plan procedure of Chapter 13 (of the same Code). The contrast in how these issues are discussed across the two systems could scarcely be starker, however. In US consumer bankruptcy literature, the question of 'chapter choice' is central and widely studied. Indeed, front page news was generated when research produced evidence that institutional racial biases make black debtors about twice as likely as white debtors to enter 'the more onerous and costly' Chapter 13.[43] In condemnations of this racial disparity, the consumer detriment associated with this diversion of debtors into long-term repayment plans (and away from the immediate discharge under Chapter 7) was assumed without much doubt. Empirical studies of comparatively negative outcomes for Chapter 13 debtors show the validity of this assumption.[44] When legislation was proposed to force more debtors into Chapter 13 and restrict access to Chapter 7, it proved 'enormously controversial' and its political passage became a 'fierce struggle'.[45] The resultant Bankruptcy Abuse Prevention and Consumer Protection Act 2005 is widely condemned in US scholarship as an 'unmitigated disaster'.[46] While the legislation has not been successful in increasing the proportion of debtors opting for Chapter 13, it has had the procedural effect of making bankruptcy filing more expensive due to the administrative workload involved, excluding many debtors from relief.[47] It is seen as representing a triumph of the political influence of the financial sector over empirical evidence and policy research,[48] to the point that one author dubbed its enactment 'one of the most shameful chapters in the history of American business.'[49]

43 T. S. Bernard, 'Blacks Face Bias in Bankruptcy, Study Suggests' *The New York Times* (20 January 2012) www.nytimes.com/2012/01/21/business/blacks-face-bias-in-bankruptcy-study-suggests.html accessed 5 November 2018, reporting on J. Braucher, D. Cohen and R. M. Lawless, 'Race, Attorney Influence, and Bankruptcy Chapter Choice', *Journal of Empirical Legal Studies* 9 (2012) 393.

44 T. Sullivan, E. Warren and J. L. Westbrook, *As We Forgive Our Debtors: Bankruptcy and Consumer Credit in America* (Beard Books, 1989); K. Porter and D. Thorne, 'The Failure of Bankruptcy's Fresh Start', *Cornell Law Review* 92 (2006) 67; Porter (n. 21); S. S. Greene, P. Patel and K. Porter, 'Cracking the Code: An Empirical Analysis of Consumer Bankruptcy Outcomes', *Minnesota Law Review* 101 (2016) 1031.

45 D. Skeel, *Debt's Dominion: a History of Bankruptcy Law in America* (Princeton University Press, 2001), 187.

46 J. J. Kilborn, 'Still Chasing Chimeras but Finally Slaying Some Dragons in the Quest for Consumer Bankruptcy Reform', *Loyola Consumer Law Review* 25 (2012) 1, 3.

47 Westbrook (n. 2) 44–9.

48 S. J Lubben, 'Do Empirical Bankruptcy Studies Matter', *American Bankruptcy Institute Law Review* 20 (2012) 715; M. Howard, 'Bankruptcy Empiricism: Lighthouse Still No Good', *Bankruptcy Developments Journal* 17 (2000) 425.

49 G. Thain, 'Consumers' in *The Oxford Handbook of Legal Studies* (Oxford University Press, 2005).

If this marks a 'retreat' of American bankruptcy law from its traditional commitment to the 'fresh start' policy, one can observe a similar retreat in English law.[50] For most debtors the personal insolvency system has moved from offering rapid debt relief with minimal or no repayment to creditors, to making discharge conditional on the completion of increasingly long repayment plans. Indeed, the position is worse for debtors in English and Wales than in the US. While the terms of Chapter 13 repayment plans are set neutrally by a court, creditors effectively impose terms under English law's contractarian IVA procedure. It is remarkable that UK creditors achieved this outcome without legislative change and without resorting to the political lobbying activities of their US counterparts, but through reshaping existing law in an incremental and barely visible manner. The remainder of this chapter describes this process and highlights the factors that have led to the orientation of bankruptcy law away from the debt relief aims seemingly embodied in the Enterprise Act reforms and the introduction of the DRO, towards the dominance of contractarian consensual negotiation mechanisms prioritising repayment. The next chapter presents the adverse public policy consequences of this position.

4.3 'Vanishing' Bankruptcy: Restricted Access to Public Provision

A significant element of the 'retreat' of English bankruptcy law has been the manner in which costs and access conditions exclude large numbers of debtors from the bankruptcy and DRO procedures. This has residualised the public provision of debt relief and forced excluded debtors to turn to market solutions for assistance.[51] The liquidity constraints of debtors mean that raising funds to pay access costs can be a primary factor in exclusion from bankruptcy procedures, exceeding even the effects of substantive access criteria such as means testing rules (which themselves often exclude more debtors through raising the costs of compliance than through the substantive application of the rules

[50] This chapter offers an alternative perspective to the perception that during the early 2000s UK Government policy 'moved in the other direction' from the measures introduced in the USA by the Bankruptcy Abuse Prevention and Consumer Protection Act 2005: P. Ali, L. O'Brien and I. Ramsay, '"Short a Few Quid": Bankruptcy Stigma in Contemporary Australia', *University of New South Wales Law Journal* 38 (2015) 1575, 1588.

[51] On residualisation of public services, see C. Crouch, *Post-Democracy* 1st edn (Polity Press 2004) 89.

themselves[52]).[53] In systems such as the American system it is the professional fees charged by attorneys that have exclusionary effects.[54] In the English system debtors seeking to access bankruptcy generally lack legal representation, and instead face exclusion due to fees charged by the state to access this procedure (currently £680). Alternatively, debtors can access the DRO procedure through debt advice agencies ('approved intermediaries', under the legislative scheme[55]) and must pay a fee (£90) to government agency the Insolvency Service (part of which is directed to the advice agencies). Debt advice charities report considerable evidence of exclusion of debtors unable to raise these respective sums,[56] with problems posed even by the £90 fee charged under the DRO procedure.[57] Difficulties are compounded by the limitation of the DRO procedure to debtors whose obligations fall under a £20,000 ceiling,[58] subjecting all debtors not meeting this condition to the barrier of bankruptcy fees. An Insolvency Service report indicated that in 2013–14 the ceiling excluded approximately 85 per cent of bankruptcy debtors from the cheaper DRO procedure, suggesting that this condition is a key factor influencing debtors to enter bankruptcy (as 77 per cent of bankruptcy debtors otherwise met the 'no income, no assets' criteria for availing of the DRO).[59] The limited

[52] n. 47 above.

[53] S. Albanesi and J. Nosal, 'Insolvency after the 2005 Bankruptcy Reform' Federal Reserve Bank of New York Staff Report No. 725 (Federal Reserve Bank of New York, 2015); P. Foohey and others, 'No Money down Bankruptcy', *Southern California Law Review* 90 (2016) [i].

[54] R. Mann and K. Porter, 'Saving Up for Bankruptcy' SSRN Scholarly Paper ID 1540216 http://papers.ssrn.com/abstract=1540216 accessed 30 January 2013 (Social Science Research Network, 2010); L. R. Lupica, 'The Consumer Bankruptcy Fee Study: Final Report', *American Bankruptcy Institute Law Review* 20 (2012) 17; Foohey and others (n. 53); P. Foohey, 'Access to Consumer Bankruptcy', *Emory Bankruptcy Developments Journal* 34 (2018) 341.

[55] See Debt Relief Orders (Designation of Competent Authorities) Regulations 2009.

[56] 'Debt Relief Orders and the Bankruptcy Petition Limit: Citizens Advice Response to the Insolvency Service' 2014 Evidence: a Citizens Advice Social Policy Publication 3 (Citizens Advice Bureau, 2014); 'Too Poor to Go Bankrupt' (Christians Against Poverty, 2014).

[57] S. Collard, C. Kinloch and S. Little, 'Debt Solutions in the UK Recommendations for Change' (Money Advice Service, 2018) 9; 'Review of the Literature Concerning the Effectiveness of Current Debt Solutions: Final Report for the Money Advice Service (MAS)' (ICF Consulting Services, 2017) 27.

[58] Insolvency Act 1986, Schd. 4ZA para. 6; Insolvency Proceedings (Monetary Limits) Order 1986/1996, Schd. 1

[59] 'Insolvency Proceedings: Debt Relief Orders and the Bankruptcy Petition Limit: Call for Evidence' (Insolvency Service, 2014) Call for Evidence https://assets.publishing.service.gov.uk/government/uploads/system/uploads/attachment_data/file/341089/Insolvency_Proceedings__Debt_relief_orders_and_petition_limits_v3.pdf, accessed 5 November 2018.

justifications offered for these barriers illustrate how ideas of austerity, individual responsibility, and market efficiency associated with neoliberalism and financialised capitalism serve to deny the debt relief that the contemporary economic regime seems to require.

From its inception, access to the DRO procedure has been narrowly limited based on debtors' income, asset, and debt levels. As a 'no income, no asset' procedure,[60] the DRO mechanism was designed as a debt relief option of last resort for debtors who could not afford bankruptcy or alternative remedies,[61] who cannot 'afford to make even token payments to their creditors [and] have no assets that could be sold to defray the debt'.[62] Access was thus conditioned on the debtor's surplus income and non-exempt assets falling below certain ceilings (£50 and £1,000, respectively).[63] A key distinction between bankruptcy and the DRO procedure is that the latter involves no repayment to creditors and no 'estate' for distribution among creditors.[64] It was enacted purely as a debt relief device, free from the aim of debt collection historically central to the bankruptcy procedure. This distinction might justify asset and income ceilings, directing debtors with resources available for repayment into the bankruptcy procedure, where these resources could be liquidated and distributed to creditors. The debt ceiling condition is more difficult to justify, however.[65] The level of debt owed seems insignificant to whether the debtor should obtain relief via bankruptcy or the DRO procedure. The Insolvency Service's rationale for including this access condition offers little insight, merely stating that 'there are other remedies available to people who get into debt', and that since the DRO aims 'to meet the needs of those with relatively low levels of debt, the total liabilities for people who enter the scheme should be restricted'.[66] As becomes clearer from analysis of the policy of bankruptcy access fees below, underlying this position seem to be a preference for market

[60] World Bank (n. 19) 99–100.

[61] The Insolvency Service, *Relief for the Indebted – An Alternative to Bankruptcy* (n. 10) 12.

[62] ibid.

[63] Insolvency Act 1986, Schd. 4ZA paras. 7–8.; Insolvency Proceedings (Monetary Limits) Order 1986/1996, Schd. 1

[64] Questions regarding the nature of the debtor's estate and the stay of creditor enforcement efforts are discussed throughout Chapter 6.

[65] See I. Ramsay and J. Spooner, 'Submission to Insolvency Service Call for Evidence: "Insolvency Proceedings: Debt Relief Orders and the Bankruptcy Petition Limit"' (2014) https://papers.ssrn.com/sol3/papers.cfm?abstract_id=2601349 accessed 5 November 2018.

[66] The Insolvency Service, *Relief for the Indebted – An Alternative to Bankruptcy* (n. 26) 25.

provision in the first instance, with public assistance to debtors to be limited to only a last resort or residual role.

Since bankruptcy applications moved online in 2016, a fee of £130 is payable to the adjudicator determining the debtor's application.[67] This is added to a deposit payable to cover the Official Receiver's 'administration fee', to the extent that the assets forming the debtor's estate will not cover the costs of administering the procedure (which occurs in most cases, since very few bankruptcies involve any assets of note).[68] This deposit is currently set at £550,[69] and while it can now be paid via instalments, all payments must be made before access to bankruptcy will be granted. Bankruptcy fees have a long history,[70] but they have been raised to such a degree in recent years as to become qualitatively distinct from past positions in their exclusionary effects. A particularly large increase (40 per cent) took place between 2009 and 2011.[71] Prior to the move to online bankruptcy adjudication, the court fee of £180 could be reduced to £5 via remission,[72] but the deposit of £525 could not be reduced. Under the new system, even this possibility of remission of part of the cost has been reduced, and so a fee of £680 is payable in all cases.

Under the prior system, a debtor's challenge on human rights grounds to her inability to obtain remission of the deposit was rejected in the case of *Regina* v. *Lord Chancellor, ex parte Lightfoot*.[73] This decision offers insight into judicial and policymakers' limited recognition of the public policy benefits of state delivery of debt relief, while demonstrating an underlying conception of bankruptcy assistance as a service to be offered on market terms, rather than as of right. The English Court of Appeal rejected the applicant's claim that the requirement to pay a non-waivable deposit infringed the debtor's common law constitutional right of access to justice and human right to a fair hearing. It held that these rights apply only to disputes in which the outcome will decide rights and

67 Insolvency Proceedings (Fees) Order 2016/692, reg. 3, Schd. 1.

68 Insolvency Proceedings (Fees) Order 2016/692, reg. 5.

69 Insolvency Proceedings (Fees) Order 2016/692, reg. 1, Schd. 1.

70 J. Tribe, 'The *Lightfoot* Paradox: Financing the Cost of Personal Insolvency Relief through Bankruptcy Revenue Stamps and Sliding Scales – Part A', *Insolvency Intelligence* 29 (2016) 97.

71 See e.g. comments of Richard Judge, Chief Executive of the Insolvency Service, in: The Insolvency Service: Oral Evidence Taken Before the Business, Innovation and Skills Committee (House of Commons, Hansard 2012).

72 Civil Proceedings Fees Order 2008/1053, Schd. 2.

73 *R* v. *Lord Chancellor, ex parte Lightfoot* [2000] QB 597 (Court of Appeal (England and Wales)).

obligations,[74] and that a debtor petitions for bankruptcy not to have her liabilities determined, but discharged.[75] Bankruptcy is thus 'a benign administration system to make fair and practical sense' of insolvent debtors' cases, 'designed both for the fair treatment of creditors and the relief of debtors', not involving concerns of access to justice.[76] According to the court, Parliament could have provided for a similar system to be provided administratively without judicial involvement;[77] and it was equally legitimate for Parliament to decide 'to make the scheme for the rehabilitation of debtors available only at a price'.[78] The Court of Appeal expressed concerns, however, at the effects of this parliamentary choice in denying rehabilitation to 'the great majority of those wishing to petition for bankruptcy', who 'face instead a lifetime of unrelieved indebtedness'.[79]

The court's finding that bankruptcy does not involve the determination or distribution of rights and obligations mirrors Professor Jackson's 'creditors' bargain' model under which the law should replicate market entitlements and pre-bankruptcy distributions of rights and obligations.[80] This is of course a theory that views the overriding aim of bankruptcy as being to maximise returns to creditors,[81] and its deployment here subordinates of the aim of debtor rehabilitation to the goal of enforcing market allocations. In *Lightfoot*, debt relief is not an independent policy goal so important as to be available as of right, but a privilege bestowed on the debtor out of some sense of 'compassion',[82] under a law otherwise concerned with debt collection. Debt discharge is seen as a means of encouraging debtor cooperation, that should only be extended to the

74 *Lightfoot*, 629, *per* Simon Brown LJ.
75 ibid, 622, per Simon Brown LJ.
76 ibid, 609, per Laws J (High Court), cited by Simon Brown LJ in the Court of Appeal, 629.
77 ibid, 609, per Laws J.
78 *Lightfoot*, 628, *per* Simon Brown LJ.
79 ibid, 617, *per* Simon Brown LJ.
80 Jackson (n. 13) 253.
81 English courts express this view elsewhere, often in ways which assimilate corporate and personal insolvency reasoning, as evidenced in Lord Hoffmann's statement that 'bankruptcy, whether personal or corporate, is a collective proceeding to enforce rights and not to establish them': *Cambridge Gas Transport Corp* v. *Official Committee of Unsecured Creditors (of Navigator Holdings PLC and Others)* (Isle of Man) [2006] UKPC 26, [2007] 1 AC 508, [15] (2006).
82 Despite rejecting the debtor's case, Simon Brown LJ hoped 'in the more compassionate times in which we now live', legislative reforms might be enacted to grant wider access to bankruptcy and so 'strike a new balance': *Lightfoot* (n. 73) 631, *per* Simon Brown LJ.

debtor 'at a price', as a quid pro quo for her benefitting creditors by surrendering her estate and paying the costs of the process which makes her assets available for creditors.[83]

Relatedly, the court reasoning in *Lightfoot* mirrors various policy statements in viewing debt relief as something to be offered to individuals on market terms, rather than having such public policy significance as to be guaranteed by the state. Standard justifications for the charging of 'user fees' for public services include the ability of fees to raise revenue without taxation (in a manner compatible with austerity policies); to restrict demand for public services and change citizen behaviour (so promoting individual responsibility); and to deter 'abuse' of public services.[84] These rationales appear in justifications offered for bankruptcy and DRO fees. Since the 1980s, insolvency policy has been 'dominated' by a determination to reduce public expenditure.[85] Conservative Government plans that ultimately led to the Insolvency Act 1986 'candidly admitted that the net consequence of [a proposed] transfer [away from the state] of the burden of financing the administration of civil bankruptcy would be a reduction in the annual number of petitions'.[86] This desire to reduce tax expenditure on public provision of debt relief, and accompanying comfort with debtors relying on market solutions, continued among New Labour policymakers through the 2000s.[87] It has intensified, however, under Coalition and Conservative austerity policies of the past decade. The steep increase in bankruptcy petition costs in 2010 and 2011 coincided with a substantial reduction in legal aid funding

[83] 'In short, the debtor obtains the protection of a bankruptcy order on terms that he delivers up his estate for administration for the benefit of his creditors . . . ' ibid, 631, *per* Chadwick LJ. For understandings of debt discharge as being conditional on maximising returns to creditors, see J. D. Honsberger, 'Philosophy and Design of Modern Fresh Start Policies: The Evolution of Canada's Legislative Policy', *Osgoode Hall Law Journal* 37 (1999) 171, 175.

[84] A. Paz-Fuchs, 'Social Rights and User Charges' in T. Kotkas and K. Veitch (eds.), *Social Rights in the Welfare State: Origins and Transformations* 1st edn (Routledge, 2017) 159–60.

[85] Fletcher (n. 1) 81.

[86] ibid.

[87] On introducing the DRO procedure the Insolvency Service considered the alternative possibility of waiving the deposit payment required to enter bankruptcy, but rejected this prospect as it did not 'believe that it is appropriate that [the cost of administering bankruptcies] should be met out of general taxation': The Insolvency Service, *Relief for the Indebted – An Alternative to Bankruptcy* (n. 26) para. 7. See also 'Impact Assessment of a Reform to the Debtor Petition Bankruptcy Process' (Technical Policy Insolvency Service, 2007) 1; *Consultation: Reforming Debtor Petition Bankruptcy and Early Discharge from Bankruptcy* (Insolvency Service, 2009) 10.

in civil claims,[88] and an increase in court and tribunal fees in areas such as employment law.[89] In line with trends of New Public Management and the commercialisation of public services,[90] the Insolvency Service is expected to operate through business principles on a cost-recovery basis, whereby Official Receiver fees, levied as a percentage of estate assets, fund case administration.[91] In a recent impact assessment identifying means of addressing the Service's operational deficit (attributed to a falling caseload), the option of funding insolvency procedures (corporate and individual) through general taxation was not even considered.[92] While mentioning briefly that insolvency proceedings should not be unaffordable to debtors, the changes to the fee structure removed progressive cross-subsidisation (i.e. levying fees as a percentage of estate assets) in favour of a regressive flat fee model. The cross-subsidisation of low-value cases by high-value cases was deemed contrary to 'Managing Public Money' principles.[93] Worries regarding government expenditure and fiscal management here seem to outweigh any concern for the law's distributional effects and the fact that this condition will impact the poorest debtors disproportionately, despite these effects being crucial to any consideration of policy problems of household debt.[94] Similar views are evident in the reasoning in *Lightfoot*. The court concluded that 'the mandatory deposit is not for access to the court but rather towards the costs of services being provided by others for the petitioner's benefit.'[95] Bankruptcy here is conceptualised as a service on offer in a personal insolvency marketplace, and like other potential options or services available to the insolvent debtor, it comes at a price. Courts expect over-

[88] It is estimated that legal aid funding for debt problems has been cut by 75 per cent: House of Commons: Business, Innovation and Skills Committee, *Debt Management: Fourteenth Report of Session 2010–12, Report, Together with Formal Minutes, Oral and Written Evidence* (HMSO, 2012) paras. 135–7.

[89] See A. Adams and J. Prassl, 'Vexatious Claims: Challenging the Case for Employment Tribunal Fees', *The Modern Law Review* 80 (2017) 412, 414–9.

[90] See e.g. C. Hood and R. Dixon, A Government That Worked Better and Cost Less?: Evaluating Three Decades of Reform and Change in UK Central Government (Oxford University Press, 2015) ch. 1; Crouch (n. 51); W. Brown, *Undoing the Demos: Neoliberalism's Stealth Revolution* (Massachusetts Institue of Technology Press, 2015) ch. 1.

[91] House of Commons: Business, Innovation and Skills Committee, 'The Insolvency Service' (House of Commons, 2013) Report No. 6 of Session 2012-3, 14–5.

[92] 'A New Fee Structure for Official Receiver Services: Impact Assessment' (Insolvency Service, 2016) IA No: BISINSS15003.

[93] ibid, 4, 8.

[94] See e.g. pages 89–93 above.

[95] [2000] QB 597, 623, *per* Simon Brown LJ.

indebted individuals (presumably considered to be commercially-minded, well-informed rational economic actors) to conduct a cost-benefit analysis of bankruptcy and only purchase this service if so doing would realise their preferences.[96] Recent changes allowing the debtor petition to be paid via instalments,[97] with bankruptcy access granted once all instalments have been paid, were accompanied by increases in the deposit amount. Policymakers justified this increase on the quid pro quo market logic that debtors should be willing to pay more highly for the 'premium' debt relief obtainable through bankruptcy compared to other insolvency products,[98] displaying an implicit idea that policymakers can (artificially) set appropriate prices for marketised public services.[99] These changes have had little impact in increasing access to bankruptcy, due to the impossibility for many debtors of making payment even via instalments. Meanwhile empirical evidence from US consumer bankruptcy cases raises serious concerns regarding the social costs and costs to individual debtors that accrue while they 'save up for bankruptcy'.[100]

Ideas of individual responsibility and a moral sense that public service users should pay for benefits received permeate both policy statements and the *Lightfoot* judgments. The court's reasoning contains an expectation that the debtor pay an individual price for the individual benefit of debt relief, and so should internalise the costs of her participation in the credit market.[101] This reasoning is consistent with the 'great risk shift' represented by neoliberalism's privatisation and marketisation of public services.[102] Government has shown little support for proposals to allow payment via instalments over the course of a debtor's bankruptcy, citing fears that debtors would 'abuse' such a position by benefitting from

[96] See e.g. Adams and Prassl (n. 89).

[97] *Reform of the Process to Apply for Bankruptcy and Compulsory Winding Up* (Insolvency Service, 2011) 18; House of Commons: Business, Innovation and Skills Committee (n. 91) 15.

[98] 'At present, individual debtor bankrupts have to pay an upfront fee of £525. Given the level of debt relief they can receive, we agree with the Insolvency Service that it would not be unreasonable to increase that fee, possibly on a sliding scale' House of Commons: Business, Innovation and Skills Committee (n. 88) para. 43.

[99] Crouch (n. 51) 86–7.

[100] Mann and Porter (n. 54); P. Foohey and others, 'Life in the Sweatbox' *Notre Dame Law Review* (94 Notre Dame Law Review 219 (2018)).

[101] See e.g. M. J. Wiggins, 'Conservative Economics and Optimal Consumer Bankruptcy Policy', *Theoretical Inquiries in Law* 7 (2006) 347, 355–6.

[102] J. S. Hacker, *The Great Risk Shift: The New Economic Insecurity and the Decline of the American Dream* revised edn (Oxford University Press, 2008).

a moratorium on creditor collection efforts while an application is pending, potentially by borrowing further.[103] This reflects concern regarding moral hazard and a general fear of abuse of bankruptcy's debt relief visible in Government comments that 'we do not believe that general taxation should pay for people to enter bankruptcy when they may have taken on debts irresponsibly'.[104] This individualised view and consequent political suppression of bankruptcy[105] either ignores, or places a great deal of trust in markets to address, the social costs of over-indebtedness and the reality of 'informal insolvency' arising when debtors are denied relief.[106] In this way it conflicts with the classic understanding that bankruptcy's fresh start 'is of the utmost importance not only because it is a fundamental private necessity, but because it is a matter of great public concern'.[107]

4.4 Individual Voluntary Arrangements: Contractual Bankruptcy

The exclusion of debtors from the publicly provided bankruptcy and DRO procedures strengthens the position of creditors who are no

[103] 'Consultation on Reform of the Process to Apply for Bankruptcy and Compulsory Winding Up: Summary of Consultation Responses' (Insolvency Service, 2012) 13. Note the similar rationale of deterring vexatious claims advanced to support employment tribunal fees: Adams and Prassl (n. 112) 438–41. The UK Supreme Court subsequently found such fees to be unlawful: *UNISON, R (on the application of)* v. *Lord Chancellor* [2017] UKSC 51 (UKSC (2017)).

[104] HC Deb 14 April 2002 Standing Committee B col. 693, *per* Ms Melanie Johnson MP. Tribe comments that the court in *Lightfoot* may have privately been concerned to avoid creating a moral hazard problem where bankruptcy provided 'a cost-free exit strategy from irresponsibly incurred indebtedness': J. Tribe, 'The *Lightfoot* Paradox: Financing the Cost of Personal Insolvency Relief through Bankruptcy Revenue Stamps and Sliding Scales – Part B', *Insolvency Intelligence* 29 (2016) 116, 120. Chapter 7 discusses further the problem of moral hazard and efforts by bankruptcy law to address it.

[105] Ramsay, '*21st Century*' (n. 5) 70.

[106] See Chapter 1, pages 20–23; Chapter 3, pages 86–93. World Bank (n. 19) 67. Recent US studies have shown how outcomes for debtors excluded from bankruptcy relief are considerably more negative than those experienced by those who can access bankruptcy: Albanesi and Nosal (n. 53); W. Dobbie and J. Song, 'Debt Relief and Debtor Outcomes: Measuring the Effects of Consumer Bankruptcy Protection', *American Economic Review* 105 (2015) 1272.

[107] This quotation is extracted from the classic statement of the 'fresh start' policy in the US Supreme Court decision of *Local Loan Co* v. *Hunt* (1934) 292 US 234 (US Supreme Court) 244. Note, however, that the Court has decided that there is no constitutional right to discharge from debts via bankruptcy: see the decision of *United States.* v. *Kras* (1973) 409 US 434, cited in *Gross* (1989), 168.

longer forced into the concessions and debt write-downs mandated by these procedures. It also creates opportunities for private sector intermediaries to sell solutions to this customer base, as debtors are forced to look elsewhere for assistance against over-indebtedness. Just as strict access requirements have seen limited use of DROs and bankruptcy, the IVA procedure has developed remarkably from a niche tool for high-end commercial debtors into a mass-marketed consumer insolvency 'product'. This process might be seen as 'organic development'[108] or 'pragmatic adjustment' of law and markets,[109] or perhaps an example of the manner by which 'capitalism expands its scope not just by developing new goods and production methods, but also by energetically pulling more and more areas of life within its reach'.[110] The development has also taken place with official support, however. As the justifications for access fees discussed above suggest, policymakers and courts have been content to see limited state intervention and expenditure in the personal insolvency system and demonstrate considerable faith in the efficiency of 'market-based debt resolution'. Furthermore, when it comes to the development of the legal nature of the IVA itself, judicial interpretations have demonstrated similar beliefs that private bargaining will produce optimal outcomes, adopting an approach of maximum contractual freedom.

4.4.1 The Market Dominance of the IVA

Authoritative accounts of the development of the IVA procedure have been produced elsewhere.[111] This section in contrast highlights key features of the growth of a personal insolvency market dominated by consensual renegotiation over statutorily mandated debt relief, with a particular focus on the understudied judicial contribution to this trend. Use of the IVA procedure was limited until it grew rapidly alongside a steep increase in use of a newly liberalised bankruptcy law in the early

[108] As suggested by the leader of one debt advice charity: J. Elson and Money Advice Trust, 'Money Advice Trust Welcomes Debt Solution Improvements' (15 January 2015) www.moneyadvicetrust.org/media/news/Pages/Money-Advice-Trust-welcomes-debt-solution-improvements.aspx accessed 5 November 2018.

[109] Ramsay, *'21st Century'* (n. 5) 104.

[110] Crouch (n. 51) 79, 81.

[111] Walters (n. 24); M. Green, 'New Labour: More Debt – The Political Response', *Consumer Credit, Debt and Bankruptcy: Comparative and International Perspectives* (Hart Publishing, 2009); Ramsay, 'A Tale of Two Debtors' (n. 16); Ramsay, *'21st Century'* (n. 5) ch. 3.

2000s, at a time when personal insolvency law became dominated by consumer (as opposed to business) debtors.[112] A primary driver of IVA growth was 'the entry of a new model of insolvency practitioner', based on high volume, low value business practices involving extensive advertising of IVAs as an alternative to bankruptcy.[113] The initial growth in consumer IVAs first produced a backlash from creditors concerned with rises in bad debts and a loss of control over their customers (whom banks would prefer to divert into 'solutions' involving lower levels of losses), with banks criticising aggressive marketing activities of 'IVA factories'.[114] What followed was 'a determined attempt by creditors ... to stiffen the criteria on which they were prepared to vote in favour of IVAs'.[115] Major banks introduced 'hurdle rates' (minimum projected dividends) of approximately 40 per cent (of the total debt owing) for the acceptance of IVA proposals, a sharp departure from the historical practice of accepting proposals offering approximately 15–25 per cent dividend.[116] A compromise was brokered between banks and insolvency practitioners by their negotiation of the IVA Protocol: 'a voluntary agreement, which provides an agreed standard framework for dealing with straightforward consumer IVAs and applies to both IVA providers and creditors'.[117] The Protocol seems to have produced an equilibrium satisfactory to both groups, as since its adoption in 2008 IVA numbers have risen consistently, particularly in most recent years (Figures 4.1, 4.2, and 4.4). Evidence is emerging of providers' expansion into new market territories, as they find ways of operating profitable IVAs for even lower-income debtors than had previously been thought possible – including the 'no income' groups for whom the DRO was designed.[118] In 2010 just 7 per cent of IVA debtors received more than half of their income from state benefits, but by 2017 this number had risen to approximately 20 per cent.[119] This trend supports

[112] Since 1994, the trend has been for approximately fewer than 5–10 per cent of IVAs to involve commercial debt: Insolvency Service, 'Improving Individual Voluntary Arrangements' (n. 37) para. 27.

[113] Ramsay, '*21st Century*' (n. 5) 87; Walters (n. 24) 25–7; Green (n. 111) 410.

[114] Ramsay, '*21st Century*' (n. 5) 94–8; Walters (n. 24) 31; Green (n. 111) 408.

[115] Walters (n. 24) 30.

[116] Green (n. 111) 408.

[117] 'IVA Protocol: Straightforward Consumer Individual Voluntary Arrangement' para. 2.1.

[118] S. Williams, 'Insolvency Numbers up – but Rising Debt Isn't the Main Cause' (*Debt Camel*, 30 January 2017) https://debtcamel.co.uk/2016-insolvency-increases/ accessed 5 November 2018. The Insolvency Service noted in the mid-2000s that creditors tended to reject low debt IVA proposals, considering that the low returns did not justify the costs involved: Insolvency Service, 'Improving Individual Voluntary Arrangements' (n. 37) para. 30.

[119] TDX Group (n. 41).

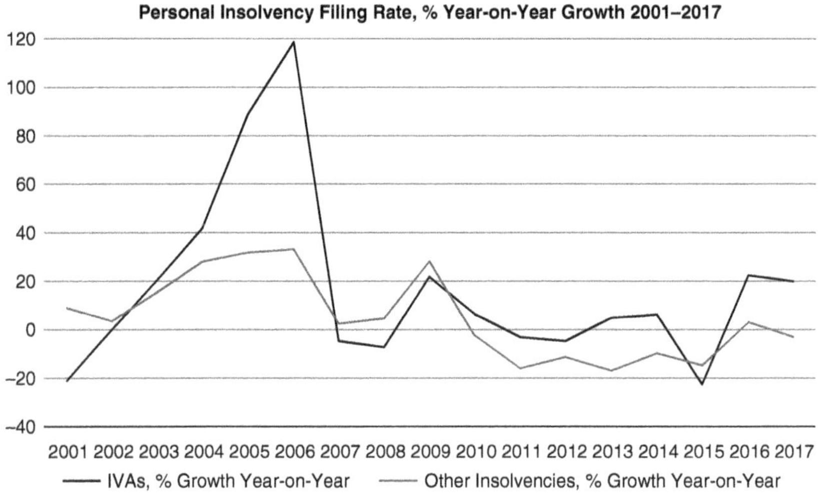

Figure 4.4: Personal insolvency percentage year-on-year growth, 2001–2017. Source: Compiled by author from The Insolvency Service data

accounts of the perpetual expansion of financialised capitalism and the potential of a 'debtfare' economy to offer opportunities for profit among markets of low-income debtors.[120] It also suggests that the bankruptcy and DRO institutions are at considerable risk of falling into a cycle of further residualisation, and increasing pressures to justify their operation, in the face of falling case numbers and accompanying budgetary pressures.[121] Such a trend can undermine the operation of the law and reduce its perceived benefit, particularly when the measure of success becomes profitability rather than the delivery of optimal public policy outcomes.[122]

4.4.2 *Facilitating the Consumer Bankruptcy Market*

The development of personal insolvency law 'from below'[123] has been facilitated by passivity among policymakers when faced with opportunities to respond to the new circumstances of mass over-indebtedness.

[120] S. Soederberg, *Debtfare States and the Poverty Industry: Money, Discipline and the Surplus Population* (Routledge, 2014) 60–5.

[121] See e.g. S. Ben-Ishai and S. Schwartz, 'Credit Counselling in Canada: An Empirical Examination', *Canadian Journal of Law and Society/La Revue Canadienne Droit et Société* 1, 29 (2014) 12–7; Ramsay, 'A Tale of Two Debtors' (n. 16) 246.

[122] Crouch (n. 51) 41–2.

[123] Ramsay, 'A Tale of Two Debtors' (n .16) 247.

Despite the transformation in scale and nature of personal insolvency procedures themselves, and the increasing economic and social significance of household debt, consumer bankruptcy has remained 'hardly conceptualised at all'.[124] Legislative inaction has been accompanied by an underappreciated active role for the judiciary in upholding marketised perspectives of the personal insolvency system and shaping the minimalist legislative framework governing IVAs into a distinctly contractarian model.[125]

The Cork Committee's review of insolvency law identified new 'demands of the consumer society'[126] and held 'no doubt ... that the most urgent need of all is for the introduction of a simple, accessible and inexpensive procedure for dealing with the ordinary consumer debtor'.[127] It recommended the introduction of a court-ordered repayment plan mechanism that would build on the existing Administration Order procedure,[128] as well as a fast track liquidation procedure for uncomplicated cases not requiring investigation.[129] The Conservative Government of the time, while enacting some Cork Committee recommendations regarding business insolvency in the Insolvency Acts of 1985[130] and 1986,[131] effectively ignored its calls for consumer bankruptcy reform, with little attention shown to household debt throughout the passage of the legislation.[132] This lack of responsiveness was part of a 'remarkable, and ominous, divergence' between the views of the Government and the Committee established by its predecessor.[133] The emerging neoliberal ideology of the Government led to drastically different views regarding the appropriate roles of state and private

[124] ibid 244.

[125] D. Milman, 'The Challenge of Modern Bankruptcy Policy: The Judicial Response.' in S. Worthington (ed.), *Commercial Law & Commercial Practice* (Hart Publishing, 2003) 397.

[126] Cork (n. 22) 11.

[127] ibid, 201, 272.

[128] This procedure was to be called the Debts Arrangement Order: ibid 272–349. The Committee also proposed that in cases of a debtor lacking significant assets and income, a court could make an Enforcement Restriction Order to prevent the enforcement of judgments against the debtor without leave of the court.

[129] ibid, 549, 585–8; Ramsay, '*21st Century*' (n. 5) 81–4.

[130] Insolvency Act 1985, ss. 110–8 (1985).

[131] Insolvency Act 1986, ss. 252–63G.

[132] Ramsay, '21st Century' (n. 5) 83; B. G. Carruthers and T. C. Halliday, *Rescuing Business: The Making of Corporate Bankruptcy Law in England and the United States* (Clarendon Press, 1998) 346–53.

[133] Fletcher, 'Bankruptcy Law Reform' (n. 1) 77.

activity in the insolvency sphere.[134] The Government rejected the Cork approach of a 'single portal' for entry to personal insolvency procedures, from which officials would direct debtors into appropriate procedures,[135] since increased judicial and administrative involvement would run contrary to the dominant policy consideration of reducing public expenditure on the system.[136] The Government was confident that voluntary solutions would be appropriate for small bankruptcy cases,[137] contrary to the Committee's proposal of the IVA as a procedure modelled on corporate voluntary renegotiation mechanisms and suitable for high-end business debtors such as company directors, professionals and unincorporated traders.[138] When the legislation introduced the IVA, therefore, it did so alongside the establishment of the Company Voluntary Arrangement procedure, as part of a general preference for consensual 'work-out' procedures.

This trend of reforming personal insolvency law with business debtors in mind continued with New Labour's Enterprise Act 2002, which removed certain punitive aspects of the bankruptcy procedure and reduced the waiting period for debt discharge to just one year.[139] These reforms were aimed squarely at business debtors as they hoped to support entrepreneurship by reducing the costs of business failure and encouraging risk taking.[140] When policymakers finally engaged with bankruptcy law as a policy solution to over-indebtedness among non-business debtors, they made clear that the resultant DRO procedure was to be limited in its application to a last resort option.[141] By this time of the mid-2000s, the Insolvency Service was won over to the IVA as 'the best product in the

[134] See also Ramsay, 'A Tale of Two Debtors' (n. 16) 245–8; Ramsay, 'Bankruptcy in Transition: The Case of England and Wales – The Neo-Liberal Cuckoo in the European Bankruptcy Nest?' (n. 25); I. Ramsay, 'Between Neo-Liberalism and the Social Market: Approaches to Debt Adjustment and Consumer Insolvency in the EU', *Journal of Consumer Policy* 35 (2012) 421.

[135] Department of Trade and Industry, A Revised Framework for Insolvency Law (Stationery Office Books, 1984) para. 17.

[136] Fletcher, 'Bankruptcy Law Reform' (n. 1) 81.

[137] ibid, 120–5.

[138] Cork (n. 22) paras. 363–97.

[139] A. Walters, 'Personal Insolvency Law after the Enterprise Act: An Appraisal', *Journal of Corporate Law Studies* 5 (2005) 65.

[140] *Productivity and Enterprise: Insolvency – A Second Chance* Cm 5234 (The Insolvency Service; Department for Trade and Industry, 2001); *Bankruptcy: A Fresh Start* (Insolvency Service, 2000) https://assets.publishing.service.gov.uk/government/uploads/system/uploads/attachment_data/file/263523/5234.pdf accessed 5 November 2018.

[141] See n. 66 above.

market for both debtors and creditors'.[142] The Service recognised that the procedure had not been designed for its current role as a consumer remedy, however, and proposed reforms to increase access to an even greater extent.[143] It advocated legislative changes that would simplify the IVA procedure and even introduce a 'cram-down' mechanism to remove the power of recalcitrant creditors to reject consumer debtor proposals. Despite the Service's initial views that legislation was necessary and that voluntary industry action would be insufficient to produce effective outcomes, a consultation process led the Government to water down proposals, before ultimately abandoning them.[144] Instead, the Service contented itself that the above-mentioned creditor-intermediary IVA Protocol had resolved relevant problems.[145] Policymakers declined another opportunity to reshape personal insolvency law to conditions of contemporary household indebtedness, and instead a commercial insolvency procedure continued to be applied to consumer debtors.

Policy has not advanced in the subsequent decade. The austerity policies of the Coalition Government saw significant cuts to Insolvency Service funding, limiting policy activity and scrutiny of the system's operation.[146] The prevailing political mood has been in favour of voluntary industry initiatives and self-regulation over government intervention,[147] and a focus on 'money advice' over legal rights to debt relief (as seen in the establishment of the Money Advice Service, and subsequently a 'single financial guidance body'[148]). Despite this typical neoliberal emphasis on financial counselling,[149] drastic cuts to debt-

[142] Insolvency Service, 'Improving Individual Voluntary Arrangements' (n. 37) para. 21.

[143] Insolvency Service, 'Consultation on IVA Regime' (n. 36) para. 4.

[144] 'Improving Individual Voluntary Arrangements: Summary of Responses and Government Reply' (2006).

[145] 'Withdrawal of Plans to Introduce Simplified IVAs and Authorised Persons – Question and Answers' (Insolvency Service, 2008) www.insolvencydirect.bis.gov.uk/insolvencyprofessionandlegislation/policychange/foum2007/plenarymeeting.htm.

[146] The Insolvency Service lost almost one third of staff and reduced its costs by a third from 2010 to 2012: House of Commons: Business, Innovation and Skills Committee (n. 91) Ev 60.

[147] 'Consumer Credit and Personal Insolvency Review: Summary of Responses on Consumer Credit and Formal Response on Personal Insolvency' https://assets.publishing.service.gov.uk/government/uploads/system/uploads/attachment_data/file/31840/11-1063-consumer-credit-and-personal-insolvency-responses.pdf accessed 5 November 2018 (Department for Business, Innovation and Skills); Ramsay, '*21st Century*' (n. 5) 76.

[148] Financial Guidance and Claims Act 2018 (2018 c. 10).

[149] J. Vass, 'Restoring Social Creativity to Immoderate Publics: The Case of the Financially Incontinent Citizen', *The Sociological Review* 61 (2013) 79, 83.

related legal aid (estimated at 75 per cent[150]) and advice mean that such assistance must be increasingly sought on market terms.[151] Changes to personal insolvency legislation – raising slightly the DRO debt ceiling and creditor bankruptcy petition threshold[152] – represent a classic example of 'legislating around the edges', rather than engaging in systemic reform.[153] These measures have had little impact, as creditor petitions increase as a proportion of bankruptcies, and DRO numbers grow more slowly than expected. Latest Government proposals to establish a 'breathing space' mechanism for debtors are tied to the proposed introduction of a consensual renegotiation procedure modelled on the Scottish Debt Arrangement Scheme.[154] This addition to the existing array of insolvency procedures would be based on voluntary debt rescheduling and full repayment, rather than statutorily mandated debt discharge.[155]

4.4.3 Judicial Shaping of the IVA 'Product': Contractual Bankruptcy and Creditors' Bargains

If policymakers and judges have shown a preference for 'market-based debt resolution'[156] at a systemic level in their non-interventionist positions, courts have more actively shaped the individual IVA procedure along similar lines. Even while basing its proposals for the IVA procedure on assumptions of efficient private business-to-business bargaining, the Cork Committee considered that the terms of IVAs could not be purely determined contractually. It proposed that in order for the instrument to

[150] Committee (n. 88) paras. 135–7.

[151] S. Kirwan, *Advising in Austerity: Reflections on Challenging Times for Advice Agencies* (Policy Press 2016); D. James, 'Owing Everyone: Debt Advice in the UK's Time of Austerity' Paper given at event *Austerity, Debt – What Alternatives?* held by LSE Works: Department of Anthropology in 2017.

[152] Insolvency Service, 'Insolvency Proceedings: Debt Relief Orders and the Bankruptcy Petition Limit: Call for Evidence' (n. 59); 'Insolvency Proceedings: Debt Relief Orders and the Bankruptcy Petition Limit – Call for Evidence: Analysis of Responses' (Insolvency Service, 2015).

[153] Graeber n. 6 above, 390–1.

[154] For an overview of this procedure and its place in the Scottish system, see D. McKenzie Skene, 'Plus Ça Change, Plus C'est La Même Chose? The Reform of Bankruptcy Law in Scotland', *Nottingham Insolvency Business Law eJournal* 3 (2015) 285.

[155] 'Breathing Space: Call for Evidence' (HM Treasury, 2017) www.gov.uk/government/consultations/breathing-space-call-for-evidence/breathing-space-call-for-evidence accessed 5 November 2018. See also Financial Guidance and Claims Act 2018 (2018 c. 10), ss. 6–7.

[156] International Monetary Fund (n. 12) 14.

achieve its objectives, certain 'mandatory terms' must apply to all arrangements. The committee limited the consensual nature of the process by proposing that a simple majority of creditors could approve an arrangement over the dissent of the minority, and that debtors should be guaranteed debt discharge after a repayment plan of a maximum of three years (mirroring the time limit then applicable to debtors' wait for bankruptcy discharge).[157] In another divergence between Committee and policymakers, the Conservative Government adopted an approach more orientated towards private ordering in its enactment of the IVA procedure. Its legislation required a super majority of 75 per cent (in value) of creditors for the approval of debtor proposals, while establishing a bare legislative framework for the procedure, without any statutorily implied mandatory terms. When faced with this 'tenuous statutory guidance',[158] courts have built the IVA mechanism along a clear contractarian model. Judges have decided that the rights and obligations of debtors and creditors are to be determined primarily in accordance with the doctrine of freedom of contract, rather than by reference to principles and policy aims of insolvency law.

In key decisions, courts have held that contractual negotiation should determine answers to central questions of bankruptcy policy, including the very granting of debt discharge under the IVA, the conditions for accessing the procedure and the finality of the procedure – in other words, the extent to which it grants the debtor a 'fresh start'. In each case, the courts reached conclusions favourable to creditor interests that were far from inevitable and in so doing frustrated the law's debt relief aim. The decision of *Johnson* v. *Davies* was a key early authority on the nature of the IVA.[159] Here the Court of Appeal held that where a debtor is granted discharge under an IVA, her co-debtor is not automatically discharged by operation of law, but her discharge 'depends entirely on the terms of the arrangement. One must look at the arrangement, and nothing else, in order to find the terms (if any) under which the debtor is discharged'.[160] Much later in the development of the IVA into a mass consumer remedy, the High Court in *Mond* v. *MBNA Europe Bank Ltd* held that the introduction of the consumer IVA Protocol did not change the contractual nature of the IVA, and the Protocol does not prevent a creditor from acting in its own self-interest in rejecting a debtor

[157] Cork (n. 22) 387, 396–7.
[158] Milman (n. 125) 397.
[159] *Johnson and Another* v. *Davies and Another* (1998) [1999] ch. 117.
[160] *Johnson*, 138.

proposal for whatever reasons it may choose.[161] In the most recent judicial statements on the nature of IVAs, the High Court and Court of Appeal held respectively that creditor claims remain live even where an IVA has ended due to 'effluxion of time' (rather than through their issuing of a certificate of termination or completion),[162] and that a compensation award in favour of a debtor in respect of mis-sold financial products should be held on trust for her creditors, even if received after completion of an IVA.[163]

All of these cases shape the IVA procedure along a contractarian paradigm. The Court of Appeal in *Johnson* cited the legislature's 'deliberate decision' that the IVA should be consensual in nature, in holding that rather than terms being imposed by law, creditors are bound under a 'statutory hypothesis' that requires dissenting creditors to be 'treated as if they had consented to the arrangement'.[164] Similarly in *Mond*, the High Court held that the IVA protocol, as a 'voluntary industry standard or a code of best practice', 'does not ... seek to set out the terms of any contract by which the IVA provider and the creditors ... are to be bound in law'.[165] In *Phillips*, the High Court asserted similarly that 'IVAs are voluntary, and obtain their force from contract', in contrast to a mandatory bankruptcy or corporate administration procedure, which 'derives its force from a court order'.[166] This leads courts to see the positions of debtors and creditors under IVAs as being 'no different from [the position] under the general law',[167] where 'the general law' seems to mean a natural order of 'neutral and rational principles' which always prevail unless legislative *intervention* clearly indicates the contrary.[168] Courts make clear their reluctance to imply terms into an arrangement, even where such terms might be necessary to ensure the discharge of debt (as in *Johnson*) or to ensure that debtors are not forced

161 *Mond and Another* v. *MBNA Europe Bank Ltd* (2010) [2010] BPIR 1167; Ramsay, *'21st Century'* (n. 5) 97–8.

162 *The Co-Operative Bank Plc* v. *Phillips* [2017] EWHC 1320 (Ch).

163 *Green (Supervisor of the IVA of Wright)* v. *Wright* (2017) [2017] EWCA Civ 111.

164 *'Johnson'* (n. 159).

165 *'Mond'* (n. 161) [29].

166 *'Phillips'* (n. 162) [37].

167 *Raja* v. *Rubin and Another* Court of Appeal, England and Wales [1999] 3 WLR 606, [2000] Ch 274, 287; D. Milman, *Personal Insolvency Law, Regulation and Policy* (Ashgate Publishing Limited, 2005) 131–2.

168 For critical discussions of reasoning of this kind, see e.g. I. Ramsay, 'Consumer Credit Law, Distributive Justice and the Welfare State', *Oxford Journal of Legal Studies* 15 (1995) 177, 196; G. Howells and S. Weatherill, Consumer Protection Law 2nd revised edn (Avebury Technical, 2005) 8–10, 78–80.

into long-term DMPs that deprive them of a 'fresh start' (an outcome the court lamented, but did little to avoid, in *Mond*).

Judicial opposition to such intervention in the natural contractual order seems based on faith in the efficiency of private ordering, and classic reactionary arguments that such interventions will in fact hurt the people they aim to protect,[169] by dissuading businesses from offering to contract with disadvantaged consumers.[170] According to the court in *Johnson*, an unregulated purely consensual IVA framework benefitted debtors as well as creditors, since without mandatory or implied protective terms a debtor is 'free' to present an IVA proposal that is sufficiently attractive to creditors as to encourage them to release the debtor from her liabilities.[171] Similarly, the *Mond* court held that where creditors rejected a debtor's proposal despite their acceptance of the IVA Protocol, 'the remedy lies in modifying the terms of the proposal';[172] in other words in the debtor raising her offer to creditors in a quid pro quo for debt forgiveness. Whether intentionally or not, both these statements show judges viewing increased contractual freedom as tending towards increased repayment to creditors. The reasoning mirrors Jackson's contractarian 'creditors' bargain model' or Adler's proposal for 'self-authored insolvency',[173] in considering that voluntary bargaining will produce flexible solutions which better serve both debtor and creditor interests than government-mandated outcomes,[174] as well as serving general welfare by allocating resources efficiently. It reveals a concurrent underlying assumption that efficient resource allocation involves making credit widely available at the lowest cost, an outcome seen to be facilitated by maximising returns to creditors.[175]

This leads to the particular and partial form of contractarianism adopted by the courts in relation to the IVA. The courts profess to be drawing on the contractual nature of the arrangement and literal interpretations. They rely extensively, however, on processes of 'deemed consent' and 'implied agreement'. Judges have been much more open to having recourse to general principle and implied terms where to do so advances the aim of maximising

169 A. O. Hirschman, *The Rhetoric of Reaction: Perversity, Futility, Jeopardy* (Harvard University Press, 1991) 11–2.

170 See e.g. *Amoco Oil* v. *Ashcraft* (1986) 791 F 2d 519 (Court of Appeals, 7th Circuit) [10], *per* Posner J.

171 '*Johnson*' (n. 156), p. 138.

172 '*Mond*' (n. 161) [80].

173 Adler (n. 13) 235–6.

174 World Bank (n. 19) para. 129.

175 See pages 77–81 above.

returns to creditors. In *Johnson*, while the court refused to imply a term guaranteeing discharge to a co-debtor, it nonetheless implied a term providing that creditors could not exercise individual remedies during the term of the arrangement, deeming this term necessary to the IVA's operation. Similarly in *Mond*, while the court found that it was not unreasonable for a creditor to act self-interestedly and without regard to the public interest in providing debt relief, it nonetheless judged whether the creditor's conduct was 'unfair towards other creditors'.[176] In both scenarios the courts interpret arrangements by reference to general principles of insolvency law, but only principles of creditor cooperation and equality of creditors central to the 'creditors' bargain' perspective and associated with maximising returns to creditors.[177] David Richards LJ in *Green* makes explicit the judicial perception that the IVA procedure serves the aim of maximising returns to creditors, and evidences clearly the failure to see a public interest in debt relief. The judge saw 'no good reason' why the trust of debtor assets held for creditors under an IVA should cease after the debtor's completion of the arrangement, given that the 'underlying purpose' of the IVA is to apply the debtor's property towards creditor repayment, in return for creditors refraining from enforcing against the debtor. This trend becomes even clearer in *Phillips*. Here HHJ Matthews departed from express wording of the arrangement providing for a maximum duration of the repayment plan. When the debtor argued that these words extinguished creditor claims after the expiry of the stated period, the judge rejected a literal interpretation of this term, stating that 'it makes no commercial sense' for creditors to agree to the debtor's release from her debts on the expiry of an agreed period of time.[178] Similarly, the court held that under an IVA the 'parties impliedly agree that for the term of the arrangement, time shall not run', so that statutory limitation periods are suspended and creditor claims do not expire. This meant that creditor claims remained live after the period specified in the arrangement, delaying any possible fresh start, with all the negative policy consequences this might produce.[179]

176 *'Mond'* (n. 161) [74].

177 Thus when asked what are necessary terms of the 'statutory hypothesis', the court produced the same answer as offered by Professor Jackson's hypothetical 'creditors' bargain': creditors would hypothetically agree to halt individual enforcement actions and cooperate in collectively sharing the debtor's resources among them: Jackson (n. 13) 10 *et seq.*

178 *'Phillips'* (n. 162) [53].

179 See e.g. D. Jimenez, 'Ending Perpetual Debts', *Houston Law Review* 55 (2017) 609.

Despite judicial statements to the contrary, these cases demonstrate an unconventional approach to contractual interpretation that appears based more on Jackson's hypothetical bargain between creditors than any true agreement of a debtor and her creditors. Outcomes depart from more obvious interpretations of the language of IVA terms. They produce situations in which creditor claims persist beyond statutory time limits and stated maximum IVA durations, and trusts of debtor property remain open after an IVA's 'completion'. Just like Jackson's theory, the hypothetical agreement excludes the debtor,[180] as the objective perspective of a rational debtor is not considered in these interpretative exercises.[181] It 'makes no commercial sense' for a debtor to waive her statutory rights under limitation legislation (as the court held to have been the case in *Phillips*), or to agree to an arrangement that does not discharge her co-debtor (as in *Johnson*). Similarly, there is every 'good reason' for a rational debtor to contract for the discharge of her debts on expiry of a fixed term (as in *Phillips*), or to exempt her property from seizure on 'completion' of the arrangement (as in *Green*). The debtor is not permitted to pursue her rational self-interest to any meaningful effect, however, as courts permit only interpretations involving the debtor agreeing to an arrangement that produces a commercially beneficial outcome for creditors.[182] The asymmetric interpretative approach reflects little of the classical contract law paradigm of mutually beneficial exchange. Instead, in aligning with what is often considered a pro-creditor English private law,[183] it strengthens arguments that our economic system is founded more on the relationship of debt than exchange, and that 'the debtor is "free", but [her] actions, [her] behaviour, are confined to the limits defined by the debt

[180] K. Gross, *Failure and Forgiveness: Rebalancing the Bankruptcy System* (Yale University Press, 1997) 137–8.

[181] This approach seems at odds with the objective theory of interpretation under English law. For a recent description of this approach, see Lord Neuberger's statement that when 'interpreting a written contract, the court is concerned to identify the intention of the parties by reference to "what a reasonable person having all the background knowledge which would have been available to the parties would have understood them to be using the language in the contract to mean"': *Arnold* v. *Britton & Ors* [2015] UKSC 36 [15], citing Lord Hoffmann in *Chartbrook Ltd* v. *Persimmon Homes Ltd & Ors* [2009] UKHL 38 [14].

[182] See also how courts have even authorised modifications to IVA proposals without debtor consent: S. Barber, 'Involuntary Arrangements' *Insolvency Intelligence* [2014] 113.

[183] L. F. O'Mahoney, J. Devenney and M. Kenny, 'England and Wales' in S. Weatherill and A. Colombi Ciacchi (eds.), Regulating Unfair Banking Practices in Europe: the Case of Personal Suretyships (Oxford University Press, 2010) 170.

[she] has entered into'.[184] Unlike theoretical views of corporate insolvency 'work-outs', these were not 'win-win' cases.[185] Courts could not produce mutually beneficial interpretations, revealing how the law cannot balance aims of maximising returns to creditors and offering debt relief to over-indebted households. The courts firmly chose to prioritise the objective of maximising returns to creditors, effectively to the exclusion of the debt relief aim. While the contrast between business-to-business corporate work-outs and consumer bankruptcy is often one between private ordering and redistributive intervention, the courts in these cases cannot even claim to offer a coherent position along this dichotomy. Judges professed the merits of contractual freedom while intervening robustly to imply terms where necessary to produce outcomes maximising returns to creditors. This is particularly concerning given the questions involved and their impact on debtors' access to relief (*Mond*) and the effectiveness of the fresh start they receive (*Johnson, Phillips, Green*).[186]

4.5 Conclusion

Policymakers, and especially courts, have created an insolvency marketplace founded on principles of consumer choice and relatively unrestricted private bargaining. Questions of 'rational sorting' as between rapid debt discharge and long-term repayment plans,[187] or between statutorily mandated debt discharge and voluntary renegotiated personal insolvency procedures, are considered 'vital considerations that should precede a discussion of formal regime design'.[188] In England and Wales, these questions are often neglected in policy discussions, while courts and

[184] M. Lazzarato and J. D. Jordan, *The Making of the Indebted Man: Essay on the Neoliberal Condition* reprint edn (Massachusetts Institute of Technology Press, 2012) 31.

[185] See e.g. S. Block-Lieb, 'Austerity, Debt Overhang, and the Design of International Standards on Sovereign, Corporate and Consumer Debt Restructuring Symposium', *Indiana Journal of Global Legal Studies* 22 (2015) 487, 536; Ramsay, *'21st Century'* (n. 5) 16.

[186] The *Green* case in particular offers a reminder of the potential macroeconomic benefits of bankruptcy's debt relief. It relates to compensation arising from a payment protection insurance (PPI) mis-selling scandal. Widespread compensation awards to mis-sold customers have been shown to have had a significant positive impact on growth: E. Kempson, 'What Explains the Low Impact of the Financial Crisis on Levels of Arrears among UK Households?' in F. Ferretti (ed.), *Comparative Perspectives of Consumer Over-Indebtedness* (Eleven International Publishing, 2016) 79.

[187] Braucher (n. 42).

[188] World Bank (n. 19) para. 127.

policymakers seem content to rely on market mechanisms to resolve them. A commercialised approach to public service provision has rationed access to mandatory, and comparatively generous, debt relief procedures of bankruptcy and DROs. By protecting creditors from the losses associated with generous such debt relief, this removes creditors from the 'shadow of the law' and strengthens their bargaining position,[189] tilting the system towards favourable creditor outcomes. Meanwhile creditors have maximum freedom to reject debtor IVA proposals or to dictate the terms on which they will accept such proposals, with courts claiming to apply neutral and literal methods while tending to interpret ambiguous arrangements in favour of maximising creditor returns.

The influence of neoliberal ideas over this shaping of an insolvency marketplace is clear.[190] The position shows hallmarks of ideas of New Public Management, as government agencies adopt the logic of business management and treat themselves as firms, delivering commercialised services on market terms.[191] For example, during parliamentary hearings the Insolvency Service did not base its concerns regarding the exclusionary effects of upfront bankruptcy fees on their impact in limiting the ability of the procedure to fulfil its public policy function. Rather, the Service was worried that debt management companies' acceptance of fee payments in instalments over the course of a repayment plan means that their product holds a competitive 'advantage' in the marketplace, meaning that the Insolvency Service attracts insufficient customers to fund itself on a cost recovery basis.[192]

A preference among policymakers and courts for voluntary renegotiation shows great faith in the efficiency of private ordering,[193] and mirrors contemporary trends towards viewing private law 'as an exclusively

[189] See e.g. R. H. Mnookin and L. Kornhauser, 'Bargaining in the Shadow of the Law: The Case of Divorce', *The Yale Law Journal* 88 (1979) 950.

[190] See also Ramsay, 'A Tale of Two Debtors' (n. 16) 245–8; Ramsay, 'Bankruptcy in Transition Neoliberal' (n. 25); I. Ramsay, 'Between Neo-Liberalism and the Social Market: Approaches to Debt Adjustment and Consumer Insolvency in the EU', *Journal of Consumer Policy* 35 (2012) 421

[191] Hood and Dixon (n. 90) ch. 1; Crouch (n. 51); Brown (n. 90) ch. 1.

[192] Business, Innovation and Skills Committee, 'The Insolvency Service' (House of Commons, 2013) Report of Session 2012–13 (n. 6) para. 42.

[193] See e.g. a statement of the Coalition Government that 'while regulation can sometimes be necessary, much can be achieved through other means. A voluntary approach can have clear benefits not just for business but for consumers as well': Department for Business, Innovation and Skills (n. 147) 3; Ramsay, '*21st Century*' (n. 5) 76.

private affair best resolved by the parties rather than being considered in the public arena of the trial'.[194] For reasons shown in the next chapter, a model of formal equality and 'free contracting' in debt renegotiation tends to produce outcomes favouring creditor interests. The model of bargaining applied by the courts in interpreting IVAs goes further, however, in departing from ideals of free exchange and moving towards a relation of debt under which debtors are subject to severe contracting constraints. Those who view the turn to neoliberal economic organisation as a political project of class power might see in the English case the substantial influence of the financial sector (and related intermediaries) over policy and practice. In the USA, the Bankruptcy Abuse and Consumer Protection Act 2005 has been portrayed as a shift of responsibility and risk from the financial sector onto households (and ultimately frequently onto the state), achieved through intensive political lobbying by financial sector interests.[195] UK banks have also exerted influence 'through their political action in the IVA marketplace' and influence over living standards in DMPs through the industry development of the Standard Financial Statement.[196] They have therefore achieved even better outcomes than their US counterparts in staving off regulation (for example in their defeat of Insolvency Service proposals to reform the IVA procedure), and restricting access to the 'legal safe havens for delinquent debtors' offered by bankruptcy and DROs.[197] This exposes debtors 'to more pronounced and prolonged market discipline' by keeping them 'servicing debt obligations both inside and outside the bankruptcy system'.[198] That the development of English law fits with critiques of neoliberal disciplinary debt markets is supported by the emphasis placed on individual responsibility both in justifying bankruptcy and

[194] Mulcahy (n. 11) 60. For similar views in relation to consumer bankruptcy, see J. Kilborn, 'Creeping Privatization of Justice – Credit Slips' (Credit Slips, 27 March 2013) www.creditslips.org/creditslips/2013/03/privatized-justice.html#more accessed 5 November 2018.

[195] L. E. Coco, 'The Cultural Logics of the Bankruptcy Abuse Prevention and Consumer Protection Act of 2005: Fiscal Identities and Financial Failure', *Critical Sociology* 40 (2014) 711; A. Roberts and S. Soederberg, 'Politicizing Debt and Denaturalizing the "New Normal"', *Critical Sociology* 40 (2014) 657; Soederberg (n. 120) 86–97.

[196] Ramsay, '*21st Century*' (n. 5) 103. For information on the Standard Financial Statement, see https://sfs.moneyadviceservice.org.uk/en/what-is-the-standard-financial-statement accessed 5 November 2018.

[197] Soederberg (n. 120) 87.

[198] Coco (n. 195) 711.

DRO access conditions and in the individualistic judicial interpretations of IVA contracts.

Those who object to these neoliberal ideas outright criticise the distortion of public services involved by their commercialisation,[199] and the conversion of 'the distinctly *political* character, meaning, and operation of democracy's constituent elements into *economic* ones.' (emphasis in original)[200] While these critiques are convincing, the approach of this book, and the following chapter, is to apply the logic of *market failure* to show that the policy equilibrium reached by English law does not succeed even on its own terms.[201] Whether by conditioning debt relief on creditor consent[202] or financial contributions of the debtor, ultimately the position arrived at in English law suggests a lack of acknowledgement of the public policy benefits of household debt relief, and that it might be worth paying for these benefits. The latest policy document considering the question of insolvency fees (treating together both corporate and personal insolvency without distinction) stated that the

> economic rationale for government intervention in insolvency and bankruptcy cases is that it is necessary to ensure a collective approach is taken by creditors when dealing with those companies in financial distress in response to the "prisoner's dilemma" faced by creditors.[203]

This is a statement drawing directly from Jackson's creditors' bargain thesis, presenting a view of bankruptcy as solely serving the aim of maximising returns to creditors. The previous chapter has shown general flaws in this contractarian theory, and the following chapter exposes its weakness when applied to the particular context of contemporary household over-indebtedness.

[199] Crouch (n. 51) 86.

[200] Brown (n. 90) 17.

[201] See e.g. page 75 above.

[202] The reasoning in the above-mentioned IVA cases reverts to the position of historical bankruptcy laws under which the debtor's discharge was not automatic, but rather depended on creditor assent: see e.g. P. Shuchman, 'An Attempt at a "Philosophy of Bankruptcy"', *UCLA Law Review* 21 (1973) 403, 451; C. J. Tabb, 'The Historical Evolution of the Bankruptcy Discharge' *American Bankruptcy Law Journal* 65 (1991) 325, 337. It was only through making discharge independent of consent that the law established an independent objective of debt relief: C. G. Hallinan, 'The Fresh Start Policy in Consumer Bankruptcy: A Historical Inventory and an Interpretive Theory', *University of Richmond Law Review* 21 (1986) 49, 60.

[203] Insolvency Service, 'A New Fee Structure for Official Receiver Services: Impact Assessment' (n. 92) 4.

5

The Limits of Contractual Consumer Bankruptcy

5.1 'Market-Based Debt Resolution' and Post-Crisis Consensus

The previous chapter has shown how English law has developed a marketised structure of personal insolvency law, based on competition between public and private debt solutions.[1] Similarly, in respect of the most commonly used options of IVAs and DMPs, a paradigm applies of maximum contractual freedom and minimal regulatory intervention in the terms of rescheduling arrangements. Undoubtedly the approach has been influenced by the historical roots of the law in corporate insolvency. In particular the judicial shaping of the IVA has treated the procedure analogously to corporate insolvency mechanisms,[2] despite its 'conversion' into a remedy for financially troubled households.[3] The previous chapter has also shown how neoliberal and financialised trends of political economy favour private ordering and minimal state involvement. The contemporary English position aligns with models of 'market-based debt resolution'[4] advocated by bodies such as the IMF, and adopted in

[1] See the discussion of the similar Canadian structure: S. Ben-Ishai and S. Schwartz, 'Credit Counselling in Canada: An Empirical Examination', *Canadian Journal of Law and Society/ La Revue Canadienne Droit et Société* 29 (2014) 1.

[2] *The Co-Operative Bank Plc* v. *Phillips* [2017] EWHC 1320 (Ch) [37]; In *Re NT Gallagher & Sons Ltd* [2002] Court of Appeal, England and Wales [2002] EWCA Civ 404, [2002] 1 WLR 2380.

[3] I. Ramsay, *Personal Insolvency in the 21st Century: A Comparative Analysis of the US and Europe* (Hart Publishing, 2017) 86–92.

[4] 'Dealing with Household Debt', World Economic Outlook 2012 (International Monetary Fund, 2012) 14 www.imf.org/external/pubs/ft/weo/2012/01/pdf/c3.pdf accessed 5 November 2018; M. Erbenova, Y. Liu and M. Saxegaard, 'Corporate and Household Debt Distress in Latvia: Strengthening the Incentives for a Market-Based Approach to Debt Resolution' IMF Working Paper, WP/11/85 (International Monetary Fund, 2011).

several countries,[5] as post-crisis responses to problems of household debt. These models promote 'out of court restructuring' as 'a speedy, cost effective, and market friendly alternative to formal insolvency procedures'. They view the role of the public sector as 'confined to (i) [securing] a reasonably predictable macroeconomic environment, including through strengthening the banking system and (ii) [implementing] legal and institutional reforms to encourage timely market-based restructuring ... including the removal of tax and regulatory obstacles.'[6] Only in exceptional crises will 'direct government intervention in private debt restructuring' be appropriate, as 'any interference in the market mechanism necessarily causes distortions and is often associated with additional budgetary outlays', while also raising concerns of moral hazard.[7]

This chapter takes issue with this perspective and questions the appropriateness of 'market-based debt resolution' in the context of contemporary household over-indebtedness. A market failure analysis highlights how key assumptions of the efficient market hypothesis do not hold under these conditions. While Chapter 3 illustrated the contracting failures that arise in *ex ante* credit markets, such failures are even more likely to arise in the *ex post* bankruptcy market. Consequently, a bankruptcy system based on debtor choice between procedures and dominated by consensual renegotiation is likely to produce a 'market friendly' approach only where the 'market' is understood as industries of creditors and intermediaries.[8] Contrary to the ideal of mutually beneficial exchange,

www.imf.org/external/pubs/cat/longres.cfm?sk=24802.0 accessed 5 November 2018; Y. Liu and C. B. Rosenberg, 'Dealing with Private Debt Distress in the Wake of the European Financial Crisis: A Review of the Economics and Legal Toolbox' IMF Working Paper WP/13/44 International Monetary Fund, 2013).

5 For accounts of US post-crisis mortgage restructuring programmes, see A. M White, 'Deleveraging the American Homeowner: The Failure of 2008 Voluntary Mortgage Contract Modifications,' *Connecticut Law Review* 41 (2008) 1107; A. J. Levitin, 'Resolving the Foreclosure Crisis: Modification of Mortgages in Bankruptcy', *Wisconsin Law Review* 2009 (2009) 565; International Monetary Fund (n. 4) 22–5; For comparison with Irish and Greek measures, respectively, see J. Spooner, 'The Quiet-Loud-Quiet Politics of Post-Crisis Consumer Bankruptcy Law: The Case of Ireland and the Troika', *Modern Law Review* 81 (5) (2018) 790–82; M. J. Mouzouraki, '(Failure to Set up an Efficient) Out-of-Court System to Deal with Debtors in Financial Distress in Greece' in F. Ferretti (ed.), *Comparative Perspectives of Consumer Over-Indebtedness* (Eleven International Publishing, 2016).

6 Liu and Rosenberg (n. 4) 7, 10, 13.

7 ibid, 17.

8 Note Crouch's distinction between 'market' and 'corporate' neoliberals, where the former are dedicated to producing perfect markets, and the latter to defending corporations

it is increasingly visible that the outcomes produced by such an approach are detrimental to debtors. Given the increasingly recognised public interest case for household debt relief, these outcomes also raise pressing public policy concerns.

5.2 The Consumer Bankruptcy Market

A central assumption of the efficient market ideal is that actors behave according to their preferences and constantly seek to maximise their utility.[9] Under rational choice models, debtors should therefore enter the debt resolution market seeking the most extensive debt relief at the lowest cost.[10] Creditors in turn can be assumed to seek to minimise losses and recover as much as possible from the defaulting debtor. Corporate restructuring models are based on the belief that the process of debtor-creditor bargaining will produce mutually beneficial arrangements and 'win-win' outcomes. As Chapter 4 illustrates, it becomes quickly apparent in the consumer context, however, that debt restructuring represents a zero-sum game between debtors and creditors.[11] This chapter illustrates the market failures that might explain why debtors are increasingly 'choosing' IVAs and DMPs over the more advantageous bankruptcy and DRO procedures, and how a marketised personal insolvency structure produces inefficient and regressive transfers from debtors to creditors.

In terms of direct costs and benefits, this behaviour does not fit with an ideal of debtor rationality.[12] While bankruptcy and DRO procedures

currently operating (and dominating) in these markets. Crouch argues that corporate neoliberalism 'fatally undermines the pure market condition and entire rhetoric about customers' freedom to choose that remains a fundamental part of the case for neoliberalism': C. Crouch, *Can Neoliberalism Be Saved From Itself?* (Social Europe Edition, 2017) 19–20.

9 M. Trebilcock, *The Limits of Freedom of Contract* new edn (Harvard University Press, 1997) 3–4.

10 S. Block-Lieb and E. J. Janger, 'The Myth of the Rational Borrower: Rationality, Behavioralism, and the Misguided Reform of Bankruptcy Law', *Texas Law Review* 84 (2005) 1481.

11 S. Block-Lieb, 'Austerity, Debt Overhang, and the Design of International Standards on Sovereign, Corporate and Consumer Debt Restructuring Symposium', *Indiana Journal of Global Legal Studies* 22 (2015) 487, 536; Ramsay, '*21st Century*' (n. 3) 16.

12 Note that many debtors indeed report that the IVA and/or DMP processes were not what they had expected and express disappointment in their decisions to enter these procedures, particularly on being informed of alternatives that had been available: B. Rowe and others, 'Financial Conduct Authority Consumer Credit Research: Payday Loans, Logbook

involve upfront fees (£680 and £90 approximately), these are substantially lower than the fees a debtor can expect to pay under an IVA or commercially provided DMP, where amounts run into several thousands of pounds. Bankruptcy and DROs offer guaranteed debt discharge after just one year, while under IVAs and DMPs discharge is subject to creditor consent and may only be made available after several years. Only approximately 15–20 per cent of debtors entering bankruptcy will be required to contribute available income to creditors, while debtors in the 'no income, no asset' DRO procedure make no contributions. This contrasts strongly with IVAs and DMPs, where debtors must make repayments as demanded by creditors for several years. Under an IVA, a debtor can expect to repay approximately 40 per cent of her debt and receive a discharge in respect of the remainder,[13] but a DMP offers no debt relief and merely extends the time during which a debtor can make full repayment. Rising bankruptcy rates generated extensive debate in US bankruptcy literature as to whether they resulted from opportunistic debtor behaviour taking advantage of overly generous laws, or merely from the good faith actions of households who had fallen into hopeless financial distress.[14] The English system raises a contrasting puzzle as to why, in a system ostensibly built upon market principles of consumer choice, debtors are opting in increasingly large numbers for options that run counter to their financial interests.[15]

Arguments have been made that IVAs hold the advantage of allowing debtors to retain assets that would be lost in bankruptcy,[16] including potentially the debtor's home.[17] This explanation loses force, however,

Loans and Debt Management Services' (ESRO, Financial Conduct Authority, 2014) 39, 41.

13 Review of the Impact of the IVA Protocol (Insolvency Service, 2009) 18; 'Living on Tick: The 21st Century Debtor' (PricewaterhouseCoopers, 2006) 3.

14 Block-Lieb and Janger (n. 10); T. A. Sullivan, E. Warren and J. L. Westbrook, 'Less Stigma or More Financial Distress: An Empirical Analysis of the Extraordinary Increase in Bankruptcy Filings', *Stanford Law Review* 59 (2006) 213.

15 By now there is an expanding bank of evidence suggesting that US bankruptcy law suffers from precisely the opposite problem to that which concerns US scholars in the above-mentioned debate – at present large numbers of debtors do not file for bankruptcy even where it would be financially beneficial and 'rational' for them to do so: P. Foohey and others, 'Life in the Sweatbox', *Notre Dame Law Review* (94 (2018) – forthcoming).

16 A. Walters, 'Individual Voluntary Arrangements: A "Fresh Start" for Salaried Consumer Debtors in England and Wales', *International Insolvency Review* 18 (2009) 5, 20–1.

17 In bankruptcy, a debtor is afforded a one-year "grace period" during which she and her family may continue to live at home. Also, the property is sold only where the debtor's interest is worth more than £1,000, meaning that for debtors in 'negative equity', the decision regarding the fate of a home lies with the relevant mortgage lender. Insolvency

when one realises that only approximately 20 per cent of IVA debtors are homeowners (compared to 75 per cent of US debtors using the Chapter 13 repayment plan procedure, where the aim of saving homes is key[18]).[19] While one must look beyond financial benefits to consider how debt solutions offer relief from stress, health difficulties, and related problems associated with over-indebtedness,[20] again the rapid debt discharge offered under bankruptcy and DROs seem to provide these benefits to a greater degree than living under the precarity of a long-term payment plan in an IVA or DMP. Feelings of shame and stigma continue to influence debtors' thinking on bankruptcy,[21] and the Financial Conduct Authority reports evidence of intermediaries leveraging 'misconceptions, or wider negative attitudes in society', in order to encourage debtors to shun bankruptcy and DROs and sign up for lucrative IVAs or DMPs.[22] Surveys have found that IVA debtors value the sense of 'doing the right thing' that they feel from making partial debt repayment.[23] This ignores, however, the ability of debtors to make affordable payments through bankruptcy's Income Payment Order/ Undertaking procedure, and the fact that a DRO is only available to debtors lacking any ability to pay. Further, given policy efforts to reduce the stigma of bankruptcy over the past two decades (see Chapter 7), it is concerning if stigma holds such influence over the delivery of debt relief.

In presenting the IVA as 'the best product in the market' for both debtors and creditors, the Insolvency Service argues that the IVA offers 'more control

Act 1986, ss. 313, 336–8; Insolvency Rules 2016/1024, rules 14.15–14.19; I. F. Fletcher, *The Law of Insolvency* 4th revised edn (Sweet & Maxwell, 2009) paras. 8–002, 8–032, 9–073.

18 K. Porter, 'The Pretend Solution: An Empirical Study of Bankruptcy Outcomes', *Texas Law Review* 90 (2011) 103, 135–7; M. B. Culhane, 'No Forwarding Address' in K. Porter (ed.), *Broke: How Debt Bankrupts the Middle Class* (Stanford University Press, 2012) 122 *et seq.*

19 'The Debt Review' (TDX Group, 2016) www.tdxgroup.com/getattachment/e09ab7a2-2e92-4218-bad6-d4f7ce22cc37/.aspx accessed 5 November 2018.

20 See e.g. R. Mann and K. Porter, 'Saving Up for Bankruptcy' (Social Science Research Network, 2010) SSRN Scholarly Paper ID 1540216 313–8 http://papers.ssrn.com/abstract=1540216 accessed 5 November 2018; Porter (n. 18) 142–4.

21 Recent US empirical research has shown that feelings of shame are particularly common among those debtors who delay entry to bankruptcy for long periods as they seek to struggle through their debt difficulties: Foohey and others (n. 15).

22 'Quality of Debt Management Advice' Thematic Review TR15/8 25 (Financial Conduct Authority, 2015).

23 Survey of Debtors and Supervisors of Individual Voluntary Arrangements (Insolvency Service, 2008) 17; B. Rowe and others (n. 12) 34. Some case studies suggest, however, that debtor feelings of stigma might not distinguish between various insolvency procedures: PricewaterhouseCoopers (n. 13) 15.

of the process' than bankruptcy.[24] One might question, however, the level of control held by an IVA debtor who must pass all income, except that required for a minimal standard of living, to an Insolvency Practitioner for several years. Indeed, the apparent recent trend of 'involuntary arrangements' illustrates that debtor input into the IVA process is so limited that creditors and intermediaries can modify her proposal without her consent.[25] When surveyed, IVA and DMP debtors report feeling trapped due to having passed on data and lender communication to intermediaries, leaving them unsure as to how to regain control of their situations when problems arise.[26] The Service further states that the IVA 'provides certainty in both repayment levels and duration, together with the opportunity for debt forgiveness'.[27] All of these elements are also provided to a much greater extent by bankruptcy and DROs, however, and through legal guarantees rather than creditor concessions. Finally, the Service argues that an IVA 'is less punitive on the debtor (in terms of the restrictions imposed) than bankruptcy'.[28] As Chapter 7 argues, reforms under the Enterprise Act 2002 mean that this factor is relevant to only a small minority of culpable and/or professional debtors.[29] It is questionable whether the sanctions imposed transparently and in a procedurally fair manner under DRO and bankruptcy procedures are more punitive than the discipline imposed by creditors, intermediaries and credit reference agencies through 'market-based debt resolution' methods.[30]

In contrast to the above account, the benefits to creditors and intermediaries of the current state of personal insolvency law are obvious. Debtors are diverted away from the bankruptcy and DRO procedures that involve greatest loss to creditors and that provide no opportunity for intermediaries to earn fees. In theory, individual creditors might have incentives to divert defaulting debtors out of collective solutions entirely,

[24] 'Improving Individual Voluntary Arrangements' (Insolvency Service, 2005) para. 21; Insolvency Service, *Survey of Debtors and Supervisors of Individual Voluntary Arrangements* (n. 23) 17.

[25] S. Barber, 'Involuntary Arrangements', *Insolvency Intelligence* (2014) 113.

[26] Rowe and others (n. 12) 40.

[27] Insolvency Service, 'Improving Individual Voluntary Arrangements' (n. 24) para. 21.

[28] 'A Consultation Document on Proposed Changes to the Individual Voluntary Arrangement (IVA) Regime' (Insolvency Service) para. 3.

[29] One 2006 study found only 5 per cent of its sample of IVA debtors were categorised as professionals: PricewaterhouseCoopers (n. 13) 17.

[30] The control exerted by creditors over IVA debtors is visible in court statements emphasising that debt relief under an IVA is conditional on the debtor performing as demanded by creditors: *'Phillips'* (n. 2) [50].

in order to pursue individual enforcement. The disproportionate costs of individual enforcement,[31] and the benefits of collective processes as enunciated in the creditors' bargain theory,[32] mean that these incentives are not great, however. In terms of collective solutions, debt management plans may advance creditor interests even more than IVAs, as well as appealing to creditors who are opposed in principle to any debt reduction.[33] The *Mond* case illustrates how creditors may wish to use the 'holdout'[34] power created by the 75 per cent IVA approval threshold to extract more value by diverting debtors into DMPs.[35] The non-binding nature of a DMP (in a collective arrangement, but especially in a bilateral DMP) gives creditors flexibility to retain crucial control over cases,[36] and permits them to adapt to changing circumstances, protecting against wasted 'self-cure' and 're-default' costs.[37] From the perspective of creditors and intermediaries, various factors may thus explain why DMPs outnumber IVAs. The development of the IVA Protocol, however, suggests that an equilibrium has been brokered regarding the operation of the IVA that is satisfactory to both these groups. The freedom afforded to creditors in setting IVA terms by a bare legislative framework and

[31] *Report on the Treatment of the Insolvency of Natural Persons* (World Bank, 2013) paras. 59–68; G. Bertola, R. Disney and C. Grant, 'The Economics of Consumer Demand and Supply', *Economics of Consumer Credit* (Massachusetts Institute of Technology Press, 2006) 14, 18.

[32] T. H. Jackson, *The Logic and Limits of Bankruptcy Law* (Harvard University Press, 1986) 10–14.

[33] Such creditor policies have caused problems in voluntary renegotiation schemes in other jurisdictions: World Bank (n. 31) para. 131.

[34] See e.g. M. L. Stearns and T. J. Zywicki, *Stearns and Zywicki's Public Choice Concepts and Applications in Law* (West Academic Publishing, 2009) 17–18.

[35] In *Mond*, the creditor in question had a policy of rejecting IVA proposals where the debtor could repay their debt within a 10-year period via a DMP. A 2009 Insolvency Service survey found that when dealing with certain creditors, IVA providers did not even propose arrangements, as they were aware of these creditors' policies of rejecting IVA proposals whenever they held veto power: Insolvency Service, *Review of the Impact of the IVA Protocol* (n. 13) 29. On creditors using holdout power to extract value, see e.g. D. A. Moss and G. A. Johnson, 'The Rise of Consumer Bankruptcy: Evolution, Revolution, or Both', *American Bankruptcy Law Journal* 73 (1999) 311, 318–19.

[36] Professor Rock's classic sociological study of debt collection explains the value of control to creditors: 'The transfer of control from the creditor to another institution is always attended by risks . . . . One of the chief difficulties . . . is [the] likelihood that a debtor will be redefined and consequently treated with what is thought to be excessive leniency.' See P. Rock, *Making People Pay* 1st edn (Routledge & Kegan Paul Books, 1973) 68.

[37] M. Adelino and others, 'Why Don't Lenders Renegotiate More Home Mortgages?' 7 (National Bureau of Economic Research, 2009), www.nber.org/papers/w15159 accessed 5 November 2018.

permissive judiciary (as described in Chapter 4) might leave them confident that they can extract any available value from a debtor through an IVA in any case, reducing incentives to divert debtors into DMPs.

5.3 Failures in the Consumer Bankruptcy Market

Far from the ideal of mutually beneficial outcomes, the marketised consumer bankruptcy system delivers positive results for creditors and intermediaries, at the expense of producing the least favourable outcomes for debtors. These results bear the hallmark of a market replete with failures, and the following discussion outlines the features of the consumer bankruptcy market that contribute to suboptimal outcomes.

5.3.1 Intermediation and Principal-Agent Problems

Studies of consumer bankruptcy place great importance on the role of intermediaries in these systems.[38] Literature has established that bankruptcy laws that require debtors to rely on the services of intermediaries to navigate the system create a new *ex post* consumer protection problem,[39] adding to the problems in *ex ante* credit markets that bankruptcy laws aim to address. The reliance of debtors on intermediaries raises classic agency problems, as the interests of intermediaries may diverge from those of the debtors they represent.[40] Starting with Jean Braucher's seminal study,[41] evidence from the US bankruptcy system shows that attorneys exert determinative influence over consumers' 'choice' between Chapter 7 (rapid discharge) and Chapter 13 (long-term repayment plan) procedures. Recent studies have confirmed these findings and added depth of insight, showing that both the financial

[38] World Bank (n. 31); I. Ramsay, 'Market Imperatives, Professional Discretion and the Role of Intermediaries in Consumer Bankruptcy: A Comparative Study of the Canadian Trustee in Bankruptcy', *American Bankruptcy Law Journal* 74 (2000) 399; I. Ramsay, 'Interest Groups and the Politics of Consumer Bankruptcy Reform in Canada', *University of Toronto Law Journal* 53 (2003) 379.

[39] W. C. Whitford, 'The Ideal of Individualized Justice: Consumer Bankruptcy as Consumer Protection, and Consumer Protection in Consumer Bankruptcy', *American Bankruptcy Law Journal* 68 (1994) 397, 403.

[40] F. McIntyre, D. M. Sullivan and L. Summers, 'Lawyers Steer Clients toward Lucrative Filings: Evidence from Consumer Bankruptcies', *American Law and Economics Review* 17 (2015) 245.

[41] J. Braucher, 'Lawyers and Consumer Bankruptcy: One Code, Many Cultures', *American Bankruptcy Law Journal* 67 (1993) 501.

interests and the moral values of attorneys direct large numbers of debtors into Chapter 13, even when this procedure appears not to serve these debtors best.[42] One paper shows that Chapter 13 filing rates are higher in bankruptcy courts that allow attorneys to charge higher fees, supporting 'the notion that lawyers can and do manipulate their client's filings to increase their revenues'.[43] Outside the USA, 'mystery shopper' research in Canada also offers evidence of intermediaries providing suspect and opaque advice, and recommending lucrative solutions that often would produce outcomes less favourable to clients than the publicly provided option of bankruptcy.[44] It is perhaps unsurprising that intermediaries have a substantial influence over the personal insolvency system in England and Wales, and on outcomes for the debtors entering it.

First, intermediary activity appears influential in the decline of bankruptcy petitions and the concomitant rise of DMPs and IVAs. The pricing structures of insolvency practitioners (IPs) and commercial debt advice agencies acknowledge the reality that an upfront fee can play a crucial role in deterring liquidity-constrained debtors from accessing bankruptcy.[45] Therefore these intermediaries accept payment staggered throughout the duration of an IVA or DMP.[46] Intermediaries lack any financial incentive to recommend that a debtor opt for the 'unmanaged' solution of bankruptcy, from which no fees can be earned.[47] In line with the expectations of principal-agent theory, a 2015 report of the Financial Conduct Authority (FCA) found that intermediaries who have a financial incentive to direct debtors into income-producing solutions tend to steer debtors into such procedures and direct them away from bankruptcy and DROs.[48] The authority found that advice firms, and particularly those charging fees, 'often failed to give fair and balanced information and advice about some insolvency solutions such as bankruptcy and debt relief orders'.[49]

42 P. Foohey and others, 'No Money down Bankruptcy', *Southern California Law Review* 90 (2016) [i]; J. Braucher, D. Cohen and R. M. Lawless, 'Race, Attorney Influence, and Bankruptcy Chapter Choice', *Journal of Empirical Legal Studies* 9 (2012) 393.

43 McIntyre, Sullivan and Summers (n. 40).

44 Ben-Ishai and Schwartz (n. 1).

45 S. Albanesi and J. Nosal, 'Insolvency after the 2005 Bankruptcy Reform' (Federal Reserve Bank of New York 2015) Federal Reserve Bank of New York Staff Report No. 725 2.

46 Insolvency Service, *Survey of Debtors and Supervisors of Individual Voluntary Arrangements* (n. 23) 9–10; Insolvency Service, *Review of the Impact of the IVA Protocol* (n. 13) 13–14; House of Commons: Business, Innovation and Skills Committee, 'The Insolvency Service' (House of Commons 2013) Report of Session 2012–13 (n. 6) para. 42.

47 Walters (n. 16) 34.

48 Financial Conduct Authority, 'Quality of Debt Management Advice' (n. 22).

49 ibid, 25.

This mirrored earlier findings of the Office of Fair Trading (OFT) that firms were not 'offering the solution that is in the best interests of the consumer but instead that which is most profitable to them'.[50] Firms have become adept at identifying more profitable clients while leaving to bankruptcy or DROs those without assets or income sufficient to generate fee income. In recent years, however, IVA firms have evolved their business practices to generate profit even from low-income clients.[51] The eligibility of such low-income debtors for the comparatively generous debt relief offered under DROs heightens concerns of mis-selling in this sector.

Intermediaries are active in recruiting clients, with regulators criticising marketing tactics bordering on aggressive.[52] The OFT found widespread misleading advertising in the debt management market, and that advisors 'generally lack sufficient competence and are providing consumers with poor advice based on inadequate information'.[53] The complexity of the consumer bankruptcy marketplace adds to these problems. Debtors do not 'shop around' for the best advice, and the FCA reported that often debtors have not even been seeking debt management services when first coming into contact with an advice agency.[54] Technological advances mean that debtors can readily be introduced to a firm through unsolicited marketing, as link generation and contact purchasing services operate widely in this sector.[55] The FCA found that these factors combine to render debtors 'susceptible to influence', leading to 'choices that are not in their best interests'. In response to its findings, the FCA has applied strict standards to debt management firms required to reapply for authorisation on the transfer of regulatory powers to the FCA from the OFT. The FCA has withdrawn authorisation from several firms,[56] while both the FCA and the Insolvency Service have taken or supported investigation and enforcement action against firms engaged in misconduct.[57] The FCA is not authorised to

50 See Office of Fair Trading, 'Debt Management Guidance Compliance Review' (2010) OFT1274 para. 1.20.

51 See pages 132–133 above.

52 Office of Fair Trading (n. 50) 7.

53 ibid.

54 Financial Conduct Authority, 'Quality of Debt Management Advice' (n. 22) 10.

55 ibid, 4.82.

56 'The Financial Conduct Authority Warns Clients of Three Debt Management Firms to Review Their Debts' (Financial Conduct Authority, 21 May 2015) www.fca.org.uk/news/press-releases/financial-conduct-authority-warns-clients-three-debt-management-firms-review accessed 23 February 2018.

57 '15 Month Suspended Sentence for Director of Debt Management Firm' (Financial Conduct Authority, 28 April 2016) www.fca.org.uk/news/news-stories/15-month-suspended-sentence-director-debt-management-firm accessed 23 February 2018; 'Debt

regulate the Insolvency Practitioners who provide IVAs, however. These practitioners are instead regulated by a range of professional bodies under the overarching supervision of the Insolvency Service.[58] This position has led some firms to engage in regulatory arbitrage, changing their business models to offer IVAs rather than DMPs in order to evade FCA regulation.[59] Meanwhile firms that offer only IVAs, and so were unaffected by changes in DMP regulation, 'have invested in marketing, acquisition and growth'.[60] The increased momentum in the rise of IVA numbers, therefore, can be linked to these regulatory trends.

In addition to principal-agent problems influencing the 'choice' of debt solution, they may also influence the substantive repayment terms of IVAs and DMPs. As a legal matter, under an IVA an intermediary's duty is not solely to advise the debtor but involves 'public duties' to creditors and the courts.[61] As a matter of business practice, intermediaries have a strong interest in maintaining good business relations with creditors,[62] who are 'repeat customers' (unlike a debtor who may use the practitioner's services only once). Due to the need to maintain low costs in a 'high volume, low value' industry, intermediaries are also incentivised to propose the repayment terms most likely to be accepted by creditors in order to save resources, rather than 'fighting' to negotiate the most appropriate terms for an individual debtor.[63] Therefore agency costs may result not only in debtors being diverted away from the lower cost and higher quality debt relief 'products' of bankruptcy and DROs, but may also contribute towards onerous repayment terms which assure even more negative outcomes for debtors once they have been diverted into an IVA or DMP.

Management Directors Disqualified for a Combined 11 and a Half Years' (Insolvency Service, 13 February 2018) www.gov.uk/government/news/debt-management-directors-disqualified-for-a-combined-11-and-a-half-years accessed 23 February 2018.

58 See e.g. L. Conway, 'Regulation of Insolvency Practitioners' (House of Commons Library, 2016) Briefing Paper Number CBP5531.

59 'Sector Views 2017' (Financial Conduct Authority, 2017) 23; 'Insolvency Market Trends: Review of 2017' (TDX Group, 2017).

60 'Insolvency Market Trends: January 2018 Update' (TDX Group, 2018).

61 See e.g. Statement of Insolvency Practice 3 (SIP3), Joint Insolvency Committee, 2007, 1.5. The Insolvency Service IVA review made it clear that the practitioner owes a duty to produce outcomes favourable to creditors: Insolvency Service, 'Improving Individual Voluntary Arrangements' (n. 24) paras. 32–5. See also D. Milman, *Personal Insolvency Law, Regulation and Policy* (Ashgate Publishing Limited. 2005) 79, discussing *Pitt* v. *Mond* [2001] BPIR 624.

62 For evidence of this problem in the market for *corporate* insolvency practitioners, see e.g. 'The Market for Corporate Insolvency Practitioners: A Market Study' (Office of Fair Trading, 2010).

63 Whitford (n. 39) 401.

5.3.2 *Contracting Failures and the Limits of Consensual Household Debt Restructuring*

Leaving aside intermediaries and adopting a simple stylised model of debtor-creditor negotiations,[64] contracting failures arising in debtor-creditor negotiations will generally lead to problems in consumer bankruptcy systems involving consensual debt restructuring. For example, if regulatory reforms of the type being pursued by the FCA succeed in producing alignment between the interests of debtors and intermediaries, certain problems remain inherent to household debt restructuring, irrespective of various market, institutional and regulatory arrangements. While the consumer protection problems relating to intermediaries are reasonably well documented in the literature and visible to policymakers, contracting failures inherent to consensual renegotiation schemes are less widely discussed. This chapter therefore argues that policymakers' continued faith in contractual household debt restructuring and 'market-based debt resolution' is misplaced.

First, a basic precondition for an efficient market is that all parties can enter and exit the market freely.[65] Debtors rarely enter the debt resolution market intentionally,[66] and have little option to leave once facing the pressures of over-indebtedness and collection efforts.[67] Exit through bankruptcy and the DRO procedure is restricted, and a debtor who finds her creditors unwilling to offer favourable terms in an IVA or a DMP cannot 'shop around' and decide to negotiate with an alternative set of creditors. Furthermore, there are no competitive pressures which could encourage creditors to offer more favourable renegotiation terms.[68] In fact creditors may fear that offering generous terms will signal

[64] While acknowledging that in practice third parties such as nominees and debt purchasers may step into the role of creditors: Ramsay, '*21st Century*' (n. 3) 74.

[65] I. Ramsay, *Consumer Law and Policy: Text and Materials on Regulating Consumer Markets* 3rd revised edn (Hart Publishing, 2012) 47; Scott and J. Black, *Cranston's Consumers and the Law* 3rd edn (Butterworths 2000) 27.

[66] As most will not have intended to fall into default, and even among defaulters many are not 'shopping' for debt solutions when they come into contact with a debt management firm: Financial Conduct Authority, 'Quality of Debt Management Advice' (n. 22) 10.

[67] On the role of debt collection activities in pushing debtors into bankruptcy, see e.g. Foohey and others (n. 15).

[68] Creditors may see reputational costs associated with harsh treatment of defaulters: see A. A. Leff, 'Injury, Ignorance and Spite – The Dynamics of Coercive Collection', *Yale Law Journal* 80 (1970) 1, 35. These concerns can be alleviated, however, by minimising the outward flow of information regarding IVA or DMP negotiations, or by using debt collection agencies and other third parties to recover their funds.

to other debtors to seek renegotiation rather than struggling to repay in full, raising 'free rider' and adverse selection problems.[69] Meanwhile creditors can freely exit the market either by refusing to accept any debt resolution offer other than full repayment, or by selling defaulted loans to debt purchasing agencies.

Secondly, while an efficient market requires that all actors hold perfect information,[70] significant information asymmetries exist between creditors and consumer debtors in the debt restructuring market.[71] Creditors are 'repeat players' in this market, while a consumer debtor is likely to be experiencing it for the first time.[72] This means that a debtor will not benefit from the 'learning effect' which is a theoretical feature of efficient markets.[73] Further, learning possibilities are limited as people tend to feel uncomfortable discussing financial affairs generally,[74] with those in financial difficulty often experiencing particular shame.[75] This means that debtors who have been through debt solutions are unlikely to communicate their experiences widely, furthering reducing information flow.[76] Consumer debtors are also likely to be uninformed regarding the range of 'products' in the market due to their lack of knowledge of often complex insolvency legislation.[77] Information regarding the 'going rate' of debt

[69] J. R. Andritzky, 'Resolving Residential Mortgage Distress: Time to Modify?' (International Monetary Fund, 2014) IMF Working Paper WP/14/226 28 www.imf.org/external/pubs/cat/longres.aspx?sk=42532.0 accessed 21 April 2015.

[70] See J. E. Stiglitz, 'The Contributions of the Economics of Information to Twentieth Century Economics', *The Quarterly Journal of Economics* 115 (2000) 1441.

[71] See e.g. Whitford (n. 39) 403.

[72] For a classic discussion of 'repeat players' v. 'one shotters', see M. Galanter, 'Why the "Haves" Come out Ahead: Speculations on the Limits of Legal Change', *Law & Society Review* 9 (1974) 95.

[73] Scott and Black (n. 65) 33; P. Lunn, 'Can Policy Improve Our Financial Decision-Making?' (Economic and Social Research Institute, 2012) Paper 8 9.

[74] See e.g. M. De Muynck, 'Credit Cards, Overdraft Facilities and European Consumer Protection – A Blank Cheque for Unfairness?', *European Review of Private Law* 18 (2010) 1181, 1194–5.

[75] See e.g. B. T. White, 'Underwater and Not Walking Away: Shame, Fear, and the Social Management of the Housing Crisis', *Wake Forest Law Review* 45 (2010) 971; P. Ali, L. O'Brien and I. Ramsay, '"Short a Few Quid": Bankruptcy Stigma in Contemporary Australia', *University of New South Wales Law Journal* 38 (2015) 1575.

[76] See, however, how online platforms have created new spaces for debtor communication and resistance: J. Deville, 'Debtor Publics: Tracking the Participatory Politics of Consumer Credit', *Consumption Markets & Culture* 19 (2016) 38; L. Stanley, J. Deville and J. Montgomerie, 'Digital Debt Management: The Everyday Life of Austerity', *New Formations* 87 (2016) 64.

[77] Surveys have shown that a majority of bankrupts (approximately 58 per cent and 64 per cent respectively) were unaware of a major reduction in the waiting period for

write-down typically offered by creditors is not available publicly, and creditors may exacerbate informational disadvantage by avoiding standardisation of debt forgiveness policies.[78] For example, IVA and DMP proposals are evaluated based on the Standard Financial Statement (SFS) developed by creditors and the advice sector. The standards used to calculate appropriate levels of debtor repayment under the SFS are unpublished, apparently due to fears that they might be 'gamed' by strategic debtors.[79] As Chapter 7 explores, creditors hold significant informational advantages in their proprietary credit scoring systems, creating circumstances under which a debtor faces an influential threat of unknowable adverse consequences unless she agrees to an arrangement favourable to her creditors.[80]

Debtor behaviour in the consumer bankruptcy market does not correspond to the rational choice model on which the efficient market hypothesis is based. The tendency of debtors to avoid bankruptcy and DROs cannot be assumed to reveal rational debtor preferences for alternative options. Instead it may simply be an effect of the liquidity constraints preventing debtors from accessing these more advantageous procedures.[81] Recent understandings of decision making under conditions of scarcity show that those lacking in resources are not necessarily less rational than their well-resourced peers, but must necessarily focus on immediate concerns to the detriment of long-term planning.[82] Behavioural economics research also points to cognitive biases that

discharge under English law: *Discharge from Bankruptcy* (Insolvency Service, 2006) 7; Tribe (n. 49) 67–8. See also A. Littwin, 'The Do-It-Yourself Mirage: Complexity in the Bankruptcy System', *Broke: How Debt Bankrupts the Middle Class* (Stanford University Press, 2012); P. Pleasence, N. J. Balmer and C. Denvir, 'Wrong about Rights: Public Knowledge of Key Areas of Consumer, Housing and Employment Law in England and Wales', *The Modern Law Review* 80 (2017) 836.

[78] For reports of inconsistencies in creditor positions, see Insolvency Service, *Review of the Impact of the IVA Protocol* (n. 13) para. 5.12. A lack of standardisation may serve to empower creditors and disempower debtors in restructuring negotiations: see J. Spooner, 'Long Overdue: What the Belated Reform of Irish Personal Insolvency Law Tells Us about Comparative Consumer Bankruptcy', *American Bankruptcy Law Journal* 86 (2012) 243, 265.

[79] See https://sfs.moneyadviceservice.org.uk/en/.

[80] White (n. 75) 1011; Stanley, Deville and Montgomerie (n. 76). Rock's studies of debt collection report that 'ambiguous threats are a … feature of [debt] collection. Enforcement would be discredited if it contained falsifiable predictions about action.' Rock (n. 36) 71–2.

[81] Albanesi and Nosal (n. 45).

[82] S. Mullainathan and E. Shafir, Scarcity: Why Having Too Little Means so Much (Times Books, 2013); J Griener, D. Jimenez and L. Lupica, 'Self-Help, Reimagined', *Indiana Law Journal* 92 (2017) 1119, 1126–1130.

may lead debtors into suboptimal outcomes. Optimism bias and time-inconsistent preferences may lead consumer debtors to overestimate their ability to comply with a rigorous repayment plan under an IVA or DMP over a number of years, leading them into an unsustainable or overly onerous arrangement.[83] Consumer debtors eager to end the stress of over-indebtedness,[84] and facing narrow time limits in which to make decisions,[85] may value the present benefits of immediate protection from enforcement over the underestimated costs of following an onerous repayment plan for several years into the future.[86]

Emotion and moral values appear to play a significant role in causing debtor decisions to depart from assumptions of rational financial calculation. Despite the financialisation and commercialisation of social life, and the demise of relational banking, debtors continue to view debt as a moral obligation founded on a relationship with their creditor. Surveys have found evidence that if a creditor has acted in a way perceived to be fair, a debtor may feel a moral compulsion to repay.[87] In a world of structural indebtedness, debtors appear to grasp for autonomy by restyling the patently unequal creditor-debtor relationship as one of reciprocal and equal exchange. Debtors similarly incur personal obligations to themselves to 'do the right thing', undergoing present sacrifice under the promise of future autonomy and 'debt freedom'.[88] While the 'self-evident' logic that 'one has to

[83] See e.g. the sources cited by C. J. Tabb, 'Of Contractarians and Bankruptcy Reform: A Skeptical View', *American Bankruptcy Institute Law Review* 12 (2004) 259, 263–4; J. J. Kilborn, 'Behavioral Economics, Overindebtedness &(and) Comparative Consumer Bankruptcy: Searching for Causes and Evaluating Solutions', *Emory Bankruptcy Developments Journal* 22 (2005) 13, 21; I. Ramsay, 'From Truth in Lending to Responsible Lending' in A. Janssen and G. Howells (eds.), *Information Rights and Obligations: The Impact on Party Autonomy and Contractual Fairness* (Avebury Technical, 2005) 52.

[84] For a discussion of the negative health effects of over-indebtedness, see *Consultation Paper on Personal Debt Management and Debt Enforcement* (Law Reform Commission of Ireland, 2009) paras. 1.11–1.15; S. Emami, 'Consumer Over-Indebtedness and Health Care Costs: How to Approach the Question from a Global Perspective', WHO World Health Report Background Paper 3 (World Health Organisation, 2010); N. Balmer and others, 'Worried Sick: The Experience of Debt Problems and Their Relationship with Health, Illness and Disability', *Social Policy and Society* 5 (2006) 39.

[85] Insolvency Service, *Review of the Impact of the IVA Protocol* (n. 13) 27–8.

[86] FCA reviews express particular concern that consumers enter debt solutions 'at their most desperate': Rowe and others (n. 12); Financial Conduct Authority, 'Quality of Debt Management Advice' (n. 22).

[87] F. Polletta and Z. Tufail, 'The Moral Obligations of Some Debts', *Sociological Forum* 29 (2014) 1.

[88] Stanley, Deville and Montgomerie (n. 76).

pay one's debts' is eternally powerful,[89] this sense of obligation to act against one's rational financial interests is particularly powerful in the political environment of austerity. Here a 'debt morality' prevails, according to which personal sacrifice is necessary and anyone unwilling to put in the 'hard work' of debt repayment risks being cast as an outsider and 'scrounger'.[90] Even the Deputy Governor of the Bank of England speaks of households 'working hard' in recent years to reduce historically high aggregate debt levels.[91] This politics entangles 'economic dependency and moral failure . . . in the form of debt'.[92] Contemporary studies show debtors feeling self-recrimination and expectations of punishment,[93] while citizens generally accept that they 'deserve' the hardship of austerity in atonement for debt-fuelled economic growth.[94] These feelings of shame or guilt might drive consumers to financially disadvantageous decisions, including entry into long-term repayment plans over the rapid discharge of bankruptcy or DROs. Creditors hold power to influence these feelings at the micro level through pleas to the debtor's moral obligations to repay,[95] and at the macro level by purveying messages of 'payment morality' in the media and public debate.[96]

Where empirical evidence exists, consumer bankruptcy literature illustrates clearly that procedures involving long-term repayment plans produce worse outcomes for debtors than those offering rapid discharge.[97]

[89] D. Graeber, Debt: The First 5,000 Years (Melville House, 2012) 2–4.

[90] K. Forkert, 'The New Moralism: Austerity, Silencing and Debt Morality', *Soundings: A journal of politics and culture* 56 (2014) 41.

[91] G. Wearden and N. Fletcher, 'UK Firms More Pessimistic about Brexit, Bank of England Says – as It Happened' *The Guardian* (28 June 2018) www.theguardian.com/business/live/2018/jun/28/bank-of-england-household-debts-cunliffe-haldane-markets-us-growth-business-live accessed 4 July 2018.

[92] W. Davies, 'The New Neoliberalism', *New Left Review* 101 (2016) 121, 130.

[93] W. Davies, J. Montgomerie and S. Wallin, 'Financial Melancholia – Mental Health and Indebtedness' www.perc.org.uk/project_posts/financial-melancholia-mental-health-and-indebtedness/ accessed 20 July 2017.

[94] L. Stanley, '"We're Reaping What We Sowed": Everyday Crisis Narratives and Acquiescence to the Age of Austerity', *New Political Economy* 19 (2014) 895.

[95] The moral authority of creditors is embedded in the credibility of their communications with debtors, which is to some degree a performance: Stanley, Deville and Montgomerie (n. 76); J. Deville, *Lived Economies of Default: Consumer Credit, Debt Collection and the Capture of Affect* (Routledge, 2015).

[96] White (n. 75) 996–1007.

[97] It should be noted that research suggests entry into bankruptcy repayment plans under Chapter 13 produces better outcomes for debtors than not entering into bankruptcy: W. Dobbie and J. Song, 'Debt Relief and Debtor Outcomes: Measuring the Effects of Consumer Bankruptcy Protection', *American Economic Review* 105 (2015) 1272.

This point appears so self-evident as not to require empirical studies to prove it, but such studies have been necessary due to the ongoing support for repayment plan options among creditors, judges, practitioners, and policymakers.[98] As ever in consumer bankruptcy studies, the most developed research comes from the US bankruptcy system, in which research has consistently found that in approximately two thirds of Chapter 13 cases, debtors do not complete the required repayment plan and so are denied the benefits of debt relief.[99] Benefits of Chapter 13 for debtors in 'failed' cases are temporary at best, and such debtors who are denied discharge also do not achieve the aims that drove their decisions to enter bankruptcy: saving their homes and lifting stress.[100] Indeed, those debtors who entered Chapter 13 specifically to avoid foreclosure were more likely to see their cases fail, along with other vulnerable groups such as African American debtors, debtors with young children, and debtors lacking medical insurance or legal representation.[101] Inability to pay the upfront attorney fees necessary to enter Chapter 7 push many liquidity constrained debtors into a 'no money down' Chapter 13 plan allowing staggered payment of fees. This diversion into a procedure less likely to produce intended outcomes makes debt discharge a more remote possibility for debtors falling into this situation.[102] Disparities in this effect fall along geographical and racial lines.

It is unsurprising that the diversion of debtors into IVAs and DMPs under the English system might produce similarly negative outcomes for debtors. Indeed, debtors are placed in a weaker position by the freedom of creditors to set the terms of IVAs and DMPs, in contrast to the position under Chapter 13 where a court sets the debtor's obligations.

Consistent with the above analysis, the limited number of empirical studies of IVA bargaining show 'general agreement that IVA terms are currently overly dictated by creditor groups'[103] and that 'the debtor is effectively powerless'.[104] Creditors have leveraged this power to extend

The following discussion therefore emphasises how Chapter 13 outcomes are less favourable to debtors than outcomes produced by Chapter 7's immediate debt discharge.

98 S. S. Greene, P. Patel and K. Porter, 'Cracking the Code: An Empirical Analysis of Consumer Bankruptcy Outcomes', *Minnesota Law Review* 101 (2016), 1031.

99 Porter (n. 18); Braucher, Cohen and Lawless (n. 42); Greene, Patel and Porter (n. 98); Foohey and others (n. 42).

100 Porter (n. 18).

101 Greene, Patel and Porter (n. 98).

102 Foohey and others (n. 42).

103 S. Morgan, 'Causes of Early Failures in Individual Voluntary Arrangements' (2008) 41.

104 M. Green, 'Individual Voluntary Arrangements Over-Indebtedness and the Insolvency Regime: Short Form Report' (University of Wales, 2002) 8.

the durations of IVAs and to extract higher levels of repayment from debtors. Insolvency Service research in the late 2000s showed creditors refusing to accept a debtor's initial proposal without requiring modifications in a large majority (between 70–97 per cent) of cases.[105] Most modifications related to dividends and distribution of repayments, the fees of the intermediary, and the levels of debtor contributions or the repayment plan duration. A 2009 Insolvency Service survey found that the average projected rate of returns to creditors in debtor proposals pre-modification was 35p in the £, but that this rose to 41p after modifications.[106] Arrangements requiring such high contributions risk becoming unsustainable, and surveys consistently identify unaffordable contributions as a primary reported cause of IVA failures.[107] Failure rates have also been rising steadily among IVAs commenced in the years since 2002, to the point that over 40 per cent of IVAs commenced in 2008 have failed (Figure 5.2).

A first significant victory on the part of creditors was the extension of repayment periods under IVAs. In the IVA procedure's early years about half of arrangements typically endured for less than one year,[108] while others tended to last for a period of up to three years.[109] This mirrored the three-year waiting period for automatic discharge from bankruptcy at the time (and the current maximum duration of repayments under a bankruptcy Income Payment Order/Agreement), and also reflected the recommendations of the Cork Committee.[110] Since the early 1990s, the durations of repayment periods have increased steadily, in a trend driven by creditors' desire to increase returns.[111] A consensus position is that IVAs now typical last for 5–6 years. Insolvency Service data show that this figure conceals significant minorities of longer-term plans, however. By the end of 2017, ongoing IVAs included over five per cent

[105] Insolvency Service, *Survey of Debtors and Supervisors of Individual Voluntary Arrangements* (n. 23) 30–4; Insolvency Service, *Review of the Impact of the IVA Protocol* (n. 13) 18, 27.

[106] Insolvency Service, *Review of the Impact of the IVA Protocol* (n. 13) 18.

[107] Morgan (n. 103) 42; Insolvency Service, *Survey of Debtors and Supervisors of Individual Voluntary Arrangements* (n. 23) 12; Insolvency Service, *Review of the Impact of the IVA Protocol* (n. 13) 18.

[108] K. Pond, 'Creditor Strategy in Individual Insolvency', *Managerial Finance* 28 (2002) 46, 56.

[109] Morgan (n. 103) 11.

[110] Sir Kenneth Cork, Insolvency Law and Practice: Report of the Review Committee (HMSO, 1982) para. 387.

[111] Morgan (n. 103) 11.

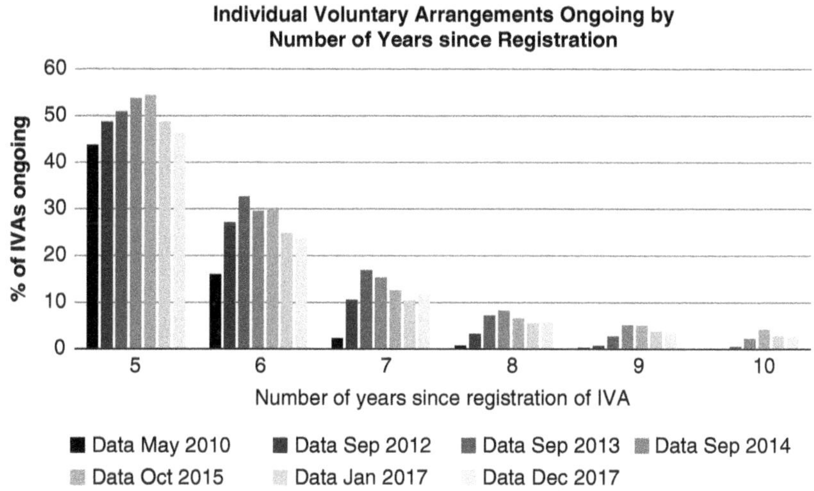

Figure 5.1: Individual voluntary arrangements ongoing by number of years since registration. Source: Compiled by author from The Insolvency Service data.

of arrangements commenced in 2009, over ten per cent of those started in 2010, and almost one quarter of those commenced in 2011. The proportion of longer-term IVAs has increased considerably compared to levels among IVAs commenced in the early 2000s (Figure 5.1).

While less evidence is available in respect of DMPs, even more concerning outcomes result from the diversion of debtors into these long-term payment plans. The FCA found many examples of fee charging debt management companies 'recommending very long debt management plans (often many decades long, some of 100+ years) when debt relief solutions are likely to have been more appropriate'.[112] The FCA also identified problems of unsustainably high repayments under DMPs, with firms for example deliberately misrepresenting debtors' income and expenditure levels in order to fit the debtor's case into a plan of sufficiently high payments to cover the firms' fees.[113] This is despite such firms being under a regulatory obligation to refer clients to non-fee-charging agencies when debtors have insufficient disposable income to pay fees. Other dubious practices involved firms using debtor payments to cover fees first before passing any payments to creditors, initially directing debtors into

[112] Financial Conduct Authority, 'Quality of Debt Management Advice' (n. 22) para. 4.55.
[113] ibid, 4.22, 4.34.

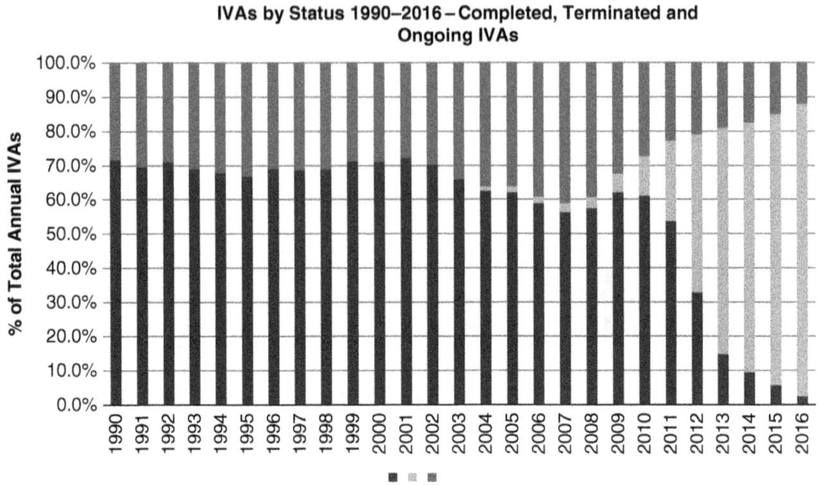

Figure 5.2: IVAs by 'Completed', 'Terminated' and 'Ongoing' status. Source: Insolvency Service

unsustainable DMPs before subsequently rolling over debtors into IVAs, and actively discouraging debtors from availing of free debt advice.[114]

Classic market failure theory acknowledges the need for regulatory intervention where markets impose negative externalities on non-contracting third parties.[115] If an insolvency procedure or non-statutory arrangement requires a debtor to participate in a prolonged repayment plan in which a large portion of her income is paid to creditors, the externalities of over-indebtedness continue to accrue.[116] When considering social costs associated with reduced consumption, poor health, lost productivity and social and political exclusion, it seems that conditions will vary little as between a debtor trapped in 'informal insolvency'[117] and a debtor who has entered into an onerous repayment plan spanning several years.[118] A consumer bankruptcy market that directs the majority of over-indebted consumers into long-term

[114] Rowe and others (n. 12) 38–43.
[115] Tabb (n. 83) 260, 266.
[116] See pages 86–93 above.
[117] Albanesi and Nosal (n. 45).
[118] Furthermore, debtors will most likely have endured considerable financial difficulty prior to seeking assistance: see e.g. Mann and Porter (n. 20) 313; Foohey and others (n. 15).

repayment plans absorbing all disposable income does little to internalise the social costs produced in credit markets.

5.4 Conclusions

Chapter 2 discusses how trends of deregulation, privatisation and financialisation mean that the formerly held belief of citizens in the state's delivery of positive outcomes has been substituted for an expectation among consumers that markets can deliver their needs. The turn to markets and the mantra of 'let them eat credit' allowed politicians to evade responsibility for adverse economic conditions and to hide from difficult distributional questions.[119] Eventually the reality must be addressed, however, that the 'privatised Keynesianism' model does not appear to deliver the prosperity necessary to pay for the expansion of household debt. policymakers in England and Wales have sought to repeat the same trick in passing responsibility to private firms and third sector agencies for addressing the inevitable problem of over-indebtedness produced by the household debt expansion.[120] By raising access fees and enacting substantive entry conditions, the state has rationed public provision of debt relief and reduced its role in addressing over-indebtedness. Financial capitalism has responded, as always, by drawing a new field of activity within its reach,[121] and developing a private personal insolvency system. While privatisation of this kind converts the state from provider to regulator, policymakers and courts have also limited public activity in this regulatory role. Legislative inaction has privatised policy making and handed responsibility for regulating the IVA procedure over to creditors and intermediaries through the IVA protocol. Judicial activism has shaped the IVA into a mechanism providing creditors with both maximum contractual freedom, and with the safeguard that any ambiguities or omissions in the contractual terms they set will apparently be resolved by reference to principles of creditor wealth maximisation. Just as prior chapters have raised questions as to the wider sustainability of the 'let them eat credit' model of economic

[119] G. R. Krippner, *Capitalizing on Crisis* Gld edition (Harvard University Press, 2012); R. G. Rajan, *Fault Lines: How Hidden Fractures Still Threaten the World Economy* (Princeton University Press, 2011).

[120] I. Ramsay, 'A Tale of Two Debtors: Responding to the Shock of Over-Indebtedness in France and England – a Story from the Trente Piteuses', *The Modern Law Review* 75 (2012) 212, 246.

[121] C. Crouch, *Post-Democracy* 1st edn (Polity Press, 2004) 79, 81.

organisation, Chapters 4 and 5 call for realism regarding the ability of a consumer bankruptcy market to deliver optimal outcomes.

Leaving aside typical criticisms that a marketised approach affords insufficient recognition to humanitarian concerns,[122] adding to the tendency of bankruptcy's technicality to de-personalise the law,[123] even those committed to the efficiency of markets must see imperfections in the consumer bankruptcy market. Conflicting incentives, liquidity constraints, information asymmetries, and behavioural issues arising in emotionally and morally fraught conditions inevitably produce market failures. A marketised system breeds complexity,[124] as seen in the introduction of a new consumer insolvency option by the conversion of the corporate insolvency IVA mechanism into a consumer remedy,[125] alongside the growth of mass-marketed DMPs, without focussing other products such as consolidation loans.[126] Limited transparency and understanding means that regulatory reviews have found that debtors often are unaware as to whether the programme in which they have enrolled in is an IVA or DMP.[127] In this context, alarms are raised by current government proposals to add further complexity through a new 'breathing space' or 'respite' mechanism coupled with another statutory debt rescheduling scheme (apparently offering a mere extension of repayment periods through contractual negotiation, without debt discharge).[128] Complexity requires consumers to engage professionals to assist in navigating the system, while increases in complexity add to the cost of such assistance in a manner that may exclude many.[129] Current regulatory efforts of the FCA to address the DMP market are promising and may produce positive outcomes. Regulation of the IVA procedure remains privatised, however. The Insolvency Service oversees practitioner

[122] See e.g. Trebilcock (n. 9) 23–4.
[123] P. Shuchman, 'An Attempt at a "Philosophy of Bankruptcy"', *UCLA Law Review* 21 (1973) 403, 420.
[124] Porter (n. 18) 113.
[125] Ramsay, *'21st Century'* (n. 3) 86–91.
[126] M. Green, 'New Labour: More Debt – The Political Response', *Consumer Credit, Debt and Bankruptcy: Comparative and International Perspectives* (Hart Publishing, 2009) 408; Rowe and others (n. 12) 33.
[127] Rowe and others (n. 12) 40.
[128] 'Breathing Space: Call for Evidence' (HM Treasury, 2017) www.gov.uk/government/consultations/breathing-space-call-for-evidence/breathing-space-call-for-evidence accessed 5 November 2018.
[129] J. Braucher, 'A Fresh Start for Personal Bankruptcy Reform: The Need for Simplification and a Single Portal', *American University Law Review* 55 (2005) 1295; Albanesi and Nosal (n. 45); Foohey and others (n. 42).

regulation carried out by a complex array of accountancy bodies, while the specific operation of the IVA is shaped by the voluntary IVA Protocol negotiated by banks and insolvency practitioners. The Insolvency Service and FCA have recently taken steps to adopt a more cooperative approach in carrying out their respective roles.[130]

Even if such regulatory efforts are wholly successful in facilitating debtors to navigate the system and enter into debt solutions best matching their preferences, in any bargaining process creditors will leverage contracting failures to achieve favourable bargains. Support for this position derives not just from the IVA experience, but also from the 'dismal failure' of the US Home Affordable Modification Program (HAMP).[131] This is another high-profile illustration of the tendency of voluntary household debt restructuring to lead to the twin problems of excluding suitable debtors from relief, while also offering to others relief composed of insufficient creditor concessions to achieve the public policy objectives of alleviating over-indebtedness. Australian experiences of the 'debt agreement' renegotiation procedure reveal similar problems to those arising in IVAs.[132] Post-crisis reforms in Ireland based on consensual renegotiation have been widely regarded as unsuccessful, even prompting legislators to depart from their initial voluntary model to introduce a limited 'cram-down' mechanism.[133] Classical contractual ideas and law-and-economics perspectives view contractual approaches as ill-suited to rectifying inequalities since contract law can only refuse to enforce contracts in limited circumstances and 'cannot compel the making of contracts on terms favourable to one party'.[134] In contrast, even the contractarian 'creditors' bargain' theory argues that the key feature of

[130] The Insolvency Service and Financial Conduct Authority, 'FCA and Insolvency Service Strengthen Relationship with MoU' (*GOV.UK*, 21 May 2018) www.gov.uk/government/news/fca-and-insolvency-service-strengthen-relationship-with-mou accessed 5 November 2018.

[131] Porter (n. 18) 114–116; International Monetary Fund (n. 4) 22–5; White (n. 5); P. A. McCoy, 'The Home Mortgage Foreclosure Crisis: Lessons Learned' (Social Science Research Network, 2013) SSRN Scholarly Paper ID 2254672 http://papers.ssrn.com/abstract=2254672 accessed 5 November 2018.

[132] V. Chen, L. O'Brien and I. Ramsay, 'An Evaluation of Debt Agreements in Australia', *Monash University Law Review* 44 (2018) https://papers.ssrn.com/abstract=3036315 accessed 5 November 2018; I. Ramsay and C. Sim, 'The Role and Use of Debt Agreements in Australian Personal Insolvency Law' (Social Science Research Network, 2011) SSRN Scholarly Paper ID 1942125 http://papers.ssrn.com/abstract=1942125 accessed 3 November 2018.

[133] Spooner (n. 5).

[134] *Amoco Oil* v. *Ashcraft* (1986) 791 F 2d 519 (Court of Appeals, 7th Circuit) [10].

insolvency law is its ability to compel optimal arrangements that the incentives of individual actors prevent from being achieved through bargaining. To view insolvency procedures purely in contractual terms misses this key element and the necessarily redistributive nature of the law,[135] and again reveals confusion regarding its core identity.

Prevailing trends of financialisation involve not just support for marketisation and contractualisation in the neoliberal belief that private ordering produces optimal outcomes, but also the idea that the economy and society benefit from maximising creditor interests. If policymakers' preferences for contractual household debt restructuring cannot be explained by reference to a 'blind spot' among policymakers as to the contracting failures that inevitably arise in *ex post* bankruptcy 'markets', perhaps they could be based on a confidence that suboptimal contracting outcomes are acceptable where benefits inure to creditors. As the early chapters of this book illustrate, justification is now thin for the idea that the economic priorities should lie with maximising returns to creditors, in the hope that this facilitates wide availability of cheap credit.[136] Whatever the merits of contractual repayment plans might be, their generation of greater returns to creditors (compared to rapid discharge procedures) can no longer be accepted as a justification. This idea remains influential, however, and Insolvency Service proposals to establish the IVA as the primary consumer insolvency remedy were strongly influenced by the consideration that the IVA is likely to produce larger returns to creditors than bankruptcy;[137] and so represents 'the best deal possible for creditors'.[138] The current law certainly benefits creditors, in extending market discipline into the insolvency system by confining most debtors to long-term repayment plans involving high creditor control and returns, even as financially troubled households turn to debt solutions as a safety net against the difficulties produced by credit markets.[139] Given the increasingly effective discipline of these markets (see Chapter 7)[140] and

[135] Fletcher (n. 17) paras. 3–002.

[136] Chapters 2 and 3 discuss how there is increasing technical consensus that 'financial deepening' and the expansion of household credit can produce more negative than positive outcomes from a public policy perspective.

[137] Insolvency Service, 'Improving Individual Voluntary Arrangements' (n. 24) paras. 22, 30, 33, 35.

[138] ibid, 33, 35.

[139] L. E. Coco, 'The Cultural Logics of the Bankruptcy Abuse Prevention and Consumer Protection Act of 2005: Fiscal Identities and Financial Failure', *Critical Sociology* 40 (2014) 711, 711.

[140] S. Soederberg, *Debtfare States and the Poverty Industry: Money, Discipline and the Surplus Population* (Routledge, 2014).

a private law singularly focused on enforcing contracts and protecting property rights,[141] it is unclear why the personal insolvency regime is directed at offering tools to maximise returns to creditors. As this book has argued, its public policy value lies instead in offering a counterbalance as a 'social insurer of last resort' or 'economic stabiliser'.[142] Rather than bankruptcy law acting as a means of reducing the problems of excessive household debt, the dominance of long-term repayment plans on onerous terms transforms the law into a pro-cyclical mechanism that exacerbates household debt difficulty and macroeconomic debt overhang problems. Given the departures of contemporary household over-indebtedness from the ideal conditions of the efficient market hypothesis, consumer bankruptcy seems a sphere of economic activity singularly unsuited to marketisation. The case for contractual bankruptcy or 'market-based debt resolution' appears increasingly unsupportable.

Political currents, path dependency, and an ambivalence of the law regarding its debt relief function pose considerable obstacles to reform, while this book only touches briefly on the further opposition produced by the influence of creditor and intermediary interest groups in maintaining the status quo.[143] Recognition of these realities should not constrain policy analysis, however, lest scholarship embed incumbent interests and ideas.[144] Studies of consumer bankruptcy in England and elsewhere offer some lessons as to the direction reforms should take. Proposals from US commentators for the creation of a single consumer insolvency portal appear equally attractive in the English context,[145] and a strong case exists for simplifying the insolvency regime by

141 On the 'pro-creditor bias' of the 'usual obligation orientation' of private law, see e.g. L. F. O'Mahoney, J. Devenney and M. Kenny, 'England and Wales' in S. Weatherill and A. C. Ciacchi (eds.), *Regulating Unfair Banking Practices in Europe: the Case of Personal Suretyships* (Oxford University Press, 2010) 170; M. Howard, 'A Theory of Discharge in Consumer Bankruptcy', *Ohio State Law Journal* 48 (1987) 1047, 1047–8.

142 See also Professor Westbrook's argument that consumer bankruptcy law should abandon any aim of collecting debts for financial institution creditors: J. Westbrook, 'The Retreat of American Bankruptcy Law', *QUT Law Review* 17 (2017) 40.

143 Several studies of collective action and public choice theory document the role of creditor and intermediary groups in shaping consumer bankruptcy law: see e.g. Spooner (n. 5); A. M. Dickerson, 'Regulating Bankruptcy: Public Choice, Ideology, &(and) Beyond', *Washington University Law Review* 84 (2006) 1861; Ramsay, 'Interest Groups and the Politics of Consumer Bankruptcy Reform in Canada' (n. 38); D. A. Skeel, *Debt's Dominion: A History of Bankruptcy Law in America* (Princeton University Press, 2001).

144 L. Zingales, 'Presidential Address: Does Finance Benefit Society?', *The Journal of Finance* 70 (2015) 1327, 1356.

145 Braucher (n. 129); Whitford (n. 39); Porter (n. 18) 154–6.

establishing a single consumer bankruptcy procedure.[146] The Debt Relief Order appears the most appropriate vehicle. This is the only English procedure designed specifically to address consumer over-indebtedness, distanced from the historical legacy of corporate law. Also, policymakers and courts have recognised this procedure as serving the purpose of 'unadulterated debt relief',[147] meaning that this aim should not be diluted by concerns of maximising returns to creditors. The most appropriate reform may be the expansion of this procedure beyond its current limited 'no income, no assets' remit to cover all personal insolvencies below a category of high net worth debtors, the insolvencies of whom may require more sophisticated procedures.[148] Asset exemptions and the Income Payment Order/Agreement mechanism applicable in bankruptcy could simply be carried over to the expanded DRO procedure. Importantly, the level of repayments would be calculated by a neutral administrative official with regard to the fresh start policy, rather than by creditors with the aim of maximising their returns (as is the case under the IVA). The approach should be 'less a matter of defining a predetermined benefit for creditors than of defining a predetermined level of sacrifice for debtors' necessary to address moral hazard concerns.[149]

Since at least the 1980s, determination to reduce public expenditure has dominated insolvency policy,[150] and such determination has been hardened by austerity policies of the post-crisis decade. There is a need to consider that the policy benefits of debt relief may be worth paying for, and a need for realism regarding the ability of a debt resolution market to

[146] The Cork Committee also proposed a 'single portal' of sorts, with multiple procedures potentially available after a common initial screening process, 'under which the court will have considerable latitude to decide upon the most appropriate method for dealing with the debtor's affairs': Cork (n. 110) paras. 272, 545–5.

[147] *R (Cooper and Payne)* v. *Secretary of State for Work and Pensions* [2011] BPIR 223 [85, *per* Toulson LJ].

[148] A useful concept might be the 'high net worth' debtor as contained in FCA regulatory rules and related legislation. Loan agreements are exempted from regulatory protection where the value is more than £60,260 and where it includes a debtor's declaration that she is a 'high net worth' individual, meaning that she earned no less than £150,000 and had net assets valued at £500,000 or more throughout the previous year. It might be appropriate to adjust these levels, particularly to allow the realisation in bankruptcy of substantial assets worth less than £500,000. See Financial Services and Markets Act 2000 (Regulated Activities) Order 2001 (SI 2001/544), art. 60H; Financial Conduct Authority Handbook CONC (Consumer Credit Sourcebook), App. 1.4.

[149] World Bank (n. 31) para. 274.

[150] Fletcher (n. 1) 81.

deliver optimal outcomes. If a marketised approach and privatised policy making can only direct debtors into arrangements that do not best meet their needs, and into long-term payment plans that only prolong over-indebtedness and debt overhang problems, then a strong case can be made for state intervention to internalise the social costs produced. This justifies the expansion of the DRO procedure to extend the availability of rapid and extensive debt relief and may make a case for increased contributions from creditors in funding debt relief procedures.[151] As well as encouraging responsible lending,[152] such developments might restore responsibility of policymakers for addressing the inevitable costs of the economic structures they have established. Given the increasing recognition of the adverse consequences of excessive household debt, this is no longer a time for 'a policy of muddling through'.[153]

151 See e.g. the levy imposed by Belgian law on consumer lenders based on the portion of their loan books in default in a given year: *Loi (du 19 avril 2002) modifiant la loi du 5 juillet 1998 relative au règlement collectif de dettes et à la possibilité de vente de gré à gré des biens immeubles saisis* (M.B. du 07/06/2002, p. 26229), art. 2 (Belgium). See also J. J. Kilborn, 'Continuity, Change and Innovation in Emerging Consumer Bankruptcy Systems: Belgium and Luxembourg', *American Bankruptcy Institute Law Review* 14 (2006) 69, 105.

152 For proposals to impose costs on lenders to sanction irresponsible lending, see e.g. J. A. E. Pottow, 'Private Liability for Reckless Consumer Lending', *University of Illinois Law Review* 2007 (2007) 405, 456 *et seq.*; J. J. Kilborn, '*La Responsabilisation de l'Economie*: What the United States Can Learn from the New French Law on Consumer Overindebtedness', *Michigan Journal of International Law* 26 (2004) 619, 669–71; V. Countryman, 'Improvident Credit Extension: A New Legal Concept Aborning?', *Maine Law Review* 27 (1975) 1.

153 Ramsay, 'A Tale of Two Debtors' (n. 120) 245.

6

The Austere Creditor: Austerity, Bankruptcy Policy and Government Debt Collection

6.1 Introduction

One factor contributing to the marketised personal insolvency structure in England and Wales is the influence of fiscal consolidation or austerity policies in shaping policymakers' preference for private solutions to debt problems (Individual Voluntary Arrangements and Debt Management Plans) over open access to public debt relief procedures of bankruptcy and Debt Relief Orders. This chapter continues to illustrate how austerity policies pursued by UK governments in the years following the global financial crisis have influenced other aspects of bankruptcy law, including the scope of the protection and debt relief offered to debtors, and the extent to which the law should be available to individual creditors as a collection tool. Austerity policies represent a continuation and acceleration of the 'loans for wages' and 'credit/welfare state trade-off' trends inherent in the financialised capitalism of recent decades, as wage stagnation and a shrinking social safety net leave the debt economy reliant on household borrowing to maintain growth and household living standards. In addition, a newfound zeal in government debt collection policies has increased the pressure on debt-laden households. These conditions challenge bankruptcy law, both in increasing need for household debt relief, and in changing the nature of problem debt from well-examined mortgage and unsecured consumer credit to understudied 'priority' debts – essential obligations such as rent arrears and debts owed to central and local government.[1] This environment provides a crucible in which to test English personal insolvency law's commitment to the 'fresh start' policy and the vision of bankruptcy as a form of social insurance.

[1] See e.g. London Assembly, Economy Committee, 'Final Demand: Personal Problem Debt in London' (Greater London Authority, 2015); 'Council Tax Debts: How to Deal with the Growing Arrears Crisis Tipping Families into Problem Debt' (StepChange Debt Charity, 2015); 'Changing Household Budgets' (Money Advice Trust, 2014).

While bankruptcy policymaking following the crisis has been notably absent,[2] this chapter aims to show that government has been shaping bankruptcy law and policy through administrative activity rather than express policymaking. As austerity policies have produced aggressive government debt collection efforts, local governments have increasingly sought to use bankruptcy law as a means of collecting council tax debts owed by home owning debtors. Similarly, the Department of Work and Pensions (DWP) has pursued an active litigation strategy in seeking to carve out an exemption from bankruptcy protection for such claims. In so doing, both local and national governments have revived an understanding of bankruptcy as a debt collection mechanism, and convinced courts to adopt an interpretation of the law as primarily serving an objective of the maximisation of creditor returns. This reopens the fissure between the law's competing objectives of debt collection and debt relief; and the divide between conceptions of the law as a commercial law tool for recovering debts, and as a redistributive social insurer of last resort. The result is the co-opting of bankruptcy into a tool for pursuing austerity policies and pro-cyclical bankruptcy policy, rather than the deployment of bankruptcy as a stabiliser against the economic, social and political pressures of austerity. In this way, we see changes in the nature of bankruptcy spurred not just by the shrinking, but also a tightening, of the social safety net.

Problems relating to government debt represent a wider issue of contemporary difficulties in relation to 'hidden' debts arising from everyday essential obligations,[3] such as rent arrears, utilities, tax debts, and debts arising through the welfare system. Consumer bankruptcy scholarship has tended to focus on the paradigm case of loans advanced by financial institutions – whether the soaring credit card lending of the pre-crisis boom,[4] or the mortgage debt crisis that followed,[5] and questions of

[2] See Chapter 1, part 1.4, Chapter 3.5.

[3] LSE Housing and Communities, 'Facing Debt: Economic Resilience in Newham' (LSE Centre for Analysis of Social Exclusion, 2014) CASE Report 83 19 http://sticerd.lse.ac.uk/dps/case/cr/casereport83.pdf accessed 5 November 2018.

[4] See e.g. I. Ramsay, 'Consumer Credit Society and Consumer Bankruptcy: Reflections on Credit Cards and Bankruptcy in the Informational Economy' in J. Niemi, I. Ramsay and W. C. Whitford (eds.), *Consumer Bankruptcy in Global Perspective* (Hart Publishing, 2003); R. J. Mann, 'Bankruptcy Reform and the Sweat Box of Credit Card Debt', *University of Illinois Law Review* 2007 (2007) 375; T. J. Zywicki, 'An Economic Analysis of the Consumer Bankruptcy Crisis', *Northwestern University Law Review* 99 (2004) 1463; E. Warren, 'The Over-Consumption Myth and Other Tales of Economics, Law, and Morality', *Washington University Law Quarterly* 82 (2004) 1485.

[5] See e.g. 'Dealing with Household Debt', World Economic Outlook 2012 (International Monetary Fund, 2012) www.imf.org/external/pubs/ft/weo/2012/01/pdf/c3.pdf accessed

whether bankruptcy laws should expand their scope to offer mortgage debt relief.[6] With some notable exceptions,[7] bankruptcy commentators and policymakers have paid less attention to how the law should treat 'hidden' debts. As these types of debt are now increasingly salient, bankruptcy law and policy must afford them new attention and find answers to the questions they pose. The framework proposed in Chapter 3 in arguing for reorientation of bankruptcy towards its debt relief goal is based primarily on a model of debt contracts advanced by a financial institution. An aim of this chapter is to extend the framework beyond this model to other categories of debt and creditors,[8] by focusing in particular on government debt. While discussing these salient policy issues, the chapter also highlights key features of bankruptcy law – the creditor bankruptcy petition procedure, and the scope of protection from debt collection and the extent of debt discharge offered to creditors. These hold great practical significance in determining the extent to which bankruptcy offers a fresh start to troubled debtors, while also raising conceptual questions regarding bankruptcy's aims, identities, and foundational ideas.

6.2 Household Debt at a Time of Austerity

6.2.1 Austerity Policies, Increased Household Financial Difficulties, and 'Priority Debts'

The shock of the financial crisis appears to have been insufficient to rupture the prevailing model of financialised capitalism that preceded

5 November 2018; M. Whittaker and K. Blacklock, 'Hangover Cure: Dealing with the Household Debt Overhang as Interest Rates Rise' (Resolution Foundation, 2014) www.resolutionfoundation.org/publications/hangover-cure-dealing-with-the-household-debt-overhang-as-interest-rates-rise/ accessed 5 November 2018; P. Bunn and M. Rostom, 'Household Debt and Spending in the UK' (Bank of England, 2015) 554.

6 See e.g. A. J. Levitin, 'Resolving the Foreclosure Crisis: Modification of Mortgages in Bankruptcy', *Wisconsin Law Review* 2009 (2009) 565; J. Taub, *Other People's Houses* (Yale University Press, 2014); J. M. Moringiello, 'Mortgage Modification, Equitable Subordination, and the Honest but Unfortunate Creditor' (Social Science Research Network, 2010) SSRN Scholarly Paper ID 1578348 http://papers.ssrn.com/abstract=1578348 accessed 5 November 2018.

7 S. Ben-Ishai, S. Schwartz and J. Barretto, 'The Role of Government as a Creditor of the Disadvantaged' in W. Backert, S. Block-Lieb and J. Niemi (eds.), *Contemporary Issues in Consumer Bankruptcy* (Peter Lang, 2013); S. Ben-Ishai and S. Schwartz, 'Bankruptcy for the Poor?', *Osgoode Hall Law Journal* 45 (2007) 471.

8 J. Spooner, 'Seeking Shelter in Personal Insolvency Law: Recession, Eviction, and Bankruptcy's Social Safety Net', *Journal of Law and Society* 44 (2017) 374.

it.[9] Rather, the pursuit of austerity policies in many developed economies perpetuated and accelerated trends that have driven the household debt expansion. As described in Chapter 2, the 'loans for wages' model has persisted and deepened during the post-crisis years of the Great Recession and beyond.[10] Real wages in the UK have stagnated and fallen, and in late 2017 remained below pre-crisis levels,[11] in what has been the worst decade for real income growth in two centuries.[12] In the absence of wage growth and in a context of reduced public expenditure, the post-crisis economy has therefore required households to borrow in order to generate aggregate demand.[13] Meanwhile at the household level, living costs continued to increase despite wage stagnation. For example, between 2010 and 2017 rents rose three times faster than incomes,[14] and electricity and gas prices rose by 75 per cent and 125 per cent respectively in the period from 2008 to 2014. This contemporary acceleration of the 'loans for wages' trend described in Chapter 2 has led to households borrowing to make ends meet, while also encountering new problems of arrears in relation to essential expenses – 'everyday', 'hidden',[15] or 'priority' debts.[16] 'Priority debts' is a term used in the money advice sector to refer to debts in relation to essential expenses, with particularly severe consequences attaching to default. These consequences include eviction (for rent[17] and mortgage debt), seizure of property (hire purchase, log

[9] I. Ramsay, *Personal Insolvency in the 21st Century: A Comparative Analysis of the US and Europe* (Hart Publishing, 2017) 24–8; W. Davies, 'The New Neoliberalism', *New Left Review* 101 (2016) 121; C. Berry, 'Citizenship in a Financialised Society: Financial Inclusion and the State before and after the Crash' *Policy & Politics* 43 (2015) 509.

[10] Chapter 2, part 2.2.

[11] 'Analysis of Real Earnings: September 2017' (Office for National Statistics, 2017) www.ons.gov.uk/employmentandlabourmarket/peopleinwork/earningsandworkinghours/articles/supplementaryanalysisofaverageweeklyearnings/latest accessed 5 November 2018.

[12] A. Corlett and S. Clarke, 'Living Standards 2017: The Past, Present and Possible Future of UK Incomes' (Resolution Foundation, 2017) www.resolutionfoundation.org/publications/living-standards-2017-the-past-present-and-possible-future-of-uk-incomes/ accessed 5 November 2018.

[13] See Chapter 1, pages 4–8; Chapter 2, pages 53–61.

[14] Comptroller and Auditor General, 'Homelessness' (National Audit Office, 2017) 7.

[15] LSE Housing and Communities (n. 3) 19.

[16] See e.g. London Assembly, Economy Committee, 'Final Demand: Personal Problem Debt in London' (Greater London Authority, 2015); 'Council Tax Debts: How to Deal with the Growing Arrears Crisis Tipping Families into Problem Debt' (StepChange Debt Charity, 2015); 'Changing Household Budgets' (Money Advice Trust, 2014).

[17] Spooner (n. 8) 393–6.

book and rent-to-own loans;[18] any debt in respect of which a County Court Judgment (CCJ) has been obtained, local and national tax debts), disconnection of utilities (energy and telecom/internet bill arrears[19]), automatic deductions from benefit payments (council tax, social welfare and tax credit overpayments, social rent arrears, utility debts) and even imprisonment (council tax).[20] When money advisors agree repayment plans with creditors on behalf of their clients, these debts are afforded privileged status and are paid before others.[21] While debt advice agencies report increases in priority debt problems generally, it is most significant for present purposes to note that the number of clients requiring assistance with debts owed to local and national government has increased more than double since the crash.[22]

Priority debts pose particularly significant public policy challenges. Given the significant consequences of default in relation to these debts, the suffering faced by debtors when repayment problems arise is profound, and externalities are significant.[23] The macroeconomic implications of such debts may also be relevant to the 'debt overhang' problem affecting many advanced economies.[24] Bank of England analysis focuses on mortgage debt, assuming that it impacts aggregate demand more significantly than unsecured consumer credit due not only to the value of this debt, but also due to the drastic cuts in consumption households are willing to make in order to avoid mortgage default and accompanying eviction.[25] Given

[18] J. Lane and H. Yusuf, 'Hire Purchase: Higher Prices' (Citizens Advice, 2016); 'High-Cost Credit: Including Review of the High-Cost Short-Term Credit Price Cap' (Financial Conduct Authority, 2017) Feedback Statement FS17/2.

[19] Money Advice Trust, 'Changing Household Budgets' (n. 1) 4.

[20] 'The State of Debt Collection: The Case for Fairness in Government Debt Collection Practice' (Citizens Advice, 2016) 11.

[21] Notably debts of this kind feature prominently in the DRO procedure: 'Insolvency Proceedings: Debt Relief Orders and the Bankruptcy Petition Limit: Call for Evidence' (Insolvency Service, 2014) Call for Evidence 9–10 https://www.gov.uk/government/consultations/insolvency-proceedings-review-of-debt-relief-orders-and-the-bankruptcy-petition-limit accessed 5 November 2018; Ramsay, *'21st Century'* (n. 9) 102.

[22] Citizens Advice, 'The State of Debt Collection: The Case for Fairness in Government Debt Collection Practice' (n. 20) 3.

[23] This is perhaps most clearly evident in the public costs of addressing homelessness arising from problems in housing markets, as recently identified by the Comptroller and Auditor General, 'Homelessness' (n. 14).

[24] A. Mian and A. Sufi, House of Debt: How They (and You) *Caused the Great Recession, and How We Can Prevent It from Happening Again* (University of Chicago Press, 2014). See pages 90–96 above.

[25] Bunn and Rostom (n. 5) 11, 18; 'Financial Stability Report: June 2017' (Bank of England, 2017) 3–4, 16.

that priority debts are defined by the severe consequences of non-payment, problems in relation to these debts may potentially generate similar consumption behaviour. Further, bankruptcy's treatment of such debts is complicated and contested – in many systems bankruptcy will not prevent secured creditors from seizing assets subject to security (such as under a hire purchase agreement), while tax debts are among those exempted from debt discharge under certain insolvency systems.[26] Meanwhile since certain of these debts arise from use of essential services and/or involuntarily (in the case of tax and some social welfare overpayment debts),[27] concerns of moral hazard and over-consumption, as well as models of bankruptcy's influence on borrowing behaviour, become less relevant.[28]

Reductions in welfare provision under austerity policies have also intensified the credit/welfare trade-off, debtfare, or debt safety net phenomena discussed in Chapter 2.[29] Household incomes have been reduced and/or interrupted by various changes to the welfare system introduced by Coalition and Conservative governments, and sources link benefit cuts quite directly to rising household debt. Commentators and the National Audit Office link rent arrears problems to government measures reducing housing benefit allowance for private tenants, 'capping' overall benefit payments per household, and placing limits on eligible rents for social tenants under the policy colloquially known as the 'bedroom tax'.[30] The Financial Conduct Authority has expressed concern regarding consumer detriment in the high interest rent-to-own market,[31] with this market's growth anecdotally linked to the discontinuation of the national Social Fund (a scheme of exceptional loans to social welfare

[26] See e.g. World Bank, Report on the Treatment of the Insolvency of Natural Persons (2013) 116–117, 120–4.

[27] D. James, 'Owing Everyone: Debt Advice in the UK's Time of Austerity', Ethnos (forthcoming – 2019).

[28] Warren (n. 2); S. Block-Lieb and E. J. Janger, 'The Myth of the Rational Borrower: Rationality, Behavioralism, and the Misguided Reform of Bankruptcy Law', *Texas Law Review* 84 (2005) 1481; Zywicki (n. 2).

[29] M. Prasad, *Land of Too Much* (Harvard University Press, 2012) 227–245; S. Soederberg, *Debtfare States and the Poverty Industry: Money, Discipline and the Surplus Population* (Routledge, 2014) 89; J. Montgomerie, 'America's Debt Safety-Net', *Public Administration* 91 (2013) 871.

[30] S. Fitzpatrick and others, 'The Homelessness Monitor: England 2015' (Crisis UK, 2015) 21–38; Comptroller and Auditor General (n. 14). For an official evaluation of the 'bedroom tax', see 'Evaluation of Removal of the Spare Room Subsidy' (Department for Work and Pensions, 2015) Research Report No. 913.

[31] Financial Conduct Authority (n. 18); Lane and Yusuf (n. 18).

recipients to meet urgent costs).[32] The abolition of national council tax benefit, and its replacement with local council tax support schemes,[33] has led to payment problems as many households becoming liable to pay council tax for the first time.[34] Another shrinking of the social safety net has been the Coalition Government's increase in the scope and severity of benefit 'sanctions' – the reduction or stopping of benefit payments in the event of a claimant's failure to comply with behavioural conditions.[35] The use of sanctions almost tripled from 2009 to 2013,[36] to the point where approximately 25 per cent of Jobseekers' Allowance claimants receive sanctions at some time.[37] Sanctions have been found to impose immense hardship on claimants (disproportionately affecting poorest groups[38]), and can cause claimants to incur emergency debt throughout the period of suspended benefits.[39] The most comprehensive welfare reform introduced in the austerity era has been the project to combine six different welfare benefits into a single programme, Universal Credit. At time of writing this project has been implemented in various pilot schemes and has been highly criticised by debt advice charities for

32 House of Commons: Business Committee Innovation and Skills, 'Debt Management: Fourteenth Report of Session 2010–12, Report, Together with Formal Minutes, Oral and Written Evidence' (The Stationery Office, 2012) 26.

33 S. Ashton, M. Francis and M. Jarvie, 'Too Poor to Pay' (Child Poverty Action Group; Zacchaeus 2000 Trust, 2015) 6 http://www.z2k.org/wp-content/uploads/2018/09/TooPoorToPay-FINAL.pdf accessed 5 November 2018; London Assembly, Economy Committee (n. 1) 19; E. Herden, A. Power and B. Provan, 'Is Welfare Reform Working? Impacts on Working Age Tenants' (LSE Housing and Communities, HAILO, LSE Centre for Analysis of Social Exclusion, 2015); E. Ollerenshaw, 'Three Years On: An Independent Review of Local Council Tax Support Schemes' (Department for Communities and Local Government, 2016); House of Commons Work and Pensions Committee, 'The Local Welfare Safety Net' (House of Commons, 2016) Fifth Report of Session 2015–16, 5–6, 34–5.

34 Ashton, Francis and Jarvie (n. 33) 6.

35 While benefit sanctions were first introduced by a Conservative Government in 1996, and supported and implemented by the New Labour Governments of the late 1990s and 2000s, the Conservative-Liberal Democrat Coalition of 2010 'expanded the range of claimants subject to conditions and increased the maximum length of Jobseekers' Allowance sanctions from 26 to 256 weeks': Comptroller and Auditor General, 'Benefit Sanctions' (National Audit Office, 2016) 7. The 2012 changes to the regime can be considered to have 'dramatically increased [sanctions'] complexity and severity': M. Adler, 'A New Leviathan: Benefit Sanctions in the Twenty-First Century', *Journal of Law and Society* 43 (2016) 195, 199–202.

36 Adler (n. 35) 211.

37 Comptroller and Auditor General, 'Benefit Sanctions' (n. 35) 7.

38 Adler (n. 35) 219.

39 E. Batty and others, 'Homeless People's Experiences of Welfare Conditionality and Benefit Sanctions' (Crisis UK, 2015); Herden, Power and Provan (n. 33) 5–12.

contributing to debt problems.[40] These relate to the payment of the benefit in arrears (creating a six-week wait for first payment) and the higher amounts that can be deducted from Universal Credit payments for the recovery of past benefit overpayments and other debts owed through the social welfare system.

6.2.2 *The Austere Creditor: Austerity and Government Debt Collection*

(i) Social Welfare Debt: A Tightening Social Safety Net

This last point highlights how policies of recent years have also involved new determination on the part of national and local government to enhance public balance sheets by collecting debts arising from the social welfare and taxation systems. This highlights the underappreciated point that the state has long held a particularly important role as creditor in the lives of lower income households.[41] Soon after coming to office in 2010, the Conservative-Liberal Democrat Coalition Government established a Taskforce on Fraud, Error and Debt to address 'enormous' and 'unacceptable' losses of public funds apparently caused by these factors.[42] This formed part of an 'Efficiency and Reform' agenda to reduce 'wasteful government expenditure' at a time when austerity demanded savings.[43] A series of policy initiatives and reports followed,[44] as well as parliamentary and National Audit Office reviews.[45] Given the focus in particular on debt arising from overpayments, fraud, or error in DWP benefits and Her Majesty's Revenue and Customs (HMRC) tax credit payments,

[40] C. Drake, 'Universal Credit and Debt' (Citizens Advice, 2017).
[41] Ben-Ishai, Schwartz and Barretto (n. 7).
[42] 'Eliminating Public Sector Fraud – Counter Fraud Taskforce Interim Report' (Cabinet Office, 2011) 3.
[43] 'Tackling Fraud and Error in the Benefits and Tax Credits System' (Department for Work and Pensions and HMRC, 2010) 5.
[44] Department for Work and Pensions and HMRC (n. 43); Cabinet Office (n. 42); Fraud, Error, Debt Taskforce, 'Tackling Debt Owed to Central Government: An Interim Report' (Cabinet Office, 2012); Department for Work and Pensions and HMRC (n. 43).
[45] House of Commons Committee of Public Accounts, 'Managing Debts Owed to Central Government' (House of Commons, 2014) Seventh Report of Session 2014–15 HC 555, incorporating HC 1061, Session 2013–14; Comptroller and Auditor General, 'Managing Debt Owed to Central Government – National Audit Office (NAO)' (The Stationery Office, 2014) HC 967, Session 2013–14 Comptroller and Auditor General, 'Fraud and Error Stocktake' (National Audit Office, 2015) HC 267, Session 2015–16; Comptroller and Auditor General, 'Fraud Landscape Review' (National Audit Office, 2016) HC 850, Session 2015–16.

a clampdown was consistent with a 'welfare reform' programme,[46] and concerns regarding the legitimacy of the welfare system and integrity of claimants.[47]

New 'uncompromising action' to produce more effective debt recovery involved government giving its agencies new collection powers. Legislation increased the maximum rate at which the HMRC and DWP can make deductions from current benefits to cover debts arising from fraud[48] – first increasing by 20 per cent,[49] and then by doubling the original maximum.[50] A Direct Earnings Attachment mechanism was introduced to allow similar deductions from earnings without a court order.[51] The government departments also committed to engaging private sector data matching and debt collection services, as well as adopting techniques used commercially in these sectors. They further indicated an intention to take more extreme steps such as 'forcing debtors to sell their houses'.[52] Central government also passed legislation disapplying the usual limitation period of six years to the recovery of overpaid benefit via deduction from ongoing payments,[53] carving out priority creditor status for itself.

This last 'most emphatic legislative statement'[54] particularly marks the determined effort of the government to depart from past government approaches to debt collection, which the Coalition Government deemed to be 'characterised by neglect and periodic large write-offs or remissions'.[55] This power to extend into the past and recover historic benefit and tax credit payments can have significant consequences for claimants who found ongoing benefit payments deducted due to historic

46 Department for Work and Pensions and HM Revenue & Customs (n. 43) 7.

47 ibid, 3; R. Patrick, 'Living with and Responding to the "scrounger" Narrative in the UK: Exploring Everyday Strategies of Acceptance, Resistance and Deflection', *Journal of Poverty and Social Justice* 24 (2016) 245; G. Valentine and C. Harris, 'Strivers vs Skivers: Class Prejudice and the Demonisation of Dependency in Everyday Life', *Geoforum* 53 (2014) 84.

48 Where 'fraud' refers to the making of a misrepresentation or the failure to disclose a material fact: Social Security (Payments on account, Overpayments and Recovery) Regulations 1988/664 reg. 16(5).

49 Social Security (Recovery) (Amendment) Regulations 2012/645 reg. 3(1)(b) (1 April 2012).

50 Words substituted by Social Security (Overpayments and Recovery) Amendment Regulations 2015/499 reg. 2(3) (6 April 2015).

51 Welfare Reform Act 2012, s. 105.

52 Department for Work and Pensions and HMRC (n. 43) 9.

53 Welfare Reform Act 2012 (2012 c. 5), s. 108.

54 *McGrath* v. *Secretary of State for Work and Pensions* (2012) [2012] EWHC 1042 [31].

55 House of Commons Committee of Public Accounts (n. 45) 6.

overpayments which they may have considered to have lapsed. Human rights law has provided little protection. In the *McGrath* case, arguments of negligence on the part of the DWP in allowing historic debts to go uncollected were unsuccessful, despite Cranston J acknowledging the undoubted 'anxiety' caused by deductions from benefits when '[f] ifteen percent of a very low income means an enormous amount to someone trying to survive'.[56] Money advice charities now complain of government creditors adopting more aggressive debt collection practices than more tightly regulated lenders in other sectors,[57] while a study of social housing tenants concluded that system errors and related overpayment recovery have 'undermined confidence in welfare as a safety net'.[58] The DWP and HMRC's determination to show it is now 'taking debt recoveries more seriously'[59] therefore adds significant pressure to financially troubled households.

(ii) Local Government Debt

Austerity has increased pressure on local government budgets and so pushed local authorities towards adopting aggressive tactics for collecting council tax debts.[60] Consistent with the use of targets for measuring public sector performance under New Public Management ideas, central government's enhanced debt collection agenda monitors local authorities' rates of recovery of local tax debts.[61] The removal of national Council Tax Benefit involved reductions in overall funding to each council,[62] and as many low-income households became liable to pay council tax for the first time, default and debt problems have grown significantly.[63] Sums that had been paid by central government fell to be paid by low-income households who lacked the means to do so, in what

56 '*McGrath*' (n. 54) [36].

57 Citizens Advice, 'The State of Debt Collection: The Case for Fairness in Government Debt Collection Practice' (n. 20) 4.

58 LSE Housing and Communities (n. 3) iii.

59 House of Commons Committee of Public Accounts, 'Managing Debts Owed To Central Government', (House of Commons, 2014) Seventh Report of Session 2014–15 para. 11.

60 StepChange Debt Charity (n. 1) 17.

61 'Council Tax and Business Rates Collection: An Update' (Audit Commission, 2014) 8–13, 19–20.

62 See notes 33–4 above.

63 Audit Commission (n. 61) 11–12; StepChange Debt Charity (n. 1); Citizens Advice, 'The State of Debt Collection: The Case for Fairness in Government Debt Collection Practice' (n. 20); 'Council Tax Arrears, Councils and Bailiffs' (Citizens Advice, 2013).

can be quite readily conceptualised as austerity's process of substituting public debt for private debt.[64]

Local authorities have responded to these pressures by adopting increasingly aggressive approaches to council tax debt collection. They have utilised particularly extensive powers unavailable to other creditors. Several advice charities have reported local authorities 'as among the most unhelpful types of creditor'.[65] They criticise their tendency to escalate quickly towards drastic (and expensive) debt collection techniques such as obtaining court orders and deploying bailiffs to seize debtors' goods (or to threaten seizure).[66] In some local authorities the number of bailiff referrals equates to half of all properties in the area.[67] Approximately 100 debtors per year are imprisoned for non-payment of council tax.[68] While regulatory guidance issued in response to criticisms of these debt recovery practices has been attributed with improvements,[69] it remains the case that aggressive local authority actions have added considerably to the financial distress of many low-income households.

(iii) The Austere Creditor in Context: Privatisation, Commercialisation and the Neoliberal State

These developments align with a 'broader shift in the state form under neoliberalism', characterised by the 'diffusion of power and resources away from national governments' and 'the growing privatisation and commercialisation of certain functions of the state'.[70] This includes the

[64] M. Lazzarato and J. D. Jordan, *The Making of the Indebted Man: Essay on the Neoliberal Condition* reprint edn (Massachusetts Institute of Technology Press, 2012).

[65] StepChange Debt Charity (n. 1) 2.

[66] Citizens Advice, 'Council Tax Arrears, Councils and Bailiffs' (n. 63); StepChange Debt Charity (n. 1); A. Pardoe and others, 'Unsecured and Insecure? Exploring the UK's Mountain of Unsecured Personal Debt – and How It Affects People's Lives' (Citizens Advice, 2015) www.citizensadvice.org.uk/Global/CitizensAdvice/Debt%20and%20Money%20Publications/UnsecuredorinsecureFinal.pdf accessed 5 November 2018; M. Kelly, 'Catching Up: Improving Council Tax Arrears Collection' (Citizens Advice, 2015).

[67] Money Advice Trust, 'Local Authorities in England and Wales Refer 1.8 Million Debts to Bailiffs in 12 Months' www.moneyadvicetrust.org/media/news/pages/local-authorities-and-bailiffs0821-6215.aspx accessed 5 November 2018.

[68] Sam Gyimah, The Parliamentary Under-Secretary of State for Justice, HC Deb, 30 September 2016, cW.

[69] Citizens Advice, 'The State of Debt Collection: The Case for Fairness in Government Debt Collection Practice' (n. 20) 15. See text to notes 150–5 below.

[70] A. Roberts, 'Doing Borrowed Time: The State, the Law and the Coercive Governance of "Undeserving" Debtors', *Critical Sociology* 40 (2014) 669, 681.

'downloading' of costs of public services from national to local level, and in turn from local authorities onto individual 'users' or 'clients' of services,[71] alongside overall increases to low-income groups' contribution to these costs. Other elements of this governance approach include the prominence of ideas of state commercialisation and the privatisation of public services. The contemporary government debt collection agenda evidences a clear desire to adopt a more 'business-like' approach. One report states that '[n]o business in the world would put up with this scale of fraudulent activity, but . . . for far too long, no one has concentrated on how to run the machinery of government properly'.[72] Similar sentiments were expressed by the House of Commons Public Accounts Committee, in criticising prior government performance in managing 'a basic business activity' of debt recovery.[73] The Coalition Government proclaimed that its 'radically' improved new system was founded on increased use of commercial debt collection services,[74] and the acquisition of 'expertise from private sector debt recovery firms'.[75]

Engagement with private sector firms has had some unexpected advantages, because collection firms must comply with Financial Conduct Authority rules and so their deployment reduces the disparity between regulated private sector debts and the less fettered government recovery practices.[76] Risks also exist, however, such as concerns identified in parliament that government-hired firms may adopt inappropriate debt collection methods, particularly against vulnerable debtors.[77] Certain fears were realised when HMRC's contracting of firm Concentrix to police fraud and error in benefit payments led to controversy.[78] Commission-based payment structures contributed to excesses such as the widespread revocation of benefits from eligible

[71] ibid., Fees charged to debtors for access to bankruptcy, as discussed in Chapter 4, also fit this trend.

[72] Cabinet Office (n. 42) 2.

[73] House of Commons Committee of Public Accounts (n. 59) 3. The National Audit Office similarly began its assessment of government debt recovery from a starting point that 'managing debtors is a normal part of most businesses': Comptroller and Auditor General, 'Managing Debt Owed to Central Government – National Audit Office (NAO)' (n. 66) 5.

[74] House of Commons Committee of Public Accounts (n. 45) para. 16.

[75] Department for Work and Pensions and HMRC (n. 43) 9.

[76] Citizens Advice, 'The State of Debt Collection: The Case for Fairness in Government Debt Collection Practice' (n. 20) 16.

[77] House of Commons Committee of Public Accounts (n. 45) 7.

[78] House of Commons Work and Pensions Committee, 'Concentrix' (House of Commons, 2016) HC 270 Fourth Report of Session 2016–17, 4.

claimants. A parliamentary inquiry concluded that it could not reconcile the approaches of HMRC and Concentrix 'with a public service ethos'. A key theme of this chapter is the difficulty in reconciling such an ethos with a clear desire by government and its departments to act as self-interested, commercially minded creditors.[79]

6.2.3 *Implications for Bankruptcy*

Austerity has caused households to incur more risk, while reducing the protection offered by the social safety net. The 'loans for wages' and 'credit/welfare trade-off' trends cause households to turn further to credit as a 'market-based social welfare program'.[80] This exposes leveraged households to greater vulnerability in the event of an 'income shock' or social force majeure of the type that causes over-indebtedness.[81] Austerity reduces the protection offered by the welfare state against such 'life accidents'. Such circumstances should increase demand for household debt relief through bankruptcy, and advance the case for bankruptcy's provision of expansive debt relief.[82] These are the conditions of a 'regulatory welfare state'. Regulatory norms and legal protections, including bankruptcy, offer a 'safety net of last resort' when the support of the traditional welfare state is insufficient.[83] European commentators have long understood generous US bankruptcy law as related to that country's limited welfare state provision, and austerity's reduction of social protections might realise their fears that European countries were following a similar route, ultimately necessitating similarly progressive debt discharge in bankruptcy.[84] At a macroeconomic level, a significant IMF report presents household debt restructuring laws and 'automatic support to households through the social safety net' as

[79] For a discussion of parallel developments in Canada, see Ben-Ishai, Schwartz and Barretto (n. 7).

[80] Teresa A Sullivan, Elizabeth Warren and Jay Lawrence Westbrook, *The Fragile Middle Class: Americans in Debt* (Yale University Press, 2000) 138.

[81] See pages 58–60 above.

[82] A. Feibelman, 'Defining the Social Insurance Function of Consumer Bankruptcy', *American Bankruptcy Institute Law Review* 13 (2005) 129; J. J. Kilborn, 'Comparative Cause and Effect: Consumer Insolvency and the Eroding Social Safety Net', *Columbia Journal of European Law* 14 (2007) 563.

[83] H. Haber, 'Regulation as Social Policy: Home Evictions and Repossessions in the UK and Sweden', *Public Administration* 93 (2015) 806, 817–19.

[84] J. Braucher, 'Consumer Bankruptcy as Part of the Social Safety Net: Fresh Start or Treadmill', *Santa Clara Law Review* 44 (2003) 1065, 1066–7.

alternative responses to financial crisis, recession, and debt overhang problems. Both policy tools can act as macroeconomic 'stabilizers' by assisting households with a high marginal propensity to consume.[85] While less necessary in countries offering automatic support to households through an expansive welfare state, 'bold household debt restructuring programs' are most appropriate for 'economies with limited scope for expansionary macroeconomic policies and in which the financial sector has already received government support'.[86] There exists a strong case for household debt relief laws to offer a counter-cyclical balance in a context of a government committed to pro-cyclical austerity policies involving reduced state expenditure.[87]

Secondly, bankruptcy literature suggests that increased debt recovery pressure from creditors should lead to increased household demand for debt relief in bankruptcy – whether manifested in increased use of existing bankruptcy procedures by households, or in political calls for more protective laws.[88] While consumer debt from products such as credit cards remains at high levels,[89] debt advice charities report that council tax has surpassed credit cards as the most frequently raised 'problem debt' among clients.[90] This might be due to the contrast between the aggressive collection techniques of local authorities and the business practices of credit card lenders who are happy to profit from customers carrying high levels of debt for long periods,[91] including through interest-free balance transfer offers.[92] Creditor debt recovery

85 International Monetary Fund (n. 5) 12–14.

86 ibid, 27.

87 See pages 92–93 above.

88 R. M. Hynes, 'Bankruptcy and State Collections: The Case of the Missing Garnishments', *Cornell Law Review* 91 (2005) 603; L. Lefgren and F. McIntyre, 'Explaining the Puzzle of Cross-State Differences in Bankruptcy Rates', *Journal of Law and Economics* 52 (2009) 367; A. E. Dawsey, R. M. Hynes and L. M. Ausubel, 'Non-Judicial Debt Collection and the Consumer's Choice among Repayment, Bankruptcy and Informal Bankruptcy', *American Bankruptcy Law Journal* 87 (2013) 1; P. Foohey and others, 'Life in the Sweatbox', *Notre Dame Law Review* (94 (2018) – forthcoming).

89 See pages 15–20 above.

90 Pardoe and others (n. 66) 13–18; StepChange Debt Charity (n. 1) 2.

91 Mann (n. 4); 'Credit Card Market Study: Interim Report' (Financial Conduct Authority, 2015) MS14/6.2 50–68.

92 A 2015 Financial Conduct Authority report stated that 0 per cent Balance Transfer offers accounted for one quarter of outstanding balances: Financial Conduct Authority (n. 91) 5. The Bank of England cautions that this may conceal risks of future debt default: 'Financial Policy Committee Statement from Its Policy Meeting, 20 September 2017' (Bank of England, 2017) 5.

practices seem to play an important role in transforming a debt into a 'problem debt', and in driving debtors to seek advice and/or enter insolvency procedures. In this way, bankruptcy law could potentially act as a counterweight to the increased aggression of government debt collection. Its social insurance function is one way to reallocate and rebalance efficiently the risks associated with the increased privatisation and commercialisation of public services in a financialised society.

6.3 Testing the Law's Insurance Function in the Face of Austerity and Recession

In its weak response to the challenges raised by these trends, bankruptcy has failed to embrace its social insurance function. The central ambivalence regarding the aims and identity of bankruptcy results in persisting conceptions of the law as a branch of the commercial law, dedicated to upholding market allocations and offering a debt collection tool to creditors. This in turn has left the law open to being shaped by government agencies increasingly determined to act as self-interested creditors, under administrative policies and practices that can be linked to ideas of commercialisation and privatisation of public services characteristic of contemporary financialised capitalism. In the absence of direct policy making and comprehensive rethinking of the system, and given the rarity of bankruptcy litigation,[93] administrative practice and court precedent can have considerable influence over personal insolvency law. Courts, regulators, and insolvency policymakers have presented limited resistance to this shaping of the law towards the prioritisation of its debt collection function. Where resistance has arisen, it has been less based upon a concern to advance the law's social insurance function, and more on a view that the law's duty is to maximise returns for *all* creditors, preventing one creditor from prevailing over others.

6.3.1 Priority Debts in Personal Insolvency

A first illustration of bankruptcy's difficulty in dealing with contemporary realities of problem debt and in addressing policy challenges lies in the law's the uncomfortable treatment of 'priority debts'. The concept of

[93] M. Galanter, 'The Vanishing Trial: An Examination of Trials and Related Matters in Federal and State Courts', *Journal of Empirical Legal Studies* 1 (2004) 459; E. Warren, 'Vanishing Trials: The Bankruptcy Experience', *Journal of Empirical Legal Studies* 1 (2004) 913; L. Mulcahy, 'The Collective Interest in Private Dispute Resolution', *Oxford Journal of Legal Studies* 33 (2013) 59.

a 'priority debt' is key in the debt advice sector, recognised by the Financial Conduct Authority in its conduct of business rules,[94] and accepted by the banking sector in the voluntary Lending Code. Yet this concept is not only unknown to personal insolvency law, but the law considers the debtor's payment of one party over other creditors as illegitimate and in many cases constituting misconduct. Under the 'creditors' bargain' model, bankruptcy is a procedural forum for replicating pre-bankruptcy allocations as best as possible, through pro rata distribution of debtor resources among creditors based on their prior market positions.[95] This view has historically voided any preferential payment of one creditor over others, returning it to the estate for fair distribution among all creditors.[96] This position conflicts clearly with the aims of debtor rehabilitation, as the maintenance of a debtor's reasonable standard of living and her receipt of a fresh start require priority payments to be made in order to retain access to essential services.

The extension of the preferences doctrine into the Debt Relief Order procedure illustrates difficulties arising from layering new policy aims into a historical framework developed for other ends.[97] Even though there is no 'estate' under the DRO procedure, and no distributions are made to creditors, the giving of a preference operates to disqualify a debtor from obtaining a DRO.[98] This provision appears to view such an action as culpable misconduct warranting the exclusion of the debtor. The traditional understanding that a preferential transaction should be undone in order to benefit other creditors but was not 'deserving of moral censure'[99] appears to have been lost in translation. Practical consequences of this rule are not insignificant, with money advice agencies reporting that approximately 5 per cent of clients must be advised against entry to the DRO procedure due to advisors finding that they have made a preferential payment.[100] Disjuncture between the rule and the reality of

[94] See *Banking: Conduct of Business Sourcebook* (Financial Conduct Authority, 2018).

[95] Jackson (n. 13) 30–1; J. Kilpi, *The Ethics of Bankruptcy* (Routledge, 1998) 14–15.

[96] I. F. Fletcher, The Law of Insolvency 4th revised edn (Sweet & Maxwell, 2009) 272–3.

[97] *R (Cooper and Payne) v. Secretary of State for Work and Pensions* [2011] BPIR 223 [78], *per* Toulson LJ.

[98] Insolvency Act, 1986 (1986 c. 45), Schd. 4ZA, paras. 9-10 (UK). Note that the giving of a preference is also grounds for a Debt Relief Restrictions Order (DRRO) and Bankruptcy Restrictions Order (BRO), as discussed in Chapter 7.

[99] Sir Kenneth Cork, *Insolvency Law and Practice: Report of the Review Committee* (HMSO, 1982) para. 1243.

[100] 'Money Advice Trust Consultation Response: Insolvency Service - DROs and the Bankruptcy Petition Limit' (Money Advice Trust, 2014) 5.

household budgeting has forced the Insolvency Service DRO team to adopt an uneasy compromise, under which it tends to exercise discretion not to reject a proposal where a preferential payment has been made to a priority creditor.[101] Administrative burdens associated with such uncertain and discretionary rules form a perennial problem in consumer bankruptcy systems, due to their potential to exclude debtors through heightened access costs.[102]

The uneasy marriage between the existing bankruptcy system of longstanding lineage and more modern policies and practices also manifests in rules relating to the essential debtor assets exempted from creditor seizure in bankruptcy (or exempted from the DRO means testing process).[103] Exemptions are part of the definition of the fresh start, which requires that a debtor exit bankruptcy not just free of debt, but with sufficient assets to live reasonably and productively.[104] Contemporary household finance conditions stretch these exemptions, as households frequently acquire even essential assets on credit, rather than owning them outright. A recent Court of Appeal case asked the court to interpret exemption rules based on these conditions, and to hold that a photographer debtor be permitted to retain the benefit of a hire purchase agreement for the purchase of a car, where a car was necessary for the debtor's trade.[105] The court rejected this argument, relying primarily on a literal interpretation of the Insolvency Act 1986 in holding that the law's protection only applied to the physical essential assets, and that what was effectively a chose in action (the hire purchase agreement) could not constitute a 'tool' or essential asset. The court

[101] 'Debt Relief Orders and the Bankruptcy Petition Limit: Citizens Advice Response to the Insolvency Service' (Citizens Advice, 2014) 2014 Evidence: a Citizens Advice Social Policy Publication 21.

[102] J. Braucher, 'A Fresh Start for Personal Bankruptcy Reform: The Need for Simplification and a Single Portal', *American University Law Review* 55 (2005) 1295. While legal representation costs are not an issue in England and Wales, administrative costs are relevant in a situation in which access to free legal advice is limited: S. Kirwan, '"Advice on the Law but Not Legal Advice so Much": Weaving Law and Life into Debt Advice', *Advising in Austerity: Reflections on Challenging Times for Advice Agencies* (Policy Press, 2016).

[103] Insolvency Act 1986 1986, s. 283, Schd. 4ZA para. 8.

[104] W. C. Whitford, 'Changing Definitions of Fresh Start in US Bankruptcy Law', *Journal of Consumer Policy* 20 (1997) 179, 180.

[105] *Mikki* v. *Duncan* [2017] EWCA Civ 57. The wording of s. 283(2)(a) Insolvency Act 1986 protects 'such tools, books, vehicles and other items of equipment as are necessary to the bankrupt for use personally by him in his employment, business or vocation'.

acknowledged that the Cork Committee reports informing the Act include the policy goal of enabling the debtor to achieve her 'rehabilitation as a useful and productive member of society', and that this requires the exemption from seizure of assets necessary for this purpose.[106] The court noted, however, that the Cork Committee had assumed the debtor owned such assets and omitted to discuss the acquisition of essential items via hire purchase.[107] In the absence of express guidance the court felt unable to extend exemption rules solely on the basis of advancing the aim of debtor rehabilitation, even in an acknowledged context of widespread reliance by households on similar financing arrangements.[108]

The decision leaves many households 'too poor for bankruptcy' in the sense that they lack assets sufficient to benefit from bankruptcy exemptions.[109] A law protecting 'chattels' becomes of limited use when essential household assets are added to the financialisation of every*thing*,[110] and the credit system erodes the assets of the debtor.[111] Westbrook argues that in 'the modern world, the fresh start includes an opportunity for debtors to keep property subject to a security interest or mortgage, including their homes and a means of transportation'.[112] While he acknowledges that the law must also respect the rights of secured creditors, the *Mikki* case shows that the position under English law may tip the balance unduly towards this objective, at the expense of advancing the law's debt relief aim. This context of a weakly established 'fresh start' policy in a system heavily infused with ideas of creditor wealth maximisation leaves the law ill-equipped to deal with challenging conditions for household finances, but also renders it susceptible to being 'manipulated by creditors' into serving their aims.[113] What is perhaps surprising is that government creditors have been among the chief manipulators.

[106] Cork (n. 99) para. 1096.
[107] '*Mikki*' (n. 105) [38].
[108] ibid, 20, 38.
[109] U. Reifner, 'Responsible Bankruptcy' in L. Nogler and U. Reifner (eds.), *Life Time Contracts: Social Longterm Contracts in Labour, Tenancy and Consumer Credit Law* 1st edn (Eleven International Publishing, 2014) 557.
[110] D. Harvey, *A Brief History of Neoliberalism* new edn (Oxford University Press, 2007) 33.
[111] Reifner (n. 109) 557.
[112] J. Westbrook, 'The Retreat of American Bankruptcy Law', *QUT Law Review* 17 (2017) 40.
[113] Roberts (n. 70) 670.

6.3.2 Government as (Priority) Creditor: Council Tax Collection and Local Authority Creditor Petitions

Despite personal insolvency law being primarily invoked by debtors as a means of obtaining relief from financial troubles and creditor collection efforts, a large minority of bankruptcy cases continue to arise from creditor petitions. While IVAs are instigated by debtors and only debtors can apply for a Debt Relief Order (which, it should be recalled, involves no distributions to creditors), over one quarter of bankruptcies result from creditor petitions (Figure 6.1). This is an 'oddity' of English law,[114] given that European consumer debt resolution procedures are generally only instigated by debtors, and that creditor petitions make up less than 0.1 per cent of Chapter 7 bankruptcies in the USA.[115] Undoubtedly debates regarding the extent to which creditors should be paid in bankruptcy are common in many systems.[116] The conflict between competing debt collection and debt relief understandings of the law is clearest, however, in a jurisdiction where many lawyers and judges consider it appropriate to invoke bankruptcy to collect a single ordinary debt.[117] A creditor in England and Wales may bring a bankruptcy petition against a debtor on showing that it is owed 'a debt which the debtor appears either to be unable to pay or to have no reasonable prospect of being able to pay'.[118] Unlike the position in other jurisdictions, there is neither a need for a creditor to show the debtor's general insolvency, nor the presence of any circumstances that might justify investigation of the debtor's affairs through bankruptcy.[119]

Government plays a significant role in keeping alive bankruptcy's debt collection function and re-establishing 'the brutal truth ... that creditors use bankruptcy to recover debts owed to them and have little interest in

[114] J. Kilborn and A. Walters, 'Involuntary Bankruptcy As Debt Collection: Multi-Jurisdictional Lessons in Choosing the Right Tool for the Job', *American Bankruptcy Law Journal* 87 (2013) 123.

[115] ibid, 124; S. Block-Lieb, 'Why Creditors File So Few Involuntary Petitions and Why the Number Is Not Too Small', *Brooklyn Law Review* 57 (1991) 803.

[116] Kilborn and Walters (n. 114) 123.

[117] ibid.

[118] Insolvency Act 1986, s. 267(2).

[119] S. Block-Lieb, 'Fishing in Muddy Waters: Clarifying the Common Pool Analogy as Applied to the Standard for Commencement of a Bankruptcy Case', *American University Law Review* 42 (1992) 337, 359–60; J. Spooner and I. D. C. Ramsay, 'Insolvency Proceedings: Debt Relief Orders and the Bankruptcy Petition Limit – Submission by Professor Iain Ramsay and Dr Joseph Spooner to the Insolvency Service Call for Evidence' (Social Science Research Network, 2014) SSRN Scholarly Paper ID 2601349 16–17 http://ssrn.com/abstract=2601349 accessed 5 November 2018.

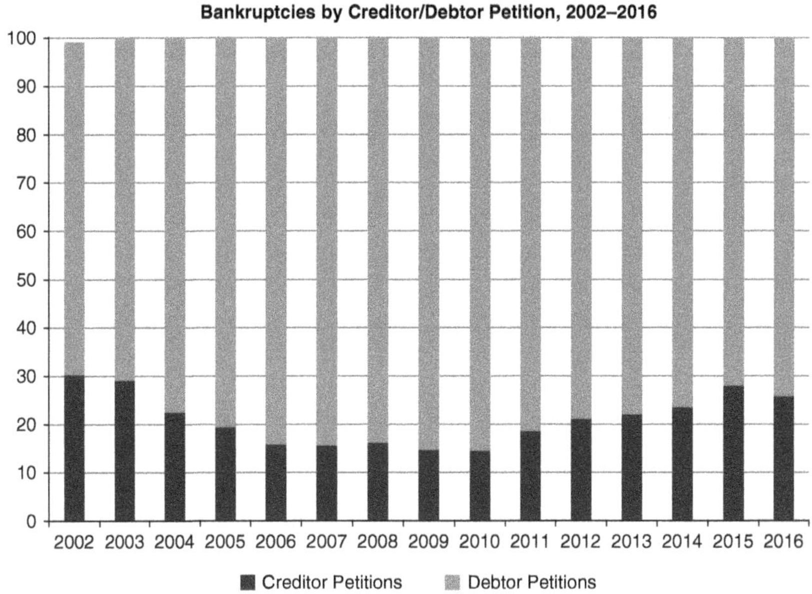

Figure 6.1: In recent years, creditor petitions have risen as a proportion of total bankruptcies. Source: Insolvency Service

addressing the wider indebtedness of the bankrupt'.[120] Available research shows that HMRC and local government authorities are responsible for approximately 40 per cent of creditor-initiated bankruptcies.[121] From 1992/3 to 2008, the proportion of creditor petition bankruptcy orders issued by local authorities rose from approximately 1 per cent to 20 per cent.[122] While it appears that local authorities subsequently reduced recourse to bankruptcy (following intervention by the Local Government Ombudsman discussed below), an accounting firm found that by 2013–14 32 per cent of local authorities were using bankruptcy as part of their debt collection practices, compared to just 20 per cent in 2009–10.[123]

[120] D. Milman, 'Reflections on Recent Cases of Interest on Bankruptcy Law: Part 1', *Insolvency Intelligence* 23 (2010) 104.

[121] Kilborn and Walters (n. 114) 143.

[122] J. Briggs, 'Council Tax Arrears and Bankruptcy: A Thorny Issue', *Insolvency Intelligence* 23 (2010) 1.

[123] M. Finch, 'Increasing Number of Councils Forced to Step up Bankruptcy Actions against Council Tax Defaulters – Moore Stephens' www.moorestephens.co.uk/news-views/june-2015/councils-forced-to-step-up-bankrupty-actions accessed 5 November 2018.

The personal insolvency system, as represented by government and Insolvency Service policymakers and the courts, has shown little resistance to these trends.[124] In fact, court decisions illustrate a prevailing understanding of creditors' petitions as legitimate uses of the personal insolvency system, and of bankruptcy as a debt collection tool. In the leading case, the Court of Appeal has held that local authorities are free to use bankruptcy as a means of recovering council tax arrears and that it was not a disproportionate measure despite its severe consequences for the debtor.[125] The Court of Appeal noted that local authorities 'are as a rule very reluctant to invoke bankruptcy as a means of enforcement', compared to the comparatively frequent use made of the threat of committal to prison for non-payment.[126] The court considered bankruptcy less draconian than committal, and found 'no objection to the use of a procedure which is permitted by statute and regulations'.[127] Emphasising the local authority's need to manage public finances and to take all necessary steps to achieve this aim, the court 'could see no reason for supposing that the use of bankruptcy ... was inspired by improper motives rather than a determination to try and collect the outstanding sum which it is the local authority's duty to collect'.[128] The Court of Appeal has subsequently affirmed this position, stating that 'it is not essential ... that the local authority should choose one remedy rather than another, and in any event it must have some measure of discretion to choose the appropriate course'.[129]

Recent reported cases show the courts adopting a similar approach to local authorities' use of bankruptcy petitions. Many of these cases are consistent with research findings that local authorities and other creditors use bankruptcy applications more frequently as a threat to encou-

[124] For example, courts have not used their general power to dismiss or stay a bankruptcy petition for any reason, or their more specific power to dismiss where a creditor has unreasonably refused a debtor's offer to settle the debt claim: Insolvency Act 1986, ss. 266(3), 271(3).

[125] *Griffin* v. *Wakefield MDC* (2000) [2000] RVR 226 (Court of Appeal). See also J. Briggs, 'Council Tax Arrears and Bankruptcy: A Thorny Issue', Insolvency Intelligence 23 (2010) 1.

[126] 'Griffin' (n. 125) [7].

[127] ibid, 8.

[128] ibid.

[129] *Lonergan* v. *Gedling Borough Council* [2009] EWCA Civ 1569 [2009] EWCA (Civ) A2/ 2007/2914, 2010 BPIR 911 [32], *per* Arden LJ.

rage payment rather than with the intention of following through with bankruptcy.[130] Several cases involve applications for annulment or rescission of a bankruptcy order after payment (or a rejected offer of payment) of a debt, or disputes regarding parties' respective bearing of litigation costs once debtor and local authority have agreed a repayment arrangement to avoid bankruptcy.[131] Given the level of discretion allocated to courts in the assessment of costs and even in the decision whether to annul a bankruptcy,[132] these cases offer opportunities for courts to cast judgment on local authorities' use of bankruptcy as a debt collection tool. Courts have not indicated any objection to bankruptcy being deployed in this manner, however. They do not see anything unusual with bankruptcy being used 'simply as a matter of debt enforcement' and accept that such bankruptcy petitions are 'very much mechanical operations'.[133] Once the local authority fulfils the statutory conditions, it is '*prima facie* entitled to such an order'.[134] Courts will make valid bankruptcy orders even where a debtor contests a council tax liability order,[135] until such an order is set aside via a bespoke appeal tribunal process.[136] Local authorities will be given leeway when courts determine the reasonableness of their decisions to reject debtor offers of compromise and continue with bankruptcy.[137] Similarly, the power to make or not to make the debtor bankrupt remains the gift of the petitioning creditor, and a seized court will not substitute its judgment for that of the creditor. Thus a creditor who presents a petition against an insolvent debtor 'is in control of the proceedings' and retains the right to

[130] Kilborn and Walters (n. 114) 140–6.

[131] *Adetula* v. *Barking and Dagenham London Borough Council* (2017) [2017] EWHC 2279 (Ch) (High Court); *Stratford-on-Avon District Council* v. *Clarke* (2015) [2015] EWHC 1539 (Ch) (High Court).

[132] Under s. 282(1)(a) Insolvency Act 1986, 'The court may annul a bankruptcy order if it at any time appears to the court that, on any grounds existing at the time the order was made, the order ought not to have been made'.

[133] '*Clarke*' (n. 131) [7].

[134] *Choudhry* v. *Luton Borough Council* (2017) [2017] EWHC 960 (Ch) (EWHC) [8].

[135] This has negative consequences for the debtor in question, as a rescinded bankruptcy (as opposed to one annulled) is not removed from the Individual Insolvency Register and so may have negative effects on a debtor's credit report: *Yang* v. *The Official Receiver* 2017 EWCA Civ 1465 [54–5].

[136] *Okon* v. *London Borough Of Lewisham* [2016] EWHC 864 (Ch) (EWHC (Ch)); *Choudhry* v. *Luton Borough Council* (n. 134).

[137] *Allen* v. *Haringey LBC* (2017) [2017] EWHC Unreported (High Court); Insolvency Act 1986, s. 271. As well as a general power to dismiss or stay a bankruptcy petition for any reason, courts have a more specific power to dismiss where a creditor has unreasonably refused a debtor's offer to settle the debt: ss. 266(3), 271(3).

withdraw the petition on reaching a satisfactory repayment arrangement with the debtor.[138] This right can be exercised over the objections of the bankruptcy trustee, even where other creditors would be affected by the withdrawal of the collective procedure instigated against the insolvent debtor.

This last position highlights the ideological confusion at the core of bankruptcy law. Even those prioritising bankruptcy's debt collection function emphasise that it is a *collective* procedure concerned with collecting debts on behalf of a group of an insolvent debtor's creditors, and this is the very basis of the 'creditors' bargain' model.[139] Thus, the non-governmental organisation JUSTICE commented in 1994 that '[t]he insolvency process, whilst incidentally giving relief to the debtor, is essentially *collective* by nature for the benefit of creditors'.[140] Under this logic, bankruptcy is appropriately invoked only when the debtor's circumstances mean that the conditions of a 'common pool' collective action problem are met.[141] English law's approach of founding bankruptcy on a debtor's apparent inability to satisfy a single claim therefore lacks theoretical justification, even if the law was viewed solely as a tool for producing returns to creditors.[142] While debtor conduct that prefers one creditor and disadvantages the creditor group is sanctioned as culpable misconduct that may disqualify the debtor from accessing relief, creditors are authorised and encouraged to act in a self-interested manner without regard to fellow creditors.

Further, an understanding of the law as a debt collection tool for self-interested creditors, with no regard to public policy objectives beyond allowing a creditor freedom to collect its debt, conflicts openly with a view of bankruptcy as a social insurance mechanism for addressing the externalities of over-indebtedness. A bankruptcy law serving this aim would design access conditions based around questions of whether

138 *Sands (as trustee in bankruptcy)* v. *Layne & Anor* [2016] EWCA Civ 1159 (EWCA (Civ)) [53].

139 Jackson (n. 95). See Chapter 3's discussion of the 'creditors' bargain' theory.

140 *Insolvency Law: An Agenda for Reform* (JUSTICE 1994) para. 3.1.

141 T. H. Jackson, *The Logic and Limits of Bankruptcy Law* (Harvard University Press, 1986) 200. For a critique of Jackson's specific policy recommendations regarding the standard for commencing creditors' bankruptcy proceedings (and particularly for its inappropriate focus on a debtor's assets, rather than income), see S. Block-Lieb, 'Fishing in Muddy Waters: Clarifying the Common Pool Analogy as Applied to the Standard for Commencement of a Bankruptcy Case', *American University Law Review* 42 (1992) 337, 345–7.

142 Insolvency Service (n. 21) 28; Kilborn and Walters (n. 114) 147–8.

externalities would otherwise arise if a debtor is not offered relief, rather than permitting proceedings to be opened according to the wishes of a single creditor. Chapters 4 and 5 of this book criticise the market model of personal insolvency prevailing in this jurisdiction, highlighting the risks of a system founded upon an illusory principle of debtor choice. If one accepts for present purposes the existence of this model, however, then the law's facilitation of involuntary bankruptcy against the debtor's opposition raises a further fundamental inconsistency. Bankruptcy in its current form involves significant costs, including a fundamental loss of autonomy on the part of the debtor, in which all her non-essential assets are surrendered alongside legal rights and control over her financial affairs.[143] Involuntary bankruptcy adds sizeable costs to debtors' already high debt burdens (with bankruptcy petitions alone accruing costs of well over £1,000,[144] and various reports offering examples of bankruptcy administration costs ranging from over £30,000 to over £100,000[145]). It also can increase pressure on debtors, impact credit histories, and may cause debtors (both homeowners and, as shown below in the context of the *Sharples* case, renters) to lose their homes.[146] Creditors' use of threats of bankruptcy (often where there is no intention or possibility of following through[147]) might also increase stigma associated with the procedure, particularly given the information asymmetries intrinsic to the relationship of creditor and defaulting debtor.[148] Creditor threats of bankruptcy may leave a troubled debtor uncertain as to whether bankruptcy is an option to be embraced or feared.

Criticism of creditor petitions might seem inconsistent with arguments elsewhere in this book that debt relief procedures of bankruptcy and DROs should be more readily accessible – shouldn't the author be happy to see more debtors accessing bankruptcy? Indeed, some debtors may wish a creditor to 'make them bankrupt' in the face of the unaffordable costs of petitioning for their own bankruptcies.[149] The above

143 For example, a debtor loses her right to bring an appeal or judicial review claim on entering bankruptcy: *Heath* v. *Tang* [1993] 1 WLR 1421 (1993) [1993] 1 WLR 1421 (EWCA); *Baljinder Singh* [2010] UKUT 174 (TCC) (15 May 2010) (UKUT (TCC)).

144 '*Clarke*' (n. 131).

145 'Reform of the Process to Apply for Bankruptcy and Compulsory Winding Up: Response by Citizens Advice to the Insolvency Service' (Citizens Advice, 2012) 11–12.

146 ibid, 9–14.

147 ibid, 10–11; Kilborn and Walters (n. 114) 140–6.

148 P. Rock, *Making People Pay* 1st edn (Routledge & Kegan Paul Books, 1973) 71–2.

149 'Help with Bankruptcy Fees' (*Debt Camel*, 23 February 2016) https://debtcamel.co.uk/help-with-bankruptcy-fees/ accessed 5 November 2018.

considerations show that negative consequences relating to bankruptcy should require that debtors have a choice in this matter, however. This is primarily a book about ideas influencing bankruptcy law and policy, and it argues that the most important aspect of the persistent application of the law as an individual creditor's debt collection mechanism is its tendency to obscure the policy benefits of the law's debt relief function and the importance of the law being understood and applied as a social insurance mechanism against the risks of a debt-dependent economy. Reforms advancing the debt relief goal have been edited into a single legislative text alongside provisions embodying and implementing a view of the law as a debt collection tool. There is now a worrying fissure between the continued invocation of the law by creditors in a large minority of cases; and the contemporary practice of the vast majority of cases in which the law is invoked by debtors of very limited means as a safety net of last resort. When judges or policymakers are faced with decisions raising a direct choice as to whether the law should prioritise the law's debt collection or debt relief aims, persistent ideas of the law as a debt collection tool undoubtedly colour their judgment. The next section discusses consequences of this trend when illustrating how important questions such as the protection of a debtor's home in bankruptcy, a key element of any fresh start, have been addressed through judicial decisions founded on the pervasive image of the law as a debt collection tool.

It was ultimately the Local Government Ombudsman, rather than the courts, which used its regulatory powers to restrict local authorities' use of bankruptcy. The Ombudsman issued a series of investigation findings that demonstrated 'a contrast in underlying attitudes' to courts' perspectives.[150] It subsequently published a report clarifying how authorities will be liable for maladministration unless they follow appropriate procedures before deciding that bankruptcy is a fair and proportionate action on the facts of any given case.[151] Central Government, through the Department for Communities and Local Government, has also issued guidance to local authorities on debt collection practices.[152] These interventions might suggest that specialist regulators are better monitors of creditor practices than the personal insolvency system and particularly its

[150] Milman (n. 120) 106.

[151] 'Can't Pay? Won't Pay? Using Bankruptcy for Council Tax Debts' (Local Government Ombudsman, 2011).

[152] 'Guidance to Local Councils on Good Practice in the Collection of Council Tax Arrears' (Department for Communities and Local Government, 2013).

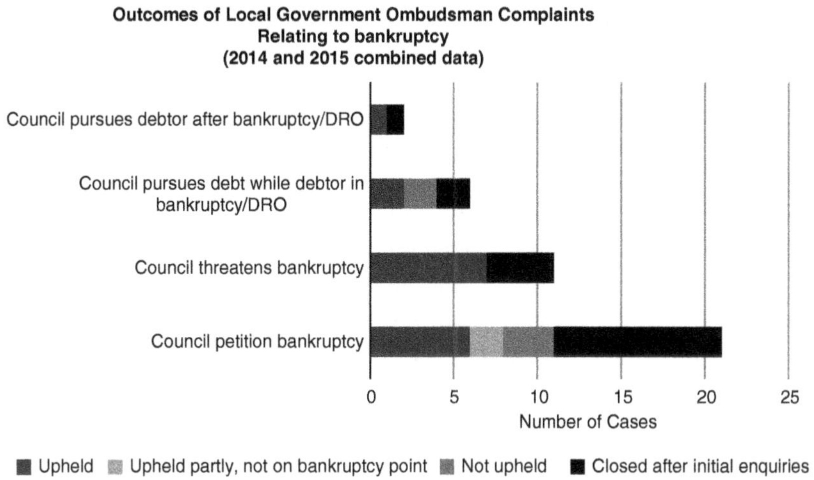

Figure 6.2: Outcomes of Local Government Ombudsman decisions in complaints relating to bankruptcy. Source: Local Government and Social Care Ombudsman

courts, which must deal with all debts without sector-specific knowledge. The effectiveness of these particular regulatory interventions remains open to question, however. Debt advice charities report that local authorities have become more cooperative.[153] A survey of the Ombudsman complaints decisions database in the years following this advice, however, shows that the institution has provided limited relief (Figure 6.2). Many cases are dismissed on procedural grounds due to complaints being raised after the expiry of the 12-month time limit, while others fail due to the ombudsman's jurisdiction not applying where a complainant has an available judicial remedy,[154] which the ombudsman deems to be the case when a debtor has the opportunity to challenge a bankruptcy order in court.[155] The result is that the Ombudsman will not intervene to correct maladministration when court proceedings are available; while courts will not police maladministration and will hold that a creditor is entitled to a bankruptcy order so long as statutory formalities are met. The courts neither allow public law values to

[153] Citizens Advice, 'The State of Debt Collection: The Case for Fairness in Government Debt Collection Practice' (n. 20).

[154] s. 26(6)(c) of the Local Government Act 1974; Briggs (n. 122) 3.

[155] See e.g. Local Government & Social Care Ombudsman, *Wolverhampton City Council* (13 003 161).

condition what counts as creditors' appropriate use of bankruptcy, nor allow the policy benefits of bankruptcy's social insurance function to limit creditors' ability to turn bankruptcy into a debt collection tool.

Recently enacted personal insolvency law reforms restrict creditor petitions by increasing the minimum debt threshold from £750 to £5,000.[156] This will have important practical consequences and may reduce local authority recourse to bankruptcy,[157] though the new threshold remains low.[158] The Insolvency Service justified the increased threshold by noting that bankruptcy was 'an extremely expensive' and 'largely ineffective' 'way of recovering low level debts'.[159] It also cautioned that given 'its potentially devastating effect upon individuals and families, bankruptcy should be used as a last resort by creditors'. The question of disproportionate use was the limit of the Insolvency Service's concerns regarding bankruptcy creditor petitions, however. The policy papers displayed no objections to the invocation of bankruptcy by creditors in higher value cases, indeed reaffirming bankruptcy as the 'strongest of debt recovery tools'. The agency entertained neither the possibility of denying an individual creditor the right to petition for bankruptcy where no collective creditor interest arises, nor more radical reforms to abandon the law's debt collection function entirely in view of its contemporary role as a safety net of last resort.[160]

6.3.3 *Litigating State Immunity from the Fresh Start*

If local government creditors must bear much responsibility as 'repeat players' for the problematic development of the law as an individual creditor's debt collection tool,[161] DWP litigation activities fit a similar pattern in relation to other core aspects of the law. The intensified collection of social welfare debt by this Department has included attempts to exempt themselves from the stay of creditor enforcement

[156] Insolvency Act 1986 Amendment Order 2015 (2015/922).
[157] Insolvency Service (n. 21) 26–7.
[158] The limits contrasts with the DRO debt ceiling of £20,000, which one might have thought represented a policy decision that cases involving debt levels lower than £20,000 have no place in the bankruptcy procedure.
[159] Insolvency Service (n. 21) 26.
[160] Chapter 3 argues for the law to abandon its debt collection function in all cases bar those of high-net worth debtors (leaving questions open in respect of that group). For support for this view, see e.g. Westbrook (n. 112).
[161] M. Galanter, 'Why the "Haves" Come out Ahead: Speculations on the Limits of Legal Change', *Law & Society Review* 9 (1974) 95.

and debt discharge. In two recent cases, the Department has taken litigation to the Court of Appeal[162] and Supreme Court[163] in efforts to exempt from these features of the bankruptcy and DRO procedures its methods of collecting social welfare overpayments via deductions from present payments. These claims fit an apparent pattern of litigation – visible before the financial crisis but seemingly intensified by the austerity agenda – brought by this government department to defend austerity policies in the courts.[164] The insolvency cases seek to reshape existing law to suit the government department's ends as a self-interested creditor seeking to maximise returns under overarching austerity policies. The DWP argued for special status due to their 'need to protect the public purse'[165] and suggested that a 'net entitlement principle' meant that a benefit claimant's right to payment is subject to any 'adjustment' made by the DWP to take into account past overpayments, with the effect that a claimant is only ever entitled to a 'net' sum of the benefit.[166] In litigating these cases based on an imperative of recovering public funds, the government seems to be abandoning a role as a public-spirited policymaker, and to be subordinating bankruptcy principles and policy to austerity's single-minded aim of reducing government deficits. This position was made clear by government's passing of legislation to overturn the Supreme Court's ultimate decision in *Cooper* that the DWP's claim to exceptional creditor status was incompatible with insolvency law.

In the first case, *Balding*, the High Court and Court of Appeal both held that a debtor's liability to repay overpaid social welfare payments (collected via deductions from ongoing government welfare payments to the debtor), was discharged by bankruptcy. In the second case, *Cooper*, the UK Supreme Court decided that the moratorium on enforcement

162 *Regina (Balding)* v. *Secretary of State for Work and Pensions* [2007] EWCA Civ 1327 [2008] 1 WLR 564.

163 *Regina (Cooper and Payne)* v. *Secretary of State for Work and Pensions United Kingdom Supreme Court* [2011] UKSC 60, [2012] 2 WLR 1.

164 For litigation concerning the 'bedroom tax', see *Daly & Ors, R (on the application of) (formerly known as MA and others)* v. *Secretary of State for Work and Pensions* [2016] UKSC 58 (UKSC (2016)); J. Meers, 'The Bedroom Tax in the Supreme Court: Implications of the Judgment', *Journal of Poverty and Social Justice* 25 (2017) 181. The 'benefit cap' policy has also been litigated, with further appeals pending at time of writing: *DA & Ors, R (On the Application Of)* v. *Secretary of State for Work and Pensions* [2017] EWHC 1446 (Admin) (EWHC (Admin)).

165 *Regina (Balding)* v. *Secretary of State* [2007] EWHC 759 (Admin) (High Court of Justice, England and Wales) [26].

166 *'Cooper UKSC'* (n. 163) [21–2].

under both the Debt Relief Order[167] and bankruptcy procedures prohibited deductions from debtor benefits to recover social welfare overpayments and sums borrowed from social fund loans.[168] While the superior courts thus reached conclusions that restrained the state's debt collection and ultimately discharged its debt, what is most significant is the reasoning of the court, which demonstrates clearly a view of personal insolvency law as serving an objective of maximising returns to creditors. This is notable in the contrasting approaches evidenced in the judgments of Davis J in *Balding* and in those of the Court of Appeal and Supreme Court in *Cooper*.

In *Balding*, both Davis J and the Court of Appeal based their decision on a literal interpretation of the Insolvency Act 1986's definitions of 'liability' and 'bankruptcy debt'. They found that social welfare legislation gave the DWP a right to recover an amount of benefits determined to have been overpaid; and imposed on the debtor a corresponding 'liability to pay money under an enactment', constituting a bankruptcy debt.[169] Since a court judgment to collect overpaid sums would undoubtedly create a bankruptcy debt, it would be illogical if recovery of the overpayment by alternative means (i.e. deducting the overpaid amount from future payments) would not.[170] Davis J's judgment is interesting, however, for aspects that deploy a purposive interpretation and so offer a judicial perspective on personal insolvency law's objectives. In reaching his conclusion that bankruptcy must bring an end to the deduction of social welfare payments from debtors, the judge described the policy underpinning bankruptcy's debt discharge as being 'to wipe the slate clean and, broadly speaking, enable the bankrupt to make a fresh start'.[171] The unacceptable vista of a debtor who has supposedly been given a fresh start remaining subject to enforcement in respect of pre-bankruptcy liabilities therefore would 'simply compel a conclusion' that the liability to repay benefits must be discharged by bankruptcy.[172] Davis J's reasoning affirms the fresh start policy and interprets the debt discharge

[167] Insolvency Act 1986, s. 251G(2).
[168] The Supreme Court overruled precedents that had prevented lower courts from including such recovery methods within bankruptcy's prohibition on enforcement (and which had meant that the scope of stay of enforcement was not at issue in the prior *Balding* case).
[169] For definitions of 'bankruptcy debt' and 'liability', see Insolvency Act 1986, ss. 382(1), 382(4).
[170] '*Balding EWHC*' (n. 165) [28].
[171] ibid, 41.
[172] ibid, 49.

as the 'essence' of a law[173] in which the provision of debt relief is a core objective shaping interpretation and application. This approach understands that the 'more debts that are excluded from the effect of the discharge, the less effective the insolvency regime can be in achieving the debtor's rehabilitation'.[174] It accordingly construes any exceptions to debt discharge narrowly. While the case did not call on Davis J to decide on the scope of bankruptcy's stay of enforcement, the judge nonetheless also offered views on the objectives underpinning this feature of the law, importantly identifying *both* debt collection and debt relief aims. The judge recognised that the orderly administration of the bankruptcy, through the protection of the debtor's estate for the benefit of creditors, 'of course' constitutes one rationale for the stay of enforcement. He identified another rationale as being to protect the debtor from proceedings, however, thus recognising the stay's debt relief function.[175] The judge appeared to recognise the 'breathing space' offered by the stay of enforcement,[176] and the centrality of such protection as 'the linchpin of bankruptcy relief'.[177]

In contrast, the Court of Appeal and Supreme Court in *Cooper* reasoned entirely on the basis that the stay of enforcement in bankruptcy serves aims of maximising returns to creditors. Under a view prioritising the law's debt collection function, the stay or moratorium represents the core of the creditors' bargain and gives the law its key *collective* nature, preventing individual advantage-taking and preserving *equality of creditors*. For reasons of precedent, the Court of Appeal's finding that the DRO moratorium on enforcement suspended social welfare payment deductions required distinguishing the purposes of the respective stays under the DRO and bankruptcy procedures.[178] Smith LJ followed the 'creditors' bargain' model in explaining that the purpose of the moratorium on enforcement in bankruptcy is 'to preserve the bankrupt's assets in order that they should be available for fair distribution'[179] to creditors, as

173 R. E. Flint, 'Bankruptcy Policy: Toward a Moral Justification for Financial Rehabilitation of the Consumer Debtor', *Washington and Lee Law Review* 48 (1991) 515.

174 World Bank (n. 26) para. 367.

175 *'Balding EWHC'* (n. 165) [52].

176 U. Reifner and others, *Overindebtedness in European Consumer Law: Principles from 15 European States* (Books on Demand Gmbh, 2010) 277. See also K. Porter, 'The Pretend Solution: An Empirical Study Of Bankruptcy Outcomes' *Texas Law Review* 90 (2011) 103, 142–4.

177 J. J. Kilborn, 'Mercy, Rehabilitation, and Quid Pro Quo: A Radical Reassessment of Individual Bankruptcy', *Ohio State Law Journal* 64 (2003) 855, 893.

178 *'Cooper EWCA'* (n. 97) [30], [54].

179 ibid, 85.

part of the process of administering the debtor's estate. In contrast, the judge saw the purpose of the DRO moratorium as simply providing 'immediate debt relief, but with a period for investigation [before final debt discharge] during which the order may be set aside'.[180] Toulson LJ clarified that 'the purpose of the DRO scheme is unadulterated debt relief, and it is entirely consistent with the nature of the scheme that from the making of the DRO a creditor to whom a specified qualifying debt is owed should have no "remedy in respect of the debt"'.[181] Therefore, the Court of Appeal saw the moratorium as serving a debt relief objective under the DRO procedure, but a debt collection aim in bankruptcy. These contrasting objectives then informed interpretations of the respective statutory provisions, justifying an extension of the moratorium under the DRO beyond the limits of the bankruptcy stay.

The Supreme Court in contrast decided that the *both* the DRO and bankruptcy procedures operated to suspend deductions from benefit payments to the debtor through their respective moratoria, before also subsequently discharging these liabilities.[182] Baroness Hale JSC accepted the Court of Appeal's logic that there is 'a major difference between the purpose of the waiting periods in each scheme'.[183] She nonetheless did 'not see any reason to distinguish the DRO scheme and bankruptcy' in respect of the scope of the stay. The court therefore affirmed the conclusion in *Balding* and applied its findings equally to the DRO regime as to bankruptcy. In contrast with the Court of Appeal's approach of treating the bankruptcy and DRO moratoria distinctly,[184] the Supreme Court considered appropriate a harmonious approach to the procedures.[185] This harmony did not result from a view that both procedures, and so the protection of the debtor from enforcement under both, have now come to serve the same debt relief objective. Though it might have, the Supreme Court did not conclude that the time has arrived to recognise that bankruptcy, just like the DRO procedure, now functions primarily as a support mechanism for financially troubled households. Rather, the Supreme Court supported the lower court's view that the sole function of enforcement protection in bankruptcy remains the preservation of the debtor's assets for creditors' benefit. The courts' recognition that the key

[180] ibid, 77.
[181] ibid, 85.
[182] *'Cooper UKSC'* (n. 163).
[183] ibid, 23.
[184] *'Cooper EWCA'* (n. 97) [54] (Toulson LJ).
[185] *'Cooper UKSC'* (n. 163) [28].

function of the stay of enforcement in the DRO procedure was one of debtor protection and debt relief did not extend to bankruptcy. Therefore, the courts in *Cooper* did not even recognise a debt relief objective of bankruptcy sufficiently to diagnose a conflict between this and the law's aim of maximising returns to creditors. Instead, for them the case turned on a tension between the law's collective nature and an individual creditor's right to collect its debt.[186]

6.3.4 *The Sharples Decision and Bankruptcy in a Housing Crisis*

Despite this reasoning, the ultimate outcome in *Cooper* was to protect debtors from collection efforts. In contrast, the consequences of the conception of personal insolvency law adopted by the courts in *Balding* and *Cooper* were starker in the case of *Sharples*, which raised a more direct conflict between the law's competing objectives.[187] Here the creditors in question were not state agencies, but non-profit housing associations of the type increasingly called upon to provide social housing in the context of privatisation and reduced state provision. The Court of Appeal heard joined appeals in two cases where housing associations wished to evict tenants who owed rent arrears and had sought insolvency protection. The Court answered negatively the key question of 'whether a bankruptcy order . . . and a DRO . . . preclude the making of an order for possession of a dwelling let on an assured tenancy[188] on the ground of rent arrears.'[189] Again the question resulted from the uncertain scope of insolvency's stay of any creditor's 'remedy in respect of a debt',[190] and the unclear effects of provisions of the Housing Act 1998 exempting the debtor's tenancy from the bankruptcy estate.[191] It would follow from the view of the stay of enforcement as serving to maximise creditor

[186] On this point, *see* Kilborn and Walters (n. 114) 123–4.
[187] *Places for People Homes Ltd* v. *Sharples; A2 Dominion Homes Ltd* v. *Godfrey* [2011] HLR 45; Spooner (n. 8), See also *Harlow District Council* v. *Hall* [2006] EWCA Civ 156, [2006] 1 WLR 2116.
[188] The tenancies were 'assured tenancies', in respect of which a court cannot make a possession order except on specified grounds. Some grounds are mandatory, while others are discretionary and allow courts to refrain from making an order where unreasonable. The relevant grounds here were the discretionary ground of rent arrears and the mandatory ground of eight weeks of unpaid rent. See Housing Act 1988 (1988 c. 50), s.7 and Schd. 2.
[189] '*Sharples*' (n. 187) [5].
[190] See Insolvency Act 1986, ss. 285, 251G(2).
[191] Insolvency Act 1986, s. 283(3A), inserted by Housing Act 1988 (c. 50), s. 117(1).

recoveries by preserving estate assets that the stay does not prevent an individual creditor from seizing an *exempt* asset such as a tenancy. Alternatively, if the stay serves debt relief aims, it must offer insurance against the debtor's eviction, since any meaningful fresh start requires stable housing and the externalities of homelessness are profound. The case thus required the court to make a stark choice between competing conceptions of the law's aims.

In reaching the conclusion that a debtor's entry into bankruptcy or the DRO procedure does not serve to protect her from eviction, Etherton LJ followed the logic of the courts in *Cooper* by reasoning that the purpose of the stay of enforcement is to preserve the debtor's estate for the benefit of creditors as a group. This meant that the stay does not prevent a landlord from seizing the tenancy where a tenancy constitutes an asset exempted from the estate. To take this asset would not disadvantage other creditors by reducing the pool of assets available for them in the estate.[192] Even though the DRO procedure does not involve repayments to creditors and so a debtor's estate, the court reached the same conclusion that the DRO stay does not prevent eviction. It acknowledged the 'broad policy point that the object of a DRO is the relief from debt of those with limited means and limited debts'.[193] Ultimately, however, it refused to allow this purpose to shape its conclusions in relation to the DRO's scope of protection. The court instead reverted to literalism in efforts to avoid giving 'an artificial meaning' to the relevant legislative provision.[194] The judge thus was comfortable adopting a purposive approach when the purpose in question was debt collection, but in contrast was unprepared to allow the debt relief objective determine legislative interpretation.[195] The decision amounts to a clear prioritisation of the law's debt collection objective, to the point of marginalising the debt relief aim. While it acknowledged this aim in providing that rent arrears are included in the debt discharge in both the bankruptcy and DRO procedures, its lack of protection against possession orders renders this finding moot, since debtors will in practice be compelled to pay arrears in order to avoid eviction.[196] In ruling that debtors entering insolvency are unprotected from eviction, it reveals the serious practical consequences

[192] '*Sharples*' (n. 187) [70].
[193] ibid, 77.
[194] Insolvency Act 1986, s. 251G.
[195] For parallels regarding judicial interpretation of IVA terms, see pages 137–143 above.
[196] Spooner (n. 8) 400.

of the idea that personal insolvency law is primarily a mechanism for collecting debts, and of efforts by public service providers to shape the law in this direction. The social costs of eviction are profound,[197] and it is difficult to argue that a law is committed to offering debtors a fresh start when it allows them to leave bankruptcy without a home.

6.5 Extending Bankruptcy's Social Insurance Function to Government Debts

These decisions form part of a wider pattern of English courts prioritising the aim of maximising returns to creditors in litigation over the discharge and stay of enforcement – central 'battlegrounds for determining the scope of a debtor's fresh start'.[198] Similar triumphs of creditor rights over debtor rehabilitation can be found in cases involving the courts' discretionary powers to discharge debts otherwise excluded from the scope of bankruptcy's discharge.[199] The *Balding, Cooper*, and *Sharples* decisions hold additional significance for a number of reasons. The cases are illustrative of trends in the development of the law over the past decade, showing that the crisis has not shocked the personal insolvency system into a re-evaluation of its core objectives and an acceptance of the need to prioritise debt relief. Rather the law may indeed have retreated from a prior position more protective of debtors. Importantly, consideration of these cases allows an extension of the framework proposed in Chapter 3 beyond the archetypal case of a loan advanced by a financial institution, to explore whether the framework applies equally to other contemporary categories of problematic debts such as those owed to government agencies. These cases led judges to offer views on policy questions of whether government debts should hold special status, and despite the outcomes reached, their comments often reveal support for the exclusion of government debt from the stay and discharge. The cases also raised questions regarding the redistributive nature of bankruptcy relief, and judicial comments are also significant in their visible discomfort at the effects of redistributing risk away from debtors and spreading it more widely in the manner required by an understanding of bankruptcy as social insurance. In this sense, judicial concerns regarding the costs for

[197] M. Desmond, *Evicted: Poverty and Profit in the American City* (Allen Lane, 2016); Spooner (n. 8) 397–8.

[198] J. S. Byington, 'The Fresh Start Canon', *Florida Law Review* 69 (2017) 115, 117.

[199] Insolvency Act 1986, s. 281(5); *Hayes* v. *Hayes* (2012) [2012] EWHC 1240; *McRoberts* v. *McRoberts* (2012) [2012] EWHC 2966 (Ch) (EWHC (Ch)).

others of assisting insolvent debtors mirror classic reactionary arguments that consumer and social protection reforms will produce opposite effects to those intended by policymakers.[200]

In *Cooper*, two Supreme Court judges expressed 'misgivings' regarding what they perceived as negative consequences of their seemingly grudging finding that the relevant social welfare debts should be incapable of collection. The courts worried that their decision would mean that overpaid claimants who

> have become bankrupt or subject to a DRO scheme, will now receive larger social security benefit payments – larger than they did prior to the bankruptcy or DRO and larger also than the social security benefits received by persons subject to such deductions who have avoided bankruptcy or a DRO scheme.[201]

This reasoning questions the legitimacy of household debt relief generally. The comments are striking, since it seems that a bankruptcy law – or any public policy intervention – should always improve the circumstances of those availing of the process, over those of someone similarly placed who does not avail of relief. Supreme Court judges similarly communicated concern that the decision they felt compelled by legislation to reach, in leading to the protection of insolvent debtors from collection, would mean that 'the social fund (a fund of limited resource designed to be replenished by repayment and thereby enabled to provide financial assistance to others in particular need) will be diminished'.[202] The judges questioned 'whether any of this is sensible or desirable', and indicated that they would not be surprised if government passed amending legislation to change this position.[203] Therefore the judges invited government to enact the subsequent legislation that overturned (in part) the Supreme Court decision.[204] This argument against debt relief reflects concerns motivating Etherton LJ's decision in *Sharples* that saving

[200] A. Hirschman, *The Rhetoric of Reaction: Perversity, Futility, Jeopardy* (Harvard University Press, 1991) 11. Baker notes that moral hazard is used similarly to caution against 'the perverse consequences of well-intentioned efforts to share the burdens of life': T. Baker, 'On the Genealogy of Moral Hazard', *Texas Law Review* 75 (1996) 237, 239.

[201] '*Cooper UKSC*' (n. 163) [44]; '*Balding EWHC*' (n. 165) [52].

[202] '*Cooper UKSC*' (n. 163) [28].

[203] ibid, 29, 44.

[204] The Insolvency (Amendment) Rules 2012 provide that the recovery of social fund loan debts is excluded prospectively from bankruptcy and DRO protection: see Milman (n. 154) 105. As discussed above, the Government subsequently abolished the social fund as part of welfare system cuts.

debtors from eviction would harm 'non-defaulting tenants who may have to pay higher rents to compensate for the landlord's lost revenue'.[205] Etherton LJ cautioned that such debtor protection

> could be financially catastrophic for [social] landlords … unable to recover possession from persistent non-payers and could threaten the availability of social housing to meet the great demand from the large number of people who are economically disadvantaged and seek suitable and affordable permanent accommodation.[206]

This mirrors the classic argument that debt relief ends up raising costs for borrowers. The social insurance theory of bankruptcy answers this concern readily, as it aims precisely to produce the outcome feared by these judges – the distribution of the risks of financialised capitalism more broadly in an effort to internalise social costs.[207]

When insurance theory poses the question of which party among the government creditor or debtor can best prevent default and bear its costs, the policy case for relieving the debtor of responsibility appears to hold. Debtors owing council tax, council tax benefit overpayments, social welfare overpayments, or social fund loans generally are in low-income groups.[208] People experiencing these debt problems are unlikely to have resources to self-insure against the risks of over-indebtedness, leading either to costs being passed elsewhere (onto family members, social welfare and healthcare systems),[209] and/or severe contractions in expenditure and a potential reduction of living standards below an accepted social minimum. This group also has a high marginal propensity to consume, meaning that significant reduced spending among affected debtors may give rise to negative macroeconomic effects.[210] Rather than inflicting 'catastrophic' costs on those debtors found to have received overpayments or who struggle to repay other government debts,[211] an approach that spread these costs among all welfare users might reduce the fear of unexpected debt problems and so restore faith in the

205 *'Sharples'* (n. 187) [5].

206 ibid, 71.

207 See pages 99–102 above.

208 One caveat is that local authorities' use of bankruptcy in the collection of council tax debt seems targeted at asset-holding debtors, though debt levels involved in reported council tax bankruptcy cases are not high.

209 C. G. Hallinan, 'The Fresh Start Policy in Consumer Bankruptcy: A Historical Inventory and an Interpretive Theory', *University of Richmond Law Review* 21 (1986) 49, 118–25; R. M. Hynes, 'Non-Procrustean Bankruptcy', *University of Illinois Law Review* 2004 (2004) 301, 340–2.

210 See text to notes 23–5 above.

211 World Bank (n. 26) para. 95.

welfare system as a safety net.[212] A wider understanding of the cost pool as including all taxpayers raises the broadest of political questions of whether taxpayers are willing to pay more for increased social protection. This leads to intractable debate, even in the contemporary context of increased technical recognition that debt and distribution 'matter' to macroeconomic prosperity,[213] and that equity and economic efficiency may be interlinked, rather than values to be traded against one another.[214]

It is almost trite to point out that government has the means to spread risks across the population, targeting taxation and regulatory burdens in order to reallocate costs efficiently.[215] Though interdepartmental conflict over budgets seems an inevitable part of government and has often constrained insolvency policy,[216] a holistic view of the overall impact of debt collection efforts can look beyond individual departments' short-term balance sheets towards the overall and longer-term economic impact of government action.[217] Such reasoning has spurred trends of reducing state priority in insolvency across several jurisdictions in recent decades.[218] Similarly in England and Wales, the Enterprise Act 2002 removed the priority status of tax debts, as government acted against its own immediate interest in order to mobilise insolvency policy as a facilitator of economic productivity.[219] The 2013 World Bank report on personal insolvency law argues that 'excluding government debts from the scope of discharge undermines the entire insolvency relief system', defeating the benefits which result from providing debtors

212 See n. 58 above.

213 G. Vlieghe, 'Debt, Demographics and the Distribution of Income: New Challenges for Monetary Policy – Speech by Gertjan Vlieghe, Bank of England' (Department of Economics and Centre for Macroeconomics Public Lecture, London School of Economics, 18 January 2016) www.bankofengland.co.uk/publications/Pages/speeches/2016/872.aspx accessed 5 November 2018.

214 'Tackling Inequality', IMF Fiscal Monitor: October 2017 (International Monetary Fund, 2017); A. B. Atkinson, *Inequality* (Harvard University Press, 2015) 243–62.

215 For analogies between taxation and regulation, see e.g. J. S. Masur and E. A. Posner, 'Should Regulation Be Countercyclical', *Yale Journal on Regulation* 34 (2017) 857.

216 Comptroller and Auditor General, *Helping Over-Indebted Consumers* (The Stationery Office, 2010) paras. 3.22–3.28; Fletcher (n. 96) 17.

217 K. Gross, *Failure and Forgiveness: Rebalancing the Bankruptcy System* (Yale University Press, 1997) 153.

218 *Report on Personal Debt Management and Debt Enforcement* (Law Reform Commission of Ireland 2010) 162–72 http://www.lawreform.ie/_fileupload/Reports/rDebtManagementsFinal.pdf accessed 5 November 2018; B. K. Morgan, 'Should the Sovereign Be Paid First – A Comparative International Analysis of the Priority for Tax Claims in Bankruptcy', *American Bankruptcy Law Journal* 74 (2000) 461, 481–495.

219 The Insolvency Service; Department for Trade and Industry (n. 26) para. 2.19.

with a fresh start.[220] Recent English developments therefore mark a departure from modern best practice in personal insolvency policy making, representing a reassertion by government of its status as a financially self-interested creditor, rather than as a supporter of (the fresh start) policy.

Secondly, in relation to the question of the most efficient preventer of losses, a strong argument can also be made that government creditors are better placed than their debtors to prevent debt problems. Any exceptional status in bankruptcy appears based on the idea that government is a deserving 'involuntary creditor', who must provide public services and levy taxes, and cannot choose to whom it extends 'credit'.[221] This argument is partly true in relation to taxation debts but does not fit well with overpayment claims of the type arising in *Balding* and *Cooper*. While public *services* must be provided by statutory entitlement, government holds significant control over the accrual of an overpayment 'debt'. Debtors do not incur government debts voluntarily through contractual borrowing, but through statutory regimes. Commentators note the complexity of these regimes and how difficulties in calculating liability (deducting benefit allowances) can lead to debt problems.[222] In relation to benefit overpayment debt, complexity is exacerbated by volatile working conditions, where a payment may turn from a legitimate entitlement to an overpayment debt based on the number of hours worked.[223] Overpayments of benefits can arise from claimant fraud, but also from administrative errors. These factors tend to be conflated and treated analogously, despite the crucial differences between debts arising from fraud and error.[224] As discussed in Chapter 7, the 'fresh start' has always been reserved for the 'honest but unfortunate' debtor,[225] and bankruptcy legislation already excludes from discharge debts arising by fraud.[226] In contrast, overpayment claims arising from error – due to the claimant's mistake, and/or especially where the error is administrative – come close to involuntary borrowing and amount often to 'debts

220 World Bank (n. 24) para. 373.
221 Gross (n. 217) 170.
222 Briggs (n. 122).
223 James (n. 27)
224 D. E. Chunn and S A. M. Gavigan, 'Welfare Law, Welfare Fraud, and the Moral Regulation of the "Never Deserving" Poor', *Social & Legal Studies* 13 (2004) 219, 228.
225 As *per* Sutherland J's classic formulation of the fresh start policy in the US Supreme Court: *Local Loan Co* v. *Hunt* (1934) 292 US 234 (US Supreme Court) 244.
226 Insolvency Act 1986, s. 281(3); *Templeton Insurance Ltd & Anor* v. *Brunswick & Ors* [2012] EWHC 1522 (Ch).

incurred to welfare agencies and the tax [authorities] without one knowing'.[227] By shifting losses away from debtors onto government agencies in these cases, bankruptcy law may encourage efficient administrative practices that reduce the occurrence of overpayment problems, in a manner analogous to the principle of 'responsible lending'.[228]

Further militating against the exceptionalism of government is the determination expressed by administrative officials to model themselves on commercial creditors in intensifying their collection efforts.[229] The Coalition Government praised new commercialised DWP and HMRC approaches to fraud and error, in stating that 'a private sector approach has been adopted, involving segmentation analysis' of debtors,[230] and measures 'to expand significantly the use of debt collection agencies [and] provide all government departments with a single route to access private sector debt services'.[231] These circumstances present a government acting as a self-interested creditor along commercial principles, and give credence to Lazzarato's assertion that under the neoliberal state the debtor-creditor relationship subsumes all others, including that between citizen and government.[232] This austere creditor increasingly adopts sophisticated technologies to enhance its collection efforts, alongside allocating itself exceptional statutory powers of recovery, and often benefitting from lighter touch regulation than that applicable to private sector actors.[233] These factors delegitimise claims that the personal insolvency system should be shaped to meet the exceptional needs of government creditors and to serve their 'duty' to recover public funds. To the contrary, they render government creditors less deserving of assistance from bankruptcy law than other creditors,[234] and appear to augment the need for the law to offer a safety net against new pressures and risks facing debtors.[235]

227 James (n. 27).

228 See also arguments of government negligence in allowing historic debts to persist for decades, only to be later revived: text to notes 54–6 above. A case for responsible lending applies even to a needs-based lending scheme such as the (now abolished) social fund, requiring realism regarding whether credit is the appropriate response to such need if repayments must be set at unaffordable levels.

229 See text to notes 70–9 above.

230 Department for Work and Pensions and HMRC (n. 43) 6. Roberts notes that segmentation practices by debt collection firms have been criticised as targeting vulnerable debtors: Roberts (n. 70) 681.

231 House of Commons Committee of Public Accounts (n. 45) para. 16.

232 Lazzarato and Jordan (n. 64) 30, 38.

233 See text to notes 48–above.

234 Morgan (n. 218) 467.

235 Ben-Ishai, Schwartz and Barretto (n. 7).

These government creditor practices again illustrate how ideas of financialised capitalism operate to increase the need for household debt relief, while influencing institutions in such a manner as to reduce relief. Similarly, judicial comments in *Balding, Cooper*, and *Sharples* regarding the exceptionalism of state debt claims suggest conversion to the logic of austerity. Mirroring statements in the creditor petition cases regarding government creditors' 'duty' to collect public monies,[236] the courts accepted an understanding that public monies – as represented by the 'ring-fenced' social fund – are constrained such that protecting a debtor necessarily reduces these funds. This view directs personal insolvency law towards austerity policy aims, rather than seeing the potential for the law to act as a counterweight to the pressures these policies place on individual households and the wider economy. To take fiscal consolidation concerns into account in bankruptcy policy reasoning ignores the credit/welfare trade-off and the policy case for treating bankruptcy as a social insurer of last resort and 'economic stabiliser'.[237] The result is pro-cyclical bankruptcy, as the law becomes an instrument of overarching trends of political economy and their problematic effects, rather than a bulwark against them.

6.6 Conclusions

The findings in this chapter have significant consequences for our understanding of English personal insolvency law, and particularly for questions of whether one can view the law as part of the social safety net. Many European systems expressly adopted rehabilitative consumer over-indebtedness laws in response to recessions of the 1990s and 2000s, conceptualising these laws as part of the social support system.[238] English law, in contrast, has through incremental reforms and market developments added rehabilitative and social support elements to a bankruptcy system originating in the commercial law. Policymakers and judges frequently persist in viewing the law in its original setting. Attitudes of courts displayed above are at one level emblematic of classic

[236] See text to notes 127, 165 above.

[237] See text to notes 85–7 above.

[238] J. Niemi-Kiesilainen, 'Consumer Bankruptcy in Comparison: Do We Cure a Market Failure or a Social Problem', *Osgoode Hall Law Journal* 37 (1999) 473, 481; I. Ramsay, 'A Tale of Two Debtors: Responding to the Shock of Over-Indebtedness in France and England – a Story from the Trente Piteuses', *The Modern Law Review* 75 (2012) 212, 234; Braucher (n. 84) 1066.

judicial preferences for facilitating market exchange and discomfort at engaging in redistributive processes.[239] They perhaps reflect the principle of early law-and-economics reasoning that private law is less efficient than taxation and welfare policies for addressing wider problems of inequality.[240] The personal insolvency system has offered little support in respect of priority debt problems, raising questions regarding its ability to offer protection to the poorest.[241] In a significant contribution to the then-nascent consumer bankruptcy literature, Niemi asked whether personal insolvency law should seek to cure a market failure or a social problem.[242] The conditions of contemporary financialised capitalism make it increasingly difficult to draw this boundary between the market and the social. The reduction in the state's role in augmenting incomes and offering public services has led households to turn increasingly to credit markets to meet essential needs and to maintain reasonable living standards. Austerity cuts have at times made this substitution of private debt for public debt particularly visible. State determination to reduce liabilities has extended from cutting expenditure to intensifying collection efforts. Human rights courts and public authority ombudsmen have shut their doors to debtors seeking protection from such efforts, reducing citizen-state interactions to a debtor-creditor relationship to be regulated by bankruptcy law. As the state has commercialised as well as privatised public services, it has sought on the one hand to act as a self-interested creditor; and on the other to plead for special status and to deploy private (insolvency) law as a tool for pursuing its taxation and welfare policies. Bankruptcy law has generally obliged on both fronts (albeit to varying degrees), revealing confusion at its core.

Extrapolating to a broader perspective, one can in this way see public debt working its way through all of society, from the macro to the micro circumstances of individual debtors.[243] Following the bail-outs of the crisis and subsequent fiscal contractions, public and private lines blur in many areas, to the point that 'it is virtually impossible to tell where the state ends and the market begins'.[244] Meanwhile debtors in financial stress turn to the personal insolvency system just as they turn to social

[239] I. Ramsay, 'Consumer Credit Law, Distributive Justice and the Welfare State', *Oxford Journal of Legal Studies* 15 (1995) 177, 179.

[240] ibid, 178; Hynes (n. 209) 328.

[241] Ben-Ishai, Schwartz and Barretto (n. 7); Ben-Ishai and Schwartz (n. 7).

[242] Niemi-Kiesilainen (n. 238).

[243] James (n. 27).

[244] Streeck (n. 1) 39.

welfare support, often due to identical causes.[245] As noted above, a key early finding of the Consumer Bankruptcy Project in the USA was that bankruptcy 'must be understood within a broad range of social support systems',[246] and that it is 'clear that many lawyers see it just that way'.[247] English lawyers, judges and government departments do not appear to share this view, seeing debt collection as 'a self-evidently appropriate use of bankruptcy'.[248] Debtors, money advisors, and perhaps also specialist regulators would recognise the US lawyers' view, however, meaning that a significant gap may exist between legal understandings and practice; between the judicial experience and the everyday life of the law. Whatever of conceptual understandings, it becomes increasingly difficult to present an empirical case for maintaining a rigid distinction between personal insolvency and the social welfare system. Bankruptcy is in the business of distribution, and must make decisions as to the direction in which it wishes to reallocate resources. In contemporary conditions of economic stagnation, inequality, and political discord, the policy argument for embracing the law's redistributive function, as a social insurer of last resort, seems compelling.

[245] See e.g. P. Ali, L. O'Brien and I. Ramsay, 'Bankruptcy and Debtor Rehabilitation: An Australian Empirical Study', *Melbourne University Law Review* 40 (2017) 688.

[246] T. Sullivan, E. Warren and J. L. Westbrook, *As We Forgive Our Debtors: Bankruptcy and Consumer Credit in America* (Beard Books, 1989) 333.

[247] Sullivan, Warren and Westbrook (n. 80) 169.

[248] Kilborn and Walters (n. 114) 123.

7

Moral Hazard and Bankruptcy Abuse Prevention

7.1 Introduction

7.1.1 The 'Very Bedrock' of Bankruptcy Law

This chapter focuses on the question of *moral hazard*. This is a key concept in insurance theory and so essential to understanding consumer bankruptcy in its role as a social insurance mechanism against the risks of contemporary financialised capitalism. In this context, the moral hazard concept concerns the risk that by providing extensive debt relief, bankruptcy law may create incentives for debtors to petition for debt relief when not in true financial difficulty, or to engage in borrowing practices which increase over-indebtedness. This chapter considers, within the framework of insurance theory and the economic concept of moral hazard, how English law guards against abuse of debt relief. This is an important subject due to the traditional importance of the maintenance of credit morality as 'the very bedrock'[1] and primary 'basic objective'[2] of English personal insolvency law, and the law's traditional concern in protecting the public from the potentially harmful actions of a dishonest debtor.[3] The historical concern around this issue means that questions of bankruptcy 'abuse' and the regulation of debtor (mis)conduct expose tensions between the origins of a quasi-criminal law[4] concerned with

[1] I. F. Fletcher, *The Law of Insolvency* 4th revised edn (Sweet & Maxwell, 2009) paras. 6–032.

[2] Sir Kenneth Cork, Insolvency Law and Practice: Report of the Review Committee (HMSO, 1982) para. 191.

[3] ibid, 1734 *et seq.*; Fletcher, *The Law of Insolvency* (n. 1) para. 11–031.

[4] C. J. Tabb, 'The Historical Evolution of the Bankruptcy Discharge', *American Bankruptcy Law Journal* 65 (1991) 325, 330; A. J. Duncan, 'From Disemberment to Discharge: The Origins of Modern American Bankruptcy Law', *Commercial Law Journal* 100 (1995) 191, 192 *et seq.*

punishing debtor deviancy,[5] and its modern operation as a social insurance mechanism of last resort for 'honest but unfortunate' debtors.[6] This issue also constitutes a 'fault line' between the law's debt collection and debt relief objectives. Policymakers, judges, and commentators who emphasise the efficiency of credit markets and prioritise the law's facilitation of debt collection will emphasise its role in compelling debtor repayment and upholding market bargains. Under this view, debtors are responsible for default and to permit them to avoid their obligations easily would erode confidence in market exchange.[7] In contrast, among those prioritising the law's aim of rehabilitating debtors and insuring against externalities inevitable in consumer credit markets (marked by information asymmetries and behavioural biases), most responsibility for default lies with lenders.

The issue of moral hazard is also a question that features prominently in political and policy debates surrounding bankruptcy.[8] The 'spectre of moral hazard is an inevitable part of accepting the broader benefits of a system of insolvency treatment', and concerns relating to debtor fraud feature regularly in discussions of bankruptcy law.[9] One of the most widely analysed (if deeply politicised) policy debates in consumer bankruptcy literature relates to changes in the US Bankruptcy Code enacted in the mid-2000s making it more difficult for debtors to access immediate debt relief under Chapter 7, instead forcing debtors into repayment plans under Chapter 13.[10] The justificatory (even if instrumentalist) argument behind this legislation was that rising bankruptcy rates were a sign of declining credit morality and 'stigma' concerning debt default,[11] and an

5 Cork (n. 2) para. 38; P. Ali, L. O'Brien and I. Ramsay, '"Short a Few Quid": Bankruptcy Stigma in Contemporary Australia', *University of New South Wales Law Journal* 38 (2015) 1575, 1576–7.

6 *Local Loan Co.* v. *Hunt*, 292 US 234, 244 (1934); L. Ponoroff and F. S. Knippenberg, 'Debtors Who Convert Their Assets on the Eve of Bankruptcy: Villains or Victims of the Fresh Start?', *New York University Law Review* 70 (1995) 235, 243; M. Howard, 'A Theory of Discharge in Consumer Bankruptcy', *Ohio State Law Journal* 48 (1987) 1047.

7 J. M. Czarnetzky, 'The Individual and Failure: A Theory of the Bankruptcy Discharge', *Arizona State Law Journal* 32 (2000) 393, 413.

8 I. Ramsay, *Personal Insolvency in the 21st Century: A Comparative Analysis of the US and Europe* (Hart Publishing 2017) 23–4.

9 World Bank, *Report on the Treatment of the Insolvency of Natural Persons* (2013) 41–2.

10 See e.g. J. Braucher, 'Theories of Overindebtedness: Interaction of Structure and Culture', *Theoretical Inquiries in Law* 7 (2006) 323, 338; A. M. Dickerson, 'Regulating Bankruptcy: Public Choice, Ideology, &(and) Beyond', *Washington University Law Review* 84 (2006) 1861; J. J. Kilborn, 'Still Chasing Chimeras but Finally Slaying Some Dragons in the Quest for Consumer Bankruptcy Reform', *Loyola Consumer Law Review* 25 (2012) 1, 2.

11 See e.g. Braucher, 'Theories of Overindebtedness' (n. 10) 338; Kilborn (n. 10) 1, 2.

accompanying abuse of bankruptcy's debt relief by opportunistic borrowers.[12] Australian debates have raised similar concerns regarding debt relief becoming available too easily, leading to legislative tightening of bankruptcy discharge criteria (although these rules appear set for loosening in the near future[13]).[14] When the 'Troika' of European Commission, European Central Bank, and International Monetary Fund directed personal insolvency reforms as part of their post-crisis financial assistance programmes across Europe, the inclusion of safeguards to address moral hazard concerns was a key policy priority.[15]

The tension between acknowledging the benefits of debt relief, while guarding against the risk of abuse, is clear in key English reforms to the bankruptcy procedure introduced by the Enterprise Act 2002. These measures offered a more generous debt discharge, after just one year, as part of measures to 'address the fear of failure and reduce the stigma of bankruptcy . . . to encourage those who have failed honestly to try again.' Policymakers balanced this aim, however, with measures 'providing a robust and effective remedy against the small minority who abuse their creditors'.[16] The chapter focuses particularly on this new 'robust and effective remedy' – the system of Bankruptcy Restrictions Orders (BROs) and Bankruptcy Restrictions Undertakings (BRUs).[17] This system is an innovative addition to a range of more traditional safeguards against abuse built into personal insolvency laws. It offers the potential for the law to establish contemporary standards of debtor conduct, and appropriate approaches to questions of debtor fault and stigma.

[12] See also E. Warren, 'The Market for Data: The Changing Role of Social Sciences in Shaping the Law', *Wisconsin Law Review* 2002 (2002) 1, 13–20.

[13] P. Ali, L. O'Brien and I. Ramsay, 'Misfortune or Misdeed: An Empirical Study of Public Attitudes towards Personal Bankruptcy', *University of New South Wales Law Journal* 40 (2017) 1098, 1107–1110.

[14] N. Howell and R. F. Mason, 'Reinforcing Stigma or Delivering a Fresh Start: Bankruptcy and Future Engagement in the Workforce', *University of New South Wales Law Journal* 38 (2015) 1529, 1530.

[15] I. Ramsay, 'Two Cheers for Europe: Austerity, Mortgage Foreclosures and Personal Insolvency Policy in the EU' in H. W. Micklitz and I. Domurath (eds.), Consumer Debt and Social Exclusion (Routledge, 2015); Ramsay, *'21st Century'* (n. 8) 158–69; J. Spooner, 'The Quiet-Loud-Quiet Politics of Post-Crisis Consumer Bankruptcy Law: The Case of Ireland and the Troika', *Modern Law Review* 81 (5) (2018) 790–824.

[16] *Productivity and Enterprise: Insolvency – A Second Chance* Cm 5234, Executive Summary (The Insolvency Service; Department for Trade and Industry, 2001).

[17] A parallel system of Debt Relief Restrictions Orders and Debt Relief Restrictions Undertakings (DRRO/Us) has also been introduced in respect of the Debt Relief Order procedure. References in this chapter to the Bankruptcy Restrictions Order/ Undertaking (BRO/U) regime generally include references to DRRO/Us.

The chapter highlights limitations of the system, however. It shows how the regime's origins and operation are heavily influenced by historical norms not designed for contemporary conditions of household indebtedness – notably the quasi-penal nature of early bankruptcy laws and the law's traditional identity as a branch of commercial law. Trends in the application and enforcement of the law – characteristic of government agency practices in the contemporary financialised state – create further limitations. They pursue contractarian and commercialised approaches that risk negative outcomes for individual debtors, as well as inhibiting the development of transparent standards of appropriate borrowing conduct. The contractarian and commercialised approach of public agencies in their enforcement of the law is consistent with a general marketisation of personal insolvency law. In this context, the chapter concludes by arguing that the law may have surrendered (moral and legal) authority over the regulation of debtor conduct to creditors and credit reporting agencies. The chapter shows how these developments fit uneasily with aims of debtor rehabilitation and an acceptance of personal insolvency law as a social insurance mechanism necessary to alleviate the risks inherent in the contemporary debt economy.

7.1.2 The Household Debt Expansion and the Reasonableness of Consumer Borrowing in a Debt-Dependent Economy

As discussed throughout this book, financial crisis and recession have led to increased recognition that the household debt expansion of recent decades has been excessive, and that the 'privatised Keynesianism' model is unsustainable due to the risks of economic stagnation, inequality, and political instability it generates. Debates on this macro question, between advocates of the 'democratisation of credit' and critics of a 'loans for wages' economic structure, are reflected in micro debates concerning bankruptcy 'abuse'. Certain authors and policymakers accuse households of borrowing excessively through 'over-consumption', facilitated by the availability of overly generous bankruptcy laws.[18] Alternative accounts point to structural reasons for increased debt and default, and external causes of financial distress.[19] In other words, discussions reflecting on the

[18] See e.g. Judge E. H. Jones and T. J. Zywicki, 'It's Time for Means-Testing', *Brigham Young University Law Review* 1999 (1999) 177.

[19] E. Warren, 'The Over-Consumption Myth and Other Tales of Economics, Law, and Morality', *Washington University Law Quarterly* 82 (2004) 1485; T. A. Sullivan, E. Warren and J. L. Westbrook, 'Less Stigma or More Financial Distress: An Empirical

household debt expansion of recent decades often turn to a question of the reasonableness of consumer borrowing. This challenges bankruptcy law to establish contemporary standards of reasonable borrowing. There is little dispute about the appropriateness of debt relief for the 'honest but unfortunate' debtor,[20] and similarly 'amoral calculators' are widely seen as worthy of censure when they lie to creditors or to courts/administrative officials or conceal assets.[21] Greatest controversy arises in the intermediate category of the 'spendthrift'[22] or 'improvident'[23] consumer debtor, in some cases an 'incurably naïve optimist'.[24] Such cases involve substantive misconduct, and scrutiny of debtor's *ex ante* pre-insolvency borrowing behaviour;[25] raising questions more difficult than those of procedural misconduct arising from the debtor's *ex post* behaviour in insolvency proceedings themselves. It is this category that produces most controversy and the most nuanced application of the concept of moral hazard, and cases of this type come closest to affording bankruptcy law the opportunity to pass judgment over decades of household debt expansion.

7.1.3 Neoliberalism, Financialisation and the Responsible Financial Consumer

Financialisation has created severe structural problems of excessive household debt and over-indebtedness, developing a strong case for the collectivisation of risk through household debt relief policies, including more generous bankruptcy laws. Yet elements of the economic regime that necessitate such policy responses also hinder their adoption. Under 'neoliberal governmentality',[26] not only official policies, but the rationality of neoliberalism itself, push individuals towards responsible

Analysis of the Extraordinary Increase in Bankruptcy Filings', *Stanford Law Review* 59 (2006) 213.

20 C. G. Hallinan, 'The Fresh Start Policy in Consumer Bankruptcy: A Historical Inventory and an Interpretive Theory', *University of Richmond Law Review* 21 (1986) 49, 65–6; L. M. LoPucki, 'Common Sense Consumer Bankruptcy', *American Bankruptcy Law Journal* 71 (1997) 461 *et seq.*

21 Fletcher, *The Law of Insolvency* (n. 1) paras. 11–007.

22 LoPucki (n. 20) 461, 464.

23 Hallinan (n. 20) 66–71.

24 Howard (n. 6) 1054.

25 Howard (n. 6), 1053–7.

26 J. Vass, 'Restoring Social Creativity to Immoderate Publics: The Case of the Financially Incontinent Citizen', *The Sociological Review* 61 (2013) 79, 86.

consumption, with society and debtors themselves attributing blame inwards for financial difficulty.[27] The process of financialisation has been founded on faith in the efficiency of financial markets, and a project of market expansion or 'financial deepening'.[28] Critics of this process of 'financial inclusion' argue that it merely involves exposing households to new risks and shifting responsibility from collective institutions to individual households.[29] Financial literacy policies can have similar effects in individualising the structural problem of over-indebtedness and pathologising the defaulting consumer,[30] so 'that relatively powerless individuals bear responsibility and consequences for fiscal decisions taken in the global financial marketplace'.[31] Contributions to this process include policy discourse (even the turn to behavioural economics and its emphasis on consumers' limited capacity for 'rational' decision making[32]), credit industry branding of struggling debtors as 'irresponsible' (and so to be offered loans only at profitable high interest rates), and media messaging.[33]

Media portrayals of consumer debtors during the pre-crisis boom highlighted extravagant 'credit binges' and the 'debt culture' gripping the UK, as well as 'sharp', 'soaring' and 'alarming' rises in personal insolvency.[34] These increases were accompanied by media criticism of the reformed law's excessive generosity, as it allegedly welcomed 'bankruptcy tourists', and caused the country's descent into a 'bankruptcy brothel'.[35] When the financial crisis struck following this period of

[27] Ramsay, *'21st Century'* (n. 8) 26–7.

[28] A. Turner, *Between Debt and the Devil: Money, Credit, and Fixing Global Finance* (Princeton University Press, 2015) 32–48.

[29] C. Berry, 'Citizenship in a Financialised Society: Financial Inclusion and the State before and after the Crash', *Policy & Politics* 43 (2015) 509, 511.

[30] Vass (n. 26) 83.

[31] ibid, 96.

[32] ibid, 86–9.

[33] ibid, 82–3; K. Porter, 'Bankrupt Profits: The Credit Industry's Business Model for Postbankruptcy Lending', *Iowa Law Review* 93 (2007) 1369.

[34] I. Ramsay, '"Wannabe WAGS" and "Credit Binges": The Construction of Overindebtedness in the UK' in J. Niemi, I. Ramsay and W. C. Whitford (eds.), *Consumer Credit, Debt and Bankruptcy: Comparative and International Perspectives* (Hart Publishing, 2009).

[35] See e.g. E. Moya 'London risks becoming "brothel" for bankruptcy tourists' *The Guardian*, 31 January 2010, www.guardian.co.uk/business/2010/jan/31/insolvency-uk-law-bankruptcy-foreign accessed 11 November 2018: A. Walters and A. Smith, '"Bankruptcy Tourism" under the EC Regulation on Insolvency Proceedings: A View From England and Wales', *International Insolvency Review* 19 (2010) 181; Ramsay, *'21st Century'* (n. 8) 179–84.

increased borrowing, it was largely 'blamed on some combination of spendthrifts, irresponsible speculators and mortgage dealers, and the financially illiterate poor'.[36] William Davies argues that the post-crisis 'punitive neo-liberalism' era entangles 'economic dependency and moral failure . . . in the form of debt',[37] to the point that debtors experience feelings of self-recrimination and expectations of further punishment.[38] Citizens may even feel that they 'deserve' the hardship of austerity in atonement for debt-fuelled economic growth.[39]

Difficulties arise from two directions for those aiming to give effect to more extensive household debt relief while guarding against the risk of abuse. On one hand, bankruptcy law's historical origins mean the persistence of ideas of bankruptcy law as a commercial law designed for debt collection, with an additional penal dimension. On the other hand, financialisation and neoliberalism extend commercial reasoning to the individual (or 'entrepreneur of the self') and the state (in the marketisation of government and public agencies) in a manner that leads bankruptcy towards procedural contractarianism, attribution of responsibility to debtors, the maximisation of returns to creditors, and a reduced moral authority of the state. Conditions of political economy that apparently make extensive debt relief essential to averting economic stagnation, alleviating inequality, and reducing political instability also work to prevent bankruptcy from providing such relief.

7.2 Moral Hazard, Debtor Misconduct and Bankruptcy 'Abuse'

7.2.1 The Politics and Morality of Moral Hazard

This chapter aims to explore the technical concept of moral hazard and its usefulness in policy design and evaluation. It acknowledges, however, that 'moral hazard has never been a straightforward, purely logical or scientific concept'.[40] The technical account detaches the 'moral' from moral hazard, focusing instead on institutional incentives and the

[36] M. Fourcade and K. Healy, 'Seeing Like a Market', *Socio-Economic Review* 15 (2017) 9–29, 12.

[37] W. Davies, 'The New Neoliberalism', *New Left Review* (2016) 121, 130.

[38] W. Davies, J. Montgomerie and S. Wallin, 'Financial Melancholia – Mental Health and Indebtedness' www.perc.org.uk/project_posts/financial-melancholia-mental-health-and-indebtedness/ accessed 20 July 2017.

[39] L. Stanley, '"We're Reaping What We Sowed": Everyday Crisis Narratives and Acquiescence to the Age of Austerity', *New Political Economy* 19 (2014) 895.

[40] T. Baker, 'On the Genealogy of Moral Hazard', *Texas Law Review* 75 (1996) 237, 239.

'universal utility-maximising subject',[41] while ignoring the question of whether an individual's moral compass might make her more or less likely to take advantage of such incentives. In the 'definitive study of moral hazard',[42] Tom Baker argues that this approach is a feature of how the concept has been used in (neo-classical economic) policy making since approximately the 1970s. He notes that the concept as it originated in the insurance context held dual aspects of both 'temptation' (loosely approximating to economists' 'incentives') and 'character'. Baker argues that the removal of character from the concept was itself political, and part of the neoliberal mobilisation of a simplified notion of moral hazard to promote a deregulatory agenda and oppose redistribution.[43]

Baker shows, however, that a careful application of the technical concept – complete with a thorough consideration of its underlying assumptions – can offer a useful and even progressive tool of policy analysis.[44] This seems particularly true when analysis incorporates advances in information and behavioural economics, as well as the increasing adoption of macroeconomic approaches in law-and-economics.[45] Furthermore, even if one acknowledges that the reconceptualisation of concepts in neo-classical economic terms has been part of the neoliberal political project ('neoliberalism's disenchantment of politics by economics'), Davies argues that this trend constrains political power as 'neoclassical economics becomes a soft constitution for government'.[46] If a technical understanding of moral hazard has been deployed by policymakers in pursuance 'of the interests of the economically powerful',[47] its use as a tool of analysis offers critics a means of holding the powerful to account, and of evaluating them against standards of governance they set for themselves. For these reasons, as well as moral hazard's central place in the insurance theory framework used throughout the book, this chapter's analysis applies the technical understanding of the concept. While

[41] A. Leaver, 'Fuzzy Knowledge: An Historical Exploration of Moral Hazard and Its Variability', *Economy and Society* 44 (2015) 91, 94.

[42] ibid, 93.

[43] Baker (n. 40) 290–2. For consideration of the centrality of the idea of moral hazard to contemporary conservative political thought, see W. Davies, 'What Are They After?' London Review of Books (8 March 2018) 3.

[44] Baker (n. 40) 291.

[45] See e.g. J. S. Masur and E. A. Posner, 'Should Regulation Be Countercyclical', *Yale Journal on Regulation* 34 (2017) 857; Y. Listokin, 'Law and Macroeconomics: The Law and Economics of Recessions', *Yale Journal on Regulation* 34 (2017) 791; J. Furman, 'How Lawyers Can Help Macroeconomists in the Wake of Three Major Challenges Keynote Address', *Yale Journal on Regulation* 34 (2017) 709.

[46] Davies, 'The New Neoliberalism' (n. 37) 128.

[47] Baker (n. 40) 291.

policymakers might not expressly use the language of moral hazard when discussing questions of condemnable borrowing or 'abuse' of bankruptcy, this chapter treats the concept of moral hazard as the most productive lens through which to view these issues.

This does not deny, however, that there is a less technical, more political aspect of 'the vague and value-laden concept' of moral hazard.[48] Leaver suggests that moral hazard is a 'fuzzy' form of economic knowledge, a concept that 'has consistently meant different things to different authors'.[49] In the bankruptcy context, at times policymakers invoke it in a non-technical sense when expressing opposition to debt relief policies,[50] rendering unclear distinctions between the technical and the political or ideological. A further complication is that policymakers, commentators, and politicians regularly appear to adopt purely value-laden approaches to questions of debtor conduct, which suggest a lack of concern for economic efficiency or any technical justification for policy positions beyond personal convictions. These include fears of a general decline in moral standards if individuals are allowed to discharge their debts too readily ('the sky will fall'),[51] often based on 'an ideological conviction that personal responsibility explains most financial misfortune'.[52] Concerns also arise that borrowers (and so voters) who are doing the 'right' thing by repaying their debts perceive an injustice in fellow citizens being rewarded with debt discharge for doing the 'wrong' thing of 'walking away' from their debts.[53] Certain insolvency law experts are open in their view that bankruptcy law rightly possesses a moral dimension emphasising individual responsibility, and must maintain 'the highest attainable standards of commercial morality and business integrity'.[54]

[48] M. McCaffrey, 'The Morals of Moral Hazard: A Contracts Approach', *Business Ethics: A European Review* 26 (2017) 47.

[49] Leaver (n. 41) 93.

[50] See e.g. the commitment of the Irish Government to the Troika to reform personal insolvency law 'with the objective of increasing the speed and efficiency of proceedings *while at the same time mitigating moral hazard and maintaining credit discipline*' (emphasis added): European Commission, *Economic Adjustment Programme for Ireland: Summer 2012 Review*, p. 61.

[51] K. N. Klee, 'Restructuring Individual Debts', *American Bankruptcy Law Journal* 71 (1997) 431, 432; L. R. Lupica, 'The Consumer Debt Crisis and the Reinforcement of Class Position', *Loyola University Chicago Law Journal* 40 (2008) 557, 604.

[52] Warren (n. 19) 1509–10.

[53] K. Gross, 'Demonizing Debtors: A Response to the Honsberger-Ziegel Debate', *Osgoode Hall Law Journal* 37 (1999) 263, 270; LoPucki (n. 20) 463–4.

[54] I. Fletcher, 'Bankruptcy Law Reform: The Interim Report of the Cork Committee, and the Department of Trade Green Paper', *The Modern Law Review* 44 (1981) 77, 78; I. Fletcher,

The chapter recognises, therefore, that it may not be possible or appropriate to separate politics from 'science' entirely.[55] There may be an important political role played by bankruptcy's claim to establish moral standards of debtor conduct.[56] The insurance industry's assurances that they could screen individuals of bad character from their markets helped to legitimise the expansion of redistribution through insurance.[57] In a similar way, bankruptcy law's claim that it establishes appropriate moral standards may legitimate the institution of debt relief.[58] The risk, of course, is that one can go too far with this legitimating process – both through sanctioning debtors too heavily and through stigmatising innocent debtors by promoting too widely the message that bankruptcy's role is to punish culpable debtors (see below).[59] The moral hazard approach has the advantage of offering an approximate means of calculating the costs and benefits of 'insurance' and calibrating safeguards proportionately. Further, while a moralistic approach treats the maintenance of standards of commercial behaviour as a discrete objective alongside the law's other aims, the moral hazard concept allows issues of debtor conduct to be integrated into the single coherent account of bankruptcy as a social insurance mechanism.

7.2.2 *Moral Hazard as a Policy Tool*

The insurance theory of bankruptcy views the law, through its key institution of debt discharge, as a means of allocating the risks of the contemporary debt-based economy in an efficient manner. In this way the law can minimise overall risk by making losses more predictable and

'"Out of Sight, out of Mind"? The Progressive Dematerialisation of Our Insolvency Procedures', *Insolvency Intelligence* 30 (2017) 81, 85.

55 J. R. Hackney, 'Law and Neoclassical Economics: Science, Politics, and the Reconfiguration of American Tort Law Theory', *Law and History Review* 15 (1997) 275.

56 For ethical analyses of bankruptcy, see e.g. K. Gross, *Failure and Forgiveness: Rebalancing the Bankruptcy System* (Yale University Press, 1997); J. Kilpi, The Ethics of Bankruptcy (Routledge, 1998); H. M. Hurd, 'The Virtue of Consumer Bankruptcy' in R. Brubaker, R. M. Lawless and C. J. Tabb (eds.), A Debtor World: Interdisciplinary Perspectives on Debt (Oxford University Press USA, 2012).

57 Baker (n. 40) 240.

58 See e.g. Levitin's argument that bankruptcy should be theorised as a mechanism for mediating political relationships: A. J. Levitin, 'Bankrupt Politics and the Politics of Bankruptcy', *Cornell Law Review* 97 (2011) 1399.

59 For recent studies of stigma in bankruptcy, see M. D. Sousa, 'Bankruptcy Stigma: A Socio-Legal Study', *American Bankruptcy Law Journal* 87 (2013) 435; Ali, O'Brien and Ramsay (n. 5); Howell and Mason (n. 14).

incentivising lending practices which reduce levels of default.[60] This perspective also acknowledges the corresponding problem of moral hazard, however, and the risk that the availability of debt relief may create incentives for borrowing practices which increase levels of default and over-indebtedness. The classic concept of moral hazard refers to the 'tendency for insurance against loss to reduce incentives to prevent or minimise the cost of loss'.[61] Reduced incentives to prevent the loss arising are conceptualised as *ex ante* moral hazard, while *ex post* moral hazard is the theoretical tendency for insurance to reduce incentives to minimise costs of recovering from loss.[62] Applied to personal insolvency law, moral hazard concerns firstly arise as to the extent to which the discharge, by relieving the debtor of over-indebtedness, creates incentives (at the *ex post* stage) for the debtor to enter an insolvency procedure at the first sign of financial difficulty without a true need for debt relief. At the *ex ante* stage, similar concerns arise regarding debt relief's tendency to create incentives for consumers to over-borrow in the first place.[63] For neo-classical economic theorists, the law must take serious account of both of these sets of incentives. Behavioural economists and socio-legal researchers are more concerned only with the *ex post* incentives,[64] as they argue that assumptions of moral hazard theory required to generate *ex ante* concerns do not hold in consumer over-indebtedness's empirical reality (see Part 7.5 below). The assumptions of moral hazard theory include:

1) Money (the reduction in a debtor's liability in the case of personal insolvency law) compensates for loss;
2) People are rational economic actors (including rational loss minimisers);
3) Taking care to prevent loss requires effort;
4) Taking care is effective;
5) The insured has control over herself, her property and her financial circumstances; and

60 Personal insolvency policy is but one of many issues which, through insurance theory, 'can best be understood as an institutional adaptation to the problems of risks and incentives'. See J. E. Stiglitz, 'Risk, Incentives and Insurance: The Pure Theory of Moral Hazard', *The Geneva Papers on Risk and Insurance – Issues and Practice* 8 (1983) 4.

61 Baker (n. 40) 239; Hallinan (n. 20) 84, 92, 103; R. M. Hynes, 'Non-Procrustean Bankruptcy', *University of Illinois Law Review* 2004 (2004) 301, 329; Stiglitz (n. 60); ibid, at 5.

62 Baker (n. 40) 270.

63 Hallinan (n. 20) 92.

64 ibid; A. J. Levitin, 'Resolving the Foreclosure Crisis: Modification of Mortgages in Bankruptcy', *Wisconsin Law Review* 2009 (2009) 565, 644.

6) Insurance payments are not conditioned on a given standard of care on the part of the insured.[65]

A further insight incorporated into personal insolvency law is the relational nature of moral hazard,[66] meaning that every legal amendment addressing the risk of debtor moral hazard may increase incentives for lenders to raise risk levels in their lending practices. One of the notable achievements of economists' explorations of moral hazard is to illustrate how 'insurance' is not simply a product provided by insurance companies as traditionally understood, but relates to any case in which the actions of one party have consequences for the risk of loss carried by another.[67] The issue of moral hazard is a two-way phenomenon, and any reduction in the debt relief provided under the law means that debtors (and ultimately wider society) are providing increased insurance to creditors in respect of their unsuccessful lending decisions. This book argues that conditions of the contemporary debt-dependent economy require personal insolvency law to play a market disciplining role in incentivising creditors to lend responsibly and internalise the social costs of credit markets. If so, measures addressing debtor moral hazard must guard against creating a moral hazard problem on the supply side of the market.

7.3 Addressing Moral Hazard under English Law

7.3.1 The Cost of Debt Relief: Designing Incentives

In both academic and political debates in which moral hazard is invoked, the point is sometimes underappreciated that the concept's value lies 'not in the recognition that insurance could have undesirable consequences . . . but rather in the claim that the undesirable consequences could be controlled'.[68] Insurance theory illustrates a number of ways in which personal insolvency law can address moral hazard, largely mirroring means through which insurance contracts can be structured to reduce perverse incentives. Ultimately the guiding principle of moral hazard is that the costs and benefits of insurance must be calculated so that an insured cannot profit from a loss. Personal insolvency laws must be structured to avoid this risk, and English law demonstrates a wide range

65 Baker (n. 40) 276.
66 ibid, 275.
67 ibid, 272.
68 ibid, 240.

of measures designed to ensure that a debtor conducting a cost-benefit analysis is not incentivised to over-borrow or otherwise fail to avoid over-indebtedness. The system relies on imposing such costs so that the procedures are attractive only to debtors carrying severe burdens of over-indebtedness, 'for whom the possibility of externalisations of those burdens are correspondingly large'.[69]

First, English personal insolvency law causes all debtors entering procedures to bear part of the costs of their default, just as an insurance contract may require the insured to pay a deductible or co-payment.[70] The law achieves this first by conditioning access on the debtor's insolvency,[71] meaning that the debtor herself will have to incur considerable costs (loss of income/assets, stress and health difficulties, shame of financial failure, etc.) from the onset of initial default until her insolvency.[72] Furthermore, English law requires a debtor in bankruptcy to surrender her non-exempt[73] assets for liquidation,[74] while the debtor may also be required to contribute excess income to creditors under an Income Payments Order/Agreement.[75] Under the insurance theory of the fresh start policy, these features of personal insolvency law address moral hazard concerns even though they differ from features of bankruptcy law traditionally seen as sanctioning misconduct, such as restrictions/incapacities and criminal law penalties.[76] Obvious and literal 'costs' of accessing debt relief are the fees payable on applying to the bankruptcy and Debt Relief Order (DRO) procedures, and the practitioner fees accompanying an IVA. At one level, these fees could be considered as designed to raise the costs of access and so address moral hazard concerns [see Part 7.6 below]. As Chapters 4 and 5 show, however, the motivations behind these fees are varied and uncertain.

[69] Hallinan (n. 20) 131.
[70] ibid, 103.
[71] The insolvency conditions for accessing the DRO, Individual Voluntary Arrangement and bankruptcy procedures all require that the debtor must 'unable to pay her debts' when applying to enter the procedure, as stated in Insolvency Act 1986, ss. 251A, 255(1) and 256A(3), 272(1) (respectively).
[72] For evidence of the hardships endured by US debtors before accessing bankruptcy, see P. Foohey and others, 'Life in the Sweatbox', *Notre Dame Law Review* (94 (2018) – forthcoming).
[73] Insolvency Act 1986, s. 282(2).
[74] On the distribution of the debtor's assets, see Fletcher, *The Law of Insolvency* (n. 1) ch. 10.
[75] Insolvency Act 1986, ss. 310, 310A.
[76] Hallinan (n. 20) 144.

For a lawyer who views personal insolvency law as a debt collection mechanism, the above analysis might seem unfamiliar. From this perspective, these features are not conceptualised as serving aims of preventing undesirable debtor behaviour, but as serving the law's purpose of maximising returns to creditors (with the debt collection perspective requiring additional sanctions to deter irresponsible borrowing and default). So, an insolvency condition is seen as necessary for defining the point at which a common pool problem arises which necessitates a collective debt collection remedy,[77] and surrender of the debtor's income and assets is seen as the key feature of the law. From this viewpoint, other features such as debt discharge are merely auxiliary facilitators of the maximisation of assets/income available to creditors, or serve an unrelated 'independent social policy' of helping debtors.[78]

The advantage of the insurance analysis of bankruptcy is that these features of the law can be explained and calibrated under a single theory, rather than relying on a range of rationales and objectives as underlying the law's different aspects.[79] Even under an understanding of bankruptcy as insurance, however, the question always remains as to whether the costs attached to debt relief are sufficient to prevent over-borrowing and subsequent insolvency from becoming utility-maximising behaviour. These concerns arise particularly in relation to the one-year waiting period for discharge in bankruptcy[80] introduced under the Enterprise Act 2002 as an express policy choice to reduce bankruptcy's costs.[81] The law recognises that additional safeguards are necessary to monitor and prohibit certain debtor conduct, so to remove incentives for actions which could reduce the costs of debt relief for that debtor. The law thus

[77] S. Block-Lieb, 'Fishing in Muddy Waters: Clarifying the Common Pool Analogy as Applied to the Standard for Commencement of a Bankruptcy Case', *American University Law Review* 42 (1992) 337, 406 *et seq*. Court decisions can be found to support this reasoning, in rejecting debtor petitions for bankruptcy as abusive where no common pool issue arises. In the case of *The Debtor* v. *Allen* the debtor owed only a single debt which he was unable to pay immediately in full, but could pay via instalments over time, leading to court to find the debtor did not meet the insolvency condition of inability to pay one's debts. See *Re A Debtor (No17 of* 1966), ex parte the Debtor v. Allen [1967] 2 WLR 1528; Fletcher, The Law of Insolvency (n. 1) paras. 5–004. See also the recent case of *Lock* v. *Aylesbury Vale District Council* [2018] EWHC 2015 (Ch), [2018] All ER (D) 136.

[78] T. H. Jackson, *The Logic and Limits of Bankruptcy Law* (Harvard University Press, 1986) 201; Block-Lieb (n. 77) 427.

[79] Howard (n. 6) 1069.

[80] Insolvency Act 1986, s. 279.

[81] See e.g. Fletcher, *The Law of Insolvency* (n. 1) paras. 11–007; D. Milman, *Personal Insolvency Law, Regulation and Policy* (Ashgate Publishing Limited, 2005) 123, 154.

prohibits (and sanctions through the Bankruptcy Restrictions Orders / Undertakings (BRO/U) regime and criminal penalties) the concealment of, or fraudulent dealing with, property by the debtor. Similarly, restrictions on the debtor's ability to borrow and trade during the bankruptcy[82] and DRO[83] moratoria further perform *ex post* and *ex ante* monitoring functions.[84] *Ex post* monitoring of the debtor's true need for relief is facilitated by the insolvency access condition, investigation of the debtor's affairs, and the duty imposed on the debtor to co-operate in the insolvency proceedings,[85] (the latter of which is punishable severely by the suspension of discharge,[86] BRO/Us and criminal liability).[87] *Ex ante* monitoring of the insured by the insurer at the borrowing stage is facilitated by excluding from debt discharge (and so from insurance coverage) debts incurred by fraud,[88] since such fraud inhibits lenders from conducting accurate creditworthiness assessments (and setting interest rates or 'premiums' to match risk levels).[89]

Where a risk falls within an insured's endogenous control so that the insured can cause the relevant loss intentionally, the only response of insurance markets may be to deny coverage. A premium accurately covering the risk could be prohibitively expensive.[90] Such acts may also be socially undesirable, so that insurance should not encourage their committal.[91] This reasoning provides another explanation for the exclusion from discharge of fraudulently incurred debts, as well as justifying

[82] See the range of prohibitions and offences outlined in the Insolvency Act 1986, Insolvency Act 1986, ss. 353–360, 390; Fletcher, *The Law of Insolvency* (n. 1) paras. 11–021, 13–001 *et seq*.

[83] Insolvency Act 1986, ss. 251K, 251N–251S.

[84] Certain of these prohibitions, such as on the debtor obtaining credit above a prescribed amount without disclosing her status as a bankrupt, or on engaging in business under a different name, facilitate *ex ante* monitoring of future borrowing by the debtor's creditors.

[85] Insolvency Act 1986, ss. 251J, 290–1, 312.

[86] Insolvency Act 1986, s. 279(1); Fletcher, *The Law of Insolvency* (n. 1) paras. 11–004-11–005. Courts have made this sanction more severe through a recent trend of issuing indefinite suspensions of discharge: see text to notes 203–5 below.

[87] Fletcher, *The Law of Insolvency* (n. 1) paras. 13–030.

[88] Insolvency Act 1986, ss. 251I(3), 281(3).

[89] *Templeton Insurance Ltd & Anor* v. *Brunswick & Ors* [2012] EWHC 1522 (Ch).

[90] Hallinan (n. 20) 103; A. Feibelman, 'Defining the Social Insurance Function of Consumer Bankruptcy', *American Bankruptcy Institute Law Review* (2005) 13 129, 137.

[91] On the link between insurance and the encouragement of undesirable conduct, see Baker (n. 40) 259–60. When considerations of the social desirability of conduct enters into the moral hazard analysis, however, they fuel criticisms that the concept involves too much moral judgment to be a tool of technical analysis.

the exclusion of criminal law fines and debts arising from tortious acts.[92] Exclusions from discharge of certain categories of debt may substitute for scrutiny of debtor conduct at the point of access to insolvency procedures.[93]

Conditions for accessing personal insolvency procedures also exclude outright certain debtors from debt relief coverage. A court may dismiss a bankruptcy case where a petition constitutes an abuse of process, or annul a bankruptcy order where it ought not to have been granted.[94] Courts for example have used this power to dismiss a petition of a debtor who has entered bankruptcy multiple times while repeatedly obtaining credit with no intention of repayment.[95] Policymakers setting the debt relief cost-balance have access to less information than debtors regarding their preferences and the price they are willing to pay for debt relief. If a debtor, by entering bankruptcy multiple times, reveals that her subjective preferences do not value the costs of bankruptcy as being too high to reduce incentives to become over-indebted (even if these costs would dissuade most debtors), then moral hazard theory justifies denying debt relief to such debtor.[96] Outright denial of insurance coverage is only rarely appropriate, however, again based on the premise that moral hazard theory does not require the denial of insurance where perverse incentives exist, but rather the structuring of insurance in a manner to reduce or remove these incentives.[97] Consistently with this position, English courts rarely exclude a debtor from accessing

[92] Insolvency Act 1986, ss. 251A(4), 281(4)–(5). An alternative explanation suggests tortious debts are excluded because these involuntary creditor claims do not fit in the insurance model of debt relief at all, since such creditors do not have the opportunity of assessing the risk of non-payment by the debtor, and of charging an appropriate risk-adjusted premium/interest rate: see e.g. Hallinan (n. 20) 107–8. English law appears to support this latter explanation in the extent to which the wide exclusion of tortious debts from discharge in bankruptcy extends beyond claims arising from deliberate acts, to include those arising from the debtor's negligence. Also, this may explain the law's exclusion of family maintenance debts from discharge.

[93] T. Linna, 'Consumer Insolvency: The Linkage between the Fresh Start, Collective Proceedings, and the Access to Debt Adjustment', *Journal of Consumer Policy* (2015) 1.

[94] Insolvency Act 1986, ss. 264(2), 266(3), 282(1)(a); Fletcher, *The Law of Insolvency* (n. 1) paras. 6–083-6–088.

[95] *In Re Betts* (1901) [1901] 2 KB 39.

[96] Though questions might arise as to whether all debtors have equal ability to recover from bankruptcy, and the extent to which some debtors find themselves having to resort to bankruptcy a second time out of necessity, despite considering the costs of bankruptcy to be very high. See Part 7.5 below.

[97] Baker (n. 40) 240.

bankruptcy debt relief entirely.[98] English law's approach is therefore one of relatively open access to debt discharge, followed by rigorous scrutiny of the debtor after her entry into the procedure. This approach is more compatible with the insurance conception of bankruptcy and the law's debt relief objective than approaches in other jurisdictions which screen debtors closely for misconduct at the point of entry.[99] Exclusion from debt discharge may be an effective safeguard against abusive behaviour, but any benefits may be outweighed by the externalities associated with the unavailability of relief to over-indebted households.[100]

Apart from the structural features described thus far, insurance contracts may also guard against moral hazard by obliging the insured to take certain steps to avoid a risk. Similarly, English law imposes obligations on a debtor not to be careless in increasing the risk of insolvency, by sanctioning the incurrence of debt without reasonable likelihood of repayment under the BRO/U regime.

7.3.2 *Bankruptcy Restrictions Orders and Undertakings*

Bankruptcy law reform and the introduction of the Debt Relief Order procedure in the 2000s reduced the costs of debt relief.[101] This was

[98] Fletcher, *The Law of Insolvency* (n. 1) paras. 6–086-6–087. Stricter access conditions attach to the DRO procedure, however, as a debtor may be excluded due to her previous participation in an insolvency procedure, or her giving of a preference or making of an undervalued transaction: Insolvency Act 1986, Schd. 4ZA, paras. 2–10. Fewer limitations attach to access to the IVA procedure, and an IVA debtor is subject to fewer restrictions and sanctions during the procedure, most likely because under this procedure creditors are given final say as to whether the costs of debt relief in a particular IVA are set sufficiently highly. See, however, the criminal liability imposed on fraudulent debtors under s. 262A of the 1986 Act.

[99] World Bank (n. 9) para. 189.

[100] Hallinan (n. 20) 130; World Bank (n. 9) para. 197; 'Dealing with Household Debt', World Economic Outlook 2012 (International Monetary Fund, 2012) 24–5, 27 www.imf.org/external/pubs/ft/weo/2012/01/pdf/c3.pdf accessed 11 November 2018.

[101] These reforms clearly aimed to make debt relief available more generously and with reduced stigma. Legislation did not remove all restrictions and incapacities applying to debtors, however, but rather limited their application by reducing the waiting period for discharge. 'Core' restrictions on debtors accessing credit or acting in certain roles of responsibility (for example as company directors and insolvency practitioners) continued to apply for the one-year period: see K. Moser, 'Restrictions after Personal Insolvency', *Journal of Business Law* (2013) 679, 684, 692–4. In addition, sectoral legislation, professional association rules and industry codes include various restrictions on debtor employment while in bankruptcy. For a comprehensive treatment of this issue in the Australian context, see Howell and Mason (n. 14).

counterbalanced by the introduction of the system of Bankruptcy Restrictions Orders and Undertakings (BRO/Us) and Debt Relief Restrictions Orders and Undertakings (DRRO/Us).[102] In prescribing certain types of conduct as giving rise to sanctions, the BRO/U system imposes additional obligations on debtors to take steps to reduce the risk of over-indebtedness, as well as not to take actions which could inhibit monitoring of the debtor, exaggerate her need for assistance, or generally skew the cost-benefit balance. In the *Randhawa* decision, the court described this function of the regime, albeit through the language of 'deterrence' rather than of moral hazard. The court commented that while 'the main object of making a BRO must undoubtedly be the protection of the public', the 'jurisdiction is also intended to have a deterrent effect'.[103] Parliament thus intended 'to impose a substantial sanction in any case where the bankrupt's conduct was shown to have fallen below the appropriate standard'. This aim of deterrence has been repeated in other judgments.[104] A Bankruptcy Restrictions Order must be made by a court where the court thinks it appropriate having regard to the bankrupt's conduct both before and after the making of the bankruptcy order (thus encompassing both substantive and procedural misconduct).[105] The court is required to take into particular account a range of specified 'kinds of behaviour' on the part of the bankrupt,[106] which are discussed below. The system therefore responds to concerns that, even though the cost-benefit balance of debt relief may be appropriate in most cases, certain actions of calculating debtors can reduce the costs of debt relief so that over-borrowing or exaggerating the need for debt relief become profitable. The restrictions regime applies to a small minority of cases, with 444 orders (35) or undertakings (409) made in 2017–18.[107]

In terms of sanctions, a BRO/U operates to impose incapacities on a debtor preventing her (on pain of criminal penalty), for a period of between 2 and 15 years,[108] from holding positions including the following:[109]

102 The Insolvency Service; Department for Trade and Industry (n. 16) paras. 1.25–1.45.
103 *Randhawa* v. *Official Receiver* [2006] BPIR 1435 [69].
104 *Official Receiver* v. *May* [2008] EWHC 1778 (Ch) [24]; *Official Receiver* v. *Bathurst* [2008] EWHC 1724 (Ch) [30]–[31].
105 Insolvency Act 1986, Schd. 4A, para. 2(1).
106 Insolvency Act 1986, Schd. 4A, para. 2(2)–2(3).
107 Insolvency Service, 'Insolvency Service Enforcement Outcomes: 2017/18'. For context, there were just over 15,000 bankruptcies and almost 25,000 DROs in 2017.
108 Insolvency Act 1986, Schd. 4A, paras. 4(2), 9(2).
109 See A. Walters, 'Personal Insolvency Law after the Enterprise Act: An Appraisal', *Journal of Corporate Law Studies* 5 (2005) 65, 87.

- Company director (unless authorised by a court);[110]
- Insolvency practitioner[111] or receiver/manager of a company's property;[112]
- Member of Parliament;[113]
- Member of a local authority.[114]

Perhaps more relevantly to the average consumer debtor, a BRO/U also prohibits a debtor from obtaining credit above a prescribed amount without disclosing her status.[115] Most importantly, details of any debtor subjected to post-discharge restrictions are entered into a public register maintained by the Secretary of State.[116] In this way, the BRO/U sanction primarily imposes costs on the debtor in her future credit market participation by damaging her credit reputation.[117] Immediate costs of debt relief are not increased, as the debtor's discharge remains unaffected.[118] The public nature of the restrictions mean that the sanction may have effects even outside of credit markets, for example potentially influencing debtors' employment prospects.[119]

This form of sanction is comparatively distinctive, taking the form of restrictions rather than entry conditions, denial of discharge, or criminal penalties.[120] It is a form of protection – of lenders and of 'the public', as mentioned below – based on information disclosure, sending messages to credit markets regarding the heightened credit risk represented by culpable, as opposed to honest, debtors.[121] The law effectively aims to sort debtors in order to alleviate information asymmetries and adverse selection problems in consumer credit markets,[122] facilitating more accurate

[110] Companies Director Disqualification Act 1986, s. 11(1).
[111] Insolvency Act 1986, s. 390(5).
[112] ibid, s. 31.
[113] ibid, s. 426A.
[114] Local Government Act 1972 (1972 c. 70), s. 81(1)(b).
[115] Insolvency Act 1986, ss. 251S(3)(b), 360(5).
[116] ibid, Schd. 4A; para. 12.
[117] See Parts 7.4, 7.6 below. On the role of this information in setting a premium to reflect a potential insured's risk, see Hallinan (n. 20) 102.
[118] Walters (n. 109) 77.
[119] See e.g. Howell and Mason (n. 14).
[120] See e.g. World Bank (n. 9) para. 114. Contrast with the limitations on access and discharge designed to address debtor misconduct in the laws of France, Belgium and Ireland: see e.g. J. Spooner, 'Fresh Start or Stalemate? European Consumer Insolvency Law Reform and the Politics of Household Debt', *European Review of Private Law* 21 (3) (2013) 747, 751–62.
[121] Walters (n. 109) 86.
[122] See e.g. Hallinan (n. 20) 102; Stiglitz (n. 60) 5.

creditor lending decisions (and more accurate pricing of risk via interest rates).[123] The personal insolvency system,[124] and particularly the BRO/U regime, thus represents an information-based regulatory response to market failure, mirroring information disclosure rules which have dominated consumer credit regulatory policy on the opposite side of the market in recent decades. It is based on the contrary assumption, however, that lenders enter the market at an informational disadvantage.[125]

The new BRO system provides a means for English law to address the controversial *ex ante* moral hazard cases of substantive debtor misconduct and 'improvident' consumer debtors, through the inclusion of borrowing without reasonable expectation of repayment as a condemnable type of behaviour. Indeed, this was the most common ground for BRO/Us in the early years of the system (Figure 7.2). From a comparative perspective, English law is unusual in investigating the reasonableness of the debtor's *ex ante* borrowing.[126] US law has traditionally not examined the debtor's pre-bankruptcy conduct (with the exception of intentional misconduct and fraud).[127] Prohibitions on irresponsible or reckless over-borrowing are much more limited in scope in the USA than under English law's questioning of the reasonableness of the debtor's expectation of payment.[128] Similarly, while French law's 'good faith' access condition extends somewhat further into an examination of borrowing conduct,[129] the French courts have confirmed that

[123] See e.g. Hallinan (n. 20) 102; A. A. Leff, 'Injury, Ignorance and Spite – The Dynamics of Coercive Collection', *Yale Law Journal* 80 (1970) 1, 28.

[124] Under a creditor protection perspective, personal insolvency law and its debt discharge can be seen as a means of reducing wasteful collection costs by providing 'a device by which creditors could efficiently discover that their debtors' financial circumstances rendered further collection efforts pointless'. See Hallinan (n. 20) 82.

[125] T. Eisenberg, 'Bankruptcy Law in Perspective', *UCLA Law Review* 28 (1980) 953, 982.

[126] World Bank (n. 9) para. 195.

[127] Hallinan (n. 20) 126; LoPucki (n. 20) 462.

[128] Certain consumer debts are presumed by US law to be non-dischargeable on the grounds of being incurred by false pretences or fraud, including consumer debts of more than $500 owed to a single creditor for luxury goods/services incurred within 90 days before bankruptcy; and cash advances under an open ended consumer credit plan exceeding $750 in value obtained within 70 days before bankruptcy: see USC Title 11 – Bankruptcy, USC s. 523(a)(2)(C)(i)–(ii). While these categories examine the borrowing conduct of the debtor, they in effect police deliberate borrowing with the intention of entering bankruptcy; rather than merely unreasonable or improvident over-borrowing.

[129] See e.g. I. Couturier, 'La Condition de Bonne Foi Pour Le Reglement Des Difficultés Liées Au Surendettement Des Particuliers', *Le Surendettement des Particuliers* (Anthropos, 1997) 77–82.

mere negligence on the part of the debtor does not amount to bad faith, so as to exclude her from accessing debt relief.[130]

7.4 Limitations of the Bankruptcy Restrictions Order/ Undertaking System in addressing Moral Hazard

Ultimately the BRO/U regime has been a problematic means of addressing moral hazard in consumer bankruptcy. Academic commentaries have subjected the system to considerable criticism,[131] while Insolvency Service evaluations also admit to failures in achieving intended objectives. The Service identifies the BRO system as being primarily 'designed to provide protection for the public',[132] and a key feature of the Enterprise Act's approach of balancing this aim with the objective of de-stigmatising bankruptcy is the drawing of distinctions by potential lenders between culpable and non-culpable debtors.[133] On evaluating the regime the Service found, however, that lenders do not distinguish between the two categories in their lending practices.[134] The regime also does not appear to contribute much towards legitimising the insolvency system in the public eye, since Insolvency Service found that less than a third of the public it surveyed agreed that the insolvency regime protected the public from dishonest or reckless bankrupts.[135] Approximately half of respondents were undecided on this question, and a lack of public awareness or opinion was confirmed by findings that only approximately one fifth of respondents thought they had heard of BRO/Us, and no respondents were able to describe them accurately. This part argues that the system's failure can be traced in part to path dependency and the application of historical commercial norms to a novel context of mass household over-indebtedness.[136] It also identifies

[130] I. Ramsay, 'A Tale of Two Debtors: Responding to the Shock of Over-Indebtedness in France and England – a Story from the Trente Piteuses', *The Modern Law Review* 75 (2012) 212, 229.

[131] Moser (n. 101); Fletcher, 'Out of Sight' (n. 54).

[132] *A Study of the Bankruptcy Enforcement Regime before and after the Enterprise Act 2002* (Insolvency Service, 2007) 18.

[133] Walters (n. 109) 86.

[134] *Enterprise Act 2002 – the Personal Insolvency Provisions: Final Evaluation Report November 2007* (Insolvency Service, 2007) 98.

[135] Insolvency Service, *A Study of the Bankruptcy Enforcement Regime before and after the Enterprise Act 2002* (n. 132) 21.

[136] I. Ramsay, 'U.S. Exceptionalism, Historical Institutionalism, and the Comparative Study of Consumer Bankruptcy Law', *Temple Law Review* 87 (2014) 947, 952–5; B.A. Hansen and M. E. Hansen, 'The Role of Path Dependence in the Development of US Bankruptcy

problems in the administration of the system and argues that these are symptomatic of trends in governance and political currents characteristic of the contemporary era of financialised capitalism.

7.4.1 Applying a Historical Commercial System to Contemporary Consumer Debtors

The ability of the BRO/U regime to establish contemporary standards of household borrowing behaviour is limited by the law's development, involving the mere layering of new ideas of debtor rehabilitation 'onto an older quasi-criminal bankruptcy law'.[137] Historically the law has operated in the commercial law sphere, where it was (perhaps appropriately in the business-to-business context) focused on enforcing contracts and collecting debts. The 'kinds of behaviour' which a court must take into account in deciding whether a BRO is appropriate[138] were not developed based on considerations of modern conditions of consumer credit use. Rather these standards are adopted almost verbatim from the Bankruptcy Act of 1914.[139] Rather than being shaped 'in the light of experience and developing commercial circumstances',[140] the BRO/U regime is based on standards of behaviour expected under a historical law which presumed misconduct and placed strict duties on debtors to maximise returns to creditors.[141] Despite occasional judicial opinions emphasising that in the period since historical bankruptcy laws were enacted 'social views as to what conduct involves delinquency, as to punishment . . . have drastically changed . . .',[142] this aspect of the legislation is inconsistent with modernisation efforts. In simply reproducing historical standards, the legislature effectively opted out of the debate

Law, 1880–1938', *Journal of Institutional Economics* 3 (2007) 203; P. Pierson, 'Increasing Returns, Path Dependence, and the Study of Politics', *The American Political Science Review* 94 (2000) 251.

137 Ramsay, *'21st Century'* (n. 8) 75.

138 Insolvency Act 1986 Schd. 4A, para. 2(1)–(3).

139 Under the 1914 legislation, courts were obliged to take into account these factors when assessing whether to discharge a debtor under that statute's conditional discharge system Bankruptcy Act 1914 (4 & 5 Geo. 5), s. 26. See also Cork (n. 2) paras. 1854–7.

140 ibid para. 1858.

141 For a consideration of how a perspective of bankruptcy prioritising debt collection might lead to certain debtor conduct being judged as culpable, see Ponoroff and Knippenberg (n. 6) 301–4.

142 *Smith (A Bankrupt)* v. *Braintree District Council*, [1990] 2 AC 215, 237–8 (1989), *per* Lord Jauncey.

relating to what might constitute acceptable contemporary household credit behaviour.

Secondly, the BRO/U regime is symptomatic of a second wider flaw in English bankruptcy law: the application of commercial standards to what is now a social insurance mechanism – a de facto consumer law, social welfare law, or more broadly a 'law of hardship'.[143] While attitudinal and legislative changes may have shifted personal insolvency out of its quasi-criminal origins, many engaged in law and policy continue to categorise bankruptcy within the field of commercial and corporate law. As consumer bankruptcies were growing in the early 1990s, an influential report written by insolvency experts expressed alarm at this 'abuse of the system', given that bankruptcy was never designed for non-business debtors.[144] More recently, a representative contemporary quote welcomes how legal and social changes have 'taken personal insolvency from the realm of crime and moral outrage and *into the commercial sphere where it more properly belongs*' (emphasis added).[145] The BRO/U emanates from such thinking, as it was introduced as part of a policy initiative designed to promote entrepreneurship, and expressly modelled on rules for the disqualification of company directors.[146]

Case law on the BRO/U regime illustrates the consequent difficulty of applying standards developed in the corporate governance context to contemporary circumstances of household debt, and to cases of debtors borrowing to fund their personal lives.[147] In the leading case of *Randhawa* v. *Official Receiver*, Sir Launcelot Henderson QC drew from the policy documents preceding the introduction of BRO/Us a 'predisposition' to construe the relevant provisions in a manner analogous to corresponding provisions relating to company director disqualifications. The judge therefore followed director disqualification cases in deciding on the level of judicial discretion available under BRO jurisdiction and on the method of calculating the appropriate duration of restriction orders.[148] He was nonetheless 'alert to . . . the inherent differences in [the] subject matter' of corporate and personal insolvency.[149]

143 J. Braucher, 'Response to Eric Posner', *Fordham Journal of Corporate & Financial Law* 7 (2001) 463.
144 *Insolvency Law: An Agenda for Reform* (JUSTICE, 1994) 15.
145 P. Patterson, 'Indefinite Suspension of Discharge from Bankruptcy – a Worrying Trend?', *Insolvency Intelligence* (2016) 21.
146 The Insolvency Service; Department for Trade and Industry (n. 16) para. 1.30.
147 See also Walters (n. 109) 89.
148 '*Randhawa*' (n. 103) [70]–[74].
149 ibid, 68; Walters (n. 109) 89.

The judge identified difficulty in applying corporate governance standards 'concerned only with conduct as a director . . . of a company, which is of course a separate legal person to which directors stand in a fiduciary relationship', to a debtor's 'own financial affairs [which do not] involve a fiduciary relationship' and which involve circumstances 'of almost infinite variety'.[150] While the list of types of conduct to be considered by the judge are not exhaustive, the court noted that it cannot 'carry out a roving inquiry into the bankrupt's conduct, but will instead have to focus on specific allegations of misconduct and decide whether they are made out on the evidence'.[151] Even given this judicial acceptance that the entire lifestyle and financial affairs of the debtor should not be on trial, uncertainties remain as to how an enquiry into the appropriateness of a consumer's conduct in her private financial affairs can be conducted under standards designed for investigating a company director's compliance with specific freely assumed duties. A director accepts the highest behavioural standards of a fiduciary, in circumstances in which such duties are justified by information asymmetries and principal-agent problems inherent to corporate management structures. This situation bears little resemblance to that of a household borrower funding personal expenditure via credit sold by an institutional creditor who holds significantly superior information and ability to prevent default and bear its costs.[152]

7.4.2 *Financialised Capitalism, New Public Management, and the Enforcement of Bankruptcy Law*

(i) Procedural Problems: Contractualisation and the Limits of Consumer Plea Bargaining

A further problematic aspect of the restrictions regime in consumer bankruptcy is that the vast majority of restrictions are actually imposed by BRUs rather than BROs. The existence of BRUs is consistent with trends discussed in other chapters in demonstrating English law's tendency to apply ideas of self-interested market bargaining to personal insolvency. Even the sanctioning of the debtor becomes a commodity for which parties should bargain. Authors such as Lazzarato identify the contractualisation of 'social relations' and public services as a feature of

150 *'Randhawa'* (n. 103) [62].
151 ibid, 66–67.
152 Ponoroff and Knippenberg (n. 6) 277–8.

contemporary financialised capitalism.[153] He argues that this is part of neoliberalism's process of individualisation and neutralisation of 'collective' logics, serving to conceal the asymmetry of power between state agents and citizens. Instead the public institution becomes a series of individual contracts, linking various actors who pursue their own self-interests and are considered formally equal.[154] This process also transforms the state-citizen relationship to a creditor-debtor relationship, as the consumer debtor signs up to an undertaking with a public official and becomes the debtor of the state. The system also exhibits the ideology of small government, and has a clear basis in an aim of reduced public spending (via the removal of court proceedings),[155] a significant theme in insolvency policy since the 1980s.[156] Consistent with the neo-classical economic underpinnings of financialised capitalism, a debtor is expected to price the risk and costs of challenging the Official Receiver's allegations in contested BRO proceedings, before reaching an arrangement that enhances both (rational economic) parties' welfare by sharing the saved costs of litigation.[157] Such a bargain, apparently reflecting the parties' best interests, is assumed to produce an efficient outcome benefitting the public interest.

This contractual approach may be appropriate to the law's original commercial context. There company directors or business debtors may have sufficient information and access to professional advice (regarding both their *ex ante* financial affairs and the *ex post* navigation of insolvency law) as to negotiate an undertaking which protects their interests. Superior access to legal knowledge may allow directors and corporate debtors to strike arrangements with Official Receivers that represent genuine consensus.[158] In the consumer debtor context, however, it is difficult to see how the undertaking system will not merely reproduce the contracting failures arising in consumer credit contracts (Chapter 3) and

[153] M. Lazzarato and J. D. Jordan, *The Making of the Indebted Man: Essay on the Neoliberal Condition* reprint edn (Massachusetts Institute of Technology Press, 2012) 101.

[154] ibid, 102.

[155] Fletcher, 'Out of Sight' (n. 54) 83.

[156] Fletcher, 'Bankruptcy Law Reform' (n. 54); J. Spooner, 'Recalling the Public Interest in Personal Insolvency Law: A Note on Professor Fletcher's Foresight', *Nottingham Insolvency Business Law eJournal* 3 (2015) 537.

[157] In this regard the assumptions underlying the BRU regime are similar to those relating to the negotiation of settlements in civil litigation and plea bargaining in criminal law proceedings: see e.g. S. Bibas, 'Plea Bargaining Outside the Shadow of Trial', *Harvard Law Review* 117 (2003) 2464, 2464.

[158] World Bank (n. 9) para. 52.

insolvency arrangements (Chapters 4 and 5). Substantial information asymmetries exist between debtors and Official Receivers, particularly regarding the content of the law and its consequences for the debtor. While a large majority of debtors obtain advice before entering bankruptcy,[159] in only a small number of cases is legal advice received. No advice is available in respect of post-bankruptcy decisions in what the debt counselling industry considers an 'unmanaged' remedy.[160] This position has been exacerbated by austerity policies and cuts to public funding.[161] Concerns arise regarding debtors' ability to challenge the Official Receiver's allegations of wrongdoing (including the official's interpretation of legislation), or alternatively to negotiate an optimal arrangement. Debtor feelings of stigma, self-blame and personal failure[162] may inhibit their ability to contest accusations of wrongdoing.

Furthermore, ideas of behavioural economics also render dubious the assumption that parties are rational economic actors who agree only to undertakings where benefits exceed costs. On the one hand, optimism bias may lead some debtors unadvisedly to challenge allegations of wrongdoing in cases in which a BRO court determination will be unfavourable.[163] On the other hand, however, time inconsistent preferences may lead a debtor to accept an undertaking which avoids immediate costs (temporal, financial, emotional) of court proceedings, but which has detrimental long-term consequences.[164] Risk aversion also means that debtors (whose financial failure particularly limits their willingness to take future risks) are likely to accept what is offered in an undertaking rather than risk a more severe punishment via a court-ordered BRO, even where a court challenge holds the potential gain of lesser punishment.[165] Even if a consumer debtor can identify that an undertaking is not in her interests, or wishes to contest the misconduct allegations, her simple lack of resources mean that a legal challenge to the Official Receiver's allegations

159 *Survey of Debtors Petitioning for Bankruptcy* (Insolvency Service, 2007) 10.

160 *CCCS Statistical Yearbook 2011* (Consumer Credit Counselling Service, 2012) 7.

161 S. Kirwan, *Advising in Austerity: Reflections on Challenging Times for Advice Agencies* (Policy Press, 2016).

162 *Enterprise Act 2002: Attitudes to Bankruptcy 2009 Update* (Insolvency Service, 2009) 8. Feelings of stigma and personal failure relating to debt difficulties are complex, however: S. A. Sandage, *Born Losers: A History of Failure in America* (Harvard University Press, 2005); Sousa (n. 59); Ali, O'Brien and Ramsay (n. 13).

163 On the application of this idea in the related area of plea bargaining in criminal law, see Bibas (n. 157) 2498–2502.

164 ibid, 2504–7.

165 ibid, 2507–12.

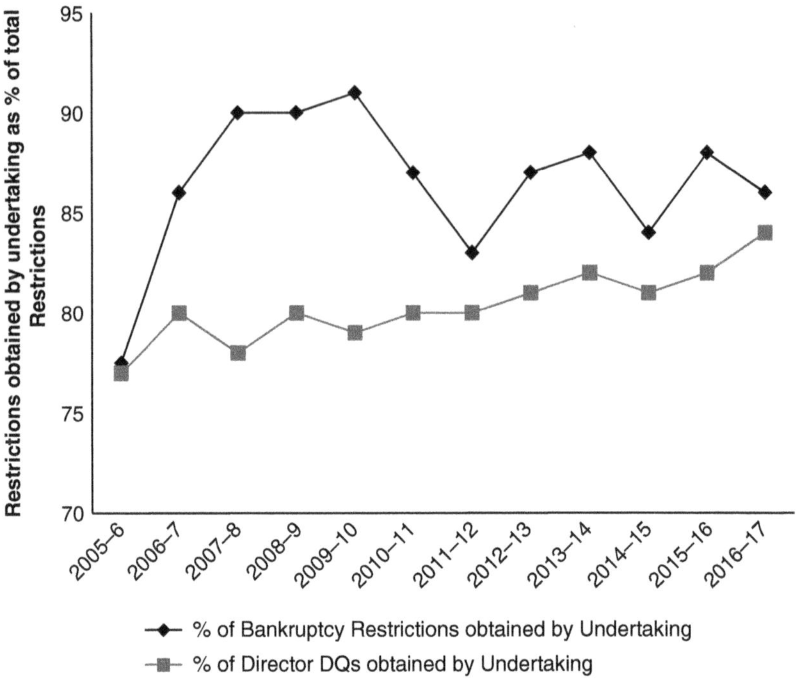

Figure 7.1: Respective percentages of bankruptcy restrictions and director disqualifications obtained via undertakings. Source: Insolvency Service

may be unaffordable.[166] In support of these theoretical predictions, not only do BRUs outnumber BROs considerably, but the BRU:BRO ratio is consistently higher than the corresponding figures for company director disqualifications, suggesting fewer bankrupt debtors than company directors challenge allegations of misconduct in court (Figure 7.1).

166 Just as debtors in bankruptcy often have to accept even dubious creditor claims as they lack the resources to fund litigation vindicating their rights: J. Braucher, 'Increasing Uniformity in Consumer Bankruptcy: Means Testing as a Distraction and the National Bankruptcy Review Commission's Proposals as a Starting Point', *American Bankruptcy Institute Law Review* 6 (1998) 1, 11. In the *Randhawa* decision, the debtor had previously entered into a company director disqualification undertaking despite contesting his culpability, as he lacked the resources to pay the legal costs of defending himself against the allegations put forward: '*Randhawa*' (n. 103) [17]. Albeit in the different context of the suspension of discharge mechanism, Nugee J notes that 'the bankrupt always has the option . . . of applying to Court, but bankrupts are often obliged to act in person, and that, and the time and costs involved in initiating an application of this sort, means that it is a far from perfect solution'. See *Weir* v. *Hilsdon* [2017] EWHC 983 (Ch) [100].

One must assume that Official Receivers act in good faith and with expert knowledge both of personal insolvency law and of the empirical reality of consumer over-indebtedness. In the opaque BRU system, however, concerns arise regarding the *potential* for inappropriate outcomes under the BRU system. Suspicion of such may undermine the regime's legitimacy, while the lack of transparency limits awareness of the standards of consumer borrower conduct being applied. Institutional factors contribute to these concerns, such as the pressures to obtain BRUs exerted on Official Receivers by annual enforcement targets.[167] While enforcement officials may decide to 'get the most bang for their buck' by focusing on the most egregiously culpable debtors,[168] enforcement targets in the presence of limited resources may incentivise officials to obtain undertakings in a number of 'easy' cases of weak resistance to a BRU.

(ii) The Bankruptcy Restriction Order/Undertaking Regime and 'Post-Democratic' Governance: Performance Targets and Political Communication

Certain commentators would view the pressures of these enforcement targets as characteristic of New Public Management techniques in the era of neoliberal governance. Davies argues that neoliberal 'reforms of public-sector bureaucracies sought to inject a spirit of enterprise into government', including by measurement of public service performance.[169] This process manifested itself, for example, in the channelling of 'normative questions of fairness, reward and recognition' into 'economic tests of efficiency and comparisons of "excellence"'.[170] Crouch worries that public services can be distorted 'when artificial attempts are made to provide indicators that can serve as the analogues of prices'.[171] In this context, temptations arise to choose indicators based on what can be readily measured, rather than conduct evaluations of whether public services are fulfilling their core objectives. Resources become channelled to work measured in indicators, while other activities are neglected 'not because

[167] These enforcement targets are specified in the Insolvency Service's annual reports: see e.g. Insolvency Service, *The Insolvency Service Annual Report and Accounts 2009–10* (The Stationery Office, 2010) 4. For an example of the pressure exerted by politicians on the Insolvency Service regarding enforcement targets, see House of Commons: Business, Innovation and Skills Committee, 'The Insolvency Service' (House of Commons, 2013) Report of Session 2012–13, 6 16–20.

[168] Bibas (n. 157) 2466.

[169] Davies, 'The New Neoliberalism' (n. 37) 128.

[170] ibid.

[171] C. Crouch, Post-Democracy 1st edn (Polity Press, 2004) 86–7.

they are intrinsically less important but because they are less measurable'.[172] Davies argues that the nature of target measurement in the public sector has accelerated and experienced a qualitative change under recent austerity policies, becoming a tool to withdraw funds rather than to allocate where needed.[173] This 'punitive target-setting' strains public services and those providing them.

These factors seem to influence the Insolvency Service's approach to administering the BRO/U regime, and so its regulation of debtor conduct. The Service saw substantial decreases of its staff under austerity, with its policy unit particularly vulnerable.[174] Funding to the agency's enforcement and investigation staff has been more stable, however. When politicians have sought to hold the agency accountable during parliamentary hearings, they have focused sharply on the Service's enforcement activities, and stakeholder ratings of the agency's performance in this area.[175] No such scrutiny of the law's achievement of its other objectives appears to take place, with little enquiry into even basic issues such as the alarming decline in bankruptcies in recent years. A risk then is that mechanisms of public service measurement may direct Insolvency Service activity unduly towards policing and sanctioning debtor conduct. It also deflects policymakers' attention away from measuring the extent to which the law delivers the debt relief this book argues is necessary to address problems of a debt-dependent economy.

Such trends may even compromise the law's ability to offer rehabilitation to debtors who manage to access the insolvency system, by perpetuating the stigma of bankruptcy. Pressures on the Insolvency Service to deliver visible results in their enforcement activities appear to influence the agency's communication strategy. The Insolvency Service's annual reports give prominence to its investigation and enforcement activities, presenting case studies of dishonest debtors who have been subjected to bankruptcy restrictions orders and whose discharges have been suspended on the grounds of dishonesty.[176] One describes how a bankrupt

[172] ibid.

[173] Davies, 'The New Neoliberalism' (n. 37) 131; 'Oral Evidence Taken before the Business, Innovation and Skills Committee: The Insolvency Service' (House of Commons, 2012); House of Commons: Business, Innovation and Skills Committee (n. 167) 16–20.

[174] J. Spooner, 'Long Overdue: What the Belated Reform of Irish Personal Insolvency Law Tells Us about Comparative Consumer Bankruptcy', *American Bankruptcy Law Journal* 86 (2012) 243, 281.

[175] See e.g. House of Commons, Business, Innovation and Skills Committee (n. 167) 16–20.

[176] On the legal use of such case studies can operate to discourage similar dishonest or irresponsible behaviour among others: see e.g. L. Johnson, 'Counter-Narrative in

debtor put more than £175,000 beyond the reach of creditors and indulged in a luxurious lifestyle involving expensive meals and extravagant tips at high end restaurants, and £4,500 sprees at escort agencies.[177] More recently, reports present descriptions of debtors found to have committed insurance fraud,[178] caught concealing an inheritance from the Official Receiver, or imprisoned for fraudulently transferring assets to relatives.[179] The Insolvency Service's press releases and Twitter feed publicise are dominated by sensationalist accounts of misconduct cases among debtors and company directors, replete with puns and hashtags such as '#dodgydirectors'.[180]

The Insolvency Service's portrayal of 'dodgy directors' and 'lavish' spendthrifts, as well as their invitations to the public to report debtor misconduct via a hotline, bear striking similarities to sensationalist condemnations of bankruptcy abusers discussed above, and fit alongside hardline political branding of welfare recipients as 'scroungers' and abusers of the system.[181] Media reports of bankruptcy tend towards the more dramatic cases irrespective of their representativeness,[182] presenting 'atrocity stories' that can sometimes spur policymakers into unwarranted policy action where other areas deserve closer attention.[183] It is surprising to see such themes and tones in communications from a government agency, however. Even more so from an agency tasked with implementing the aims of debtor

Corporate Law: Saints and Sinners, Apostles and Epistles', *Michigan State Law Review* 2009 (2009) 847, 851–2; 860–74.

177 Insolvency Service, *Report 2009–10* (n. 167) 27.

178 Insolvency Service, *The Insolvency Service Annual Reports and Accounts 2016–17* (The Stationery Office, 2017) 18.

179 Insolvency Service, *The Insolvency Service Annual Reports and Accounts 2015–16* (The Stationery Office, 2016) 27.

180 See e.g. 'Plymouth baker is toast after failing to ensure payment of taxes to HMRC', Insolvency Service Twitter Account, 3 November 2017.

181 Similar strategies in relation to social welfare fraud have been strongly criticised by commentators as undermining public confidence in the welfare system and conveying 'the impression that fraud [is] rampant, and that every person on welfare needs to be watched and reported and tested'. See D. E. Chunn and S. A. M. Gavigan, 'Welfare Law, Welfare Fraud, and the Moral Regulation of the "Never Deserving" Poor', *Social & Legal Studies* 13 (2004) 219, 230. J. Hills, *Good Times, Bad Times: The Welfare Myth of Them and Us* (Policy Press, 2014); R. Patrick, 'Living with and Responding to the "scrounger" Narrative in the UK: Exploring Everyday Strategies of Acceptance, Resistance and Deflection', *Journal of Poverty and Social Justice* 24 (2016) 245.

182 Ali, O'Brien and Ramsay (n. 13) 1108–1110.

183 World Bank (n. 9) 55; O. Ben-Shahar and C. E. Schneider, *More Than You Wanted to Know: The Failure of Mandated Disclosure* (Princeton University Press, 2014) ch. 9.

rehabilitation and stigma alleviation embodied in the Enterprise Act 2002, and which itself professes to run a 'myth busting' campaign to reduce bankruptcy stigma.[184] The Insolvency Service here appears to be following and perhaps partly fuelling ideas of 'neoliberal governmentality' and prevailing political ideas of individual responsibility and condemnation for those in financial difficulty (as manifested in the pressure exerted on the agency by scrutinising politicians).[185] Again the agency's approach seems consistent with critiques of neoliberal government communication in the 'post-democratic' era. Crouch argues that contemporary political communication by commercialised governments mirrors tabloid newspapers in modelling itself on advertising copy, consisting of very brief messages and high-impact images, rather than 'arguments appealing to the intellect'.[186] Governments modelling their communications on product marketing prioritise 'extreme simplification and sensationalisation'.[187] Consequently government agencies discuss, without nuance, complex issues of responsibility for debt and default in a financialised economy, in a manner unsuited to the establishment of serious standards of appropriate consumer borrowing. Sensationalist communication of this type may contribute towards inappropriate stigmatisation of those turning to the insolvency system for debt relief, particularly given the lack of distinction drawn by the public (or by institutional lenders) between innocent bankrupts and debtors subjected to BRO/Us. Messaging by social and economic institutions encouraging debtor repayment may add to the costs of debt relief and discourage debtors from accessing procedures even where to do so might bring wider public policy benefits.[188] In addition, the emphasis on (and funding of) enforcement in an unrepresentative minority of cases, in the context of a withdrawal of resources to enable the Insolvency Service to conduct empirical research,[189] also may contribute to indeterminate and inappropriate standards of debtor conduct.

[184] Insolvency Service, *Report 2016–17* (n. 178) 14.
[185] Ramsay, '*21st Century*' (n 8) 26–27; Berry (n. 29) 511.
[186] Crouch (n. 171) 26.
[187] ibid, 47.
[188] B. T. White, 'Underwater and Not Walking Away: Shame, Fear, and the Social Management of the Housing Crisis', *Wake Forest Law Review* 45 (2010) 971, 996–1007.
[189] 'Debt Relief Orders: Interim Evaluation Report' (Insolvency Service, 2010) 4.

7.4.3 *Indeterminate Standards and Difficulties in Determining* Reasonable *Borrowing Behaviour*

A classic response of policymakers to fears of debt relief abuse is to attribute subjective powers to decision makers under vague standards, which risks both inappropriate outcomes and inconsistency.[190] As the discussion so far has been revealing, this is an overarching problem of the BRO/U regime. There is scope for considerable inconsistency in judging the responsibility of consumer borrowing behaviour, as one person's high-flyer or spendthrift[191] is another's unfortunate victim of volatile economic conditions and a 'credit culture'.[192] Contested spaces at the margins of empirical studies of over-indebtedness suggest a complexity of credit use that renders individual judgments difficult.[193] Judges and Official Receivers are human decision makers and may be subject to factors such as hindsight bias, under which people tend to overestimate what could have been anticipated in foresight.[194]

On introducing the BRO/U system, government representatives responded to doubts regarding the practicality of distinguishing between honest and culpable debtors with assurances that 'case law will develop over time and previous judgments will provide guidance on what constitutes culpability'.[195] Approximately 80–90 per cent of restrictions are obtained by BRUs rather than court order (Figure 7.1), meaning that this expectation has not been fulfilled. Private determinations of Official Receivers, rather than public court decisions, set standards of debtor culpability.[196] Courts have shown little willingness to seize control of setting standards of debtor conduct. In relation to the suspension of

190 J. L. Westbrook, 'Local Legal Culture and the Fear of Abuse', *American Bankruptcy Institute Law Review* 6 (1998) 25.

191 It might be useful to heed Professor Ramsay's warning that '[t]here is the danger that criticism of bankrupts as "bad planners" may simply be middle-class moralising dressed up as a technical judgment'. See I. Ramsay, 'Models of Consumer Bankruptcy: Implications for Research and Policy', *Journal of Consumer Policy* 20 (1997) 269, 275.

192 I. Ramsay, 'Comparative Consumer Bankruptcy', *University of Illinois Law Review* 2007 (2007) 241, 245.

193 I. Ramsay, 'Consumer Credit Society and Consumer Bankruptcy: Reflections on Credit Cards and Bankruptcy in the Informational Economy' in J. Niemi, I. Ramsay and W. C. Whitford (eds.), Consumer Bankruptcy in Global Perspective (Hart Publishing, 2003) 25.

194 ibid.

195 HC Deb 14 April 2002 Standing Committee B col. 638, *per* Ms Johnson MP.

196 While the relevant legislation (Insolvency Act 1986, Schd. 4A, para. 7) states that a debtor may *offer* a bankruptcy restrictions undertaking to the Secretary of State, in practice a BRU involves an Official Receiver presenting the debtor with allegations of

discharge mechanism for regulating procedural misconduct, they have delegated considerable power to private trustees by making indefinite suspension orders which persist until a trustee has reported to the court that the debtor has cooperated to the trustee's satisfaction.[197] Even the minority of cases which are litigated (and the smaller number reported) are not likely to be representative.[198] Due to issues of both debtor and Official Receiver resources, high value and complex cases involving well-resourced debtors are likely to be overrepresented, which arguably hold the greatest potential for strategic and opportunistic behaviour.[199] This may influence the perceptions of judges, giving a misleading impression as to the proportion of bankruptcy cases involving such complicated financial arrangements requiring close scrutiny. Concrete standards for 'normal' consumer borrowing are unlikely to emerge from this process.

Courts and Official Receivers have encountered difficulty in sharpening the historical and commercial norms outlined in legislation into standards of behaviour for modern consumer debtors. In the leading case of *Randhawa* v. *Official Receiver*,[200] the High Court noted that no express guidance is given as to the applicable standards, but that all of the listed grounds 'involve some element of misconduct or neglect or financial irresponsibility'. Sir Launcelot Henderson QC suggested that this must amount to 'a failure in some significant respect to live up to proper standards of competence or probity in the conduct of one's financial affairs'.[201] In this case, the judge condemned the debtor's conduct, 'a self-confessed act of folly' as 'reckless and irresponsible', and so justifying the making of a BRO.[202]

The guidance provided in this decision is limited, as illustrated in the consumer bankruptcy case of *Official Receiver* v. *Southey*,[203] in which the

misconduct, which a debtor then accepts and agrees to an undertaking for an appropriate period: see Insolvency Service, *Report 2009–10* (n. 167) 20.

197 Patterson (n. 143). The Court of Appeal has slowed this judicial practice somewhat by suggesting that courts should 'hesitate' before making such an order, since 'it is not only in the interests of bankrupts, but also in accordance with the policy of the reforms introduced by the Enterprise Act, that a bankrupt should be able to tell with some precision when their discharge will take place, so that they can move on and rebuild their financial lives'. *See Weir* v. *Hilsdon* [2017] EWHC 983 (Ch) [100].

198 See e.g. P. Shuchman, 'An Attempt at a "Philosophy of Bankruptcy"', *UCLA Law Review* 21 (1973) 403, 406.

199 Bibas (n. 157) 2466.

200 '*Randhawa*' (n. 103).

201 ibid, 66–8.

202 ibid, 78–9.

203 *Southey* v. *Official Receiver* [2009] BPIR 89.

court disagreed with the relevant Official Receiver's opinion that the debtor had borrowed without reasonable expectation of repayment. Here an actor borrowed substantial sums of money while in financial difficulty and casual employment, expecting to repay when his employment recommenced on the second series of a TV show on which he had been playing a prominent role. When the entire cast of the TV show was changed for the second series, the debtor was left without employment. The Official Receiver sought a BRO on the basis that the debtor's expectation of repayment on borrowing was not reasonable, as there was no guarantee that actors in a TV show would be retained for a subsequent series.[204] Chief Registrar Baister rejected the application for a BRO in finding that on the evidence, the debtor's prospect of repayment was reasonable.[205] First, the Chief Registrar noted that the law does not require certainty regarding repayment and that here the prospect 'was not so remote that no reasonable person could have concluded that the extra indebtedness could never be repaid'. In contrast, a series of factors pointed towards the reasonableness of the expectation, including the debtor's history of living a similar lifestyle for the past decade and ability to meet his monthly repayments until close to bankruptcy, and the fact that his acting career, though not secure, was progressing positively. Registrar Baister then cited both *Randhawa* and directors' disqualification case law as establishing 'a relatively high test' for the making of a BRO. Despite the debtor's admission that he borrowed without 'sufficient thought'[206] and that he was 'slightly naïve' in assuming re-employment for a second series, such errors of judgment did not satisfy the standard of misconduct required for a restriction. The Registrar summarised his judgment of the debtor's conduct as follows:

> Putting it at its highest, the respondent misjudged his ability to repay. Putting it at its lowest, he was doing nothing wrong in managing his modest affairs as best he could.

The divergence of opinion between Official Receiver and court in this case demonstrates the potential for contrasting subjective standards in judging consumer debtor culpability.[207] This is an important divergence,

204 '*Southey*' 8.
205 '*Southey*' (n. 203) [23].
206 ibid, 11.
207 For a discussion of the difficulties and inconsistencies arising in judicial decision making based on vague standards see Ponoroff and Knippenberg (n. 6) 292.

since the number of BRO/Us based on this once most common ground has fallen dramatically since 2008–9.[208] The causes of this trend are unclear, but if it is the case that the *Southey* decision has had a corrective effect in illustrating that BRUs should not be made in analogous cases,[209] this worryingly suggests that BRUs were being made inappropriately for several years in cases similar to *Southey*. The indeterminacy of the legislative standards may therefore have led to serious practical consequences of inappropriate BRUs being issued.

Of course, the problem of indeterminacy is exacerbated in a system heavily reliant on BRUs rather than court-issued BROs. More transparency is a first step towards any serious attempt by the law to develop determinate standards of appropriate borrowing conduct. While this may be an exercise fraught with difficulty,[210] the following section uses the *Southey* case as a frame and suggests that the concept of moral hazard can offer guidance as to how the law should approach this question of reasonable consumer borrowing.

7.5 Moral Hazard and Judging the Reasonableness of Consumer Borrowing Behaviour

7.5.1 Household Borrowing in the Debt Economy

A preliminary task in this enquiry is to consider typical uses of credit.[211] Theoretical accounts of household credit use and the expansion of debt in recent decades offer perspectives through which to develop standards.[212] The facts of the *Southey* case resemble a typical case of household borrowing which conforms both to conventional explanations of the purposes of household borrowing and standard accounts of causes of over-indebtedness, rather than some exceptional case of deviancy. Empirical studies repeatedly identify 'income shocks' as significant causes of over-indebtedness, including the debtor's unemployment, income reduction, or inability to work due to ill health. Even the most orthodox neo-classical economic model of consumer credit would explain Mr Southey's conduct as a standard case of short term 'consumption smoothing'. In this sense credit is used rationally as a form of

[208] See Figure 7.2.
[209] Ramsay, '*21st Century*' (n. 8) 91.
[210] Ramsay, 'Reflections on Credit Cards' (n. 193) 25.
[211] Hynes (n. 61) 360.
[212] See Chapter 2, text to notes 105–26; and Chapter 3, text to notes 97–138.

insurance during a temporary deviation from the long-run trend of income.[213] Departing from the criticised assumption of rational choice which underlies the 'consumption smoothing' model, behavioural economics might explain a financially troubled debtor's borrowing in the expectation of future employment as a standard example of a decision influenced by optimism bias and time-inconsistent preferences. Ultimately inopportune household borrowing to supplement 'modest means' in the face of volatile low-earning employment also represents a standard case under the alternative 'loans for wages' model of household debt,[214] rather than an example of exceptional abusive conduct.

Reflecting the increased turn to macroeconomics in contemporary law-and-economics thinking,[215] the law's regulation of borrower behaviour must also be assessed in light of the macroeconomic function performed by household borrowing. Under the 'privatised Keynesianism' model, household debt sustains the demand and consumer spending necessary for economic growth, particularly at times of stagnant incomes for much of society. Cautious calls for tighter regulation of borrower behaviour may understate the point that wider society, and not just consumer borrowers, benefits from economic growth associated with increased consumer spending. While championing entrepreneurial risk, policymakers are less ready to see that current economic growth structures require households to borrow at unprecedented levels despite volatile living and working conditions,[216] and so to take risks historically treated as irrational, dangerous or reckless.[217] The law must accept the perhaps uncomfortable reality that the people closest to the category of the improvident over-borrowing debtor may also represent those households with a higher marginal propensity to consume and so to contribute to economic growth.[218] Contemporary macroeconomic conditions might require the law to afford greater leeway to borrowers

[213] See e.g. A. Barba and M. Pivetti, 'Rising Household Debt: Its Causes and Macroeconomic Implications – a Long-Period Analysis', *Cambridge Journal of Economics* 33 (2009) 113, 120.

[214] Barba and Pivetti (n. 213).

[215] Masur and Posner (n. 45); Listokin (n. 45).

[216] See e.g. M. Crain and M. Sherraden, *Working* and Living in the Shadow of Economic Fragility (Oxford University Press, 2014); G. Standing, *The Precariat: The New Dangerous Class* new edn (Bloomsbury Academic 2016); J. Morduch and R. Schneider, *The Financial Diaries: How American Families Cope in a World of Uncertainty* (Princeton University Press, 2017).

[217] Hallinan (n. 20) 66–7.

[218] International Monetary Fund (n. 100) 9–10.

in regulating the reasonableness of their behaviour than would be the case under an economy less dependent on high household debt levels.

7.5.2 Moral Hazard and the Allocation of Responsibility for Consumer Insolvency

Doubts arise as to the extent to which the assumptions of moral hazard hold in the context of contemporary household over-indebtedness. Firstly, moral hazard theory assumes the sufficiency of *financial* compensation for loss. This means that in order for bankruptcy to create moral hazard concerns, it must be the case that the financial benefits of debt relief compensate the debtor for any losses incurred up to the point of receiving a debt discharge. An individual's over-indebtedness, however, may lead to costs which cannot be compensated by the reduction in the individual's debt burden alone.[219] These include stress and health difficulties, strained family relationships, and/or a sense of stigma or shame due to financial failure.[220] The debtor's sense of moral obligation may lead to non-financial costs of entering an insolvency procedure,[221] while the loss of a debtor's home involves many costs which cannot be compensated by improvement to a balance sheet.[222] Secondly, for a classic moral hazard situation to arise, the insured's person, property or financial circumstances must lie within her control, and taking care must be effective in preventing loss. Empirical studies of over-indebtedness, however, show that its primary causes include factors external to the debtor and against which taking care will not protect, such as unemployment/income reduction, ill health, and relationship breakdown.[223] As argued in a World Bank Report, 'no matter how carefully and responsibly one manages one's finances, one can never be sure when financial distress will strike unexpectedly as a result of distant and perhaps unexpected forces'.[224] Therefore those who seek to raise moral hazard concerns in a case of alleged unreasonable insolvency such as

[219] K. Porter, 'The Damage of Debt', *Washington and Lee Law Review* 69 (2012) 979.

[220] K. Porter, 'The Pretend Solution: An Empirical Study of Bankruptcy Outcomes', *Texas Law Review* 90 (2011) 103, 142–4. For recent reviews of literature on bankruptcy stigma, see e.g. Sousa (n. 59); Ali, O'Brien and Ramsay (n. 5); Howell and Mason (n. 14).

[221] Hallinan (n. 20) 141–2.

[222] M. B. Culhane, 'No Forwarding Address' in K. Porter (ed.), *Broke: How Debt Bankrupts the Middle Class* (Stanford University Press, 2012) 129–34.

[223] See Chapter 2, text to notes 158–67.

[224] World Bank (n. 9) para. 96.

Southey must relax key conditions of the moral hazard concept to an unsustainable degree.

These factors illustrate a certain inevitability of default and indeed the desirability of default risk under the contemporary economic model. The social insurance theory identifies bankruptcy law as a means of allocating this risk efficiently, through rules requiring risk to be borne by the party best placed to prevent default from occurring and to bear the costs of default should it occur.[225] Traditional perspectives considered borrowers to have superior ability to prevent default due to their unique knowledge about their own propensity to repay.[226] In current conditions, however, technological advances mean that institutional consumer lenders possess sophisticated means of determining the likelihood of repayment through processes such as credit scoring.[227] In *Southey*, the Official Receiver argued that the employment prospects in the debtor's industry are such that it was unreasonable for the debtor to believe he had a realistic prospect of repaying, a position which places responsibility for such assessments on the debtor.[228] In a calculation of industry-wide employment prospects, however, 'the knowledge needed to assess the risk of default is actuarial, not individual'.[229] The calculations necessary to determine accurately whether the benefits of a loan outweigh the costs 'are intractable for even the most sophisticated, diligent, and unbiased of decision makers',[230] and the decision making of unadvised household borrowers falls quite short of this ideal of rationality.[231] It is therefore more efficient to impose the costs of evaluating the debtor's employment prospects on the institutional lender, so that the expert professional risk assessor, rather than a household debtor, is responsible for conducting the necessary actuarial analysis to assess a credit transaction's risk.

225 In this section I focus on the factors making the institutional lender better positioned to prevent default than the consumer debtor. For a discussion of why the institutional lender is better placed to bear the costs of default, see Part 2.2(B)(III) above.

226 T. Eisenberg, 'Bankruptcy Law in Perspective', *UCLA Law Review* 28 (1980) 953, 983.

227 See e.g. J. A. E. Pottow, 'Private Liability for Reckless Consumer Lending', *University of Illinois Law Review* 2007 (2007) 405, 432–4; D. G. Baird, 'Technology, Information, and Bankruptcy', *University of Illinois Law Review* 2007 (2007) 305, 311–4; P. A. McCoy, 'Rethinking Disclosure in a World of Risk-Based Pricing', *Harvard Journal on Legislation* 44 (2007) 123; J. Niemi-Kiesilainen, 'Consumer Bankruptcy in Comparison: Do We Cure a Market Failure or a Social Problem', *Osgoode Hall Law Journal* 37 (1999) 473, 477.

228 '*Southey*' (n. 203) [19].

229 Howard (n. 6) 1063.

230 L. E. Willis, 'Will the Mortgage Market Correct – How Households and Communities Would Fare If Risk Were Priced Well', *Connecticut Law Review* 41 (2008) 1177, 1230.

231 See Chapter 3, text to notes 118–30.

Furthermore, efforts of personal insolvency law to modify consumer borrower behaviour are likely to be unsuccessful. Evidence abounds of limited understanding of credit contracts amongst the general population and of behavioural biases in decision making. Consequently, even if consumers were strongly incentivised to make optimal borrowing decisions, their ability to respond to those incentives is limited. Furthermore, it is unlikely that personal insolvency law could ever have such an incentivising effect on borrowing behaviour. Consumers tend to ignore the possibility of default (and so the content of bankruptcy law) when making borrowing decisions, while even if they attempt to account for the risk of default, decision-making biases cause them to undervalue this risk (and so the likelihood of the law ever applying to them).[232] Knowledge of personal insolvency law is low even among debtors in the system,[233] not to mention among the general borrowing population.[234] It might in theory be desirable to provide sufficient levels of education and de-biasing training to convert the general population into better borrowers and subsequently hold them to higher standards of behaviour. The effectiveness of such programmes has been strongly questioned.[235] From a policy making perspective the aim of educating the entire borrowing population to act as economically rational responsible borrowers is likely to be expensive and limited in effect, and ultimately an impractical means of promoting reasonable borrowing behaviour. Any pragmatic policymaker must realise that 'creditors are likely to be more fruitful regulatory targets for reforming behaviour'.[236]

Moral hazard is a relational concept, and where the law holds a debtor liable for the consequences of her over-indebtedness (by raising costs of insolvency debt relief), this reduces creditors' incentives to prevent over-indebtedness.[237] If the BRO/U regime deters debtors from entering

[232] Willis (n. 230) 1230.

[233] Surveys conducted in England and Wales show that a majority of bankrupts had not been aware of a major change in the English debt discharge regime's leniency before entering bankruptcy: see e.g. *Discharge from Bankruptcy* (Insolvency Service, 2006) 7; J. P. Tribe, 'Bankruptcy Courts Survey 2005 – A Pilot Study: Final Report – January 2006' [2006] SSRN eLibrary 67–8 http://papers.ssrn.com/sol3/papers.cfm?abstract_id=1329109 accessed 10 November 2018.

[234] P. Pleasence, N. J. Balmer and C. Denvir, 'Wrong about Rights: Public Knowledge of Key Areas of Consumer, Housing and Employment Law in England and Wales', *The Modern Law Review* 80 (2017) 836.

[235] L. E. Willis, 'Against Financial-Literacy Education', *Iowa Law Review* 94 (2008) 197.

[236] Pottow (n. 227) 430.

[237] Baker (n. 40) 274.

insolvency procedures, this raises concerns that lenders may be left free to lend profitably and lower their monitoring costs by reducing the quality of creditworthiness assessments, while avoiding the write-off of losses in bankruptcy.[238] These monitoring costs can be externalised and borne by other parties (e.g. the state's welfare system, the debtor's family, other creditors, and society in general).[239] Indeed, concerns of creditor moral hazard may be more significant than that of debtor moral hazard, since well-advised financial services firms are aware of incentives created by the law,[240] respond to financial incentives,[241] and are judged by profitability rather than being held to moral standards (thus having few moral costs of the kinds which might restrain individual debtors from engaging in opportunistic behaviour).[242] A bankruptcy system that sanctions 'unreasonable' borrowers, while providing for no equivalent sanction for unreasonable or irresponsible lending (often assisting creditors by maximising their returns), may fail in a basic duty of reinforcing market discipline and so correcting market failures.[243] If a BRO/U signals debtor culpability in a case in which lenders have taken insufficient care to prevent default, the market message of the inappropriateness of a lender's conduct is suppressed. If policymakers wish to prevent the making of loans involving unreasonable prospects of repayment, it may be more effective to place responsibility on lenders, rather than consumer borrowers, to avoid such transactions. This realisation has led to the development of the regulatory principle of *responsible lending*,[244] but the idea seems yet to be accepted in the insolvency field. Instead, the BRO/U regime's asymmetric view of moral hazard clings to principles of market individualism and *caveat emptor*, viewing departures from creditor freedom to lend and

[238] LoPucki (n. 20) 466.
[239] World Bank (n. 9) paras. 91–2.
[240] ibid, para. 52.
[241] LoPucki (n. 20) 466; Hallinan (n. 20) 110.
[242] White (n. 188) 972, 1009.
[243] W. C. Whitford, 'The Ideal of Individualized Justice: Consumer Bankruptcy as Consumer Protection, and Consumer Protection in Consumer Bankruptcy', *American Bankruptcy Law Journal* 68 (1994) 397, 403.
[244] See e.g. I. Ramsay, 'From Truth in Lending to Responsible Lending' in A. Janssen and G. Howells (eds.), Information Rights and Obligations: The Impact on Party Autonomy and Contractual Fairness (Avebury Technical, 2005); K. Fairweather, 'The Development of Responsible Lending in the UK Consumer Credit Regime' in J. Devenney and M. Kenny (eds.), Consumer Credit, Debt and Investment in Europe (Cambridge University Press, 2012); T. Wilson, 'The Responsible Lending Response' in T. Wilson (ed.), *International Responses to Issues of Credit and Over-Indebtedness in the Wake of Crisis* (Ashgate Publishing Ltd, 2013).

subsequently enforce market bargains as extraordinary 'redistributions' to be avoided by courts.[245] In its imposition of fiduciary-style duties and information-disclosure sanctions, the system clings to outdated understandings that saw creditors as lying at the wrong side of the information asymmetries and principal-agent problems inherent in debt contracts. A regime built on historical ideas of commercial law, and constrained by the limitations of government agencies in the era of financialised capitalism, has only limited utility in addressing the policy challenges raised by market distributions increasingly recognised as being inefficient as well as unequal.

The above analysis suggests that the law indeed may have no role to play in sanctioning the 'improvident' debtor, who commits substantive misconduct by over-borrowing in an unreasonable manner. Rather, the optimal policy approach may be to limit the disciplining of debtors to those engaged in intentional misconduct, while incentivising creditors to lend more responsibly so that the paradigmatic improvident debtor (engaged in unintentionally unreasonable borrowing) never has the opportunity to over-borrow. Such an approach is consistent with this book's argument for the overall reconceptualisation of the law as a social insurance mechanism for providing the more equal and efficient allocations – and market discipline – which imperfect markets fail to produce.

7.6 Forgiveness, Discipline and the Privatisation of Credit Morality

The discussion suggests that within the BRO/U mechanism, legislators and courts have eschewed responsibility for determining reasonable standards of borrowing behaviour. The approach of the insolvency administration, as represented by Official Receiver practice, has involved non-transparent sanctioning of debtors, an apparent reduced pursuit of consumer borrowing misconduct,[246] and a sensationalised approach to publicising the enforcement regime that inhibits the development of serious standards of conduct (while also potentially stigmatising debtors in such a manner as to blur distinctions between the innocent and culpable). These trends, coupled with the fact that the BRO/U regime

[245] See Baker (n. 40) 275; I. Ramsay, 'Consumer Credit Law, Distributive Justice and the Welfare State', *Oxford Journal of Legal Studies* 15 (1995) 177; G. Howells and S. Weatherill, Consumer Protection Law 2nd revised edn (Avebury Technical, 2005) 8 *et seq.*

[246] Moser (n. 101) 701–2.

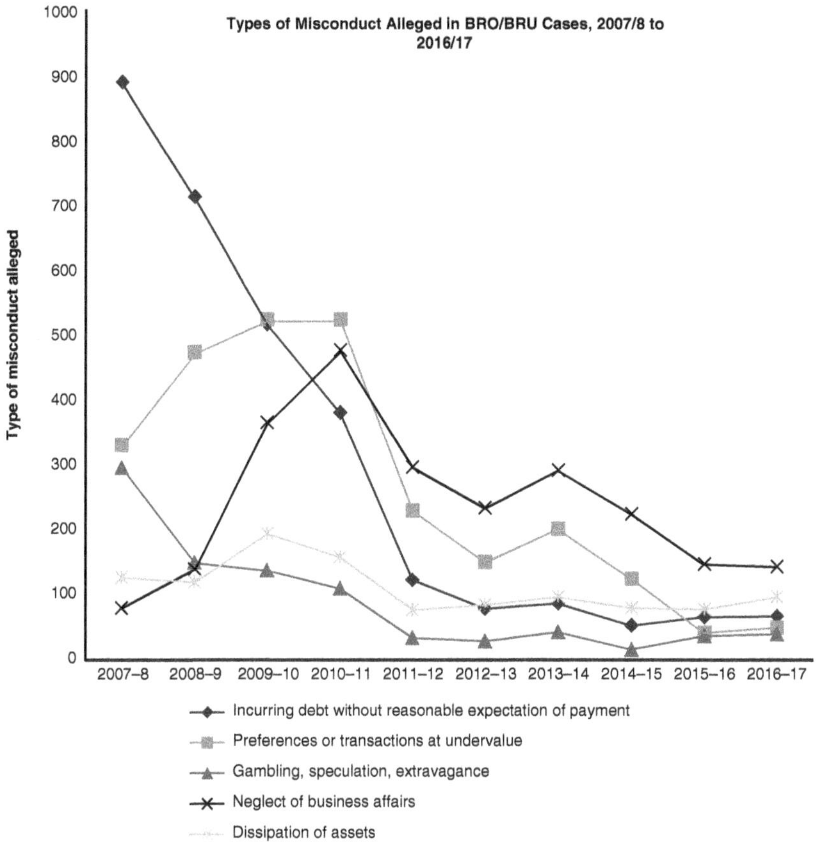

Figure 7.2: Types of misconduct alleged in BRO/U cases. Source: Insolvency Service

does not apply to the large majority of debtors entering into the alternative Individual Voluntary Arrangement or Debt Management Plan procedures, may amount to an abrogation of responsibility in the insolvency system for regulating the morality of credit use and default. At first, a removal of moral censure from bankruptcy might seem welcome. Difficulty arises, however, from the fact that debtors appear to remain subject to moral judgments, but from actors other than public officials, and based on standards other than those democratically determined. Significant and opaque costs imposed on debtors by disciplinary credit markets make it difficult for bankruptcy legislation to calibrate safeguards against moral hazard appropriately.

7.6.1 *'Market-Based Debt Resolution' and Forcing Debtors to 'Do the Right Thing'*

Despite the apparent centrality of the BRO/U to the personal insolvency system, it is increasingly bypassed as debtors are diverted out of bankruptcy and DROs into Individual Voluntary Arrangements (IVAs) and Debt Management Plans (DMPs) (see Chapters 4 and 5). The personal insolvency system, or the policymakers shaping it, do not seem to have complete faith in its ability to set appropriate incentives or pass moral judgment over borrowing behaviour (through the BRO/U regime or otherwise). If this was the case, then policymakers would be comfortable with debtors freely availing of bankruptcy and DROs, satisfied that the collection of safeguards – access conditions, restrictions, criminal sanctions and suspension and/or denial of discharge – would regulate use effectively. Instead policymakers show an apparent distaste for consumers 'resorting' to bankruptcy, and so justify debtors being charged high access fees on the grounds that many of them have incurred debts irresponsibly and should not be assisted at taxpayer expense.[247] Policymakers also imagine the DRO procedure as a residual measure for the 'deserving poor', to be accessed only through debt counsellors and means testing, by debtors whose indebtedness falls below a debt ceiling and so evade suspicions of misconduct and over-borrowing.[248] The Insolvency Service cites, as a reason for its support of the growth of the IVA as a consumer remedy, the ability of the procedure to teach debtors how to manage money responsibly.[249] This position clearly evokes neoliberal ideas of individual responsibility and the disciplinary attribution of blame for over-indebtedness on financially incompetent debtors.[250] Under the 'can pay, should pay' coda that looms over the English system,[251] debt relief itself is viewed with suspicion, and

[247] Note the comments of the New Labour Government in defending the existence of high bankruptcy deposit costs: 'we do not believe that general taxation should pay for people to enter bankruptcy when they may have taken on debts irresponsibly'. HC Deb 14 April 2002 Standing Committee B col. 693, per Ms Melanie Johnson MP.

[248] Ramsay, '*21st Century*' (n. 8); J. Spooner and I. D. C. Ramsay, 'Insolvency Proceedings: Debt Relief Orders and the Bankruptcy Petition Limit – Submission by Professor Iain Ramsay and Dr Joseph Spooner to the Insolvency Service Call for Evidence' (Social Science Research Network, 2014) SSRN Scholarly Paper ID 2601349 http://ssrn.com/abstract=2601349 accessed 11 November 2018.

[249] 'A Consultation Document on Proposed Changes to the Individual Voluntary Arrangement (IVA) Regime' (Insolvency Service) 45–6.

[250] Vass (n. 26); Berry (n. 29). See text to notes 26–39 above.

[251] Ramsay, '*21st Century*' (n. 8) 70.

policymakers express a preference for debtors entering into long-term repayment plans on creditors' terms. This trend is documented in Chapters 4 and 5 above. Policymakers' preference for IVAs and DMPs mirror the 'affinity' of US policymakers for Chapter 13, with repayment plan mechanisms maximising returns to creditors and offering the moral appeal of requiring debtors to 'do the right thing' and repay as much as possible.[252] The fact that IVA and DMP terms are set by creditor agreement appeals to those who favour 'market-based debt resolution' and oppose statutory debt relief measures *on any terms*, under the view that *any* evasion of contract enforcement necessarily creates a problem of moral hazard.[253] These positions are leveraged by actors with an interest in diverting debtors from bankruptcy and DROs into long-term repayment plans. Financial Conduct Authority reports show intermediaries relying on 'misconceptions, or wider negative attitudes in society' in encouraging debtors to opt for profitable IVAs or DMPs.[254] Insolvency Practitioner association R3 has long argued that bankruptcy is 'too easy' for debtors.[255] It has advocated that bankruptcy should be made more onerous and punitive, in this way 'incentivising repayment of debts via procedures such as Individual Voluntary Arrangements (IVAs) by making the bankruptcy process a more robust procedure'.[256]

Economically, this subjects debt relief to creditors' right to maximise their returns. Creditors may frustrate the law's public policy aims in setting the costs of debt relief beyond levels necessary to address moral hazard and instead at levels that maximise creditor returns. Morally, this position tends to conceptualise debt relief as falling within the gift of

[252] S. S. Greene, P. Patel and K. Porter, 'Cracking the Code: An Empirical Analysis of Consumer Bankruptcy Outcomes', *Minnesota Law Review* 101 (2016) 1031, 1031–1032; J. Braucher, D. Cohen and R. M. Lawless, 'Race, Attorney Influence, and Bankruptcy Chapter Choice' *Journal of Empirical Legal Studies* 9 (2012) 393.

[253] Czarnetzky (n. 7) 413.

[254] 'Quality of Debt Management Advice' (Financial Conduct Authority, 2015) Thematic Review TR15/8 25.

[255] The association has even called for the use of insolvency law to police fraud, with insolvency practitioners to be given investigatory roles in 'light of cutbacks to Government resources to fight fraud': 'The Fraud Landscape: Insolvency and the Fight against Fraud' (R3: Association of Business Recovery Professionals, 2015) 3 www.r3.org.uk/what-we-do/policy-and-public-affairs/policy-and-briefing-papers accessed 16 July 2018.

[256] R3: Association of Business Recovery Professionals, 'Redressing the Balance: Strengthening the Bankruptcy Process and Recognising Prior Behaviour' 5 www.r3.org.uk/what-we-do/policy-and-public-affairs/policy-and-briefing-papers accessed 16 July 2018.

creditors to grant, mirroring justifications of debt discharge founded upon a societal virtue of forgiveness.[257] This view of debt relief as 'debt forgiveness' is problematic. Its starting assumption is that default always amounts to debtor wrongdoing, and that any debt 'forgiveness' is subjectively 'based on the sympathetic will of the person excusing'.[258] In contrast, any debt discharge founded in a legal institution must create and enforce rights which apply uniformly to all, irrespective of their attitudes.[259] The approach of directing debtors into consensual repayment plans on the general suspicion that their borrowings may have been irresponsible privatises the maintenance of moral standards in bankruptcy, subordinating such standards to creditor interests.[260]

English law's increasing subjection of debtors to creditors' conditional forgiveness through the IVA procedure adds credence to accounts of the disciplinary nature of (legal) debt relations under financialised capitalism.[261] Typically critiques of the 'debtfare' economic structure and contemporary debt markets' disciplinary effects argue that their exploitative nature is concealed by 'the seeming neutrality of the law and consumer protection'. The promotion of ideas such as financial inclusion or the democratisation of credit serves 'to depoliticise and naturalise debt relations among the poor'.[262] Making generous debt discharge available under bankruptcy and the DRO, only to limit access artificially based on nebulous moral objections, seems consistent with this account. English policymakers have not quite advanced ideas of debtor discipline in such express terms as, say, Troika (ECB, European Commission and IMF) policymakers when 'recommending' personal insolvency law reforms in countries receiving post-crisis financial

[257] Gross (n. 56) 91–134; Hurd (n. 56).

[258] Kilpi (n. 56) 67–8.

[259] ibid, 68.

[260] The subjection of traditionally political questions to judgment of financial market actors is a feature throughout the financialised societies of 'debt states': W. Streeck, *Buying Time: The Delayed Crisis of Democratic Capitalism* (Verso Books, 2014) 79–90; Lazzarato and Jordan (n. 153) 99.

[261] See e.g. Lazzarato and Jordan (n. 153); T. Mahmud, 'Debt and Discipline: Neoliberal Political Economy and the Working Classes', *Kentucky Law Journal* 101 (2012) 1; S. Soederberg, *Debtfare States and the Poverty Industry:* Money, Discipline and the Surplus Population (Routledge, 2014); A. Roberts, 'Doing Borrowed Time: The State, the Law and the Coercive Governance of "Undeserving" Debtors', *Critical Sociology* 40 (2014) 669; L. E. Coco, 'The Cultural Logics of the Bankruptcy Abuse Prevention and Consumer Protection Act of 2005: Fiscal Identities and Financial Failure', *Critical Sociology* 40 (2014) 711.

[262] Soederberg (n. 261) 61.

assistance.[263] As this book shows throughout, however, the current policy position, fails on its own terms, can be condemned using the neo-classical economic principles it appears to be founded upon, and uses moral arguments to suppress rapid debt discharge in favour of long-term repayment on creditors' terms.[264] In this way, justifications for the current state of English bankruptcy law are limited, making the law vulnerable to accusations of merely forming part of a disciplinary structure of debt that entrenches unequal market and class positions.[265]

7.6.2 Credit Reporting in Contemporary Surveillance Capitalism

Bankruptcy law's regulation and judgment of debtor conduct has been superseded also by market systems of credit reporting and credit scoring. These systems constitute further key structures of discipline and neoliberal self-governance in the contemporary financialised economy. They offer an alternative non-juridical system of monitoring and evaluating debtor behaviour – addressing moral hazard concerns at both the *ex ante* and *ex post* levels by raising substantially the costs of default for debtors. Policymakers appear preoccupied with the moral hazard risk posed by bankruptcy, and reform efforts often involve painstaking development of complicated, finely calibrated and sometimes heavy-handed safeguards to prevent 'abuse'. These efforts, and for example the BRO/U regime discussed in this chapter, may be rendered redundant by the expansive reach and force of credit reporting systems.

To the extent that they largely rely on the disclosure of information to potential lenders, sanctions and prohibitions imposed by the BRO/U system are dependent on, or subordinate to, credit reporting and lending practices. The reach of credit reporting systems almost guarantees that information offered by the bankruptcy system in this way is superfluous, as it is already available to credit reference agencies and lenders. Disciplinary procedures such as the BRO/U regime apply to only a small proportion of even the narrow subset of debtors who enter insolvency, and are limited in the blunt distinctions they can draw between 'honest' and 'culpable' debtors. In contrast, the 'big data' revolution and the increased influence of algorithmic decision making have

263 Spooner, 'The Quiet-Loud-Quiet Politics of Post-Crisis Consumer Bankruptcy Law: The Case of Ireland and the Troika' (n. 15).

264 Ramsay, '*21st Century*' (n. 8) 70.

265 Coco (n. 261).

established an unprecedented reach and influence of credit reporting and credit scoring systems.[266] In the present era of 'surveillance capitalism',[267] aggregate analyses and individualised records are combined, and individuals are ranked based on 'a precise set of digital records, drawn from a wide range of sources and allowing for customisable scoring possibilities'.[268] Contemporary credit scoring systems have moved beyond historical distinctions between 'good' and 'bad' risks, between those offered and denied credit. Instead the development of these systems has as its ideal the availability of credit for (almost) all at the right price, with Big Data and algorithmic calculation enabling advanced market segmentation.[269] The credit reporting system, like other forms of algorithmic decision making, is supported by advocates for removing 'human beings and their flaws from the assessment process'.[270] In this way it can be perceived as avoiding the apparent subjective judgments of courts and bankruptcy officials. Credit scoring claims the promise of removing questions of 'character' from assessments of credit risk,[271] and of offering objective measures based on behaviour,[272] rather than tortured legal enquiries into borrowers' intentions. In this way market rankings and categorisation even claim an 'ethically meaningful' moral dimension typically seen as the reserve of the law. A consumer's ranking or score is 'defined against particular standards of behaviour, which its promoters and users see as desirable'.[273] This leaves the consumer feeling judged, and causes her to self-police and carry out the labour necessary to improve herself into

[266] J. Lauer, *Creditworthy: A History of Consumer Surveillance and Financial Identity in America* (Columbia University Press, 2017) ch. 9; C. O'Neil, *Weapons of Math Destruction: How Big Data Increases Inequality and Threatens Democracy* reprint edn (Broadway Books, 2017) ch. 8; F. Pasquale, *The Black Box Society: The Secret Algorithms That Control Money and Information* reprint edn (Harvard University Press, 2016); D. K. Citron and F. Pasquale, 'The Scored Society: Due Process for Automated Predictions Essay', *Washington Law Review* 89 (2014) 1.

[267] S. Zuboff, 'Big Other: Surveillance Capitalism and the Prospects of an Information Civilization', *Journal of Information Technology* 30 (2015) 75.

[268] Fourcade and Healy (n. 36) 11.

[269] Fourcade and Healy here refer to 'the economist's dream of perfect price discrimination': ibid, 23. See also M. Cooper, Family Values: Between Neoliberalism and the New Social Conservatism (Zone Books – The MIT Press, 2017) 149–51.

[270] Keats Citron and Pasquale (n. 266) at 4. See also Lauer (n. 266) at 232–41.

[271] Lauer (n. 266) ch. 7. Note the parallels with the process Baker describes of neo-classical economists of the neoliberal era removing the element of 'character' when adopting (from the insurance context) the concept of moral hazard: Baker (n. 40) 267–75.

[272] Fourcade and Healy (n. 36) 24.

[273] ibid, 19.

a more efficient 'entrepreneur of the self'.[274] Bad outcomes are presented as 'the mechanical translation of bad habits and behavioural failures', as a 'dispassionate, impartial and objective' system allocates to consumers their just desserts based on 'morally deserved positions'.[275]

These developments raise concerns for those who still consider the maintenance of credit morality to be the 'bedrock' of bankruptcy law, and more broadly believe that democratically determined standards should establish standards of appropriate credit use. The credit reporting system not only extends beyond bankruptcy's breadth and depth of debtor supervision, but also imposes sanctions of greater import than those imposed by the legal system. Credit scoring follows neoliberal era trends of market institutions' increasing use of actuarial techniques 'to split and sort individuals into *classification situations* that shape life-chances'.[276] In a financialised society in which credit funds essential purchases for much of the population, market access conditions are crucial. A debtor's credit history determines her future ability to access credit (as well as – through 'off label' use[277] – her opportunity to rent an apartment, access utility facilities, make purchases consistent with her economic and social status,[278] and even in some cases to gain employment[279]).[280] The impact of bankruptcy on a debtor's credit history appears to be one of the most significant determinants of whether the law offers the debtor a true 'fresh start'.[281] The combination of credit history with other digital data risk 'negative spirals' in which a consumer's ranking in one index relating to

[274] ibid, 20, citing M. Foucault, *The Birth of Biopolitics: Lectures at the Collège de France, 1978–1979: Lectures at the College De France, 1978–1979* A. I. Davidson (ed.) G. Burchell (trans.) 2008 edn (Palgrave Macmillan, 2010).

[275] Fourcade and Healy (n. 36) 25.

[276] M. Fourcade and K. Healy, 'Classification Situations: Life-Chances in the Neoliberal Era', *Accounting, Organizations and Society* 38 (2013) 559.

[277] Lauer (n. 266) 227; Fourcade and Healy (n. 36) 12.

[278] R. Dyal-Chand, 'Human Worth as Collateral', *Rutgers Law Journal* 38 (2006) 793, 811.

[279] *McGuffick* v. *Royal Bank of Scotland plc* [2009] EWHC Comm 2386 [29]. For perspectives from other jurisdictions, see Howell and Mason (n. 14); T. Cain, 'The Bankruptcy of Refusing to Hire Persons Who Have Filed Bankruptcy', *American Bankruptcy Law Journal* 91 (2017) 657.

[280] Claimants in suits against lenders and credit reference agencies in respect of alleged misreporting of credit history data provide evidence of considerable costs of negative credit reports, including the loss of businesses and homes: see e.g. *Gatt* v. *Barclays Bank plc, Mark Williams* [2013] EWHC 0002 [2]; *Smeaton* v. *Equifax plc* [2013] EWCA Civ 108, 3, 36; *Durkin* v. *DSG Retail Ltd and another* [2014] UKSC 21 [8], [36]–[38].

[281] D. Thorne, 'Personal Bankruptcy and the Credit Report: Conflicting Mechanisms of Social Mobility', *Journal of Poverty* 11 (2008) 23. See also Will Dobbie and others, 'Bad Credit, No Problem? Credit and Labor Market Consequences of Bad Credit Reports'

credit markets can reduce her opportunities in other apparently unrelated markets.[282] All lenders become secured lenders from the debtor's perspective, as creditors hold as collateral the debtor's reputation – an asset subject to value fluctuation via the communication of relevant information.[283] Credit reporting does not just function as a means of overcoming adverse selection problems in lending decisions, but encourages debtor repayment on creditors' terms by sanctioning a defaulting debtor through the destruction of value held in her credit history asset.[284] Credit scoring may extend beyond merely reflecting disadvantage and discrimination in existing market positions, in fact *producing* outcomes,[285] and generating 'consequential forms of social categorisation and price-differentiated opportunities'.[286] Credit scoring and the (largely neo-classical economic) ideas justifying its use have a performative aspect, often producing the financial difficulty they claim to describe.[287] Even regulators have come to reify credit scores and fulfil their prophecies by using them as a measure for consumer harm, with the Financial Conduct Authority justifying regulatory interventions on the reductions in credit scores associated with use of certain credit products.[288]

Credit reporting systems have seized the role of judge of debtor conduct, but the normative standards they apply are based on profitability rather than the pursuit of public policy objectives. Bankruptcy law has effectively tried to develop a system of distinguishing 'good' and 'bad' debtors. Under the social insurance framework of bankruptcy, this corresponds roughly to a system of distinguishing between risks within and outside a debtor's control. While members of the public, and even regulators, assume that consumers too have 'good' and 'bad' credit scores, this understanding may not reflect the reality that every consumer

(National Bureau of Economic Research, 2016) Working Paper 22711 www.nber.org/papers/w22711 accessed 12 July 2018.

282 Keats Citron and Pasquale (n. 266) 32–3.

283 Leff (n. 123) 26–33; Dyal-Chand (n. 278); White (n. 188) 1005.

284 Dyal-Chand (n. 278) 808. In the English High Court case of *McGuffick* v. *RBS*, a consumer debtor's representatives argued that credit reporting is 'overtly a tool of enforcement. Indeed ... it enable[s] a creditor to enforce an agreement in the most effective way, by threatening the debtor that if he [does] not pay ... the default would be reported to [Credit Reference Agencies]': '*McGuffick*' (n. 279) [28].

285 Keats Citron and Pasquale (n. 266) 10.

286 Fourcade and Healy (n. 36) 10.

287 ibid, 14; Keats Citron and Pasquale (n. 266) 18–9.

288 'High-Cost Credit Review – Update' (Financial Conduct Authority, 2018) Feedback Statement FS17/2.

merely has a price – 'a person with a "bad" score . . . might nevertheless be valuable *for that very reason*' (emphasis in original) to a particular lender.[289] Advanced data collection allows lenders to monitor borrower behaviour throughout the contractual relationship, which in theory should reduce moral hazard concerns. In practice this allows lenders to nudge debtors towards maximum profitability and creates such a lopsided information asymmetry as to risk dramatic divergences of borrower and lender interests under debt contracts. Price differentiation and market segmentation may involve identifying 'under-sold' prime customers and encouraging them to borrow more,[290] or offering high-cost credit to subprime but profitable customers.[291] Such processes of judgment based solely on profitability may facilitate suboptimal practices productive of externalities – expanding household debt to produce 'debt overhang' problems; 'subprime' lending that contributed to the financial crisis;[292] or the 'sweat box' lending model of trapping customers in persistent default.[293]

Further critiques from a procedural justice perspective argue that not only do contemporary credit reporting practices shift power increasingly from democratic institutions to markets, but they also move decision making from visible to invisible fora or 'black boxes'.[294] Credit scoring mechanisms are proprietary in nature, meaning that the algorithms that produce final scores, and the manner in which lenders incorporate scores into their decisions, are confidential. Consumers and even regulators lack knowledge of the basis of assessments, meaning that consumers cannot become aware of the criteria under which they are being judged, and of 'the optimal credit utilisation strategy'.[295] The lack of transparency may conceal arbitrary decisions inevitably produced by the 'blunt instruments' of scoring.[296] It may also hide human biases built into algorithms, and their discriminatory effects.[297] The accuracy of credit reporting

[289] Fourcade and Healy (n. 36) 22.
[290] Lauer (n. 266) 209.
[291] ibid, 209–210.
[292] ibid, 210; Fourcade and Healy (n. 36) 12; Keats Citron and Pasquale (n. 266) 9–13.
[293] Lauer (n. 266) 250–2; R. J. Mann, 'Bankruptcy Reform and the Sweat Box of Credit Card Debt', *University of Illinois Law Review* 2007 (2007) 375.
[294] Lauer (n. 266) 266–7; Keats Citron and Pasquale (n. 266) 10–11; F. Ferretti, 'Consumer Credit Information Systems: A Critical Review of the Literature. Too Little Attention Paid by Lawyers?', *European Journal of Law and Economics* 23 (2007) 71.
[295] Keats Citron and Pasquale (n. 266) 11.
[296] Fourcade and Healy (n. 36) 25; Keats Citron and Pasquale (n. 266) 11–3.
[297] Lauer (n. 266) 233–41; Keats Citron and Pasquale (n. 266) 13–6.

systems is nothing close to that produced by judicial standards of evidence, with the FCA finding average variations of 24 per cent in the information held by two different UK credit reference agencies for the same individuals.[298] If the theorists of Chapter 2 make a valid argument that credit should now be understood as substituting for wages and social transfers, then it is wholly inappropriate that the process for its allocation lacks the procedural transparency and fairness warranted in respect of employment rights and expected in public service provision. While other sources are more appropriate for consideration of the regulatory issues raised by credit reporting and scoring,[299] it appears the legal system largely draws a line at monitoring data security and privacy, without regulating the algorithmic use of (properly obtained and secured) data.[300] English law does not appear, however, to acknowledge the role of credit reporting as a de facto control of debtor behaviour and sanction against default.[301] In a case in which consumer protection legislation rendered the relevant credit agreement unenforceable, the English High Court rejected as 'somewhat pejorative' 'any suggestion that the bank is using ... its continued reporting of the state of the claimant's account to [credit reference agencies] ... as a coercive tool to persuade the claimant to pay the outstanding amount of the loan'.[302] Rather, according to the court, 'the reporting has been for the legitimate purposes ... of

[298] 'Preventing Financial Distress by Predicting Unaffordable Consumer Credit Agreements: An Applied Framework' (Financial Conduct Authority, 2017) Occasional Paper No. 28 9.

[299] See e.g. O. Lynskey, *The Foundations of EU Data Protection Law* (Oxford University Press, 2015).

[300] Currently credit reference agencies are licensed and supervised (Financial Services and Markets Act 2000 (Regulated Activities) Order 2001/544, art. 89B), while the law requires accuracy in credit reporting and the disclosure to consumers on request of their file (General Data Protection Regulation (Regulation (EU) 2016/679); Consumer Credit Act 1974, ss. 157–9). Lenders are obliged to conduct creditworthiness assessments as part of their responsible lending duties, having regard to sufficient information, which may include credit histories: Financial Conduct Authority *Handbook of Rules and Guidance, Mortgage and Home Finance: Conduct of Business Sourcebook* (MCOB), 11.3; Financial Conduct Authority Handbook CONC (*Consumer Credit Sourcebook*), 5.3.1; see 'Assessing Creditworthiness in Consumer Credit: Proposed Changes to Our Rules and Guidance' (Financial Conduct Authority, 2017) Consultation Paper CP17/27 19–20.

[301] Certain actions such as reporting/threatening to report a debt which in fact is not owed are regulated, either as unfair commercial practices or as breaches of data protection rules respectively: *Office of Fair Trading* v. *Ashbourne Management Services Ltd* [2011] EWHC 1237 (Ch); *Grace & Anor* v. *Black Horse Ltd* [2014] EWCA 1413.

[302] '*McGuffick*' (n. 279) [36].

sharing credit performance data with other financial institutions through the CRAs to promote responsible lending.'[303]

It seems again that the law has ceded its role of making the decisions that matter in relation to debtor conduct. Private actors in opaque fora control the extent to which a moral hazard problem exists in credit markets, and the safeguards against such problems. Chapter 2 showed how many commentators argue that the 'democratisation of credit' has been used to compensate for stagnating wages and a shrinking social safety net, and absolve policymakers from responsibility for guaranteeing the public's economic well-being. Similarly, policymakers have supported the expansion of credit scoring as a technological solution to the intractable political problems of determining who deserves credit, and how the resource of credit access should be distributed.[304] The unaccountability of the process leading to such crucial decisions seems consistent with Davies' argument that under advanced neoliberalism elite power is exercised through a 'juridical deficit', as 'unconscious' processes of non-human systems are elevated above 'discursive spheres of politics and judgment'.[305] Holders of elite power are shielded from juridical and political control, and those adversely affected are directed to blame machines, or their own behaviour for leading the – objective and impartial – machine to find that they deserve a 'bad' score. The inequality produced by credit markets and credit scoring techniques therefore becomes difficult to challenge politically.[306] A socially and economically critical role, and more narrowly a prized function of bankruptcy law (perhaps even its 'bedrock'), has been handed over to particularly opaque and unaccountable market processes.

7.7 Conclusion

Classically, problems of moral hazard are generated when there is information asymmetry between the insured and insurer, limiting the insurer's ability to monitor the insured's conduct and insert contractual provisions which foresee and control the insured's actions.[307] Conditions

303 ibid.
304 Lauer (n. 266).
305 W. Davies, 'Elite Power under Advanced Neoliberalism', *Theory, Culture & Society* 34 (2017) 227.
306 Fourcade and Healy (n. 36) 25.
307 Stiglitz (n. 60) 5.

of contemporary consumer credit markets mean that lenders' ability to monitor borrowers' conduct is greater than ever. In trends visible in the UK and elsewhere, creditors exert considerable control over borrower behaviour both outside of personal insolvency (through credit reporting systems) and through the increasing retreat of the law to long-term repayment plans and creditor-controlled renegotiation procedures. Nonetheless, policymakers continue to identify moral hazard problems associated with allowing insolvent debtors to access expansive debt relief, and to fear abuse of the benefits of bankruptcy. This perspective is fuelled by residues of bankruptcy history as a quasi-penal code and a commercial law (meaning that consumer borrowing traditionally drew suspicion), and by trends of political economy characteristic of contemporary financialised capitalism. Bankruptcy laws are generally replete with safeguards which limit access to debt relief, control and restrict behaviour of participating debtors, and sanction debtors for misconduct. This chapter seeks to show how moral hazard theory suggests these measures can be excessive and can limit the ability of bankruptcy to fulfil the role demanded of it as an insurance mechanism against the risks of the contemporary debt economy. Moral hazard theory merely requires that insurance should not be structured so that its benefits exceed its costs. Where markets impose significant and opaque costs through credit scoring systems and onerous debt restructurings, the primary concern of the law should be in quantifying and regulating these costs so that the safeguards against abuse of debt relief can be efficiently calibrated. Judgments passed by lenders and credit scoring algorithms may not produce positive public policy outcomes, given the belated lesson offered by the financial crisis that the public interest and financial sector profitability are not synonymous. Policymakers therefore seem preoccupied with establishing safeguards against abuse of debt relief at a time when they should more appropriately be concerned with alleviating the disciplinary structures of credit markets which discourage debtors from accessing debt relief and deny a 'fresh start'. Given the high levels of over-indebtedness in this country, English bankruptcy law is significantly underused. The high costs imposed by credit markets through disciplinary mechanisms such as credit scoring may play as powerful a role in deterring debtors from accessing bankruptcy as any legal rules or financial obstacles.

Using this framework of bankruptcy as insurance, this chapter probes the concept of moral hazard and applies it to the disciplinary features of bankruptcy in a more comprehensive and theoretically developed manner than is often the case in policy and political discussions. A key insight from moral hazard theory is not that insurance has negative consequences, but that these negative consequences can be controlled and limited through insurance contract design.[308] The chapter shows how many aspects of bankruptcy law conform to such design features, both demonstrating the explanatory power of moral hazard as a concept, and the extent to which the law guards strongly against the risk of perverse incentives being generated by bankruptcy's debt relief. Further, many of the assumptions of moral hazard theory are absent in the circumstances of contemporary consumer credit markets. Shifts in the creditor-debtor relationship brought about by technological developments, changing business models and transformations of wider economic conditions mean that creditors are now better placed than debtors to prevent default in cases not involving deliberate debtor misconduct. A detailed application of moral hazard theory offers little support for the sanctioning of unreasonable (as opposed to dishonest or intentionally culpable) consumer borrowing, given that key assumptions of moral hazard theory are absent in this context. Outside of cases of intentional misconduct (against which safeguards can be put in place readily), this chapter removes the moral hazard argument as a serious policy objection to debt relief through bankruptcy. For policymakers or politicians persisting in opposing debt relief, the technical concept of moral hazard should not be an available tool.

This is not to say that there is not a political dimension to the 'fuzzy' concept of moral hazard.[309] This book does not make an ethical case for debt relief, and it acknowledges that moral objections will always persist.[310] Indeed, this chapter acknowledges that essentially political questions are raised regarding the availability of debt relief and the price that should be paid for this benefit. It is concerning that such questions have been divorced from politics by the privatisation of bankruptcy and its regulation of debtor conduct. The analysis in this chapter suggests, however, that policymakers' and politicians' moral objections to debt relief should be openly and clearly expressed as such, rather than cloaked in the technical legitimacy of the concept of moral hazard.

[308] Baker (n. 40) 240.
[309] Leaver (n. 41).
[310] This book notes, however, that convincing ethical justifications for debt relief have been advanced: Kilpi (n. 56).

An application of moral hazard theory suggests that economic policy has little to fear, and much to gain, from offering expansive access to debt relief through bankruptcy. In contrast, the limited scope of application of bankruptcy law under current English law, and its ceding of moral authority over the setting of standards of appropriate borrowing behaviour (and so of the conditions of crucial credit market access), limit its ability to fulfil its potential as an insurance mechanism against the risks of a debt-dependent economy. Instead, it may do little to release individuals from market disciplinary structures built upon privately determined norms that risk perpetuating contemporary problems of economic stagnation, inequality, and political disquiet.

8

Conclusion

A consensus is emerging that the perceived benefits of finance, upon which much of our contemporary model of financialised capitalism has been built, decline when aggregate debt levels grow too high.[1] Mainstream policy institutions increasingly recognise that excessive household debt can increase the likelihood of financial crisis and that debt overhang problems can reduce economic growth. Over recent decades, capitalism has sought to use household debt to square the circle of increasing the share of growth diverted to capital while maintaining the aggregate demand necessary to maintain growth. This 'privatised Keynesianism' model eats itself when historic debt reduces present consumption, and the model is revealed as having merely shifted future demand forward to the present.[2] It becomes clear that the 'problem with viewing the future as territory to be plundered is that eventually we all have to live there'.[3]

Advanced economies now live with the stagnation generated by borrowing of the past. The 'democratisation of credit' did not deliver on its promise of widespread wealth and prosperity for middle and working classes, and a heavily indebted society is an unequal one. The inequality created by orientating policy towards supporting financial markets extends beyond economic imbalances to 'differential access to political power'.[4] A combination of deteriorating material conditions and

[1] See e.g. 'Household Debt and Financial Stability', *Global Financial Stability Report* October *2017* (International Monetary Fund, 2017) 53.

[2] C. Crouch, 'Privatised Keynesianism: An Unacknowledged Policy Regime', *The British Journal of Politics & International Relations* 11 (2009) 382.

[3] W. Davies, 'The Big Mystique' London Review of Books (2 February 2017) 19.

[4] C. Crouch, *Post-Democracy* 1st edn (Polity Press, 2004) 52. For discussion of the role of financialisation and the political prioritisation of finance in generating inequality, see J. Hopkin and K. A. Shaw, 'Organized Combat or Structural Advantage? The Politics of

unresponsiveness of mainstream institutions to debtor voices may have contributed to the considerable political instability in many countries that had allowed the development of 'creditors' paradise' economies.[5]

8.1 Bankruptcy as Social Insurance in a Debt-Dependent Economy

This book argues that bankruptcy law has an important role to play as a social insurance mechanism against the risks inherent in the debt-dependent economic structure of financialised capitalism. In so doing, the book opens conversations between bankruptcy literature and macro-economic policy, inequality studies and political science; hoping to show what the law can offer in demonstrating how wide ideas of debt relief can be implemented through concrete legal rules. It also hopes that its findings extend globally beyond its focus on England and Wales. While the acceptance of the need to tackle problems of excessive debt is now widespread, international institutions do not necessarily see the potential of bankruptcy as a policy solution. The World Bank report on personal insolvency is rare in capturing both these policy challenges and the role that bankruptcy can play in addressing them.[6] Various international organisation reports arguing the need for household debt reduction continue to advocate 'market-based debt resolution' mechanisms that rely on the same market dynamics productive of debt problems.[7] Chapters 4 and 5 have drawn on the English experience of Individual Voluntary Arrangements (IVAs) and Debt Management Plans (DMPs) to argue that such mechanisms are inappropriate in the context of household over-indebtedness. Public policy would be better served by bankruptcy law's guarantee of open access to effectively designed rapid debt relief procedures. Bankruptcy law is also well equipped to incorporate

Inequality and the Winner-Take-All Economy in the United Kingdom', *Politics & Society* 44 (2016) 345.

5 M. Blyth and M. Matthijs, 'Black Swans, Lame Ducks, and the Mystery of IPE's Missing Macroeconomy', *Review of International Political Economy* 24 (2017) 203.

6 *Report on the Treatment of the Insolvency of Natural Persons* (World Bank, 2013).

7 'Dealing with Household Debt', *World Economic Outlook 2012* (International Monetary Fund, 2012) www.imf.org/external/pubs/ft/weo/2012/01/pdf/c3.pdf accessed 11 November 2018; J. R. Andritzky, 'Resolving Residential Mortgage Distress: Time to Modify?' (International Monetary Fund, 2014) IMF Working Paper WP/14/226 www.imf.org/external/pubs/cat/longres.aspx?sk=42532.0 accessed 11 November 2018; 'Fiscal Monitor – Debt: Use It Wisely' (International Monetary Fund, 2016) www.imf.org/external/pubs/ft/fm/2016/02/fmindex.htm accessed 4 January 2017.

carefully designed safeguards against moral hazard, and so overcome perennial objections raised against proposed debt relief policies (Chapter 7). Certain international policy documents seem only to see household debt in terms of Non-Performing Loans (NPLs) on bank balance sheets. These documents in turn tend to discuss bankruptcy under an implicit assumption that it is a debt collection tool for maximising returns to investors.[8] A lesson from this book is that conceptions of bankruptcy as a debt collection tool are inappropriate in a context of widespread over-indebtedness and pressing debt overhang problems. In this context, bankruptcy's public policy value lies as an insurance mechanism against the risks of excessive debt. A bankruptcy law focused on contract enforcement and upholding market allocations perpetuates and exacerbates the problems of a debt-dependent economy. Finally, European Union proposals now venture into the area of consumer bankruptcy law, but arrive there only through policy initiatives primarily focused on corporate insolvency law.[9] This book has sought to highlight the dangers of applying ideas and assumptions from the field of corporate insolvency to the distinct area of personal insolvency law. It argues for a departure from the common understanding that there is a single body of 'insolvency law' shaped by common ideas and policy considerations. Of course, the United Kingdom's imminent exit from the European Union colours these issues and the relationship of English law with international norms and standards, in bankruptcy as in almost all policy areas.

Certain key features must be established in a bankruptcy law that acts as a social insurance mechanism of last resort against the risks inherent to a contemporary economy reliant on high levels of household debt. Bankruptcy law must offer open access for debtors in all cases where externalities would otherwise arise. An 'insolvency' condition is an effective criterion for access, operating as a screen to ensure the benefits of debt relief are available to debtors only where their exclusion would lead to social costs.[10] The point at which a debtor is unable to meet her

[8] S. Aiyar and others, 'A Strategy for Resolving Europe's Problem Loans' (International Monetary Fund, 2015) IMF Staff Discussion Note SDN/15/19.

[9] 'Initiative on Insolvency: Inception Impact Assessment' (European Commission, 2016) 2016/JUST/025 – Insolvency II 5; 'Proposal for a Directive of the European Parliament and of the Council on Preventive Restructuring Frameworks, Second Chance and Measures to Increase the Efficiency of Restructuring, Insolvency and Discharge Procedures and Amending Directive 2012/30/EU' (European Commission, 2016) 2016/0359 (COD) COM(2016) 723 final 14.

[10] C. G. Hallinan, 'The Fresh Start Policy in Consumer Bankruptcy: A Historical Inventory and an Interpretive Theory', *University of Richmond Law Review* 21 (1986) 49, 131.

obligations seems a logically inarguable time for the law to switch its focus from compelling repayment to addressing the externalities of over-indebtedness. Arguments for even more expansive access and earlier legal intervention can be made, particularly given the policy problem of debt overhang among heavily leveraged solvent households.[11] The insurance theory of bankruptcy makes clear, however, that creditor consent or financial costs should not act as barriers to access (Chapters 4 and 5). Once a debtor has entered a bankruptcy procedure, further costs should apply in order to address moral hazard concerns. Debtors can be required to sacrifice excess assets and income, but with the clear aim of safeguarding against moral hazard problems, rather than in pursuit of an objective of maximising returns to creditors (Chapter 7). In turn, the debt relief offered should be extensive and comprehensive. Little argument exists for exempting from discharge debts of 'deserving' creditors such as government agencies. Significant social costs arise from the exemption of 'priority' debts or debts linked to creditors' property rights, the most glaring of which is the lack of protection provided to a debtor's home under a law that claims to offer debtors a 'fresh start' (Chapter 6).[12] The insurance theory of bankruptcy recognises the significant problem of moral hazard, and the need for carefully designed safeguards to ensure that the benefits of bankruptcy's debt relief do not exceed its costs. Such safeguards must reflect the realities of contemporary credit markets, however, where lenders have unprecedented information and control over debtor behaviour, and market failures often make it inappropriate to attribute responsibility for default to debtor misconduct (Chapter 7).

8.2 The Logical and Political Limits of English Bankruptcy Law

This book shows how English law has much distance to travel in order to align itself with the social insurance theory of bankruptcy. Path

[11] A. Mian, A. Sufi and F. Trebbi, 'Resolving Debt Overhang: Political Constraints in the Aftermath of Financial Crises', *American Economic Journal: Macroeconomics* 6 (2014) 1, 21.

[12] A question for further analysis is how mortgage debt should be addressed in bankruptcy: A. J. Levitin, 'Resolving the Foreclosure Crisis: Modification of Mortgages in Bankruptcy', *Wisconsin Law Review* 2009 (2009) 565; J. Taub, Other People's Houses (Yale University Press, 2014); A. Mian and A. Sufi, *House of Debt* (University of Chicago Press, 2014); For discussion of Irish personal insolvency reforms allowing the restructuring of mortgage debt, including a limited 'cramdown' mechanism, see J. Spooner, 'The Quiet-Loud-Quiet Politics of Post-Crisis Consumer Bankruptcy Law: The Case of Ireland and the Troika', *Modern Law Review* 81 (5) (2018) 790–824.

dependency seems influential in the English bankruptcy system, in which key stakeholders persist in holding views of the law as part of the commercial law and/or a quasi-criminal procedure. The politics of debt also raise considerable obstacles to reform. In a financialised economy, banks represent a powerful lobbying force, and several studies document their influence over bankruptcy law.[13] Under collective action theory, the diverging interests of a large group such as consumer debtors tend to lose out in the marketplace for regulation to the concentrated interests of an organised group such as the financial sector.[14] Even when crises or scandals create a window of opportunity for weaker interests to demand policy responses,[15] this opening quickly shuts and strong interests resume influence over 'quieter' technocratic policy making.[16] Popular demands for bankruptcy law reform can be weakened by concerns of fairness as between repaying debtors and those seeking relief. Creditor interest groups have often succeeded in broadcasting the powerful legitimating narrative that offering debt relief to the few will hurt the many by raising the costs of credit.[17] A powerful political morality of debt also prevails, particularly in an era of austerity.[18] The 'self-evident' logic that 'one has to pay one's debts' is influential,[19] and seems to have contributed significantly to public acceptance of austerity policies that have harmed

[13] See e.g. D. A. Skeel, *Debt's Dominion : A History of Bankruptcy Law in America* (Princeton University Press, 2001); I. Ramsay, 'Interest Groups and the Politics of Consumer Bankruptcy Reform in Canada', *University of Toronto Law Journal* 53 (2003) 379; A. M. Dickerson, 'Regulating Bankruptcy: Public Choice, Ideology, &(and) Beyond', *Washington University Law Review* 84 (2006) 1861; I. Ramsay, *Personal Insolvency in the 21st Century: A Comparative Analysis of the US and Europe* (Hart Publishing, 2017) 189–91; M. Olson, *The Logic of Collective Action: Public Goods and the Theory of Groups*, revised edn (Harvard University Press, 1974); Spooner (n. 12).

[14] Olson (n. 13).

[15] L. Kastner, '"Much Ado about Nothing?" Transnational Civil Society, Consumer Protection and Financial Regulatory Reform', *Review of International Political Economy* 21 (2014) 1313.

[16] P. D. Culpepper, Quiet Politics and Business Power: Corporate Control in Europe and Japan 1st edn (Cambridge University Press, 2010). Note that in the example of post-crisis Ireland, policy positions advanced by the 'Troika' of the IMF, European Central Bank and European Commission were notably less favourable to debtor interests than those taken in reports published by these institutions: Spooner (n. 3).

[17] Ramsay, *'21st Century'* (n. 13) 190; T. A. Sullivan, 'Debt and the Simulation of Social Class' in R. Brubaker, R. M. Lawless and C. J. Tabb (eds.), *A Debtor World: Interdisciplinary Perspectives on Debt* (Oxford University Press, 2012) 83.

[18] K. Forkert, 'The New Moralism: Austerity, Silencing and Debt Morality', *Soundings: A journal of politics and culture* 56 (2014) 41.

[19] D. Graeber, *Debt: The First 5,000 Years* (Melville House, 2012) 2–4.

their interests and the wider economy.[20] Meanwhile the prevailing neo-liberal logic of individual responsibility argues against debt relief policies. These factors tend to push bankruptcy law towards equilibria favouring creditors and other strong interest groups such as insolvency intermediaries. The story of industry success in fending off debtor-friendly reforms of the IVA procedure evidences this trend (see Chapter 4). Key questions have been removed from the political sphere, involving the level of sacrifice to be made by debtors in exchange for debt relief (Chapters 4 and 5), and the sanctions imposed on debtors judged to have contravened market norms (Chapter 7).[21] Restricted access to bankruptcy and DROs undoubtedly suits the preferences of interest groups, but may also reflect a lingering public distrust of bankruptcy and an unwillingness to direct public funds towards assisting a group still perceived by many as financially irresponsible. A perception that these views are widespread may drive the activities of a commercialised Insolvency Service in pursuing and publicising debtor misconduct, though questions arise as to whether the agency here is responding to, or creating, public suspicion regarding the bankruptcy system (Chapter 7). If the social insurance theory offers a convincing technical case for expansive debt relief in bankruptcy, there is no guarantee of its political success.

Outside of politics, an investigation of the English experience shows courts to be particularly unsupportive of the social insurance function of bankruptcy.[22] This book shows examples of judges applying bankruptcy law as a debt collection tool, prioritising the maximisation of returns to creditors. This position might again result from interest group influence, as 'repeat players' such as banks and government creditors can be expected to enjoy litigation success and win courts around to their views.[23] UK banks have proved strategically canny in choosing when to settle cases and when to persevere through the courts in pursuit of favourable precedents.[24] In a financialised world, litigation may be just

[20] L. Stanley, '"We're Reaping What We Sowed": Everyday Crisis Narratives and Acquiescence to the Age of Austerity', *New Political Economy* 19 (2014) 895.

[21] World Bank (n. 6) para. 212.

[22] The book therefore extends beyond much comparative consumer bankruptcy literature, which has tended to neglect studies of court decisions: K. Anderson, 'The Explosive Global Growth of Personal Insolvency and the Concomitant Birth of the Study of Comparative Consumer Bankruptcy', *Osgoode Hall Law Journal* 42 (2004) 661, 675–6.

[23] M. Galanter, 'The Vanishing Trial: An Examination of Trials and Related Matters in Federal and State Courts', *Journal of Empirical Legal Studies* 1 (2004) 459.

[24] H. Collins, 'Regulating Contract Law' in C. Parker and others (eds.), *Regulating Law* (Oxford University Press, 2004).

another game – alongside meta-level competitions for legislation and public opinion (both discussed in Chapter 4) and micro-level individual debt restructuring bargains (Chapter 5) – in which financial institutions hold the best hands.

The book also suggests a role for ideas in shaping judicial positions. It highlights court decisions showing utmost faith in the efficiency of private contracting and marketised exchange. This stance may arise from traditional judicial discomfort at engaging in what they perceive as redistributive activities, and a view of the courts' role being to concentrate on applying a perceived 'neutral' private commercial law, leaving other institutions to address social issues.[25] It also suggests the prevalence of neoliberal ideology among the judiciary.[26] Many examples can be found of decisions where English courts assume the efficiency of the activities of incumbent businesses in the manner of Crouch's 'corporate neoliberals',[27] rather than seeing the important role (even under neoclassical economic perspectives) that courts play in enforcing market discipline and correcting failures.[28] The *Abbey National* litigation offers a classic example of this approach, in which the UK Supreme Court protected overdraft fees and a 'reverse Robin Hood' business model from regulatory control, partly on the basis that banks relied on such charges for a large portion of their income.[29] The court has approved similar 'free for most, expensive for some' business models in other consumer markets as compliant with contract law's rule against penalties.[30] Recently the Supreme Court upheld land registration rules and applied them for the benefit of banks even where this outcome both

[25] I. Ramsay, 'Consumer Credit Law, Distributive Justice and the Welfare State', *Oxford Journal of Legal Studies* 15 (1995) 177; M. Cooper, *Family Values: Between Neoliberalism and the New Social Conservatism* (Zone Books – The MIT Press, 2017) 57–8.

[26] P. S. Atiyah, 'Freedom of Contract and the New Right', *Essays on Contract* (Oxford University Press, 1986).

[27] Crouch's describes 'market' neoliberals as being dedicated to producing perfect markets, while 'corporate' neoliberals defend corporations currently operating (and dominating) in these markets. Crouch argues that corporate neoliberalism 'fatally undermines the pure market condition and entire rhetoric about customers' freedom to choose that remains a fundamental part of the case for neoliberalism': C. Crouch, *Can Neoliberalism Be Saved From Itself?* (Social Europe Edition, 2017) 19–20.

[28] See e.g. I. Ramsay, *Consumer Law and Policy: Text and Materials on Regulating Consumer Markets* 3rd revised edn (Hart Publishing, 2012) 103.

[29] *Office of Fair Trading* v. *Abbey National plc and Others* [2010] 1 AC 696 [2], [105]. See Chapter 2, text to notes 81–3.

[30] *Cavendish Square Holding BV* v. *Talal El Makdessi; ParkingEye Ltd* v. *Beavis* [2015] UKSC 67.

allowed vulnerable consumers to be defrauded and propped up a sale-and-rent-back market renowned for dubious (and in this case criminal) practices.[31] Baroness Hale questioned this outcome, however, asking whether there should 'come a point when the claims of lenders who have failed to heed the obvious warning signs that would have told them that this borrower was not a good risk are postponed to those' of defrauded consumers?[32] If the events of financial crisis and recession over the past decade have not caused this point to come, however, one is left to wonder when the time will arrive where English courts are willing to adopt market correcting rules such as lender liability,[33] rather than assuming the efficiency of every market they encounter.[34] Courts even adopt a minimalist approach to the application of consumer protection laws,[35] often finding that they set similar standards to the common law rules they were enacted to augment.[36] This approach seems consistent with a judicial view that such legislation constitutes 'a political intervention into a natural pre-political market, structured by a set of legal principles which were simply a deduction from the principle of freedom of contract'.[37] In this context, it is perhaps unsurprising to see English courts support contractual bankruptcy (Chapters 4 and 5) and allow the law to be used as a tool for creditors to enforce their contracts (Chapter 6).

8.3 Social Insurance of Last Resort or a Right Not to Pay One's Debts?

The book argues that consumer bankruptcy should be considered as a social insurance mechanism *of last resort*, and makes clear that it is

31 *Scott* v. *Southern Pacific Mortgages Ltd & Ors* [2014] UKSC.

32 ibid, 122.

33 J. Wadsley, 'Bank Lending and the Family Home: Prudence and Protection', *Lloyds Maritime and Commercial Law Quarterly* (2003) 341.

34 J. Kwak and S. Johnson, *Economism: Bad Economics and the Rise of Inequality* (Pantheon Books, 2017) 3.

35 C. Willett, 'General Clauses and the Competing Ethics of European Consumer Law in the UK', *The Cambridge Law Journal* 71 (2012) 412.

36 In *ParkingEye*, the majority held the opinion that 'the same considerations which show that the . . . charge is not a penalty, demonstrate that it is not unfair for the purpose of the [unfair contract terms legislation]': *'ParkingEye'* (n. 30) [104]. See also a recent High Court case holding that legislative control of 'unfair credit relationships' applied similar standards to the common law doctrine of misrepresentation: *Carney & Ors* v. *NM Rothschild & Sons Ltd* [2018] EWHC 958 (Comm), 50.

37 Ramsay, 'Consumer Credit Law, Distributive Justice and the Welfare State' (n. 25) 185.

not a panacea. For both individuals and society, a sorry position has been reached when bankruptcy is the appropriate solution. Bankruptcy carries severe costs, even beyond the onerous legal conditions and restrictions imposed on debtors to safeguard against moral hazard (Chapter 7). It can involve stigma,[38] mental health problems,[39] and punishment by the credit reporting systems that increasingly determine debtors' future life chances.[40] While little empirical evidence exists in respect of the English system, studies from other jurisdictions present a complex picture of the ability of bankruptcy to deliver a 'fresh start' to debtors.[41] Certain US studies find that many debtors continue to experience financial problems after bankruptcy,[42] and that it may take several years after discharge before they return to the standards of the general population.[43] Debtors can face discrimination in credit and labour markets following bankruptcy.[44] Worst outcomes arise under the long-term repayment plans of Chapter 13, where debtors often fail to complete the procedure and obtain a debt discharge, and often do not succeed in the procedure's aim of preventing foreclosure.[45]

[38] M. D. Sousa, 'Bankruptcy Stigma: A Socio-Legal Study', *American Bankruptcy Law Journal* 87 (2013) 435; P. Ali, L. O'Brien and I. Ramsay, '"Short a Few Quid": Bankruptcy Stigma in Contemporary Australia', *University of New South Wales Law Journal* 38 (2015) 1575; P. Ali, L. O'Brien and I. Ramsay, 'Misfortune or Misdeed: An Empirical Study of Public Attitudes Towards Personal Bankruptcy', *University of New South Wales Law Journal* 40 (2017) 1098.

[39] F. R. Addo, 'Seeking Relief: Bankruptcy and Health Outcomes of Adult Women', *SSM – Population Health* 3 (2017) 326.

[40] M. Fourcade and K. Healy, 'Seeing like a Market', *Socio-Economic Review* 15 (2017) 9. See Chapter 7, part 6 above.

[41] I. Ramsay, 'Towards an International Paradigm of Personal Insolvency Law? A Critical View', *QUT Law Review* 17 (2017) 15; P. Ali, L. O'Brien and I. Ramsay, 'Bankruptcy and Debtor Rehabilitation: An Australian Empirical Study', *Melbourne University Law Review* 40 (2017) 688, 694–701.

[42] K. Porter and D. Thorne, 'The Failure of Bankruptcy's Fresh Start', (2006) 92 *Cornell Law Review* 92 (2006) 67.

[43] J. L. Zagorsky and L. R. Lupica, 'A Study of Consumers' Post-Discharge Finances: Struggle, Stasis, or Fresh-Start', *American Bankruptcy Institute Law Review* 16 (2008) 283.

[44] D. Thorne, 'Personal Bankruptcy and the Credit Report: Conflicting Mechanisms of Social Mobility', *Journal of Poverty* 11 (2008) 23; K. Porter, 'Life After Debt: Understanding the Credit Restraint of Bankruptcy Debtors', *American Bankruptcy Institute Law Review* 18 (2010) 1; M. Maroto, 'The Scarring Effects of Bankruptcy: Cumulative Disadvantage Across Credit and Labor Markets', *Social Forces* 91 (2012) 99; W. Dobbie and others, 'Bad Credit, No Problem? Credit and Labor Market Consequences of Bad Credit Reports' (National Bureau of Economic Research, 2016) Working Paper 22711 www.nber.org/papers/w22711 accessed 12 July 2018.

[45] K. Porter, 'The Pretend Solution: An Empirical Study of Bankruptcy Outcomes', *Texas Law Review* 90 (2011) 103; S. S. Greene, P. Patel and K. Porter, 'Cracking the Code:

Scholars viewing bankruptcy from critical theory perspectives argue that the procedure improperly individualises the problem of over-indebtedness, denying its structural nature and concealing the need for collective responses.[46] Bankruptcy may in this way be a tool of financialised capitalism and the 'privatised Keynesianism' economic order, rather than a counterweight to its trends. The perceived assistance it offers to debtors may legitimate the contemporary regime, while its increasingly harsh aspects (including long repayment plans and the disciplinary force of credit reporting of bankruptcy) extend market discipline even to those debtors fleeing the market for sanctuary in bankruptcy. Macroeconomists emanating from quite different theoretical approaches raise similar criticisms of the limitations of individualistic remedies to address structural problems of a debt dependency.[47]

Despite these shortcomings, empirical evidence suggests that debtors entering bankruptcy nonetheless seem to benefit from better outcomes than the severe hardships suffered by similarly placed debtors denied access to bankruptcy.[48] Bankruptcy procedures offer valuable assistance to certain groups of debtors, particularly those earning reasonable incomes,[49] and having access to human and social capital.[50] Studies from the UK, USA and Australia seem to converge around a finding that bankruptcy offers less assistance to debtors suffering from unemployment, ill health or persistently low incomes.[51] Bankruptcy is no substitute for a robust welfare state and an economy that offers a broader share of prosperity through more equitable distributions of

An Empirical Analysis of Consumer Bankruptcy Outcomes', *Minnesota Law Review* 101 (2016) 1031; P. Foohey and others, 'No Money down Bankruptcy', *Southern California Law Review* 90 (2016) [i].

46 S. Soederberg, *Debtfare States and the Poverty Industry: Money, Discipline and the Surplus Population* (Routledge, 2014); L. E. Coco, 'The Cultural Logics of the Bankruptcy Abuse Prevention and Consumer Protection Act of 2005: Fiscal Identities and Financial Failure', *Critical Sociology* 40 (2014) 711.

47 R. Kuttner, *Debtors' Prison: The Politics of Austerity Versus Possibility* (Vintage, 2015).

48 W. Dobbie and J. Song, 'Debt Relief and Debtor Outcomes: Measuring the Effects of Consumer Bankruptcy Protection', *American Economic Review* 105 (2015) 1272.

49 Porter and Thorne (n. 42); S. Ben-Ishai, 'The Gendered Dimensions of Social Insurance for the Non-Poor in Canada', *Osgoode Hall Law Journal* 43 (2005) 289.

50 L. Palmer and V. Bhargava, 'Forms of Wealth Associated with Attaining Peer Group Net Worth Following Bankruptcy', *Social Science Quarterly* 99 (2018) 97.

51 Porter and Thorne (n. 42); G. Atfield, R. Lindley and M. Orton, 'Living with Debt after Advice' (Friends Provident; Institute for Employment Research, University of Warwick, 2016); Ali, O'Brien and Ramsay, 'Bankruptcy and Debtor Rehabilitation' (n. 41). Note that Chapter 6 highlights how the legal benefits of bankruptcy are reduced for low-income debtors.

income, wealth and security. There is every reason, however, for bankruptcy to aim to offer better outcomes for those debtors who turn to it for assistance. Bankruptcy should recognise the policy benefits it can provide within the constrained economic order in which it operates. A wider availability of extensive debt relief might be one solution we need in order to address the excesses of a debt-dependent economy, even if it alone cannot change the nature of this regime. Following the tumult of crisis and recession, the political consensus that created the current economic order has been ruptured. If one is optimistic, one might see the potential for a new politics of debt. Bankruptcy will have a role to play, if more radical reforms allow departure from the contemporary 'privatised Keynesianism' model – even if there is to be a jubilee, it will have to be justiciable. For now, bankruptcy might at least hold powerful symbolic value through its unique status as a social institution bestowing on debtors in need a right not to pay one's debts.[52]

[52] E. Carrère, D'autres vies que la mienne (Folio, 2010) 167, cited in Ramsay, '*21st Century*' (n. 13) 105.

INDEX